Series preface

The Centre for Caribbean Studies at the University of Warwick was founded in 1984 in order to stimulate interest and research into a region of the world which is now receiving academic recognition in its own right. In addition to the publication of papers from annual symposia which reflect the Centre's comparative and inter-disciplinary approach, other volumes in the series are published in a wide range of disciplines within the arts and social sciences. The present volume is the fruit of a two-year research project in the Centre.

This is the first book in the series to concentrate on Cuba and it does so at a moment when the Revolution faces its most serious crisis since 1959. The hypothesis advanced here is controversial. Without West European links the Revolution might well have floundered.

Refusing to submit to US pressures to cut links with Cuba, West European powers made a significant and hitherto largely unacknowledged contribution to the Revolution's survival. The links between Cuba, Britain and Spain, the three powers considered in detail, were not due to ideological affinities but to commercial pragmatism and to a different perception from the US as to the nature of radical nationalist movements. This is discussed, as well as those European ideas which have contributed towards the Revolution's ideology. However, the main chapters of the book concentrate on diplomatic, economic and commercial relations and include contributions by leading British, US and Cuban specialists. The Epilogue considers future scenarios and the dilemma facing Cuba in the 'New International Order'.

Alistair Hennessy
Series Editor

Warwick University Caribbean Studies

Series Editor: Alistair Hennessy

Behind the Planter's Back – Lower Class Responses to Marginality in Bequia Island, St Vincent
Neil Price   0–333–47460–0

The Bloodstained Tombs – The Muharram Massacre in Trinidad 1884
Kelvin Singh   0–333–47177–6

The Commonwealth Caribbean in the World Economy
Ramesh Ramsaran   0–333–49867–4

Europe and the Caribbean
Editor: Paul Sutton   0–333–48785–0

Explanation in Caribbean Migration – Perception and the Image: Jamaica, Barbados, St Vincent
Elizabeth M. Thomas-Hope   0–333–53503–0

Financing Development in the Commonwealth Caribbean
Editors: Delisle Worrell, Compton Bourne, Dinesh Dodhia   0–333–55204–0

From Dessalines to Duvalier – Race, Colour and National Independence
David Nicholls   0–333–46389–7

Hindu Trinidad – Religion, Ethnicity and Socio-Economic Change
Steven Vertovec   0–333–53505–7

In Miserable Slavery – Thomas Thistlewood in Jamaica, 1750–86
Douglas Hall   0–333–48030–9

Intellectuals and Society in the Twentieth Century Caribbean
Editor: Alistair Hennessy
Vol. 1: Spectre of the New Class – The Commonwealth Caribbean
                                                     0–333–53509–X
Vol. 2: Unity in Variety – The Hispanic and Francophone Caribbean
                                                     0–333–56939–3

Warwick University Caribbean Studies

The Fractured Blockade
West European-Cuban Relations during the Revolution

Edited by

Alistair Hennessy and George Lambie

First published 1993

Published by THE MACMILLAN PRESS LTD
London and Basingstoke
Associated companies and representatives in Accra,
Auckland, Delhi, Dublin, Gaborone, Hamburg, Harare,
Hong Kong, Kuala Lumpur, Lagos, Manzini, Melbourne,
Mexico City, Nairobi, New York, Singapore, Tokyo.

ISBN 0–333–58365–5

Printed in Hong Kong

A catalogue record for this book is available from the
British Library.

Cover based on a painting by Aubrey Williams presented to
The Centre for Caribbean Studies, University of Warwick.

The Jamaican People 1880–1902
Patrick Bryan   0–333–55125–7

Labour in the Caribbean – From Emancipation to Independence
Editors: Malcolm Cross and Gad Heuman   0–333–44729–8

Land and Development in the Caribbean
Editors: Jean Besson and Janet Momsen   0–333–45406–5

The Literate Imagination – Essays on the Novels of Wilson Harris
Editor: Michael Gilkes   0–333–49518–7

The Powerless People – The Amerindians of the Corentyne River
Andrew Sanders   0–333–45096–5

Teachers, Education and Politics in Jamaica, 1892–1972
Harry Goulbourne   0–333–47331–0

Trinidad Ethnicity
Kevin Yelvington   0–333–56601–7

The Autobiography of a Runaway Slave: Esteban Montejo
(Editor: Miguel Barnet; Introduction: Alistair Hennessy) 0–333–53507–3

Caribbean Revolutions and Revolutionary Theory – Cuba, Nicaragua and Grenada
Brian Meeks   0–333–57759–0

The Fractured Blockade – Western Europe and Cuba During the Revolution
Alistair Hennessy and George Lambie   0–333–58365–5

Noises in the Blood – Orality, Gender and the 'Vulgar' Body of Jamaican Popular Culture
Carolyn Cooper   0–333–57824–4

The United States and The Caribbean
Anthony Maingot   0–333–57231–9

Woman Version – Theoretical Approaches to West Indian Fiction by Women
Evelyn O'Callaghan   0–333–57837–6

Contents

Acknowledgements

Our major debt is to the Tinker Foundation which provided the grant making it possible to appoint a full-time Research Fellow for two years. It is rare to find the Foundation making awards outside the Americas and the Iberian world and we are most grateful to them for showing confidence in us and hope that they will be gratified by the products of our labours.

Both George Lambie, who was appointed Research Fellow, and who is responsible for the four core chapters of the book, and Antoni Kapcia, an Associate Fellow of the Centre, have been teaching the history of Cuba at Warwick for many years. From the popularity of their courses it is clear that interest in Cuba is far from dead among the current generation of students, and although they may not sport Che Guevara T-shirts, their interest is more profound than in the heady days of the 1960s when my classes on Cuba were filled by Guevarists avid for tips on what made a good guerrilla.

The present book encapsulates many hours of Cuban talk over the years and it has been a rewarding experience to work with such dedicated and enthusiastic Cubaphiles. Inevitably, in studying a controversial area it is sometimes difficult to steer a middle course and at times our pendulum may have swung too far this way or that. There have been moments when one has wondered if the weeks closeted with *Granma* have been worth it but in spite of the exasperation which Cuban Studies can provoke, at the end one is buoyed up by what has been, and at the time of writing, still is, one of the most significant political, social, economic and cultural processes of the twentieth century. We would not have embarked on this project had we not believed that the Cuban Revolution has lessons for both Left and Right which should not be ignored. The thesis of the book, that Western Europe played a far more important role in accounting for the survival of the Revolution than has hitherto been realised, may provoke surprise and disagreement. We hope it does.

We have been fortunate in associating with our project some of the foremost Cuban specialists in Britain, in the US and in Cuba itself. We regret, however, that we were not able, through financial constraints, to include French and Spanish specialists, but hope that the book may stimulate future collaboration, as well as with Cuban specialists elsewhere in Europe. We would, however, like to thank French and Spanish firms for their unstinting help and in particular Paul Berliet of the Foundation Marius Berliet and Manuel Lage of Pegaso as well as those British firms, in particular British Leyland, which tolerated our importunities. We are only too aware that we have just scratched the surface of the controversial topic of the commercial relationship, the reasons for which are outlined in the Preface.

Of the contributors, Gareth Jenkins was always ready to put his vast knowledge of Cuban commerce at our disposal. His *Cuba Business* has justifiably become the most respected and well-informed coverage of Cuban commercial affairs. Gerry Hagelberg and Tony Hannah's first-hand experience and unrivalled knowledge of the international sugar trade is reflected in their definitive analysis of Cuba's position within it. We were particularly fortunate in being able to persuade Professor Andrew Zimbalist to take time off from his many other commitments to contribute his authoritative chapter. We were pleased, as well, to have him here for the Cuba conference (R. Gillespie (ed.) (1990) *Cuba after Thirty Years: Rectification and the Revolution*, London, Cass.) when exchanges with other specialists on the Cuban economy made that a memorable occasion. We welcome the collaboration of Dr José Luís Rodríguez, Deputy Director of the Centre for the Study of the World Economy, Havana, a Cuban economist, much respected in US academic circles, who found time from his many labours at the sharp end to visit us and to contribute a Cuban view of the economy. He has also been a stimulating speaker to those groups who visit Cuba as part of the programme here in Open Studies. We would like to thank the Nuffield Foundation for its support of our Associate Fellowship programme, and the University of Warwick for its support over the years, especially the library which has had to cope with our expanding and difficult to manage Cuban press collection. Our thanks also to Shirley Hamber for all her patient help and advice, and to Barbara Croucher for her painstaking care. Finally, our thanks to Barbara Owens for coping with the illegibility of one of the editors who persists, in spite of all evidence to the contrary, in believing that the pen is mightier than the floppy disk.

The Contributors

G.B. Hagelberg is the author of *The Caribbean Sugar Industries: constraints and opportunities* (1974) and of many other publications on sugar and Cuba. Now resident in England, he was sugar adviser to the Government of Barbados from 1950–1986.

Anthony Hannah is Head of the Economics and Statistics Division of the London-based International Sugar Organisation.

Alistair Hennessy is Director of the Centre for Caribbean Studies at the University of Warwick, where until 1990 he was Chairman of the School of Comparative American Studies which he founded in 1974. Originally a specialist in Spanish History, on which he has published *The Federal Republic in Spain: Pi y Margall and the Federal Republican Movement* (1962) and numerous articles, he has since specialised in the history of the Americas on which he has published *The Frontier in Latin American History* (1978), and co-edited *The Land that England Lost: Argentina and Britain, a special relationship* (1992), and of a forthcoming edition of M. Barnet, *Autobiography of a Runaway Slave*.

Gareth Jenkins is an economic consultant based in London. He has prepared many research studies both for companies doing business with Cuba and for Cuban trade enterprises. Since 1987 he has published the report *Cuba Business* from London, which is now published from Washington. He is an Associate Fellow at the Centre for Caribbean Studies, University of Warwick, UK, and is Vice-President of the Washington trade consultancy Carib Export.

Antoni Kapcia lectures in Latin American history at the University of Wolverhampton and has been researching and publishing on Cuban intellectual and political history since 1971. His work on ideology in Cuba has resulted in several articles and chapters in recent years, including contributions to R. Gillespie, *Cuba after Thirty Years: Rectification and the Revolution* (1990) and A. Hennessy, *Intellectuals in the Twentieth Century Caribbean* (1992). He is a member of the Centre for Caribbean Studies of the University of Warwick.

George Lambie is Senior Lecturer in Politics in the Business School of de Montfort University, Leicester, and is a Visiting Fellow of the Centre of Caribbean Studies at Warwick where he teaches Cuban history and where he has been an undergraduate, graduate and Research Fellow. His book on César Vallejo, the Peruvian intellectual, *César Vallejo and the Spanish Civil War*, will be published in 1993. He is presently working on Peruvian political thought, and on contemporary developments in Cuba.

José Luís Rodríguez is the Deputy Director of the Centre for the Study of the World Economy in Havana and is one of Cuba's leading economists. Among his many publications are *Eradicación de la Pobreza en Cuba (1987), Crítica a Nuestros Críticos* (1988) and *Estrategía del desarrollo económico en Cuba* (1990).

David Thomas is a former British Ambassador to Cuba and Assistant Under-Secretary of State for the Americas at the Foreign and Common-wealth Office. He is an Associate Fellow of the Centre for Caribbean Studies at the University of Warwick and a member of the Council of the Royal Institute of International Affairs. He contributed the chapter 'The United States factor in British relations with Latin America' in V. Bulmer Thomas (ed.) *Britain and Latin America: a changing relationship* (1989), published by that Institute.

Andrew Zimbalist is Robert A. Woods' Professor of Economics at Smith College and is one of the leading economists on the Cuban economy, visiting Cuba on many occasions. He has published ten books and several dozen articles on comparative economic systems and economic development. His many studies on Cuba include *The Cuban Economy: Measurement and Analysis of Socialist Performance* (with Claes Brundenius) (1989) and 'Teetering on the Brink: Cuba's Post-CMEA Economic and Political Crisis', *Journal of Latin American Studies*, May, 1992. He has also published with John Weeks *Panama at the Crossroads: Economic and Political Development in the 20th Century*, (1991). He has just published *Baseball and Billions: a probing look inside the big business of our national pastime*, (1992), a study of the economics of the baseball industry in the US. He is currently editing a volume on the transformation process in former and current socialist societies.

Foreword

David Thomas

The wheel has come full circle. Thirty years ago a beleaguered revolutionary Cuba, cut off from its economic hinterland in the US and not yet fully integrated into the trade and aid mechanisms of the Soviet bloc, sought to develop its commercial relationships with Western Europe as one means of circumventing the US embargo. Today, as it faces perhaps its most desperate crisis following the effective collapse of its Soviet lifeline, Cuba is again looking to Western Europe (along with Canada, Japan and Latin America) for the increased trade and investment on which the regime's strategy for survival depends.

Revolutionary Cuba, which once appeared exciting, romantic and dangerous, is now seen as an increasingly irrelevant anachronism, an object of curiosity as almost the last tattered remnant of the vanished world communist system. In Cuba itself the mixture of inspiration and coercion which mobilised popular support for revolutionary change has been dissipated by time and hardship. The revolution, it has been said, gave the people of Cuba their dignity, but the system has taken it away again. The social gains are real, but the inspiration has gone; and an ageing leadership, resistant to radical reform and perceiving itself under siege from external forces beyond its control, is likely to resort more and more to coercion.

In one respect at least, this Cuban perception has some justification. Victory in the Cold War has not diminished the unrelenting hostility of the US towards Cuba. The Bush administration made it clear that it was not seriously interested in dialogue with Castro; it tightened the economic embargo and it persisted in its efforts to dissuade other countries from trading with or investing in Cuba. A bill before Congress would turn the clock back to the 1960s by imposing sanctions on third countries trading with Cuba (and, perhaps, leave the way clear for US commercial interests when US-Cuban relations are eventually restored). The British government, for one, (and not for the first time), has made it clear that it is not disposed to recognise the extra-territorial pretensions of the US Congress. Predictably, Cuban emigré organisations in Miami have sought to deter would-be foreign investors in Cuba by threatening that their investments could be declared invalid 'once democracy arrives on the island'. Such posturings deserve equally short shrift. Over the years the embargo has undoubtedly hurt Cuba and continues to do so. But whether or not US policy is based on the politically and morally questionable calculation that eventually the embargo will cause sufficient misery to provoke an uprising against the regime, its principal political effect has been and remains to provide an easy and effective vehicle for Castro to stimulate popular patriotic support against hostile US actions.

History and geography have locked Cuba and the US into a relationship of reciprocal paranoia in which each side almost automatically makes a worst case assessment of the other's actions and motives. Given Cuba's history since 1898, Cuban suspicions are understandable. But, notwithstanding memories of the 1962 missile crisis, Western European and other observers find it hard to comprehend the enduring strength of US hostility and distrust towards the Castro regime. The image which springs to mind is not so much David and Goliath as that of Walt Disney's elephant driven hysterical by a mouse. To be sure, the US was not the only Western country to be alarmed by the implications of the Soviet Union's acquisition of a strategic foothold in the Western hemisphere, and by the challenge posed by Cuba's triumphalist revolutionary rhetoric. Britain and France kept a wary eye on Cuba's destabilising potential in the Caribbean; and from the mid-1970s the projection of Cuba's military power into Africa in concert with Soviet aims and interests alarmed the West as a whole and caused Cuba's remarkable aid and technical co-operation effort in the Third World to be viewed with deep suspicion. But for Western European governments Cuba was essentially a fairly low priority foreign policy problem, to be dealt with in the context of East-West competition with due but not excessive regard for American susceptibilities.

For the US, by contrast, the defiant survival 90 miles from Key West of a Marxist-Leninist regime pursuing a militantly 'anti-imperialist' policy dedicated to undermining US interests around the world is a standing affront which has made Cuba a perennially sensitive domestic political issue, effectively exploited by the Cuban emigré lobby. This attitude has its roots much further back than the 'triumph of the revolution' in 1959. From early in the nineteenth century American leaders contemplated Cuba's inclusion in the westward and southward expansion of the US. By the middle of the century the US had become the dominant economic power in Cuba. When, in 1898, American intervention delivered the *coup de grâce* in the long wars of independence which the Cubans had been waging against Spain since 1868, Cuba became to all intents and purposes a protectorate of the US, and remained so until 1959. Quite early on Americans could be easily exasperated by the Cubans' failure to display the deferential gratitude for their liberation which the US felt was due to it. President Teddy Roosevelt wrote in 1906:

I am so angry with that infernal little Cuban republic. . . . All that we wanted from them was that they should behave themselves and be prosperous and happy so that we should not have to interfere. And now, lo and behold . . . we have no alternative save to intervene.

Old habits of thought die hard, so it is not after all so surprising that when Fidel Castro turned to the Soviet Union his action was seen not merely as a challenge to US interests but as a betrayal of American values, and his removal acquired for successive US administrations the status of a moral imperative.

Cuba, the self-proclaimed '*territorio libre en América*', has arguably never been independent. After four centuries as a colony of Spain, followed by more than half a century subject to US neo-colonialism, Cuba under Castro achieved a measure of freedom of action, but constrained by economic and military dependence on the Soviet Union (although it was never quite the compliant Soviet proxy it has often been painted). Now the country faces the bleak freedom of self-reliance in an effort to preserve a regime whose days appear to be numbered. Change must come, even though it is likely to take longer than the optimists in Miami expect; and it remains an open question whether the process will turn out to be peaceful or bloody.

Western Europe's willingness to trade with Cuba in the 1960s played, as is argued in this book, an important part in underpinning the consolidation of the Revolution and deserves to be studied for that reason. It is more doubtful that European trade and investment can make a comparable contribution to the regime's survival in the 1990s (and the social repercussions of its attempt to establish separate internal and external economies in Cuba could serve to strengthen the very pressures for reform which the authorities are trying to stifle). Cuba's future is not an issue of conspicuous concern to Europeans: they have far graver and more pressing problems closer to home. European governments and companies are likely to respond to Cuban overtures with the same calculations of pragmatic self-interest they have displayed in the past. To the extent that political considerations inform their decisions, these are likely to have to do, not with the survival of the present Cuban regime, but with encouraging an orderly transition to democratic institutions and a market economy and with keeping open their access to the new commercial opportunities which may then ensue.

Introduction

Alistair Hennessy

This book appears at an opportune moment. Embargoed for over thirty years by its nearest and natural trading partner, the US, and stranded by the ebbing of the ideological tide of communism, Cuba is turning to Western Europe. Why? It is the thesis of this book that the past survival of the Cuban Revolution cannot be understood if the Western European dimension is ignored, and that in the necessary diversification of Cuba's trade patterns, Western Europe will assume an increasing importance.

In this study we attempt to explain the reasons why the UK, France and Spain were prepared to go on trading with Cuba in spite of continued requests and pressure by the US not to. That they did so was due to a mixture of motives: legal, diplomatic, commercial and political. Differences of attitudes in assessing the communist threat and of the best way to deal with volatile radical nationalist movements, reflect fundamental differences in perception between US and European policymakers. Europeans did not share the Americans' view of the sanctity of the Monroe Doctrine and the idea of 'America for the Americans', nor did they view Cuba as being in the frontline of the Cold War, apart from the aberration of the missile crisis. In the view of many Europeans Cuba was an American problem which had been created by ingrained attitudes inherited from the past, by inflexibility in the face of unexpected challenge and by early hostility to the Revolution which forced the island into the arms of the Soviet Union. Such a view has been fiercely contested, and controversy still rages and will continue to do so over whether the break between the US and Cuba was inevitable, and once it had occurred who had been responsible for it. We do not attempt to address that issue but concentrate on the situation after the break became a *fait accompli*.

When criticising American attitudes it should be remembered that the English have been as obtuse in their attitudes towards Ireland. It was Captain Mahan whose book, *The Influence of Sea Power on History, 1660–1783* (1890), influenced *fin de siècle* American attitudes towards security issues and who, in stressing the strategic importance of Cuba, first pointed out the similarity with Ireland. However, the perceived security threat from off-shore islands was not only a matter of geopolitics but was deeply rooted in cultural and religious antipathies. A reluctance to confront differences and to understand the sensibilities of the Irish has been a leitmotif of

English history for centuries and still persists: that of the US towards Cuba is of more recent origin.

The American argument that an embargo would have forced the Revolution to collapse was based on the belief that Cuba, Americanised for so long, could not survive once it had been cut off from its source of supply and denied access to its major market. One of the greatest shocks which the Americans had to face was the way in which ordinary Cubans rose to the challenge of living in an economy of scarcity. Few Americans believed that the tyranny of distance could be tamed, and that the Eastern bloc could replace the US which accounted for some 70 per cent of Cuba's export and import trade. The heroism of the Revolution has been the heroism of improvisation under pressures of a blockade unique in modern history. An economy of scarcity and a siege mentality bred a morality of self-abnegation and of heroic endeavour, involving a re-ordering of priorities, not least of which was the questioning of those individual liberties which Americans took for granted, as well as of commonly accepted definitions of 'democracy'. With the New International Order, 'democracy' is coming to be reformulated in terms which permit the markets to operate unhindered. With such revamping it seems hypercritical to condemn Cubans for their lack of democracy and for choosing a different set of priorities.[1]

A major weakness in the Americans' historical assessment of Cuba has been to compare it with the US rather than with other Latin American countries, with their widening gap between rich and poor. This is understandable in view of the way Cuba had been drawn into the North American cultural and economic orbit of the US from as early as the 1790s. Cubans looked northwards rather than to the rest of Hispanic America. Not the least of the Revolution's achievements has been to Latinamericanise the island, and in this they were to be inspired by José Martí, their nineteenth-century nationalist mentor.[2]

For Americans, however, it was not Latin Americanisation but Sovietisation which seemed the greater threat. Cubans have always contended that theirs is an indigenous revolution. Cuban communism was a consequence of Castro's choice and not, as in other instances, a consequence of Soviet occupation or of the dislocation caused by total war. This has given to the regime an enviable flexibility denied to other communist states. However, from reading fulsome adulations of Soviet achievements and of communism generally in the Cuban press, foreign observers might be excused for assuming that it had been embraced wholeheartedly and uncritically, with accompanying thought-control, secret police, censorship, central planning, militarisation and lack of democratic accountability. Only the most dedicated Cubanologist could detect the nuances of the way in which Popular Power, Popular Courts or Rectification functioned. What is still difficult to say with any certainty (although the opening of Soviet archives might provide an answer), is the extent to which constraints imposed by the USSR have limited the Cubans' freedom of action or strengthened Castro's propensity to authoritarianism.[3]

Visitors and exiles

For foreigners visiting Havana, where 25 per cent of Cubans lived and beyond which few Americans ventured, the capital was a sophisticated city, far outstripping in size and magnificence other Caribbean capitals. It was also a mirror-image of Miami, with most of the accoutrements of American living. Brainwashed by consumer fetishism, most Americans could not conceive of social revolution on their doorstep which would question the way of life upon which their culture rested. This perception may well have been shared by many of the Cuban middle class, especially rentiers hit by the Urban Reform Law which limited income derived from rented property, a favourite investment of the Cuban middle-classes.

One of the major factors in accounting for the Revolution's political stability has been that potential opposition has been siphoned off by the safety valve of emigration which, because of the long-established Cuban-American communities in Florida, has been less traumatic than in the case of other revolutions. As many of the first wave were largely middle class, American attitudes were reinforced.

Cubans in the US have been the most successful and dynamic of the expanding Hispanic community and now number some 700,000, constituting a powerful lobby which cannot be ignored.[4] They do not speak with one voice, but the most vociferous argue for a tightening of the blockade on the assumption that this would bring down the regime. The presence of such a large exiled community keeps the Cuban issue alive, whereas in Europe it has long been dormant.

Those Cubans who did not or could not go into exile included culturally frustrated nationalists and the dispossessed. These latter entered a world from which they had been excluded: Cuban wealth could be redistributed in the form of imaginative (but increasingly costly) education, health and housing programmes. Foreigners have tended to generalise about the Revolution's shortcomings from the seedy run-down appearance of Havana which has had to pay for the sins of the forefathers as resources have been put into rural renewal, to the disgruntlement of many *habaneros*. Without understanding this rural populist thrust the Revolution makes little sense.[5]

Western Europe and the blockade

It is not too much of an exaggeration to say that had Europeans joined the embargo, as most states of the Americas, pressured though the OAS were to do (Mexico excepted), and Canada (which was not a member of the OAS), the Revolution might have collapsed. Nevertheless, West Europeans were to make a substantial contribution to the economy, especially in the early years, in the key area of transport. Without chartering West European tankers, it is doubtful if the Soviets would have been able to transport sufficient oil to Cuba which, lacking coal, hydro-electric or nuclear power, was totally dependent upon oil. Later there were to be other specialised areas of the economy to which European goods and services were qualitatively, although not necessarily quantitatively, significant.

Even in Britain with its 'Special Relationship' to the US, there was strong bipartisan resistance to joining the blockade, as Harold Macmillan wrote:[6]

> Eisenhower could now only rely on economic pressure, in which he urged us to join, to rally the Cuban people against their new oppressors. While accepting the President's analysis I expressed doubts as to whether economic hardship would encourage opposition to Castro, especially if it could be blamed on the Americans and mitigated by Russian help. Nor could I agree to operate any blockade, whether of tankers or other ships. In peacetime, we had no legal power to prevent tankers taking Russian oil to Cuba. I might have added that we had encountered quite a lot of difficulty in operating a blockade even during two world wars.

Realism and pragmatism have been the hallmarks of British diplomacy since George Canning formulated the principles of recognition policy at the time of Spanish-American Independence in the 1820s. In the case of blockades, British attitudes have been rooted in the principle of 'freedom of the seas' – a view to which Americans themselves subscribed during the war of 1812 when Britain claimed the right of search on the High Seas.[7] British foreign policy has lacked that ideological thrust which, it has been argued, has underpinned that of the US – 'one could note innumerable occasions', writes Christopher Lasch,[8] 'in which American idealism – the pursuit of ultimate instead of limited objectives, the tendency to think in terms of morality rather than in terms of power, the disavowal of national advantage in favour of altruistic internationalism – stood out in sharp contrast to European realism: and one could plausibly argue that American 'imperialism' was a function of the very eagerness with which American statesmen have tried to substitute for the old balance of power, a new world order based on universal democracy'.

French and Spanish diplomacy share a similar pragmatism to that of the British except that in the former, there is an additional cultural dimension. In the French case, the philosophical absolutes and moral imperatives of their own Revolution make them sympathetic to revolutionary movements elsewhere which they see reflecting, however dimly, their own experience, and to this must be added in Latin America strong French influences in law, republican institutions, and culture. In the Spanish case, history, language, religion and shared social values have created a sense of community between Hispanics throughout the Americas. This finds a reflection in foreign policy, whether in the liberal '*Hispanismo*' of the early years of the twentieth century, the '*Hispanidad*' of the Franco years, or in the contemporary projection of Spain as a bridge between Latin America and Europe. In the curious relationship between revolutionary Cuba and Franco Spain, pragmatism prevailed although still fortified by a strong sense of shared language, culture, family links and historical distrust of the US.

Europe and the Cuban Revolution

Over the past thirty years there has been an explosion in Cuban Studies but it is difficult to find, in the ever lengthening bibliographies, books or articles on the European connection. It is almost as if there has been a conspiracy of silence. This is a curious omission, especially as in the two peaks of the Revolution's popularity in the early- and late-1960s Cuba captured the imagination of a large number of the West European intelligentsia and students. That it should have energised the enthusiasm of this group is one of the Revolution's most significant features. It was, in a sense, the writing on the wall, presaging the generational conflicts which were to be one of the most distinctive trends of the 1960s.

Those few articles which do exist on the European connection tend to concentrate on the response of intellectuals and to ignore the nuts and bolts of the commercial relationship which, in the long run, may have been more important. The one major exception is Morris Morley's, *Imperial State and Revolution: The United States and Cuba 1952–1986*, (1987) which analyses in great detail the embargo strategy of the US once other ways of overthrowing the Castro regime had failed. Rich in theoretical ideas and in the documentation of the commercial and political complexities of US-Cuban relations, it is fundamental for an understanding of the Revolution. It appeared after our study was under way but although pursuing similar lines of enquiry the focus of this study is different.[9]

We are not concerned with the theoretical issues raised in Morley's book, but with an analysis from a European perspective of the different national contexts within which trade was conducted. The Americans' attempt to embargo Cuba was a consequence of the challenge which they faced from a reconstructed Europe and from an emergent Japan and, as Morley suggests, Cuba provides an interesting case-study of examining the way in which capitalist nations contested US hegemony. For the wider global implications readers are referred to Morley.

One of the reasons why scholars have previously not studied the West European connection with Cuba from a European perspective is partly because the subject remains sensitive and many doors still remain closed. There is an abundance of statistics on Western European-Cuban trade and much press reportage on the relationship, especially in the 1960s, but when one comes to study at source the vital commercial connections Cuba established with European firms information is scarce and often inaccessible. Although Western Europe has always defended its commercial relations with the Castro government on the grounds of pragmatism, the US has never accepted this view and often retaliated against those governments and firms which flouted the blockade, as in the case of blacklisting ships trading with Cuba. In such circumstances some firms are understandably secretive about their dealings with Cuba and prefer to keep skeletons they may have in the cupboard firmly locked away.

On several occasions representatives of firms who had done business with Cuba, commented that 'there was a story to be told' but that it could not be revealed because of prejudicing individuals who had worked, or were still working, for the firm, or because it might damage the firm's present reputation. This attitude was most common in England and to a lesser extent in Spain and France. Access to company documentation on Cuba is problematical and also not very rewarding. There were exceptions and some companies and individuals were forthcoming with valuable material. Because of these constraints the commercial chapters do not pretend to be definitive. Similarly, there is a hidden history of shared intelligence activity which remains to be uncovered. Although the US may have reluctantly accepted Britain's free trade argument for doing business with Cuba, at least there was some compensation as Britain could provide a conduit for acquiring information which might not otherwise have been available.

Historical antecedents

Our study concentrates on Britain, France and Spain. Constraints of time and finance prevented our extending the analysis to other West European powers, which will have to wait for a further study, but these three countries were the most significant and because of their long historical association with Cuba the most interesting.

Historical links between Cuba and Spain have naturally been the closest and most persistent and are discussed later (pp. 32–4). Although British and French links have been minimal by comparison, both countries played an important role in the eighteenth and nineteenth centuries, contributing towards Cuba's economic take-off as the world's major sugar producer.[10] The beginning of the modern period of Cuban history is often dated to the 11 months' occupation of Havana by the British in 1762–3 at the end of the Seven Years' War when the island was opened up to the slave trade. Having contributed to the labour force necessary for the Sugar Revolution, the British were to play an important role later in trying to undermine it by their abolitionist activity which reached a climax in the Turnbull affair of 1840, and the publication in London of a translation of the remarkable *Autobiography of a Slave* by Francisco Manzano.[11]

It is pertinent to recall that British abolitionists in the 'New World Order' of the 1840s, based on free-trade and free labour, encouraged conspiracies abroad much as Cuba was to do in the 1960s. Also, it is worth recalling the inefficacy of an earlier blockade of Cuba when British attempts in the 1830s and 1840s to curtail the slave trade were unsuccessful. Of the 550,000 slaves imported into Cuba between 1811 and 1870, 184,000 were imported after 1850.[12]

British machinery powered many of Cuba's mills and until 1900, 70 per cent of capital in public railways was British. Fernando Ortiz described Cuban railways as 'symbols of the economic domination, indirect but effective, of English imperialism'.[13] However, with the decline of abolitionist sentiment and as imperial interest shifted to India and later Africa, the British came to accept US hegemony in the Caribbean, interested not in who ruled in Cuba, but in how they ruled, only wanting satisfactory conditions for trade. Thus in the Cuban Ten Years' War (1868–78) and in the war between Spain and Cuba from 1895 to 1898, British policy supported the US, although often in opposition to that of other European powers.[14]

Nostalgia for a lost British opportunity was expressed in one of Winston Churchill's articles from Cuba where he was a correspondent in 1898 on leave from the army:

> I sympathise with the rebellion – not with the rebels. It may be that as the pages of history are turned, brighter futures and better times will come to Cuba. It may be that future years will see the island as it would be now, had England never lost it – a Cuba free and prosperous under just laws and a patriotic administration, throwing open her ports to the commerce of the world, sending her ponies to Hurlingham and her cricketers to Lords, exchanging the cigars of Havana for the cottons of Lancashire and the sugars of Matanzas for the cutlery of Sheffield. At least let us hope so.[15]

In so far as the British public was to have any consciousness of Cuba it would have been through music (although until recently this was always subsumed under the 'Latin beat'), through the lurid reputation of Havana, purveyed by seamen of the sexual delights of its brothels, or through Havana cigars, a symbol of affluence (with their distinctive decorative boxes), for which the young Winston Churchill acquired a lifelong taste.[16]

After independence, sugar and tobacco continued to be the major exports and Britain remained Cuba's second best customer in the 1920s and 1930s, but the interests in railways and tobacco declined, so that by the time of the Revolution, investments were limited to a few insurance companies and a stake in oil refining.

One issue, however, strained relations between the two countries. In 1913 the expansion of the sugar frontier into Oriente compelled the Cuban government, under pressure from plantation owners, to reverse the legislation prohibiting black immigration by admitting immigrant workers from the British West Indies. This was to be a bone of contention until the Cubanisation Law of 1933 stemmed the flow, as West Indians were continually complaining to the consuls of bad treatment, whilst the Cubans complained of the activities of the Garveyites. However, many West Indians settled in Cuba, often moving to the towns, where they became comparatively prosperous. Many were to be repatriated in the early-1960s when the Revolution threatened their businesses.

British culture, unlike that of France, made little impact on Cuba. Writers were not attracted to the island, apart from Graham Greene whose *Our Man in Havana* (1958), (the film version of which was shot on location the next year), although an 'entertainment' anticipated in a curious way the missile crisis of four years later. Earlier, D.H. Lawrence encapsulated the spirit of 1920s Havana, commenting on Americans coming down to the city in the days of Prohibition simply to get drunk. 'Ah, *Los americanos!* They are so good. They own us. They own Havana. We are a republic owned by the Americans. *Muy bien*, we give them drink, they give us the money, Bah! and he grinned with a kind of acrid indifference. He sneered at the whole show, but he wasn't going to do anything about it.'[17]

France's historical links have taken a different form to that of either Britain or Spain. Diplomatically less influential than Britain, French influences were significant in both economics and culture. The collapse of French power in St Domingue in the 1790s left a vacuum in world sugar production which the Cubans were quick to fill – aided to a considerable extent by French refugees from Haiti who provided the technical skill to build some of the largest sugar mills in the Havana-Matanzas region. At the same time coffee production in Oriente expanded largely due to French planters, many of whom brought their slaves with them and whose cultural legacies are still reflected in black folk customs. French cultural influences were considerable: in names, in language, and may be traced in the introduction of lithography in the 1820s and the subsequent domination of mid-nineteenth century printing shops by Frenchmen, in the extensive coverage of Cuba by French geographers, in the influence of French literature on Martí and others, and in the magnetic attraction of Paris for writers and for exiles, in particular Alejo Carpentier who lived in Paris from 1929 to 1939.[18]

Conclusion

One of the most striking features of the Revolution has been the interplay between a triumphalist rhetoric and a keen pragmatic sense of where Cuba's interests lie in order to ensure survival in the face of unremitting blockade. Pragmatism is a language which Western European powers understand but the Cubans are not prepared to trade the very considerable social gains of the Revolution for a mess of pottage. The future problem will be how to balance the socialist aims of the Revolution with the economic imperatives of doing business with capitalist powers. It may be that if and when the wheel turns, Cuba will once again become a model for the Third World which it was in the past, but this time shorn of the accretions of an irrelevant dogmatism.

Notes

1   The US perception of democracy in Third World nations, would seem to be shaped more by its own self-interest rather than by any consistent criterion or philosophic definition. See Noam Chomsky, *Deterring Democracy*, London, Verso, 1992.

2   See José Martí, *Our America*, (ed.) Philip S. Foner, New York Monthly Review, 1977. As he spent most of his life in exile, in Mexico and Venezuela and the US and wrote for the Latin American press, he had a continental vision which has been fully exploited in the Revolution's propaganda. Because of censorship he was better known outside Cuba during his lifetime.

3   For Castro's mind-set see Eduardo González and David Ronfeldt, *Castro, Cuba and the World*, Santa Monica, Rand, 1986.

4   See issues of the *International Migration Review* and *Cuban Studies* and Richard R. Fagen, *Cubans in Exile: Disaffection and Revolution*, Stanford, Stanford University Press, 1968. For a comparative analysis see Alejandro Portes and Robert L. Bach, *Latin Journey: Cuban and Mexican Immigrants in the United States*, Berkeley University of California Press, 1985.

5   José Yglesias, *In the Fist of the Revolution*, New York, Pantheon, 1968, reflects small town attitudes. There is an echo of Tchekov in the longing of one of his informants to get to Havana at whatever cost.

6   Harold Macmillan, *At the End of the Day* (Memoirs, Vol. 6) 1961–63, Macmillans, 1973, p. 181. The blockade of Beira during the Rhodesia conflict would seem to contradict this.

7   Recognition policy can be traced in Canning's despatches in R.K. Webster, *Britain and the Independence of Latin America, 1812–30*, 2 volumes, London,

Oxford University Press, 1938. The contrast with the American approach can be savoured in Manning, *Diplomatic Correspondence of the United States concerning the Independence of the Latin American Nations*, Washington, Carnegie Endowment, 3 vols., 1925. The spoils system as a reward for political services often conflicted with the ideological thrust of US foreign policy. Canning resolutely set his face against any political or financial interest on the part of ambassadors or consuls in the countries to which they were accredited.

8 Christopher Lasch, *The New Radicalism in America 1889–1963*, London, Chatto and Windus, 1966, p. 308. Lasch argues that Latin America, and Cuba in particular, were blind spots of the 'new realism' of the Kennedy administration due to Kennedy's European-oriented cosmopolitanism. Kennedy's first book was on appeasement in England in the 1930s.

9 Morris Morley, *Imperial State and Revolution: the United States and Cuba 1952–86*, Cambridge, Cambridge University Press, 1987. See also his 'US and Global Economic Blockade of Cuba', *Canadian Journal of Political Science*, xvii, 1 March, 1984. Jorge Domínguez, *To make a World Safe for Revolution: Cuban Foreign Policy*, Cambridge, Mass., Harvard University Press, 1989, is fundamental. See Nicanor León Cotayo, *El bloqueo a Cuba*, La Habana, Ediciones de Ciencias Sociales, 1983.

10 By far the best account is in Moreno Fraginals, *El Ingenio*, 3 vols., Havana Editorial de Ciencias Sociales, 1978.

11 Manzano's autobiography was translated by Richard Madden, and published in London in 1840; the original Spanish was not published in Cuba until 1937. British attempts to abolish the trade by naval blockade proved unsuccessful. See David Murray, *Odious Commerce: Britain, Spain and the Abolition of the Cuban Slave Trade*, Cambridge University Press, 1980 and Robert L. Paquette, *Sugar is Made with Blood: the Conspiracy of 'La Escalera' and the Conflict Between Empires over Slavery*, Middletown, Wesleyan Univ. Press, 1988.

12 Philip Curtin, *The Atlantic Slave Trade: a census*, Madison, University of Wisconsin, 1969, p. 157. Part of the failure was due to the superior speed of the better built American ships. Superior US technology was also to replace British locomotives in Cuba within ten years of their introduction.

13 See Gert Oostindie, 'La burguesía cubana y sus caminos de hierro, 1830–1868', *Boletin de Estudios Latinoamericanos y del Caribe*, No. 37, Dec. 1984.

14 Christopher J. Bartlett, 'British Reactions to the Cuban Insurrection, 1868–78', *Hispanic American Historical Review*, 37(3), August, 1957; and for 1895–8, R.G. Neale, 'British and American Relations During the Spanish American War: Some Problems', *Journal of Historical Studies* (Australia/New Zealand), Vol. 6, January, 1953.

15 Randolph Churchill, *W. S. Churchill*, Vol. 1. Companion, part 1, 1874–96, London, Heinemann, 1967, pp. 617–18.

16 This can now be savoured through the writings of Enrique Cabrera Infante as in *Infante's Inferno*, London, Faber and Faber, 1984.

17 From his unfinished story, 'The Flying Fish', in *St Mawr and Other Stories*, London, Grafton Publishing, 1983, pp. 282–4.

18 For French influence see Jean Lamore (ed.), *Cuba et la France – Francia y Cuba*, Bordeaux, Presses Universitaires de Bordeaux, 1982 and Olavo Alen, 'La sociedades de Tumba Francesa en Cuba', *Anales del Caribe*, 2/1982 and W.R. Lux, 'French Colonisation in Cuba, 1791–1809', *Americas*, Vol. 29, 1972. For exiles in Paris during the War of Independence see Paul Estrade, *L'émigration cubain a Paris, 1895–98, Caravelle*, 16:1:1971.

CHAPTER 1

Cuba, Western Europe and the US: An historical overview

Alistair Hennessy

The Cuban Revolution ushered in a new era of world politics. It challenged orthodoxies of the left; it extended the Cold War to the Americas; it popularised a new revolutionary strategy of armed struggle in which the rootless would be leaders; it energised the concept of Third World solidarity, displacing the priorities of East-West conflict by the urgencies of the North-South divide and revived faith in socialism, canalising anti-imperialist sentiment by equating it with resistance to US hegemony. Policymakers in the US were unprepared for the suddenness and the originality of the challenge, and were forced to face up to these novelties for the threat they posed to national security and to the domination of the US throughout Latin America and the Caribbean.

Perceptions and decision-making

In confronting these challenges, policymakers could receive little help from academics; there was no established tradition of American scholarship on Cuba – in marked contrast to the situation after 1959 when Cuban Studies in the US became an industry, professionalised to an extent without parallel on a country of such small size.[1] The reasons for this dearth of interest before 1959 can be related to the way in which Cuba was taken for granted, as in the much quoted phrase of John Quincey Adams in 1823 that Cuba will fall, in the 'gravitation theory' like a ripe apple into the lap of the US.[2]

For most Americans, even academics, Cuba was not a subject for serious research so much as a playground where puritanical inhibitions could be thrown to the winds. The absence of specialised knowledge meant that early interpretations of the Revolution lacked historical and sociological depth and showed little understanding of the dynamics of Cuban development, or how it differed from revolutionary changes elsewhere – as, for example, the Guatemalan Revolution (1944–54).[3]

The absence of a historical dimension, in interpreting the Revolution, raises a problem that is not unique to Cuba. Revolutions do not wait for the niceties of historical scholarship which inevitably, given the mass of archival material, as well as the lack of availability of key documents, has its own meandering momentum. Political decisions, therefore, tended to be made according to the nostrums of those with vested interests which could not convincingly be challenged or modified, or were made under the influence of the current fashionable social science paradigms of academic advisers.[4] Decisions were also taken, and attitudes formed, in the light of those perceptions which had long conditioned American foreign policy in its dealings with Cuba and Latin America generally. Latin America was, in the homely metaphor, a 'backyard problem' and as such was not given a high priority. This was reflected in the low prestige accorded to Latin American Studies in comparison with those on other areas. Nor did the Cuban desk in the State Department carry much weight and ambassadors to Havana tended to be political appointments.[5]

The consequent lack of broader understanding was particularly unfortunate as Cuban nationalism had developed into a distinctive and dynamic force deeply rooted in the nineteenth century colonial experience.[6] In contrast to the rest of Latin America where, with the premature achievement of independence, 'State' had preceded 'Nation', resulting in a confused sense of identity, in Cuba, in contrast, the longer and tighter control of Spanish colonialism had created a keener awareness of nationhood.

The confusion and complexities of mainland Spanish America in the nineteenth century may be largely attributed to the absence of a clear nationalist strategy, as personalist cliques under regional *caudillos* struggled for control of the weak state apparatus. In Cuba, the contradictions rising from the rapid expansion of the sugar revolution in a colonial economy, and the imbalance between economic and political power which this generated, heightened the tension between '*criollos*' and '*peninsulares*'.

Of all Latin American countries, Cuba was the one which should have attracted attention as its nationalism had been forged in the fires of an extended war of independence.[7] As in the Thirteen Colonies in the eighteenth century, so in nineteenth century Cuba, the idea of the nation existed in the minds of the people before independence was achieved. The frustration of the nationalist drive by the limitations imposed during the American occupation after the defeat of Spain in 1898, and by the Platt Amendment, together with increasing dependence on the US economy, gave a distinctive cast to the vocal expression of Cuban nationalism in the aftermath of the First World War.

Had the works of José Martí been read, some understanding might have been gained of the nature of Cuban nationalism.[8] His perceptive comments on American society and his prescience on the future role which the US would play in Latin America went virtually unstudied and unheeded at a time when the US was flexing its industrial muscles and seeking foreign markets, coinciding with the closing of the frontier and apocalyptic foreboding that only expansion abroad could preserve democracy at home.[9] Such was the ignorance of Cuban history and scorn for national susceptibilities that, on the infamous occasion in 1947 when a drunken American sailor climbed to the top of the Martí monument in Havana and urinated over the statue of the national hero, universally revered as the 'Apostle', the ambassador, in apologizing for the incident on television the next day, forgot his name.

Had Cuban history been studied; had its writers been read or translated, some understanding might have been gained of the wealth of Cuban culture and of the longevity of its radical nationalist tradition, with roots in the nineteenth century, of its explicit anti-imperialism and a redemptive messianic strain which was to become one of the most distinctive aspects of the Revolution's ideology.[10] Nevertheless, without some knowledge of these historical imperatives and the sustaining myths of the Revolution – as important in the Cuban psyche as those of the American Revolution have been for Americans – it is difficult to understand the Revolution's early years, and resort has to be made to conspiracy theories or to communist subversion as interpretation. In explaining the Revolution's survival, primacy has been given to Russian support at the expense of the Cubans' own efforts: Castro was regarded as a deceitful crypto-communist and Cuba as a satellite, surrogate or client state of the Soviet Union, deprived of its own independent judgement and autonomy of action. This may be illustrated by the way in which Castro's declaration of being a Marxist-Leninist was taken at face value (although explicable in the context of the Cold War, and of Khrushchev's forward policy), with the assumption that this implied total conversion to Soviet communism. The 1960s saw a number of revisions of Marxism worldwide in order to explain not only the weaknesses and failures of the left in the industrialised world, but also to accommodate revolutionary theory to the revelations of Khrushchev at the twentieth party congress, as well as to the needs of ex-colonial countries.[11] Marxism came to mean different things to different people, especially in Latin America where the left has always couched its ideas in Marxist terminology.[12] For Castro, Marxism was what he intended it to mean when he called for a 'creative approach' to Marxism in the early-1960s.

Differences between the American and European left

Americans were at a disadvantage in assessing and interpreting the Revolution's rapid radicalisation by having no deeply-rooted socialist movement themselves. When to this is added the McCarthyite legacy, it is not surprising that Castro's beliefs and his socialist and Marxist avowals were regarded with suspicion and hostility and as a betrayal of his earlier views. Europeans and Americans are deeply divided by their different perceptions of socialism which strikes at the root of the self-help ethic.[13] Living in the 'backyard' of the USSR, Europeans had learnt to co-exist with communism, and to take its presence, however unpalatable, for granted.

Marxism and communism grew and were nurtured in European soil and were indeed comparable in American eyes to those other corrupting European influences of monarchy and aristocracy. Every Western European country had a socialist left and flourishing socialist sub-culture, each varying according to national traditions, whether Chartist, Christian socialist, guild socialist, social democratic, syndicalist, anarchist, Marxist, or non-Marxist. Debate on the left over the nature of socialism was not simply an academic exercise, but a matter of public concern in societies where the socialist option was always open, in contrast to the US where socialists were confined to academic and ethnic enclaves, with no prospect of being treated seriously as a potential government.

In Europe relations between social democrats and communists were rarely harmonious as they were competing for the same constituency. Their leaders were divided by temperament, tactics, strategy and ideology, as well as in differing assessments of the Soviet Union and in sectarian interpretations of Marxist texts. But although regarding each other with suspicion, they generally enjoyed liberty to proselytise. Whereas the frustrations of the American left rose from an awareness that power was beyond their reach and that they were condemned for ever to be one of many competing pressure groups, at least they were spared the disillusionment of having their Utopian dreams destroyed by the harsh realities and the compromises of office. The frustration of the European left, in contrast, rose from departures from principle once socialists came to power, and a sense of being betrayed by the leadership, and by the fading of the Utopian dream in the labyrinths of bureaucracy. Both saw Cuba as an escape from the cul-de-sac in which the left found itself in the late-1950s.

Whether in fact a deeper knowledge of Cuban history and culture would have altered the course of Cuban-American relations by changing US policy raises the question of whether the breach was inevitable, and once it had occurred who had been responsible for it. There is an element of unpredictability in all nationalist movements as they feed on historical grievances, real, imagined or invented, but in the case of Cuba the process of Americanisation had gone so far and was so pervasive that it is difficult to see how any programme of national revindication could have progressed without a break of some sort. As a liberal capitalist society, Americans have no sympathy with the socialisation of property, but this was an integral part of all nationalist movements in the 1950s and 1960s, as was the acceptance of single party rule to ensure national unity so as to avoid the divisive influences of party conflict.

Five factors in particular made a rift unavoidable: the summary justice meted out to '*batistianos*', the refusal to hold free elections; the nationalisation of property with agrarian reform; urban reform (striking at the rentier middle class); the nationalisation of oil; and finally the infiltration of communists into the administration – necessitated by the amorphous nature of the 26th of July Movement.[14] The last was particularly galling to many 26th of July militants in view of the communists' close association with Batista in the late-1930s and 1940s and their unheroic role in the Revolution, when many were 'under their beds', in Castro's words, when there was fighting in the hills.[15]

The imperatives of student power

One factor which has made Cuban and Latin American nationalism so volatile and so difficult to contain and predict is that it finds its most ardent expression among university students. Not normally regarded in Europe, or the US, as a political force to be reckoned with (at least not until 1968), in Latin America students have exercised an importance out of all proportion to their numbers. This derives from the compulsive attraction of the University Reform Movement, which originated in the attempt by students in the Argentine University of Córdoba in 1918, to reform the university to meet the needs of modern society, but their programme went beyond pedagogic reforms to embrace nationalism, anti-imperialism and panlatinamericanism.[16] For the Reformists, students were to be the vanguard leading revolutionary change whilst the university itself would become a model republic in which students, graduates and professors shared power in the democracy of co-government. At the core of the reform movement was the myth of the incorruptibility of youth, as well as an implicit elitist assumption that students were the natural leaders of political change.

Revolutionaries always tend to be youthful – gerontocrats cannot vault the barricades, only lead from the shadows. Nevertheless, Cuban nationalism was unusual, even by Latin American standards, for the way in which students articulated nationalist grievances and influenced national politics, as had been shown in 1933 when they were to be represented in the revolutionary government of Grau San Martín, himself a university professor. To the American incomprehension of Cuban nationalism was therefore added the difficulty of taking seriously a group who, until the middle-1960s, Americans, from their own experience, had never considered to be a serious political force.

The mirage of Monroism

The globalisation of politics caused by the Cuban Revolution's extension of the Cold War to Latin America called into question the principles of the Monroe Doctrine on which US foreign policy toward Latin America had been based and which had become central to the American foreign policy psyche. When, during the missile crisis of 1962, Khrushchev had boasted that the Monroe Doctrine was dead he was striking at a fundamental belief which had, until then, not been challenged in such uncompromising terms. Mary Baker Eddy, the head of the Christian Science Church, expressed this belief graphically in 1923, a hundred years after the Doctrine's promulgation, by declaring as an article of faith that she believed 'strictly in the Monroe Doctrine, in our Constitution and in the laws of God'.[17]

When it had been originally formulated in 1823 the Doctrine had been conditioned by an acute awareness of the potential threat posed to the security of the US by the political vacuum left by the break up of Spain's empire. With the Russians already in Alaska, and with British and French Caribbean colonies and the British established in Canada as a springboard for further incursions, and with memories of the 1812 British invasion, the threat seemed real enough, finding some confirmation in 1832 when the British occupied the Malvinas Islands. But behind the pragmatic warning to European powers not to interfere lay ideological assumptions which run throughout subsequent American history. These are encapsulated in the New World – Old World dichotomy. Europeans had been the first to employ the phrase 'New World' for Columbus' landfall, projecting on to it Utopian fantasies, both religious and secular, envisaging ideal societies where the irredeemable sins of the Old World could be sloughed off and life started afresh. The newly-independent nations of both North and South America were inheritors of eighteenth century ideas of perfectibility. But whereas in the US these beliefs were enshrined in the Constitution and in the concept of the 'first new nation' becoming a beacon for the dispossessed of the Old World, the nations of Spanish America, fragmented in spite of the efforts of Simón Bolívar with his Utopian vision of an independent and united Spanish America, so far from heralding a new dawn ushered in a twilight of anarchy and violence.

Implicit in the Doctrine was the view that the US would be the protector of the Americas from the corrupting influences of the Old World, exercising a tutelary function. To Latin Americans, the Doctrine is widely regarded as a cloak for US expansionism, unimpeded by European interference. Although lacking any status in international law, the Monroe Doctrine was to be regarded by conservatives as a bulwark against international communism.

US attitudes to Europe and to Latin America

For us the important point to notice is how US attitudes to Latin America and Europe often coincide. This can be related to the continued involvement of Europe in Latin America throughout the nineteenth century. The challenge of expanding frontiers, the harnessing of science and technology to conquer territory, defeating indigenous inhabitants and settling immigrants generated its own dynamism in the US (Argentina is the only comparable example in Latin America). In Spanish America, in contrast, the new nations were unable to rise to this challenge without the aid of British finance (and increasingly, North American technology). To economic dependence was added cultural dependence. Whereas the writers of the American Renaissance of the 1840s were exploring new forms and themes, those in Spanish America tended to look to Europe for an example, and in Sarmientos' *Civilisation and Barbarism* (1845), a key text for Spanish American intellectuals until the 1920s, it was argued that salvation would come from Europe.[18] Without resources to dominate the wilderness, and unable to compete with the US in attracting immigrants, Spanish Americans regarded Europe with nostalgia; its writers bemused by Paris. Spanish Americans shared little with Spain in the nineteenth century beyond an addiction to rule by soldiers and the distinctive Hispanic phenomenon of *caudillismo*, with its accompanying '*pronunciamiento*', '*cuartelazo*', '*machetazo*', and other refinements of military intervention. Nor had Spanish America been liberated from European cultural tutelage; thus it continued to share many of the attributes which Americans associated with the Old World, regarding Latin American states as an extension of Europe or relics of colonialism rather than as 'new nations'. They remained mired in those political vices which Americans regarded, hypocritically perhaps, with abhorrence.

This was no more apparent than in religion. Americans were heirs to the Black Legend of Protestant historiography. The Manifest Destiny expansionist ideology of the 1840s and 1850s was shot through with the language and presuppositions of Protestant superiority. The US had a divine mission to liberate Spanish Americans from the benighted influences of Spanish Catholicism, introducing to it Protestantism and the work-ethic. These legitimations for expansion were to find further expression, linked to pseudo-scientific social Darwinism with racial overtones from the 1880s, and would provide much of the ideological justification behind US intervention in Cuba in 1898.[19]

Behind the rhetoric of Panamericanism – the union of sister republics canvassed at the first Panamerican Conference in 1889 – was the awareness of the potentialities of the Latin American market for American industry. José Martí sounded a warning that it was not an alliance of equals but a device, through reciprocity treaties, to tie Latin American exports to the US market in return for free entry of American industrial products. The commercial thrust of the US into Latin America was to antagonise sections of the elite there, who feared the democratic implications of increased American influence. The best illustration of this fear was in the popularity of the Uruguyan Enrique Rodó's *Ariel*, with its echoes of classical, European, aristocratic values, which was published in 1900, in the aftermath of US intervention in Cuba.[20]

It may be described as an ideology of sublimation for small states which claim spiritual superiority in the face of overwhelming material power and wealth. The extraordinary popularity of the work is indicative of the hold which European ideas still had for the Latin American elite but no one can tell from the text that the majority of the continent's population was African, Indian, mulatto, or mestizo.

In his appeal to youth, Rodó anticipates the vanguardism of the University Reform Movement. Students' political protests came to be tolerated by the public at large as often they constituted the only form of political opposition to dictators. They were accepted by the elite as a form of '*rite de passage*' through which their sons prepared for later political careers. Ideology, in this context 'is not so much a matter of deep conviction but is perceived as an individual pragmatic tool for patron-linked advancement, rather than as a legitimation of a collective world view to which one adheres out of an inner and, in principle, durable conviction'.[21] In this view, the use of Marxian language is part of the rhetoric of political exchange in intra-elite conflict and should not necessarily be taken at its face value, and certainly not as a commitment to communism.

Mutual perceptions – Latin America and the US

If the Latin American view of the US was conditioned by the perception of an uncomprehending, materialist, expansionist 'hovering giant', that of Latin America by Americans was often of a region of 'gunslinging guerrilleros and moral degenerates'.[22] It must not be forgotten that the vision each had of the other was asymmetrical, with American travel literature and commentary far outweighing that of Latin American writers on the US. However, far more significant than reading matter has been the influence of Hollywood, not only for its images of Latin Americans purveyed to American audiences, but to Latin American audiences of the American way of life. The image most people in the US had of their neighbours to the South was generalised from that of Mexico, which tended to predominate not only because of geographical proximity, but also because of the extension to Mexico of the genre of the Western and of colourful bandits such as Pancho Villa who in Hollywood films, rides again, and again and again. Those few American films set in Cuba used Havana as a back-drop for acting out fantasies in an environment similar to Miami, but one where lazy stereotypes were perpetuated. When the MGM film, *Cuban Love Story* (1931), was released the Cuban Minister of the Interior was flooded by complaints from Cubans that the film depicted the island as an 'uncivilised country where the natives are half clothed and bare foot, and the local magistrates impose absurd penalties on foreigners'.[23]

With a common frontier, which was constantly being crossed, it was Mexico and not Cuba which dominated the American imagination, and through the influence of European powers it was perceived to pose a threat to security, especially during the First World War and to American investments, as in the oil nationalisation of the late-1930s. But policymakers need not have worried about repercussions in the rest of Latin America as the furious intensity of internal conflicts distracted Mexico from actively spreading the Revolution. Added to which was the cardinal principle of Mexican foreign policy of non-intervention. Nevertheless, the Mexican Revolution's influence in the rest of Latin America was profound, although not as in the later Cuban case through guerrilla activity, but by revindicating hitherto despised Indian populations, by its agrarian reform measures and as part of the wider nationalist '*prise de conscience*' throughout Latin America in the 1920s, which saw the growth of 'New Worldism' of which isolationism in the US was itself a part.

If the US thought that isolation would be a reversion to the idea of America for the Americans they were to be mistaken. The First World War may have given a powerful impetus to American economic expansionism in Latin America, particularly at the expense of the British, whose economic dominance was challenged in every Latin American country except Argentina. But this was not accompanied by an acceptance of American cultural influence. Films may have raised envy among cinema audiences but it tended to confirm the elite in their feelings of disdain for American values. Nor could isolationism seal the Americas off from pernicious European influences such as Bolshevism, refracted through the prism of the Parisian Left Bank in the writings of Henri Barbusse and the Clarté group, and in more practical terms by the appearance of Bolshevik agents such as M.N. Roy in Mexico and the foundation of communist parties such as that in Cuba in 1923.[24]

The form which 'New Worldism' took in Latin America was paradoxical. Firstly, the repudiation of Europe which had been torn apart in the First World War stimulated interest in Latin America's Spanish heritage. By remaining neutral during the war, Spain's influence had increased among those disillusioned and horrified at the 'European Civil War', in which the gods they envied had torn themselves apart. More important, though, was the influence of Spanish writers who, after the Generation of 1898 and the self-questioning after the loss of Cuba, had reinvigorated Spanish culture.[25] The values of the Hispanic legacy began to be critically assessed and better appreciated. For the first time since independence Spain provided a positive cultural model. Relieved of the burdens of empire, Spanish intellectuals tried to forge a new relationship between Spanish-speaking nations throughout the Americas. It became quite respectable for writers to idealise Spanish culture as a way of offsetting encroaching Americanisation in a way which would have been impossible when Spain was still a colonial power.

Secondly, Latin American intellectuals, in distancing themselves from a discredited Europe began to discover the 'Other' within their midst. The Mexican Revolution's vindication of Indians gave a powerful impetus to this view, but the African legacy began to be taken seriously in Brazil by Gilberto Freyre and in Cuba by Fernando Ortiz, Alejo Carpentier, Nicolás Guillén, Wilfredo Lam and others. 'Negrismo', the use of Africanisms in poetry by white poets, became a vogue in the 1920s (paralleling the European discovery of the 'Other' and the use of African motifs by European painters). Afro-Cubanism began to popularise the idea that the distinguishing feature of Cuban culture lay in its African roots. This was paralleled in the US by the Harlem Renaissance, together with the more political and commercial expression of Garveyism.

Afro-Cubanism, especially in musical forms, was one way of asserting distinctiveness but it was not a consensus view. It was not shared by Spanish immigrants, nor by the white Cuban elite, many of whom had welcomed the Platt Amendment of 1901, which allowed for the US to intervene in Cuba should American interests be threatened, seeing this as a safeguard against a resurgence of black radicalism. The Cuban communist party proselytised among blacks, as the most exploited section of the community, thus they became suspect, bringing to the surface the existence of a submerged racial problem.

The extent of black support for the 26th July Movement in the revolt against Batista has been questioned. However, the claims that the Revolution liberated blacks and the identification of the Revolution with the cause of blacks in the US at a time when the racial problem there was reaching a climax in the late-1950s and 1960s, was an additional factor in widening the gulf of misunderstanding.[26]

The security problem

Such was the background against which the Revolution must be viewed, but it was not the fact of Batista's overthrow in 1959 which posed the challenge. Without the moral support of many in the US and the arms embargo of the US government against Batista, it is doubtful if the Revolution could have succeeded. It was, rather, the unpredictability of Fidel Castro, his apparent back-tracking on his original programme, coupled with his deliberate decision to exploit the strengths of the Cuban communist party and their disciplined cadres and their Moscow contacts which constituted the threat. For the US, a country which had not been directly menaced since the British invasion in the War of 1812, which had fought its own wars on foreign soil (excepting the Indian wars, and the fratricide of the Civil War), whose frontline of defence had always been on other people's territory and which had never heard the whine of bombs, to have a communist base 90 miles off-shore was an original and unnerving prospect.

What gave such a sense of urgency to the US assessment of the Revolution was the speed of radicalisation and the shock that for the first time in the Caribbean a coup was turning into a full-scale social revolution which was out of the Americans' control. When previously such a threat had occurred, in 1933, the most extensive revolutionary outbreak in Latin America in the 1930s, the Americans were able to find in Batista, 'that extraordinarily able and brilliant fellow' in the words of Sumner Welles the US Ambassador, someone who would support their interests. Batista's coup in January 1934 ushered in ten unheroic years of political stability during which, as part of Batista's consensus policy the communists became respectable.[27] That they should later go on to make a crucial contribution to the consolidation of Castro's revolution in the 1960s is one of the more ironical features of the US earlier support of Batista.

There were other dimensions of the national security issue beyond the direct threat from Soviet missiles and a militarised island. There was, firstly, the threat of a chain reaction throughout Latin America which the Cubans considered, mistakenly, to be ripe for revolution. Seduced by the ease with which Batista had been overthrown they believed that the strategy which had been successful in Cuba would be successful in the rest of the continent. The escalating involvement of the Soviet Union in an area where previously its influence had been minimal (partly propelled by the need to counter Chinese influences although, in retrospect this was grossly exaggerated except in the case of Peru's Sendero Luminoso) appeared to pose the real challenge.

Secondly, Moscow's involvement in Cuba was graphic confirmation of the Soviet Union's naval *Weltpolitik* foreshadowed in a massive naval building programme from the 1950s.[28] Until the 1950s, the Soviet Union's strategic interests had been concentrated on consolidating its position in Eastern Europe. To extend control and to make World Revolution feasible a Soviet presence had to be seen throughout the world's oceans – a view forcibly expressed from 1956 by Admiral Gorshkov, arguably the greatest naval administrator of the twentieth century. Naval ships in the ports of uncommitted nations of the Third World would be the visible expression of Soviet power as well as posing a threat to the oil lifeline of Western Europe round the Cape of Good Hope and through the Suez Canal. Trade strategy and ideology dictated the need for an ocean-going navy similar to that during the period of Anglo-German naval rivalry in the pre-1914 era. Cuba could provide facilities to complement those in Mogadishu, Conakry and later Luanda.

Thirdly was the security threat which a Soviet naval presence posed in the Caribbean itself. Such a threat revived historical memories. Military intervention by the US in various islands during the opening decades of the twentieth century were ostensibly debt-collecting exercises, but also to prevent political instability which might prompt European intervention, especially by Germany. Strategic need was also an argument for retaining Puerto Rico as well as for securing a naval base at Guantanamo in Cuba which would serve to guard the Panama Canal. The latter, in an era of expansionism, was crucial to the US' new world-wide commitments.

The Second World War had served to underline the vulnerability of the Caribbean region to submarine attack. It is not often realised that German 'U' boats sank some 500 allied ships in the Caribbean and its approaches. Cuba, Puerto Rico, and the Chaguaramas Base in Trinidad had played a key role as bases for anti-'U' boat patrols. By the 1960s the vulnerability of the US to naval attack had been increased by the dependence of the East coast on Caribbean sea lanes for perhaps a third of its domestic oil supplies. Also, it was estimated that some 60 per cent of reinforcements for NATO would have to pass through the Caribbean, thus providing Americans with an argument for linking the Cuban problem to European security. Soviet submarine bases in Cuba, together with radar and air surveillance, was a disturbing prospect.[29] Cubans might riposte that small powers have security problems too but in an asymmetrical relationship these are not usually recognised.

Fourthly, and most insidious because so unexpected, was the undermining of internal security. For a variety of reasons connected with social, technological, sexual, racial and educational changes, there was a small but vocal constituency of the disaffected and alienated within the US for whom Cuban criticism of the shortcomings and contradictions of American society struck resonant chords. What made this criticism more compelling than the traditional critique from foreigners of the old left was that it stemmed from Cuban familiarity with American society through experience in 'the bowels of the monster' in José Martí's phrase, and from direct contact with the behaviour of Americans in Cuba. These criticisms echoed many of those made within the US itself.[30] From the early years of the Revolution the Cubans were determined to occupy the moral high ground, subjecting

American society to savage criticisms which were to be taken up enthusiastically on American campuses. Politicised students, a fact of life in every Latin American country, were, for the first time, to become actors in American domestic politics, although this was not to be a major factor until the escalation of the Vietnam War after 1965. The Revolution's initial impact in the US could also be related to the new style of politics it represented which threatened to undermine established patterns and upset the workings of the two-party system.

Cuba's proximity to the US ensured high media coverage. The Revolution was more immediately accessible to the viewing and listening public than any previous revolution had been. Cubans themselves, Americanised for decades, had absorbed the importance of publicity. It was the first revolution to exploit television, with Castro using the media and the helicopter, as effectively as Hitler had used radio and the aeroplane before him in the 1930s. Cuba, therefore, was of central concern not only to policymakers trying to contain the revolution but to the wider population as well. For the first time in the US at peace, a foreign policy issue became a matter of widespread concern to a population which had been brought up on the established 'truths' of Monroism – the principle of non-colonisation in the Americas by a European power: the Two Spheres policy by which the US would not become involved in wars which only related to Europe and finally, the crucial 'hands off' principle by which any attempt of Europeans to promote their system anywhere in the Americas would be regarded as a threat to the safety of the US.[31]

There was, however, a paradox in American attitudes. If the Soviet Union (as a European power) had no place in the New World, Western Europe had to be brought in to redress the balance – to reverse Canning's famous dictum – by joining the blockade to break the Revolution and so destroy Soviet influence. This takes us to the heart of the difference in perception. To Europeans Cuba was an American problem but to the US it was part of the global crusade against communism.

It was clear that the US could not prevent European powers from pursuing their interests in Latin America and especially in the Caribbean, with the residual colonial legacies and responsibilities of Britain, France and the Netherlands.[32] European and US interests were not necessarily antagonistic and indeed, coincided in the wish to contain the spread of Cuban interest (although there were differences over how to achieve this, and given the US global strategy of containment the US expected greater co-operation from Europe). More recently, Britain and the US have co-operated closely in countering the drugs menace, and the European Community, through the Lomé convention, has become involved in aid programmes and has also aspired to play a mediating role in Central America.

The European dimension

Europeans were in no better position to assess or understand what was happening in Cuba. Unlike the US where there was at least the semblance of a tradition for studying Latin America on which to build, in Europe serious study scarcely existed. In the post-war period Latin America was for Europeans the least known and least important of the world's major regions. This was partly because the energies and attention of Britain and France were directed towards Africa and Asia and the problems of decolonisation and withdrawal from empire, whilst Italy, Germany and the Soviet Union were distracted by problems of reconstruction. Spain had close ties through language, religion, culture and emigrants of Spanish descent, especially in Cuba where as many as a quarter of a million had Spanish passports. However, until the death of Franco in 1975, Spain's attitude was represented by the doctrine of *Hispanidad*, harking back to a great Imperial past, with a patronising attitude which Latin Americans resented. In general, though, Latin America counted for little in Europe.

The subservience of the continent to the US was reflected by the way in which it could count on the support of Latin American countries in the United Nations. The dislocation of trade links and a falling off in investment and the withdrawal of funds had helped to consolidate American domination. The British connection with Argentina was the one exception, but even this was to be broken during the Peronist period. Nor were Europeans well-informed about Latin America. Tourism and travel writing scarcely existed; journalistic coverage was minimal; publishers avoided commissioning books on the region.

All this was to change with the Cuban Revolution. By the mid-1960s Latin America had been rediscovered. Rather like the boom of interest in the 1820s, the continent was seen to offer limitless possibilities for investment and trade.

Part of this new attitude reflected a disillusionment with Africa, Asia and the Middle East. As Latin Americans were largely of European stock and had been independent for a century and a half, it was felt that they could more easily become commercial and diplomatic partners. In the Caribbean both Britain and France feared Cuban subversion – fears which were to be temporarily laid to rest by the massive US intervention in the Dominican Republic in 1965 which was to deter Cuba for over a decade from a forward policy in the Caribbean.

The newly-revived interest was encouraged (if not actually promoted) by the US.[33] Europe could not only assist in the economic development of the continent, without which it might follow the Cuban example, but Europeans could act as a lightning conductor deflecting hostility away from the US. Hence Latin American Studies became the fastest growing of all area studies programmes, with Foundation and government funds pouring in to new centres of academic activity.

The spin-off in Europe was considerable and nowhere more so than in Britain where six Centres of Latin American Studies were established, five directly from government funds. Although the purpose of official support was the recovery of lost markets and influence, academic interest focused on the repercussions of the Cuban Revolution in Latin America and the problems of economic development. But in the mid-1960s, the heyday of the counter-culture, links between universities and commerce were distrusted.

Whereas this revival of interest quickened the flow of Latin Americans to European universities it did not extend to Cubans, and Cuban Studies were not to be a major beneficiary of this development. Research in Cuba could be hedged round with difficulties. In Britain books were slow to appear.[34] Ten years were to elapse before Hugh Thomas's massive key history of Cuba was published. In France, by contrast, there was a flood of books on Cuba and a much more thorough press coverage.[35] The reasons for this contrast may perhaps have been because of the relative ease with which Batista had been overthrown in comparison to the long drawn-out colonial revolts in Indo-China and Algeria. Cuba was a new wind providing a compelling example of revolutionary praxis for a disillusioned, implacably anti-American, French left. There was, too, the attraction to intellectuals of a Revolution in which they appeared to play a key role, both as guerrilla leaders and in the formulation of a revolutionary culture. With the imprimatur of Jean-Paul Sartre and Simone de Beauvoir, the Revolution was to receive the almost unqualified support of the French left.

In Spain the position was more complex. Censorship restricted press coverage, but the Revolution did not have the repercussions which might have been expected. The Spanish left derived little inspiration from Castro in the anti-Franco struggle, and no practical help. Spain was the one European country to receive a considerable influx of Cuban exiles, many of Spanish extraction, so unlike France and Britain, there was an active anti-Castro lobby. Most markedly was the absence of any expansion of academic interest in either Cuba or contemporary Latin America. These were dangerous subjects to introduce into universities at a time when they were becoming the major source of disaffection and opposition to Franco.[36] More important, perhaps, was the convergence of both the left and right in Spain in their dislike of and opposition to the US and the humiliating Platt Amendment. The curious relationship between Cuba and Franco Spain was one between two pariahs.

European Cuban trade links

At no time since 1959 have the links between Western Europe and Cuba been severed. Had the US succeeded in breaking those links, as on many occasions it tried to do, Cuba would have been deprived of technical advice, of sources of credit, of access to transport, of moral support deriving from the knowledge that although the US could enforce its will throughout the Americas – with the important exception of Canada and Mexico and, until 1975, when the OAS lifted the embargo, by other Latin American states – it could not corral Europe into wholehearted support of its anti-Castro policies. As late as September 1991 the traditional view was being reiterated by the British Secretary of Trade: 'It is for the British government not the US Congress, to determine the UK's policy in trade with Cuba. We will not accept any attempt to superimpose US law on UK companies'.[37]

The significance of Western European trade must be put into the context of US strategy to isolate and finally destroy the Revolution. Once US-Cuban relations had been severed and internal and external attempts to subvert the regime had proved ineffective culminating in the 'perfect failure' of the Bay of Pigs invasion of 1961, the option of enforcing an embargo on trade became the top priority of US policy. In view of the almost total dependence of the pre-revolutionary economy on the US market and on US imports, an embargo seemed practicable because of the distance and difficulties involved in the Eastern bloc trying to fill the vacuum left by the collapse of commercial links.

Had Western Europe not been prepared to trade with Cuba in the early-1960s, at a period before Eastern bloc aid had been organised, and before its technology had adapted to tropical conditions, the Revolution might well have foundered.

This may be strikingly illustrated in the case of transport. Once the break with Western oil companies had occurred in June 1960 and Cuba became dependent on Soviet oil, the Soviets could not have transported that oil to Cuba had they been unable to charter tankers from Western Europe. Although the Soviet Union had one of the world's largest tanker fleets in terms of tonnage, most were under 12,000 tons and designed only for coastal and river traffic. Before 1960 there had been little need to have an ocean-going tanker fleet as the bulk of oil exports went overland to Eastern Europe and Central Asia. Until the late-1970s the Soviets had no tanker over 175,000 tons.[38]

The second instance concerns the internal crisis caused by the deterioration of the Havana transport system as no spare parts could be obtained for the US buses on which the system depended. The Leyland deal of 1964, whereby Britain re-equipped the Havana system with 600 buses, was a graphic indication of the way in which the embargo could not be enforced.[39] Given the way in which urban transport breakdown has been a potent source of public discontent in Latin America, the bus deal was a great morale booster, as shown by the enthusiastic dockside reception for the first delivery. But its significance went much further. The fact that the British government had been prepared to guarantee Leyland export credit was evidence of official British support for normal trade relations. This had wider repercussions, giving an impetus to other Western powers, particularly France, to follow where Britain had led. Other less spectacular examples, but none the less important, contributed specialised expertise and goods which otherwise might not have been available. They concerned the dredging of harbours and construction of harbour works in order to meet the expansion of trans-Atlantic trade, plant protection, shipbuilding, animal genetics, etc.

Determining factors in the European-Cuban relationship

In considering the West European connection with Cuba six main factors can be highlighted. Firstly was the official attitude of Western European governments. Although at no time expressing unqualified support, they implicitly recognised the Revolution's right to survival by refusing to submit to US pressure. This attitude was determined by legal considerations; in International Law their subjects could not be forbidden to trade with Cuba. Advice to desist might be given by the US Department of Commerce but as trade was legitimate no further action could or would be taken by Western governments. Trading was also determined by commercial pragmatism, the 'Crumbs from the rich man's table' view or, as the *Financial Times* commented, 'One factor stimulating British trade interest is the attraction of doing business in America's back garden without having to compete with US companies'.[40] In addition to legal arguments and commercial pragmatism, the British questioned the effectiveness of embargos to bring about the desired result. Finally, there was a difference in perception of the nature of the Cuban Revolution. In general Europeans refused to accept the American view that the Cuban problem was an integral component of the Cold War which would obligate NATO powers to support US policy. In the Europeans' view Cuba was a problem specific to the Americas until Khruschev's provocative action over the missile crisis in 1962. Before this many Europeans regarded US actions as self-defeating, driving Cuba further into the communist orbit.

Secondly was the moral and ideological support given to Castro by the West European left, in particular by those disillusioned by the bureaucratic rigidities of the old left, whether Stalinists or social democrats. From this stand-point the Revolution broke the log jam and injected a new optimism, inspiring the hope that the Cuban example might revivify the left in the industrialised West where it had lost the initiative. In particular, the non-communist left was attracted to a revolution in which the communists seemed to have been taken over rather than doing the taking over themselves. Cuba was also sufficiently Western in culture, tradition and history to have relevance for other Western societies. It lacked the religious, cultural, and sociological unfamiliarities which militated against other non-European models. Early enthusiasm, however, began to wane after the Padilla affair and when human rights caused increasing concern in the 1970s, and as Cuba became 'sovietised' and firmly integrated into the Eastern bloc after its inclusion in Comecon (Council for Mutual Economic Assistance, also CMEA) in 1972.[41]

Thirdly, it appealed to the stirring consciousness of Third Worldists with their awareness of the Third World's different problems. The Revolution's unequivocal anti-imperialism made a resounding impact in Third World countries, immediately in Latin America but soon to be followed in Africa where the Cuban presence was felt as early as 1963 when aid was given to Algeria. There was a difference in emphasis between the Latin American and African cases. In the first, the Revolution's impact was partly due to its condemnation of the established and cautious Latin American left, especially the communists who through a policy of co-operating in parliaments had become co-opted into the system and in the process had been corrupted by it. Cuban voluntarism, the emphasis on action, and the *via armada* of guerrilla activity as well as a revolutionary theory which allocated a key role to intellectuals, struck a responsive chord among a powerless, although vocal, left-wing intelligentsia who had tired of waiting for the objective conditions for revolution to mature.[42] In Africa, in contrast, it was not so much revolutionary strategy which was attractive as the implicit condemnation of those successor elites who were still so influenced by the political and cultural hegemony of the ex-colonial powers that they were unable to initiate development programmes relevant to their country's real needs.[43] Although Western European intellectuals contributed to the wider Latin American debate, and in the case of Régis Debray provided the theoretical underpinning for Cuba's revolutionary strategy, the legacies of the recent colonial past in Africa engaged their attention and concern to a greater extent than Latin America with which they were not so familiar.

Fourthly, the Revolution appealed to peripatetic technical experts who, although they might be sympathetic to the Revolution's aims, were often untroubled by ideological niceties. For this group technical problems such as how to increase agricultural productivity, and how to diversify the economy to escape from monoproduction, provided the challenge. One important attribute of this group was that some had the experience of working in tropical conditions which Soviet bloc technicians tended to lack. Later, some were to fall foul of Castro. Western economists also were to contribute to the debate on economic planning and the moral versus material incentives debate.[44]

Fifthly, the Revolution appealed to a diverse constituency of the nominally apolitical who were attracted by its novel off-beat character, by the charismatic quality of the leadership, by the satisfactions of total involvement in communal effort, and by the Revolution's purposefulness and joyous enthusiasm – 'Communism with the cha-cha' in one phrase, the spirit of which was captured in *Cuba Si* an early French documentary directed by Chris Marker in 1960.[45] In particular, this group was won over by the Revolution's youthfulness which struck resonant chords in the industrialised West which in the 1960s was being swept by a wave of generational consciousness and of youthful rebelliousness. For this group, Che Guevara was the idolised hero.

Sixthly, the cultural aspect attracted writers, artists, dramatists and film makers to whom the Cuban emphasis on the importance of culture and education was a marked contrast (especially in Britain) to their own societies, although ironically Castro himself has never shown great interest in literary culture.[46]

From the Cuban point of view, support from whatever source under the conditions of a tightening embargo was welcome. However, in the long term and in hard reality, commercial pragmatism and practical advice were worth more and proved more lasting than the sympathy of intellectuals whose symbolic support although valuable, proved to be a broken reed after the Padilla affair of 1971, and who, in common with the youthful constituency, could be seduced by fashion. Supping with the capitalist West may have provided more nourishment than the eulogies of the 'tourists of the Revolution'. Hence the emphasis in this book on aspects of the commercial relationship and the practical problems which these engendered. Admiration for the Revolution passes from the literary/humanist intelligentsia of the 1960s, the 'political pilgrims' of the whirlwind visit, flattered and cosseted by their hosts, to those whose extended tours of duty spent at the sharp-end solving practical problems gave them a deeper appreciation of the extent and difficulties which confronted Cubans under their siege conditions.[47]

In the context of the current debate throughout the ex-communist world on the need for democratic control, the alienation of foreign intellectuals quite apart from those in Cuba, removed a source of informed and not necessarily anti-revolutionary criticism and was to be detrimental to the Revolution's progress.[48]

British attitudes to Cuba

Of the three countries studied, the most puzzling response was that of Britain, the closest to the US to whom it was bound, at least in rhetoric, by a 'Special Relationship'. What value was this relationship if Britain could contribute towards bequeathing to the US its most intractable foreign policy problem?[49]

Although the British had played a significant role in Cuba's early history and during the opening decades of this century when it was Cuba's second largest market, by the 1950s British interest, and interests, in Cuba had declined. Hence the British attitude was not due to relations with Cuba being close. Britain had no reason to welcome Batista's overthrow – it had sold 17 Sea Furies to the dictator (which prompted a strongly worded letter from Graham Greene to *The Times*) at a time when the US had put an embargo on arms sales. At the subsequent enquiry by a Select Committee in the House of Commons, on the reasons for the sale, it was clear that the Embassy had little knowledge of what was happening in the Sierra Maestra, excusing themselves on the grounds of understaffing and hence poor information.[50] Havana did not have a high priority in Foreign Office postings (as it was to have later).

If the conflict with communism was a global phenomenon, as the US contended, and had to be contained and fought wherever it appeared, the attitude of Britain, so it seemed to many in the US, was poor recompense by an ally who had been saved by American intervention in two World Wars. However, the Anglo-American relationship was beset by ambivalence. In spite of being outwardly amicable and co-operating in almost every field of activity, there were still pockets of anti-Americanism. The left, whether communist or anti-communist, distrusted American economic infiltration and there was considerable cross-fertilisation between the American and British New Lefts in their shared critique of American society and American action. But anti-Americanism was not confined to the left. Businessmen who normally voted conservative were prepared to trade with Cuba, professing to be 'uninterested in politics'. Indeed, many businessmen in conversation have been enthusiastic about this trade. In spite of difficulties in obtaining payment and bureaucratic delays, the absence of corruption was a contrast and relief from experiences elsewhere in the region. American hostility to embargo breakers, and the punitive measures against those firms which traded with Cuba, together with the ban on subsidiaries of American companies which did so, was attributed by many businessmen to American resentment at losing a market which they had previously taken for granted as being traditionally theirs. British firms which have expanded their trade with Cuba fear that their share of this market could be lost at the restoration of US-Cuban relations, and with good reason, for businessmen are among the most vocal lobbyists in the US for renewing trade with Cuba, believing that they are now losing more than they gain in persisting with the embargo.

There is also a residual anti-Americanism on the right. Historically this is rooted in an aristocratic disdain for the populist expressions of mass democracy. Scorn for American values and the Americanisation of British life can also stem from their free-spending ways, still vivid in folk memories of the war years. Anti-Americanism was also an expression of post-imperial malaise. The British have resented criticism of their colonial past by the Americans, whom they considered were in no position to be critical. Bemused by their own revolutionary past, many Americans consider themselves better able to empathise with colonial and ex-colonial peoples than the British, forgetting that the American Revolution has a hollow ring in the Third World when it is recalled that the Declaration of the Rights of Man could coexist with the continuance of slavery.

French attitudes

The case of France is easier to understand. There was no 'Special Relationship' but a deep resentment at the inroads made by the US after the Second World War as well as suspicion of the presumed collusion between Britain and the US, bound by similar traditions, history and language which in de Gaulle's view precluded Britain from ever becoming 'European'. The issue of language and the displacement of French as the language of diplomacy and international cultural exchange was particularly keenly felt. The concept of 'francophonie' and the doctrine of assimilation, stemming from the moral imperatives and the philosophic absolutes of the French Revolution, engendered a need to challenge any other competing universalist creed. The primacy placed on French culture and the importance attached to the role of intellectuals, particularly after the Dreyfus affair, contributed to make Paris the cultural capital of Latin America and the chosen venue for exiles. The decadence of Spain in the nineteenth century had enabled the French to take the cultural initiative in Latin America. After the Second World War French politicians had planned to capitalise on racial and linguistic affinities with Hispanic peoples. They also planned to benefit from Franco's unpopularity in Latin America among the liberal intelligentsia so Cuba occupied a special place in the affections of the French left which was not to be matched in any other Western European country.[51]

Although Britain and Holland both have residual responsibilities in the Caribbean, the establishment in 1946 of Martinique and Guadeloupe as 'Départements d'Outre Mer' (DOMS), making them constitutionally integral parts of France, meant that France is a Caribbean power in a way which marks it off from both Britain and Holland, thus giving it a closer interest in Cuban affairs. As far as Cuba was concerned the French West Indies, like Puerto Rico, were colonies and thus a legitimate target for anti-colonialist propaganda and, in the opinion of the French secret service, for terrorist subversion as well. Another source of Franco-Cuban tension was in Africa where Cuban support for the break-away Katangese in Shaba province of Zaïre provoked France and Belgium to dispatch paratroops.

With the polarisation of the Caribbean region under Reagan and with the establishment of the Caribbean Basin Initiative in 1982, President Mitterand sensed an opportunity for France and the EC to increase its influence as an independent third force. However, French diplomatic and commercial activity in the early-1980s was to be seriously constrained by the human rights issue. It was, however, a reflection of the importance which Castro placed on France's diplomatic influence that he yielded to French overtures for the release of Armando Valladares in October 1982 through the intermediary of Régis Debray and later, in 1986, in permitting the release of the dissident Ricardo Bofill, a university professor who had taken refuge in the French Embassy in Havana.[52]

Spanish attitudes

Spanish relations were closest with Cuba and need to be put into historical context.[53] From the mid-eighteenth century and after the Haitian Revolution, Cuba was to become the richest colony for its size possessed by any European power, but Cuba's economic expansion was so rapid that the role of colony and metropolis threatened to be reversed. Cuba experienced an industrial revolution in sugar production in the first half of the nineteenth century at a time when Spain was convulsed by civil wars and was becoming increasingly dependent economically on other European powers. Cuban economic importance was matched by its strategic position, especially after 1819 when the cession of Florida by Spain brought Cuba within 90 miles of the US. But, like Turkey in Europe, a weak Spain was able to retain control of Cuba because to Britain and the US, this was preferable to occupation by one or the other.[54]

Cuba fulfilled an important economic and political function for Spain in the nineteenth century. Economically, it provided a market for Spanish textiles, wheat and shipping whilst remittances sent back to Spain contributed to a debilitated Spanish economy. Politically, it provided an opening for an impoverished middle class with restricted openings in industry and commerce at home, whereas in Cuba, Spaniards monopolised business, the administration and the army. Tensions between the politically dominant *peninsulares* and the economically powerful but politically disfranchised *criollos* created tensions to which the movements of annexationism, reformism and finally independence were Cuban responses. Although nineteenth century Spanish culture had little to offer Cubans, exposure to Spanish Krausism was to have an important influence on José Martí, whose experience in Spain as an exile from Cuba convinced him that no political reform and certainly not independence, could be expected even from the most radical Spanish government.

What made differences irreconcilable was the increasing dependence of Cuba on the American market and the inability of Spain to protect it from hostile US tariffs.[55] In 1895 the final three-year war of independence broke out, which was to be finally terminated by US intervention in which superior naval power was the decisive factor. This intervention was the turning point in Cuban history, bequeathing bitter memories which have not been erased either in Spain or Cuba. Spaniards, especially those supporting Franco's doctrine of *Hispanidad*, resented the fact that the US had humiliated Spain by administering the *coup de grâce* to the empire. For Cubans, US intervention deprived them of genuine independence and resentment was felt at the way in which Americans ignored the Cuban contribution to the defeat of the Spanish army in the bitter guerrilla warfare before intervention. Cuban historiography has been devoted to correcting the American version in which they saw themselves as liberating Cubans from Spanish oppression, rather than as the Cubans see them, as depriving them of genuine independence, reflected most glaringly by their exclusion from the peace-treaty negotiations.

One aspect of the war which has been underplayed and has only recently been stressed is the role played by liberated slaves in the war, and how one consequence of American intervention and occupation was the introduction of US-style racist views. Contemporary American cartoons reveal the patronising attitude and the need for 'Uncle Sam' to exercise stern control over recalcitrant Cubans, depicted as unruly piccaninnis. Americans generally felt that Cubans owed them a debt of gratitude for freeing the island from despotic rule.

Surprisingly, in view of the war's savagery, the Spanish connection was not broken. On the contrary, as the new Republic adopted a whitening policy, Spanish immigration was actively encouraged, so that by the 1930s some 16 per cent of Cuba's population were Spaniards. Two consequences flowed from this. Firstly, whereas in the colonial period government was monopolised by Spaniards, during independence it became the preserve of Cubans, while Spaniards dominated commerce. Through family and regional links, the proprietors of Spanish businesses in Cuba employed other Spaniards – hence the importance of the Cubanisation Law of 1933 by which at least 50 per cent of the employees of every business had to be Cuban citizens. Secondly, because of their exclusion from many businesses, Cubans turned to government for employment and profit, thus encouraging the development of the spoils system.

Of all Latin American countries, Cuba was not only the closest to Spain geographically, facilitating constant interchange between its peoples, but the European component of its population was overwhelmingly from

Spain or the Canary Islands. Thus, with the outbreak of the Spanish Civil War, Cuba became more deeply involved than any other Spanish American country.[56] Returnees from the war were to exert an important influence on the course of Cuban politics in the turbulent 1940s and 1950s. Close family ties and nostalgic memories have influenced attitudes – including those of Fidel Castro, whose father came from Galicia. In the 1960s and early-1970s both countries were outcasts; Cuba in the Americas and Spain in Europe, and links were strengthened during the Revolution when Spain became Cuba's major trading partner in the non-communist world. The relationship was more than a marriage of convenience, but was based on a dense network of familial relationships and shared affinities. Although Franco's death in 1975 marked a watershed in Spanish domestic history, it did not mark a fundamental break in Spanish-Cuban relations, which have shown a remarkable continuity since the early-1960s.

Cuba and the West European left

The policies of Britain, France and Spain were determined primarily by a commercially inspired pragmatism whereas the attitudes of the left stemmed from diametrically opposed premises. These were far removed from the capitalist orientation of Western governments rooted in a rationality completely at variance with those of leftist views, who were reacting against the dullness, apathy and disillusionments of the 1950s.

If governments were important for the contribution they made to the physical survival of the Revolution, the amorphous groups on the left were important for symbolic reasons, for boosting morale, for instilling a sense of international solidarity, for ideological legitimation and for keeping the Cuban issue alive whenever it began to flag. Through access to the media, the liberal and left-wing intelligentsia made an important contribution towards breaking the enforced isolation and moral quarantine caused by the US blockade. Whether their views tell us more about themselves and their own societies than about Cuba has been much debated, but it is certain that the popular image of the Revolution struck deep resonances among both those with committed left-wing sympathies who were disillusioned with the failures of the European left as well as with those who had no political affiliations. The Revolution's impact on the left was due to its startling originality and heterodoxy which broke the log-jam of both theory and practice. 'Cuba's example', commented an article in the *New Left Review* in 1961, 'can shatter one of the oldest and strongest of the Cold War myths – that socialist power is synonymous with communism, and that only under the leadership of a disciplined communist elite is it possible to expropriate the capitalist class and to found an economy on common ownership'.[57]

Two groups were to be critical. In the early days communist parties, especially the French, distrusted the pace of change, suspecting the revolutionary credentials of the 26th July Movement, and their 'bourgeois putschism'. Later, as the Revolution developed, some criticism was levelled against the regime's tendency towards 'state capitalism' in which workers were regarded as being exploited in the interests of the state. The early purging of the unions and the tight control of the party over official unions was looked at with disfavour by some visiting unionists, who suspected that interests of party, state and unions did not necessarily coincide.[58]

However, the explanation of the Revolution's impact does not lie solely in the impatience and frustration with the attitudes and policies of the Old Left, but also in what might be termed *Zeitgeist* factors – those developments which were to make the 1960s a watershed in modern intellectual, cultural and social history. These were to widen the fissure within the left generally which had been growing since the mid-1950s, and which was to find its most graphic expression in the emergence of the New Left.[59]

National contexts

The New Left was the description given to a tendency, a mood, transcending national frontiers; a sharing of views in reaction both against the way in which international relations had been polarised by the Cold War and against the failures of the left, both communist and non-communist. Although sharing certain common assumptions, New Left groups in each country were conditioned by the context of national politics. First, in point of time, was the French *nouvelle gauche* founded by Claude Bourdet whose *France Observateur* was the mouthpiece of his views. Bourdet had been a leading Resistance fighter who was seeking a third way, independent of Stalinism (entrenched in the French Communist Party) and social democracy with its compromises, and between the Warsaw Pact and NATO. In Britain, the New Left emerged in 1956 in the aftermath of Suez and the Hungarian Revolution. In the US alone, in contrast to Europe, the New Left emerged specifically as a response to the Cuban Revolution.

In Spain, conditions under Franco were not conducive to the emergence of a New Left, although a comparable tendency was to emerge during the university disturbances of the mid-1960s, but censorship, repression and residual legacies from the Civil War were to be serious inhibiting factors. The political context in Spain was so distinctive that it needs to be spelt out in some detail.

Whereas in the rest of Western Europe Castro's heterodox, polycentrist Marxism appealed to a left-wing intelligentsia disillusioned by the bureaucratic and Muscovite tendencies of orthodox Communist parties, in Spain the intelligentsia had been scattered throughout Europe and the Americas in the post Civil War diaspora. The Spanish Communist Party (PCE) itself regained some of the prestige it lost in the war by spearheading much of the underground opposition to Franco. In the 1960s and 1970s it had a broader organisation than any other leftist party, aided by a clear organisational model and financial backing. Castroism failed to dent traditional leftist attitudes. The anarchists, for example, were wary of a revolution that condemned even those few Cuban anarchists who survived into the 1960s. For Cubans, anarchism was irrelevant – the more so as orthodox Soviet views prevailed.

If Castroism was limited, even more limited was the influence of the increasingly bureaucratised Cuban Communist Party (PCC) from the mid-1960s on. The reasons for this stem from the PCE's assertion, under the leadership of Santiago Carrillo, secretary-general of the party since 1960, of the strongest Euro-communist line of any European communist party after the Italians. Whereas Castro had defended the Soviet invasion of Czechoslovakia in 1968, Carrillo had openly opposed it. Unlike the Portuguese Communist Party under Alvaro Cunhal, with a Leninist view of its vanguard role, the PCE, faced with strong socialist and anarchist traditions and saddled with memories of its civil war record, had to be much more flexible. There was, therefore, not much empathy between the PCC and the PCE and even less so after Franco's death and the legalisation of the PCE. Then Santiago Carrillo's independent Euro-communism became even more explicit. In 1975 he said in a meeting in East Berlin: 'For years Moscow was our Rome. We spoke of the Great October Socialist Revolution as if it were our Christmas. That was the period of our infancy. Today we have grown up.' The next year, in Moscow, he was refused permission to deliver a speech at the sixtieth anniversary of the October Revolution.[60]

The New Left

One difficulty with the term New Left is that it gives an impression of coherence which did not exist and which, for many of its adherents was not desirable.[61] In each country it was a loose coalition of divergent groups, united in rejection of bourgeois consumer mass society, and disillusioned with the lack of revolutionary fervour of the industrial working class which seemed unaware of the historical role, assigned to it in Marxist theory, of acting as the vanguard of the Revolution. New Leftists were also united in their repudiation of the Old Left which, in its acceptance of hierarchy and centralised party discipline, seemed to share many of the suppositions of the capitalist society it was professing to overthrow. The New Left was totalist and global in its analysis of society and of its cultural expressions. The politicisation of those who had previously been untouched by conventional politics marked it off from most older forms of radicalism. Its cosmopolitanism marked a break, in the British case, with insular attitudes. There could be no piecemeal solutions to world problems; those of the Third World, especially, were inseparable from those of advanced capitalist societies.

The New Left's concern with community and participation was a reaction against the atomisation of liberal individualism and of the impersonality and monotony of industrial society: 'alienation' was a key word in their political vocabulary. The demonstration and the 'happening' and other forms of spontaneous protest were liberating experiences in themselves. Their emphasis on culture and especially on popular culture, which has been one of their most lasting legacies, reflected the erosion of the old working class tradition of self-education and a creeping philistinism which was seen as a consequence of the manipulation of the media. The growth of television especially, so far from liberating and opening up new vistas had the opposite effect. Hence it was in the cultural and educational fields that the Cuban Revolution was to make its most striking impact, serving as an emotional escape hatch from the apathy of the 1950s and the years of the 'end of ideology'.

In reformulating theories of socialism and political strategies, elements of the old outsider left, Trotskyists and anarchists jostled, at times uneasily, with newer elements as they sought points of agreement in their conflict with society and with the Old Left. One of the areas of fiercest debate was over the role which students should play in the new revolutionary equation. Were they a surrogate proletariat who would be the vanguard in alliance with those marginal groups who had not been corrupted by affluence? Or must they play a subordinate role as a new working-class militancy gathered momentum?[62]

Students and intelligentsia

In Western Europe, the Cuban Revolution struck a resounding chord in universities which were experiencing an unprecedented expansion of numbers due to the need to meet technological challenges, and the demands of increasingly complex administrative systems.[63] Universities were expected to become more receptive to the needs of society, and governments encouraged the strengthening of links between universities and industry. Universities and other forms of higher education were becoming a mass industry, knowledge factories subordinated to the needs of privileged groups. The threat of being compromised by being drawn in to the military/industrial complex or of becoming subordinated to multi-national corporations were to be the cause of many disturbances. Within universities vocational degrees to meet new requirements threatened to erode older humanist disciplines, which had previously guaranteed access to elite positions. At the same time, outside universities new technical demands were eroding old-established skills and traditional class loyalties.

Faced with accelerating change and expansion of knowledge many professors continued to teach outmoded courses or were slow to respond to the demands for 'relevance'. Syllabuses often failed to include the study of an increasingly vocal Third World. Specialists to teach these were either not available, taught from a Eurocentric viewpoint, or forced Third World societies into irrelevant theoretical moulds.

To academic tensions were added other strains. Upward social mobility into an elite could lead to identification with that elite's values and a repudiation of past and of parents, thus widening the 'generation gap', which became a cliché to describe a complex phenomenon which few understood. Margaret Mead argued that society had moved into a culture in which elders must now learn from their children, unlike preceding ages, in which the young learned from their elders or from their elders together with their peers. 'All of us', she wrote, 'who were born and reared before the 1940s are immigrants. . . .' fearful that the 'young are being transformed into strangers before our eyes, that teenagers gathered at a street corner are to be feared like the advance guard of an invading army'.[64] It was the fear of a new and little understood phenomenon which promoted the violent reaction of adults, resentful of youth's spending habits, envious of their sexual mores and bruised by their refusal to accept established concepts of authority. Nowhere was this felt more acutely than in universities, where professors were de-sacralised, their political ideas subjected to scrutiny and their persons even brutalised.

Industrial societies were being riven by conflicts which had been endemic in the Third World where since early in the century traditional elites had been challenged by modernising 'young Turks'. The youthfulness of the Cuban revolution was not its unique feature – the old after all do not make efficient guerrillas. What was original and resonated through the early 1960s was the constant emphasis by Fidel Castro on the regenerating role of youth. 'Nobody under thirty', Castro once remarked, 'can understand what the Revolution is about'.

The impact of Cuba

It has been cogently argued that the Cuban Revolution was welcomed by the left with a fervour comparable to that given to the USSR in the 1930s and that, in similar fashion, there was a suspension of critical faculties on the part of sympathetic visitors to both countries. There may be parallels but the differences are equally striking. Attitudes in the 1930s were conditioned by the Depression and the belief that the Soviets were providing a rational solution to problems which Western capitalism had been unable to solve. Although this was to involve sacrificing large numbers of the peasantry and purging political opponents, these were either unknown at the time, or explained away. Whereas the Old Left had been bemused by the apparent successes of Soviet communism the New Left were to be repelled by its failures.

In the 1960s Cuba was viewed not merely as an alternative society but *the* alternative society with a Utopian vision embodied in Che Guevara's 'New Man' where the corruption, compromises and ideological rigidities of communism would be expunged, and where moral would replace material incentives.[65] Cuba would be the model and inspiration for the rest of the Third World – Havana was a lode star much as Madrid had been for European progressives during the siege in 1936. The 'discovery' of the Third World had a particular potency for the New Left and pro-Cuban sympathisers. The irrelevance of the Soviet model: the Soviet's lack of understanding of and empathy with the problems of underdeveloped countries except in abstract formulations, reflected the Eurocentric views of Marx himself. Moreover, the ease with which Batista had been overthrown seemed to suggest that the revolutionary equation of *déraciné* intellectuals, peasants and marginalised groups could provide an alternative model for Third World revolution, although Vietnam and Central America were to show how misleading the Cuban experience could be, rooted in a specific socio-economic and historical mould, and how inappropriate even for Latin America, where it might seem to have had most relevance.

Ignorance about Cuba on the eve of the Revolution was even greater than ignorance about Spain in 1936. Cuban politics were not susceptible to easy categorisation. What was known about the resistance to Batista, especially after Herbert Matthews' famous article in the *New York Times*, was that a corrupt and brutal dictatorship, tolerated when not actively bolstered by the US, was being challenged by a small band of middle-class revolutionaries with the support of the local peasantry.[66] The phenomenon of a guerrilla uprising spearheading a revolution was sufficiently novel to attract the attention of the heterodox left. How such a small group was able to defeat a well-equipped army and to overthrow Batista was to exercise commentators for many years to come and still attracts academic analysis.[67] At the time, the David and Goliath image was sufficient to command attention and rally support, especially when the conflict widened to include opposition to the US. Fidel Castro was able to capitalise on deep currents of anti-Americanism in the rest of the continent as well as in those expressions of anti-Americanism in Europe which blamed the US for the Cold War and where, for a variety of complex reasons, '*Le Défi Américain*' was feared.[68] Resentment at accelerating Americanisation and the threat which this posed to cultural values – more acutely felt in France and Spain which lacked the cultural affinities of the British-American connection – found an outlet in pro-Cuban sentiment, especially among intellectuals, traditional defenders of cultural values, who were to be targeted by Castro in a deliberate attempt to rally foreign support.

Intellectuals have always enjoyed high prestige in Hispanic societies as legitimators of alternative ideologies to that of Roman Catholicism.[69] Their role had been enhanced by their opposition to military rule and the domination of *caudillos* who filled the legitimacy vacuum left by the demise of Spanish imperial power. In Cuba, intellectuals matured as the thaumaturges of nationalism, during the long colonial domination by Spain throughout the nineteenth century. José Martí had been the supreme example of the '*intelectual comprometido*'. The rediscovery of his ideas in the 1920s and 1930s, especially among politicised university students, exalted the role of intellectuals as national regenerators.

The seduction of foreign intellectuals

The deeply-entrenched Cuban tradition of the committed intellectual partially explains the high priority given to culture and to the intellectuals' role in raising revolutionary consciousness. By attracting back writers of stature after 1959, such as the exiled Alejo Carpentier, and by drawing on hitherto untapped reserves of Cuban culture, creative energies would be released to liberate Cubans from the suffocating hold of American influences. Without raising consciousness, radical change would be stillborn. Intellectuals were therefore mobilised and given a freedom to experiment which visitors to Cuba in the early days felt was one of the Revolution's most impressive features. Almost without exception, intellectuals accepted the challenge and few were to be found among the first waves of Cubans to go into exile. With such a tradition, Carlos Franqui, the editor of *Revolución*, had little difficulty in persuading Castro to enlist the support of foreign intellectuals.[70] The foundation of the review *Casa de las Americas* in 1960 as a Latin American rather than a narrow Cuban journal, and the invitation to European writers to sit on the Casa's prize-awarding panels, as well as Castro's appeal to foreign intellectuals to break with the US, revealed the extent to which the international intellectual community was to be harnessed to the support of revolution. This official recognition had a strong attraction for foreign writers, with its flattering exaltation of their importance. The French, predictably, were attracted, as it confirmed the post-Dreyfusard role of intellectuals.[71]

In Britain and the US, intellectuals, 'eggheads' in the depreciatory phrase, traditionally distrusted, even despised, were envious of the importance accorded to them in Cuba.[72] In Spain the *pensador* had always enjoyed high prestige although this was to be tempered by Francoist censorship as well as by one of the largest intellectual diasporas of modern times. One of these exiles, Juan Goytisolo, a leading Spanish novelist, living in Paris, was an early enthusiastically pro-Cuban supporter.[73]

The most important early example of an intellectual identifying himself with the Revolution was C. Wright Mills whose *Listen Yankee* (1960) sold some 400,000 copies and provided one of the most accessible sources on the Revolution available to Europeans.[74]

Mills, the independent neo-Marxist radical, professor of sociology at Columbia University, became something of a cult figure among university students on both sides of the Atlantic where his books became academic best-sellers. Unconcerned with theoretical niceties, his purpose in *Listen Yankee* was to alert Americans to the originality and significance of the Revolution as a new model for democratic socialism. The book was in the form of letters, as if written by a Cuban explaining the Cuban viewpoint, based on a three-week visit throughout the island, some of it in Fidel Castro's company. In the final 'Notes to the Reader', he summed up the nature and future prospects of the Revolution. It was, he suggested, a genuine revolution in contrast to that in Mexico (which was increasingly to be promoted in the US as a counter-example of a 'safe' Revolution and as an alternative model for the rest of Latin America to follow). The hostility of the US had been responsible for forcing Cuba into the arms of the Soviet bloc against Castro's original intentions: the government was a revolutionary dictatorship of peasants and workers in which authoritarian features could be justified by the needs of socialist reconstruction and by the enthusiastic support from the majority of the Cuban people. The absence of elections to which Americans objected could be explained by the widespread distrust of them due to the past corruption of the electoral process. Elections would, it was alleged, have been seen as a return to corrupt prerevolutionary days evaporating mass support for Castro overnight.

These views were to become the stock-in-trade of sympathisers of the Revolution whilst Mills' other books, especially *The Power Elite* (1951), were exposés of US corporate capitalism, corrupted through power, and of the military-industrial complex which, in his view, made the US incapable of empathising with or aligning itself with radical movements in the Third World.

With Cubans convinced of the importance of securing the support of European intellectuals, Franqui recounts how as early as 1959 he had been instrumental in persuading Jean-Paul Sartre and Simone de Beauvoir to visit Cuba, which they were to do in February and March 1960. The Cuban visit was to relieve their deep depression caused by the recent death of Albert Camus, and for Simone de Beauvoir 'the gaiety of the place exploded like a miracle under the blue sky'. It was carnival time and she commented at being 'witness to happiness that had been achieved by violence' – the contrast to the paralysing hopelessness of the Algerian conflict could not have been more marked. Sartre's views from this visit were immediately published in 16 articles in *France Soir* in June, and then a few months later in an English paperback edition. This was to become the European equivalent to Wright Mills' book, and complementary to it.[75]

Sartre's book incorporated substantially the same arguments but with a strong emphasis on the non-ideological and existential aspect of the Revolution as reflected in the voluntarism of Castro and the revolutionary leadership. Castro exerted an almost hypnotic influence on Sartre who admired his inexhaustible energy. Castro and Guevara were 'Renaissance Men', modern heroes through whose exercise of will the course of world history could be changed. At a moment when communist influence in Cuba was increasing, Sartre's support legitimated the revolution in the eyes of the non-communist left, offsetting the existential gloom caused by France's seemingly endless colonial wars.

For the French left, which had been embroiled in 15 years of colonial wars, (Indo-China, 1947–1954 and Algeria, 1954–1962), the striking success of the Cuban 'war of liberation' was a cause for hope and optimism. Both Mills' and Sartre's emphasis on the Revolution's lack of doctrinal rigidity and of its existential nature attracted foreign intellectuals, although for some Cubans, recalling Lenin's dictum that there could be no revolution without a revolutionary ideology, this was a cause of concern.

In its early days the Revolution was described as 'Humanist' but the declaration of it as socialist in 1961 marked the decisive shift leftwards presaging, on the one hand, the erosion of the transclass nature of the Martían inspiration of the early years and, on the other, the construction of an official party (eventually to become the Cuban Communist Party) although it was not to hold its first congress until 1975.[76] The purge of Anibal Escalante and communists who were accused of infiltrating the new party in 1962 was reassuring to those foreign sympathisers who were alarmed at growing communist influence; the purge seemed to indicate that it was still 'Castro's Revolution' and that he was sufficiently wilful in the Hispanic caudillo tradition to resist communist blandishments.

The Soviets themselves were surprised and embarrassed by the declaration of the Revolution to be socialist. It was to tie them to a wayward ally who until 1967 pursued an independent '*via armada*' line of guerrilla strategy which ran counter to the official policy of Latin American communist parties. In the context of the Sino-Soviet struggle the Soviet Union had no option but to support Cuba for fear of losing face in the Third World. In the early-1960s the combination of Cuban heterodoxy, the pursuance of an independent foreign policy and the romanticism of the guerrilla fascinated a large section of the Western intelligentsia.

Castro's ability to follow an independent line lasted until the death of Che Guevara in Bolivia in 1967 and the collapse of the guerrilla strategy, ironically in the same year that Régis Debray's book, *Revolution in the Revolution*, was published. Not only did the book appear at the moment of disaster, but there is additional irony in that the author of what has been the most authoritative statement of Cuba's revolutionary strategy should have been by a Frenchman, whose subsequent political career has been a 'long march' away from the ideals expressed in this book.[77]

The high point of Cuba's wooing foreign writers came in the opening days of 1968 with the Congress of Intellectuals in Havana.[78] Four months later, Castro supported the Warsaw Pact's intervention in Czechoslovakia. 1968 ushered in the Year of the Barricades and worldwide student revolt, in which as Castro had predicted, the dead Che would be more potent than the living Guevara. The reasons for the worldwide outburst, comparable, although on a global scale, to the 'Revolution of the Intellectuals' of 1848, were rooted in those *Zeitgeist* factors alluded to earlier, but by 1968 the corrosive influence of Vietnam had radicalised large swathes of the hitherto apolitical, especially in the US but also large sections of Western youth. Che's total identification with Vietnam (with his exhortation to create two or three more Vietnams), inevitably associated Cuba with the protests, although the Revolution was lost among many other issues. Through the potent image of the martyred Che it enjoyed a brief burst of popularity, although now it was the myth of an earlier Cuba and not that of 1968.

The New Left had become swamped by the accretions of the counter-culture but iconoclasm, obscenity, irrationalism and the babel of different voices alienated those who were otherwise sympathetic to the Revolution. Many now reversed their views, repelled by the currents of anti-rationalism with overtones which bore a resemblance to fascism. Liberal ideas were to be undermined by Herbert Marcuse's concept of 'repressive tolerance'. The demonstrations which mobilised the comparatively affluent middle-class students had little mass support and were far removed from Cuba's demonstrations which were becoming more disciplined and regimented. Nor did the hedonist counter-culture have anything in common with the serious, committed, ascetic Cuban revolutionary in whom light-hearted effervescence often co-existed with a high moral earnestness. The views of Wilhelm Reich enjoyed a certain vogue, popularising the view that political liberation was consequent on sexual liberation – a view which earned the riposte that most past revolutionaries had tended to be ascetic puritans.

The student revolts were not confined to the West but erupted in the Eastern bloc, in particular Poland and Czechoslovakia, but students there were rebelling in the name of those liberal values which were being repudiated by their peers in the West. In supporting Soviet intervention in Czechoslovakia, Cuba was to be on the side of the state apparatus. Nearer home, the Cubans were to remain silent over the Tlatelolco massacre in Mexico.[79]

The fading of the dream

The role which intellectuals had played in the Prague Spring of 1968 was a warning of the potential threat posed by dissidents. This threat came to a climax in the Padilla affair in 1971 when those foreign writers, hitherto sympathetic to the Revolution, signed public letters criticising Cuba for its 'Stalinist' excesses, prompting a savage response from Castro condemning them as a 'mafia of pseudo-Leftist bourgeois intellectuals'. His intemperate attack marked the end of support by the majority of those who had hitherto been among Cuba's staunchest and most articulate supporters.[80]

The hard line against freedom is understandable in the context of Castro's frustration at the failure of the ten million ton sugar harvest and of the changing relationship with the Soviet Union. With the increasing dependence on Soviet aid, and Cuba's admission into the CMEA (Council for Mutual Economic Assistance, also known as COMECON) in 1972, it would have been suicidal to permit freedoms to flourish when these were being suppressed in the Soviet Union.[81] Although there had been indications of Castro's ambivalence towards intellectuals earlier, this had been overlooked by foreign sympathisers but after Czechoslovakia, and the Padilla Affair, the increasing sovietisation of Cuban society, accompanied by the army's hard line (reflecting Raul Castro's views) and coupled with Castro's scorn towards foreign advisers during his wilful pursuance of the ten million ton harvest, the enthusiasm of outsiders waned. The militarisation of the labour force during the harvest paralleled the militarisation of attitudes towards free-ranging criticism, however sympathetic the critics may have been towards the Revolution's aims, as in the case of René Dumont and K.S. Karol.[82]

Castro's dismissal of Western liberals' reservations as bourgeois scruples has to be put into an international context but it also obscured those temperamental incompatibilities between, on the one side, cautious, unimaginative bureaucrats, fearful of change and of taking initiatives or being too critical, who are bound by the iron hoops of precedent and, on the other, the writer's free-ranging imagination. Cuba was no longer a guerrilla state with internalised constraints but one with a growing paranoic siege mentality, a centralised command economy, the largest army in Latin America and an increasingly institutionalised state structure. The loss of the valued support of foreign intellectuals increased the sense of isolation. The idea of the Cuban Revolution being a 'third way' which had proved so attractive to foreign sympathisers – 'socialism in liberty' – in the early days of the Revolution now gave way to a repudiation of the 'two imperialisms' thesis. The closer dependence on Soviet models, in culture as well as in economics, seemed to be backtracking on that earlier openness when Castro had called for a creative Marxism and not one which accepted foreign models uncritically.

The significance of the Cuban reformulation of the intellectual's role lay in the assertion that the Third World intellectual had no choice. Commitment, and by implication contentment, meant dirtying one's hands, which in an ex-slave society where manual work was despised was a revolutionary act in itself. Castro wielding a machete in the sugar harvest has a symbolic significance far beyond the press publicity stunt.[83]

New Left enthusiasm waned as the New Left itself declined in influence in the early-1970s. The Utopian visions of foreign visitors of the 1960s were replaced by the official party line. The 'New Man' and moral incentives gave way to hard-line vanguardism and by Cuban attempts to swing the Non-Aligned Movement behind the Soviet Union, a repudiation, it would seem, of independent Third World unity exemplified in the Tricontinental Conference of 1966.

The myth of the Third World united under Cuban leadership, lost its imaginative pull among the Non-Aligned nations as the island became increasingly identified with the Soviet Union, especially after Cuba's support for Soviet intervention in Afghanistan. The mistake, perhaps, was to assume that the Eastern bloc would take aid programmes to the Third World as seriously as the Cubans did themselves. In the West, it was noticeable how more attention was paid to Cuba's military adventurism than to the scale and extent of its civilian aid programmes.

Cuban foreign policy in the 1970s and its impact on Europe

i) Africa

The 1970s also saw a marked change in Cuban foreign policy. Guerrilla strategy in Latin America was discredited both by Che's failure in Bolivia and by the accession to power of reforming regimes, whether by military coup as with Velasco in Peru or by election as with Allende in Chile. In addition, Cuban isolation was ended by the OAS decision to lift sanctions in 1974 (except for the US). The collapse of Portuguese power in Africa in 1975 and the subsequent threat to Angola from South Africa provided Cuba with a new opportunity to recapture the moral initiative. The falling away of Western intellectuals' support and their criticisms of human rights issues could now be ignored as involvement in Africa provided a new moral crusade against apartheid – the 'Last Great Cause' which could inject new life into the Revolution, refurbish its image and inspire enthusiasm among a new generation who had not known the heroic days of the guerrilla struggle.[84]

Guevara's experiences in Africa in the mid-1960s had underlined the complications of becoming enmeshed in African politics with its tribalist overtones, and this may partly account for the shift away from guerrilla strategies and the adoption of more conventional military action. It was ironical that Jonas Savimbi, an admirer of Guevara who had absorbed his military (although not his social) teachings, should confront a Cuban army deployed along traditional lines. The lessons of Soviet military advisers had been well absorbed.[85]

However, Africa posed problems as it was in the European sphere of influence in a way which the Americas were not and hence the Cubans had to tread warily so as not to damage their relationship with Belgium, Britain and France, all of whom retained a network of financial, technical, military and educational links with their ex-colonies. African countries comprised a large proportion of the British Commonwealth and French links with her ex-colonies were even tighter and more pervasive. The French retained a garrison in Djibouti and on a number of occasions French troops intervened in the course of civil wars as in Chad, or in the crisis of 1978 in pro-Western Zaïre's province of Shaba when French and Belgian troops defeated an invasion by Shaban exiles, reputedly supported by Cuba.[86] For the British, Rhodesia was the sensitive issue. The Cubans supported Joshua Nkomo's ZAPU, partly to offset ZANU's links with China as Sino-Soviet competition for influence in the Third World had now shifted to Africa. Some guerrillas received training but Cuban interference in the Rhodesian question did not become a serious issue in Cuban-British relations.

The assertive African phase of Cuban foreign policy had positive advantages domestically, both in the Third World and for the Soviet Union, where the Cubans were able to advance Soviet interests in places where their influence had hitherto been restricted. In the West, however, it had adverse effects. Sweden, for example, which had been described in the Cuban press as 'the Western nation friendliest to Cuba' cut its aid, and trade between the two countries declined in the late-1970s. If Cuba could afford expensive overseas commitment, why should it receive aid? The Dutch also reduced their aid programme after Cuban involvement in Ethiopia which was qualitatively different from Angola, as in the former Cuban troops were operating directly under Soviet command. With the rise in world sugar prices in the 1970s the Cuban economy prospered. This was reflected in the inflow of Western credit and in the growth of Cuban indebtedness to the bankers, with the consequence that the prospect for future relations with Western Europe and Japan was to be impaired. As Dominguez comments: 'Cuba lost an opportunity for excellent relations with Western Europe and Japan in the mid-1970s: that opportunity has not been regained'.[87]

ii) The Caribbean: Grenada

Nearer home, in the Caribbean and Central America, Cuba's foreign policy had adverse effects as well. In 1979 the New Jewel Movement under Maurice Bishop, a close friend of Castro, came to power in Grenada. Although the revolution there was to be destroyed by internal dissension it had roused some alarm in Western circles, as it reflected a more active Caribbean policy following on from the initiative of the major Commonwealth Caribbean countries in establishing diplomatic links with Cuba in 1972 (three years before the OAS voted to allow its members to do so). The election of Michael Manley in that year, with a democratic socialist, Third Worldist programme, presaged the forming of close links with Cuba. Castro's visit to Jamaica in November 1977 was followed by the signing of commercial, technical and educational agreements. These links were to be weakened by Cuba's increasingly pro-Soviet stance in foreign policy and by economic failure in Jamaica itself. When, in the general election of 1980, Edward Seaga defeated Manley it was largely by exploiting fear of growing communist influence.[88] Within a year diplomatic relations had been severed and with Manley's fall and the attractions of Reagan's Caribbean Basin Initiative in 1982 Cuba was friendless in the Caribbean apart from Grenada.

The Grenada case illustrates very well the different perceptions by the US and Britain of the dangers of Cuban influence. British-American relations were to be strained over the US intervention in Grenada. As in the case of the Dominican Republic in 1965, intervention overthrew what were considered to be Cuban-inspired regimes. It had been customary for Britain and the US to consult each other and exchange information on Caribbean matters, as in the case of the 1962 missile crisis when Macmillan and Kennedy were in constant communication with each other, but this did not happen in the case of Grenada, a member of the Commonwealth, with which Britain had normal relations. However close Reagan and Thatcher might have been, the Grenada incident revealed the extent to which the US was prepared to act on its own without consulting its closest ally. 'Over and above the British government's objection of principle, forcibly expressed by Mrs Thatcher after the event, what really hurt was the realisation that not only had it not been taken fully into the administration's confidence, but it had to some extent been misled as to US intentions'.[89] Although the British government looked with some alarm at Cuban attempts to increase their influence in the region, 'it did not share the more extreme US perception of the threat to regional security represented by the Cuban presence and the construction by Cuban workers of Point Salines Airport, with participation by a British contractor and (a detail frequently overlooked) a US dredging company'.[90]

iii) Central America

It was not that the British government did not share US views about the undesirability of a Marxist takeover in El Salvador or in Nicaragua, but there was a difference of opinion about how the threat should be treated. 'The British were not convinced by the more apocalyptic vision of the nature and extent of the threat to US security' which had been voiced in Washington.[91]

The US view of the Central American imbroglio was vitiated by an exaggerated perception of Cuban and Soviet subversion (echoing the Guatemalan Revolution of 1944–54), but this was to misread the very different historical roots and the differing social, political and economic contexts within which the two revolutions operated. Three features in particular marked off the Nicaraguan from the Cuban experience.[92]

The first concerned the comparative strengths of the respective communist parties. That in Cuba was one of the strongest (as well as being the largest per head of population) in Latin America, whereas the Nicaraguan communist party was minuscule. There was, thus, in the case of the latter, no hard core party with rigid ideological, sectarian links to Moscow or to Cuba, which could impose its view on the government. Like the Cubans the Nicaraguans could draw inspiration from a nationalist hero, although Gregorio Sandino was no José Martí, lacking both the literary resonance and the political prescience which was to make the latter a Latin American figure. The second feature was the role of the Catholic church and of popular Catholicism – a factor which may have influenced Castro in taking the church more seriously as a force for social change than he had done in the past. Third, was the involvement in Nicaragua of both the European community and of the Contadora powers. As a condition of their support and aid the Nicaraguans accepted the principle of political pluralism. This was to have a practical effect in the elections when the Sandinistas handed over power.

In contrast to Cuba, where Western Europe's role was low-key, in Nicaragua their involvement, both diplomatically and in terms of aid agencies, was more overt, and was an important factor in mediation both between extremes in Nicaragua itself and between Nicaragua and the US.

One factor which the two revolutions had in common was the primacy placed on cultural factors, although in the case of Nicaragua, the presence of poets in the government was one reason why European intellectuals could be weaned away from Cuba. For the idealist left in Europe, Nicaragua was in the 1980s what Cuba had been in the early-1960s.

Present trends

After the 1960s Cuba was never again to figure prominently in the imagination of the European left or in the calculations of European chanceries.[93] Interest shifted elsewhere, not so much to other countries (not even Nicaragua) as none could repeat the enthusiasm and hope with which the Revolution had been greeted in the early-1960s, so much as to causes such as the environment and green issues which has focused on the North-South divide more effectively than any previous revolutionary movement. Only in the US is the Cuban question alive and at no time more so than now as groups jostle for influence as they wait for the collapse of the regime. The debate as to ways and means and of possible scenarios rages within the exile community, and between them and those with an interest in Cuba, and among the Cubanologists who now comprise a significant sub-grouping among academic Latinamericanists with their own journals and associations. Whereas in the US exiles are many, successful, vocal and influential, in Europe they are few and although articulate, are without a constituency to which to appeal.[94]

Whereas in the US the Cuban exile community, its divisions and its influence as a pressure group has been exhaustively analysed, in Europe few studies of exiles exist. One that was based on a very small cross-section of exiles in Spain in 1989 revealed the extent to which, in spite of their number, they have been a forgotten group.[95] The close relationship between Spain and Cuba meant that they did not enjoy the privileged position of those in the US (at least until Mariel). Their very existence in Spain could be an embarrassment to a government whose relationship with Cuba was determined by pragmatic considerations. Those who are unable to join members of their family in the US have not found their life in Spain to be easy. Intellectuals, however, are atypical, being admitted to the charmed circle of their peers where anti-Castro sentiments can be articulated.

European interest lapsed when writers' enthusiasm waned in the aftermath of the Padilla affair, with the haemorrhage of many of the ablest Cuban writers, and with the publication of the prison memoirs of Armando Valladares and others. The human rights issue soured relations with both France and Spain. As the Gay Rights movement became more assertive, so Cuba's harsh treatment of homosexuals (given high visibility by the unceremonious expulsion of Allan Ginsberg in 1965), was widely publicised. Even two of the most vaunted social achievements of the Revolution – the improvement in the position of women and blacks, came to be questioned. Awareness of Cuba in Europe is kept alive by visits from Cuban musicians and groups who frequently perform in prestigious venues such as Ronnie Scott's Club in London's West End, by film festivals in Europe, and by the annual film festival in Havana which is still the most important gathering for Third World film-makers and others. Cuban sportsmen have inevitably made an impact, especially in the Olympics, but playing neither soccer nor cricket, their impact in Europe is limited, unlike in the Americas, where they are pre-eminent in basketball, baseball, and boxing.

Although there have been few pro-Cuban associations comparable to the Fair Play for Cuba Committee, there are groups such as the British Cuban Resources Centre which over the years has organised, and continues to organise, an annual brigade to cut cane or take part in community activities – the equivalent of the American Venceremos Brigade. At their meetings younger left-wing militants can mingle with ageing enthusiasts. Those who still display Che Guevara posters betray their age and his name is more likely to give distinction to a fashionable boutique, although the customers may have been at a loss to know who he was.

Havana may no longer be a magnet attracting revolutionaries of the Third World, attending solidarity congresses, but it has become one of the world's major conference centres, especially in the fields of medicine and bio-technology, which are among the Revolution's most notable achievements.[96]

With the collapse of the Soviet bloc, Cuba has been left as the standard bearer of revolution, together with North Korea, and China, the despised enemy of the 1960s but now a major trading partner and ideological bedfellow. Exhortations and stress on moral incentives in the absence of material goods recall the heady days of the 1960s, but now with only the moral support of a dwindling band of well-wishers. However, an interesting prospect is opening up with the projected tourist boom, primarily of Western Europeans. Tourism as a hard-currency earner, has now become a key factor in diversifying the economy, but by creating a form of apartheid where tourists get preferential treatment it may come to foment discontent and with emerging 'sex tourism' it may offend revolutionary susceptibilities as well.[97]

Whether visitors will be impressed by the Revolution's achievements, and encouraged to make invidious comparisons with their own societies; whether tourism will introduce the corrupting ways of the affluent West and subtly undermine Cuban morale; or by opening up a society which has been sealed off from outside influences will contribute to its downfall, are questions to which we will have to await an answer.

Notes

1   A useful overview of revolutionary historiography is Louis Pérez Jr., 'Toward
    a New Future, From a New Past: The enterprise of history in socialist Cuba',
    Cuban Studies, 15(1) winter 1985. C.E. Chapman, *A History of the Cuban
    Republic*, New York, Macmillans, 1927, commissioned by the State Depart-
    ment, reflects official views of the early years of Cuban independence. It
    remained a standard reference book for many years. *Problems of the New
    Cuba*: Report of the Commission on Cuban Affairs, New York, Foreign Policy
    Association, Inc. 1935, was prepared as a consequence of the 1933 Revolution
    and is a fundamental text. Lowry Nelson, *Rural Cuba*, Minneapolis, University
    of Minnesota Press, 1950, was a key but, I suspect, little read, book. Fernando
    Ortiz' thought-provoking cultural analysis was translated as *Cuban Counter-
    point*, New York, Knopf, 1947. Leyland Jenks, *Our Cuban Colony*, New York,
    Vanguard Press 1928, was a rare early analysis of US economic penetration of
    Cuba. See also Russell H. Fitzgibbon, *Cuba and the United States, 1900–35*,
    New York, Russell and Russell, 1964 (first published 1935). The most influen-
    tial early interpretation of the Revolution was the 'middle class revolution
    betrayed' thesis of Theodore Draper, see his *Castro's Revolution: Myths and
    Reality*, London, Thames and Hudson, 1962 and also his *Castroism: Theory
    and Practice*, New York, Praeger, 1965. The first was written as a corrective to
    a number of left-wing interpretations such as Leo Huberman and Paul M.
    Sweezy, *Cuba: anatomy of a Revolution*, New York, Monthly Press, 1960 and
    J. Morray, *The Second Revolution in Cuba*, New York, Monthly Review Press,
    1962. Morray had spent 21 months in Cuba and had taught for a time in Havana
    University. An influential account of US policy to Cuba was William A.
    Williams, *The United States, Cuba and Castro*, New York Monthly Review
    Press, 1962. In Britain, the Revolution was discussed in *Encounter*, July 1961,
    which published Draper's article on the US' 'perfect failure' in Cuba, arguing
    from Cold War assumptions, followed in August by Anthony Hartley criticis-
    ing the 'disastrous adventure' of the Bay of Pigs. Herbert Matthews published
    'Dissent over Cuba' in July 1964, protesting at the perils of being a non-
    conformist over Cuba in the US. For a discussion of the Congress of Cultural
    Freedom, *Encounter and the Cold War*, see Christopher Lasch, *The Agony of
    the American Left*, London, Andre Deutsch, 1970, Chap. 3 'The Cultural Cold
    War: a short history of the Congress for Cultural Freedom'. An excellent
    overview of foreign studies of the Revolution is Louis Pérez, '25 Years of
    Cuban Historiography: Views from Abroad', *Cuban Studies*, 1988.

2   'There are laws of political as well as of physical gravitation; and if an apple
    severed by the tempest from its native tree cannot choose but fall to the ground,
    Cuba, forcibly disjoined from its own unnatural connection with Spain, and
    incapable of self-support, can gravitate only towards the North American
    Union, which by the same law of nature cannot cast her off from its bosom'.
    J.Q. Adams to N. Nelson, 29 April 1823, *The Writings of John Quincey Adams*,
    Vol. VII, (ed.) W.C. Ford, New York, 1917, p. 373.

3   It is striking to note how little impact the Guatemalan Revolution (1944–54)
    made on Latin American Studies, attracting little scholarly attention until the
    1960s, due perhaps to the ease with which it was snuffed out by the CIA-
    supported invasion of Castillo Armas (a baleful influence on the Bay of Pigs
    invasion of 1961), although its relevance (the presence there of Che Guevara,
    Czech arms shipments, CIA involvements) was greater for the Cuban ex-

perience than the 'successful' Bolivian Revolution of 1952.

4   Current academic concerns in the early-1960s included modernisation theory usually based on quantitative analysis. W.W. Rostow's 'stage-theory' of economic growth, exerted considerable influence. The Alliance for Progress reflected the current view that injections of capital would promote the development of an entrepreneurial bourgeoisie and would be the key to successful reform and antidote to Cuban-style revolution. Its failure and that of the 'trickle-down' effect focused attention on structural blockages, on culturally-induced investment habits and on an analysis of the middle class(es) or 'middle sectors' – see J.J. Johnson, *Political Change in Latin America: the emergence of the middle sectors*, Stanford, Stanford University Press, 1958. Some of the most interesting work in the 1960s can be found in the papers of the American University Field Service, mostly written by anthropologists working at the grass-roots level. The key to understanding Latin American societies lay with social anthropologists – Eric Wolf, Sidney Mintz *et al.*, rather than the practitioners of political science, then enjoying unchallenged supremacy. The writings of Kal Silvert and Richard Morse, both gadflies to establishment academics, repay study, although neither were able to work in Cuba. For the Oscar Lewis affair see below, note 81. Two key volumes are those edited by Claudio Veliz, *Obstacles to Change in Latin America*, London, Oxford University Press, 1965 and *The Politics of Conformity*, London, Oxford University Press, 1967 – the latter containing an analysis of the Cuban middle class by Hugh Thomas. 'Dependency-theory' became a paradigm of the left, as in the writings of Gunder Frank and others. From a huge literature see Phillip O'Brien, 'Dependency Revisited', in C. Abel and C. Lewis, *Latin America: Economic Imperialism and the State*, London, Athlone Press, 1985. The concept of the 'lumpenbourgeoisie' emerges from an analysis of the failure of middle-class revolutions to take off in Latin America. The concept of populism was one attempt to explain the unique features of Latin American politics. See Hennessy in E. Gellner and G. Ionescu, *Populism: its Meanings and National Characteristics*, London, Weidenfeldt and Nicolson, 1969. 'Convergence Theory' was to have some relevance later to the 'two imperialisms' thesis – i.e. that there was little to choose between the US and the USSR, a view to which many Non-Aligned nations subscribed but which the Cubans attempted to refute in the 1970s. One of the best books in the early-1960s on Cuban society was Wyatt MacGaffey and Clifford Barnett, *Cuba: Its History, Society and Culture*, New Haven, HRAF Press 1963. The Cuban Revolution revolutionised the Latin American academic establishment in the US – in some ways 'revolutionising the counter-revolution' to borrow Debray's term from another context. One of the few people to address the fundamental Cuban issues of corruption and violence was W.S. Stokes in 'The Cuban parliamentary system in action', 1940–7, *Journal of Politics*, May 1949 and 'National and local violence in Cuban politics', *South-West Social Science Quarterly*, 34, No. 2, September 1953.

5   For this see S.G. Hanson 'Footnotes to the Castro Story': from the papers of A.A. Berle in – *Inter-American Economic Affairs*, 30(1), 1976, 'the best mind, almost the only first-rate mind applied to the problems of inter-American relations from Roosevelt to Johnson was A.A. Berle'. The quality of one US ambassador to Cuba may be gauged from Earl T. Smith, *The Fourth Floor: an account of the Castro Communist Revolution*, New York, Random House, 1962. Arthur Gardner, another ambassador, remarked of Batista: 'I don't think

we ever had a better friend'. Quoted in Hugh Thomas, *Cuba or the Pursuit of Freedom*, London, Eyre and Spottiswode, 1970. This is the key history on Cuba in English and is particularly good on the background of US officials concerned with Cuba. By far the most interesting and perceptive account of the Revolution by a US official is that by Wayne S. Smith, who was in charge of the US Interests Section in Havana after the blockade, *The Closest of Enemies: a personal and diplomatic account of US-Cuban relations since 1957*, New York, Norton, 1987. This is required reading for a sympathetic but critical view of the Revolution.

6   For an analysis of the Cuban nationalist tradition see the chapters by Hennessy, Kapcia and Díaz Quiñones in A. Hennessy (ed.) *Intellectuals in the 20th Century Caribbean*: Vol. II, *The Hispanic and Francophone Tradition*, Warwick University Caribbean Studies, Basingstoke, Macmillans, 1992.

7   For a short guide to the vast bibliography on nineteenth and twentieth century Cuba, see Louis A. Pérez, *Cuba: an annotated bibliography*, Westport, Greenwood, 1988 and for a useful general history his *Cuba between Reform and Revolution*, New York, Oxford University Press, 1988.

8   Two useful discussions of José Martí are P. Turton, *José Martí: Architect of Cuba's Freedom*, London, Zed Books, 1986, and C. Abel and N. Torrents (eds) *José Martí: Revolutionary Democrat*, Durham, N.C., Duke University Press, 1986.

9   For the Turner thesis and its relevance to Latin America see A. Hennessy, *The Frontier in Latin American History*, London, Arnolds, 1978.

10 Two translations of biographies of Martí had been published in the United States: Felix Lizaso, *Martí, martyr of Cuban Independence*, Westport, Greenwood Press, 1974, (reprint of 1953 edition) and Jorge Mañach, *Martí Apostle of Freedom*, New York, Devin Adair, 1950.

11 'Polycentrism' which has dropped out of the political vocabulary was widely used in the 1960s. See the special issue of *Survey*, No. 58, Jan. 1966.

12 For example, the Peruvians J.C. Mariátegui and C. Vallejo in particular, although the influence of Haya de la Torre who tried to break away from Marxist categories was to be an important influence in Cuba which he visited in 1923 as a representative of the University Reform Movement.

13 A stimulating discussion of the problems of the American left is Christopher Lasch, *The Agony of the American Left*, London, Andre Deutsch, 1970. Two quotations are relevant to the argument: 'In a world divided between Communism and Liberalism, American radicalism tended to become increasingly shrill, increasingly desperate and increasingly bizarre as it searched for some third position, independent of both' (p. 288), and: 'it is difficult for Englishmen to understand or sympathize with the desperation which underlines American radicalism and the sense of futility in a gigantic country in which political debate is dominated by the organs of mass communication, and in which public opinion, misinformed or even deliberately misled, seems at once powerless, when it is a question of persuading government to pursue more liberal policies, and when it is a question of compelling it to pursue politics even more illiberal than the ones it wants to pursue (as in Cuba) – the sense of sheer futility, in such a country, which afflicts those who seek to check the suicidal impulse the American people seem bent on pursuing' (p. 335, n. 7).

14 Free elections were a crucial issue. Castro's view of elections was expressed in his May Day speech of 1961 thus: 'A revolution expressing the will of the people is an election every day, not every four years; it is a constant meeting

with the people, like this meeting. The old politicians could never have gathered as many votes as there are people here tonight to support the revolution . . . What do they [in the US] want? Elections with pictures on the posts. The revolution has changed the conception of pseudo-democracy for direct government by the people. There had to be a period for abolition of the privileges'. Quoted in M. Zeitlin and R. Scheer, *Cuba: an American Tragedy*, Harmondsworth, Penguin Books, p. 255. In view of Cuba's corrupt electoral history free elections could have dissipated Castro's mass support overnight. For a useful discussion of the PSP in the early 1960s see S. Farber, 'The Cuban Communists in the early stages of the Cuban Revolution: Revolutionaries or Reformers? *Latin American Research Review*: 18(1), 1983. R.R. Fagen *The transformation of political culture in Cuba*, Stanford, Stanford University Press, 1969. Richard Nixon's memo to Eisenhower after meeting Castro was quite perceptive: 'Fidel Castro is either incredibly naive, or under Communist discipline. My guess is the former. . . . His ideas as to how to run a government or an economy are less developed than those of almost any world figure I have met in fifty countries'. Stephen Ambrose, *Nixon: The Education of a Politician, 1913–62*, New York, Simon and Schuster, 1987, p. 515. This tallies with the view that he turned to the PSP for their expertise, rather than because he was a crypto-communist.

15   This phrase comes from a speech on the occasion of the observance of the 13 March assault on the presidential palace in 1957 when José Antonio Echevarría was gunned down. Castro's anger was roused by the communists writing off Echevarría as a Catholic. However, Castro's ambivalent attitudes towards the communists will exercise academics for many years to come.

16   For the context of the Reform Movement see J. Maier and R. Weatherhead, *The Latin American University*, Albuquerque, University of New Mexico Press, 1979, and for Cuba J. Suchlicki, *University students and Revolution in Cuba 1920–68*, Coral Gables, University of Miami Press, 1969. For the US see S.M. Lipset, *Rebellion in the University: a history of student activism in America*, London, Routledge Kegan Paul, 1972, (6).

17   Quoted in W. La Feber, *The American Age: United States Foreign Policy at Home and Abroad since 1750*, New York, Norton, 1989, p. 340. From a huge literature on the Doctrine one of the best – and provocative – accounts is Richard van Alstyne, *The Rising American Empire*, Oxford, Blackwells, 1957.

18   Domingo Sarmiento, *Facundo: Civilisation and Barbarism*, first published in 1845, was translated in 1868 as *Life in the Argentine Republic in the Days of the Tyrant*. It is an extraordinary, and some would say a pernicious book, dominating intellectual discourse until the 1920s but Sarmiento was more ambivalent than many commentators allow. He was a rare example of a nineteenth-century Spanish American intellectual who admired the US, comparing its frontier experience with that of Argentina. Unlike so many of his contemporaries, he was not seduced by French example, except possibly by their policy in Algeria. The civilization-barbarism dichotomy influenced the Cuban historian Ramiro Guerra y Sánchez and the Puerto Rican Antonio Pedreira whose key works on the origin of nationality were published in 1927 and 1934 respectively. For this see Arcadio Díaz Quiñones, 'Hispanic-Caribbean national discourse: Antonio Pedreira and Ramiro Guerra' in A. Hennessy (ed.) *Intellectuals II, op. cit.*

19   The Protestant impulse behind Manifest Destiny ironically coincided with the first wave of Irish Catholic immigration. For the Social Darwinist thrust see

R. Hofstadter, *Social Darwinism in American Thought*, New York, Braziller, 1965.

20 See the edition by G. Brotherston, *Ariel*, Cambridge, Cambridge University Press, 1967.

21 H. Hoetink in A. Hennessy, *Intellectuals II, op. cit.* p. 135.

22 L. Schoultz, *National Security and United States' Policy toward Latin America*, Princeton, Princeton University Press, 1987, p. 126, which includes a useful discussion of the slippery concept of political culture.

23 Quoted in A. Woll, *The Latin Image in Hollywood Cinema*, UCLA, 1977, p. 35. See also Arthur G. Pettit, *Images of the Mexican American in Fiction and Film*, College Station, Texas A. and M. University Press, 1980.

24 M.N. Roy was an Indian nationalist who had been sent to Mexico by the Comintern to establish a communist party in return for Russian support for the nationalist movement in India. For the Comintern in Latin America see Manuel Caballero, *Latin America and the Comintern 1919–43*, Cambridge, Cambridge University Press, 1986. See also Ilya Prizel, *Latin America Through Soviet Eyes: the Evolution of Soviet Perceptions during the Brezhnev Era*, Cambridge, Cambridge University Press, 1990. In Cuba a Polish Jew, Yunger Semjovich, whose pseudonym was Fabio Grobart was a founder member and *éminence grise* of the Cuban Communist Party.

25 For Cuban intellectuals see the chapter by Kapcia here and those of Kapcia, Hennessy and Miller in *Intellectuals, op. cit.*

26 The issue of black support for the 26th July Movement is discussed very forcibly in C. Moore, *Castro, the Blacks and Africa*, Los Angeles, Centre for Afro-American Studies, University of California Press, 1988.

27 For the 1934–44 period, the silent unheroic years, see S. Farber, *Revolution and Reaction in Cuba, 1933–60*, Middletown, Wesleyan University Press, 1976.

28 The growth of Soviet naval power, especially submarines, with useful commentaries can be followed in the annual publications of *Janes' Fighting Ships*, London. A useful overview is by Captain J.E. Moore, pp. 121–172 in *Soviet War Power*, (ed.) Ray Bonds, Salamander Books, London, 1980. For Soviet naval strategy, see B. Dismukes and J. McConnell (eds) *Soviet naval diplomacy*, New York, Pergamon Press, 1979 and P.J. Murphy (ed.) *Naval Power in Soviet Policy*, Vol. 2, Studies in Communist Affairs, USAF, Washington, 1978. For a useful overview see Hedley Bull in *Problems of Communism*, March/April 1981. There was increased emphasis put on surface ocean-going vessels after the missile crisis of 1962, both to protect Soviet merchant ships and to cover possible landings of Soviet troops. For the USSR merchant marine see B. Bock and B. Klaus, *Soviet bloc merchant ships*, London, Janes, 1981. From 1959–65 the USSR rose from being 12th to 6th among the world's maritime fleets, and by 1975 the USSR merchant fleet had overtaken that of the US.

29 See L. Schoultz, *op. cit.*, Chaps. 4–7. These are fundamental to an understanding of lines of communication, oil supplies, military bases, etc. For regional security issues see also Peter Calvert (ed.) *The Central American Security System: North-South or East-West?*, Cambridge, Cambridge University Press, 1988.

30 J.K. Galbraith, *The Affluent Society* (1958) questioned the premises of capitalist society, albeit from a liberal perspective. T. Veblen *The Higher Learning in America: a memorandum on the conduct of universities by businessmen* (1918) was reprinted in 1957. This foreshadowed the critiques of US universities in

the 1960s. Popular sociologists like Vance Packard, *The Status Seekers* (1959), and *The Waste Makers* (1960), and W.H. Whyte, *The Organisation Man* (1956) all created a critical climate without being specifically 'left'. The most influential of this genre was C. Wright-Mills, *The Power Elite* (1956).

31   Various later corollaries of the Doctrine make explicit the implicit assumptions of the original declaration. In 1845 President Polk expanded the concept of European non-intervention by forbidding external powers to intervene diplomatically in inter-American relations, and prohibited any government in the Americas from ceding territory to an outside power, claiming the right of the US to oversee relations between American nations and the rest of the world. In 1904 the Roosevelt Corollary, in response to the threat of European debt-collecting expeditions (e.g. the Anglo-German blockade of Venezuela in 1902 – the Doctrine had also been invoked in 1895 in the Anglo-Venezuelan dispute over the frontier of British Guyana). The Corollary legitimated the US role (in US eyes at least) as regional arbiter intervening when necessary. The modification of this by F.D. Roosevelt's acceptance of the resolution, as part of his 'Good Neighbor' policy at the 1936 Inter-American Conference, forbidding any kind of unilateral intervention was quantified by the US conceding the principle only if other American countries recognised collective responsibility. If they refused to do so, the US felt free to act unilaterally. For an overview, see M. Erisman 'The US perception of Western Europe's role in the Caribbean', P. Sutton (ed.), *Europe and the Caribbean*, Warwick University Caribbean Studies, Basingstoke, Macmillan Press Ltd, 1991.

32   The most recent and striking is the case of the Falklands/Malvinas war which divided opinion throughout the Americas and became a touchstone for Monroist attitudes. In spite of the lack of ideological affinity with the military dictatorship in Argentina, Castro supported Argentina. US support for Britain, without which the war might well have been lost, was, of course, a reversal of traditional Monroist attitudes.

33   For example, by the Ford Foundation's support for a 5-year Chatham House programme on Latin America with its regular seminars and the key volumes edited by Claudio Véliz, *Obstacles, op. cit.* and *The Politics of Conformity, op. cit.*, and also support for the Latin American programme at St Anthony's College, Oxford. The Astor Foundation funded visits to Latin America including one by the author to Cuba in 1961.

34   Hugh Thomas visited Cuba in 1961 to write a Penguin Special on the Revolution but recognising that it was inexplicable without understanding the historical background spent the next ten years researching it. *Cuba, or the Pursuit of Freedom* is still a fundamental history.

35   For French Press coverage see Liliane Hasson 'La Révolution Cubaine et la Presse Française' in *Cuba et la France*, (ed.) J. Lamore, Presses Universitaires de Bordeaux, 1983, based on a detailed content analysis for a Paris doctoral thesis. An exhaustive, and hostile, treatment of French writers on Cuba is J. Verdès Leroux, *La Lune et le Caudillo; le Rêve des Intellectuels et le Régime Cubain*, Paris, Gallimard, 1989. For a hostile coverage of general press treatment see W. Ratliff *et al.*, *The Selling of Fidel Castro: the Media and the Cuban Revolution*, New Brunswick, Transaction Books, 1986.

36   For university and student disturbances, in which there was some Castroist influence, see J.A. Maravall, *Dictatorship and Political Dissent: Workers and Students in Franco's Spain*, London, Tavistock, 1978.

37   *Cuba Business*, Oct. 1991, V.v.

38 For figures on Western shipping visiting Cuban ports, see Morley, *op. cit.*, appendix 2, table 2, p. 374. In the peak year 1964, 383 West European (including Cyprus and Lebanon) ships called in at Cuban ports of which 180 were British. For the USSR's tanker fleet, see the various copies of the *Tanker Register*, Clarkson Research Studies Ltd., London. By 1967, the USSR had only 3 tankers of 150,000 tons.

39 See Chapter 6. The history of the subsequent failure of British motor exports to Latin America remains to be written. It may be that US pressure played a part in Leyland losing orders in Latin America – for example in Peru where the contract to re-equip the Lima transport system, considered to be certain, was lost at the last moment.

40 *Financial Times*.

41 For the Padilla affair, see *Index*, Summer, 1972, 'Cuba: Revolution and the Intellectual: the strange case of Herberto Padilla'. For a succinct account, putting the affair into context see Nicola Miller's chapter in *Intellectuals*, *op. cit.* See also Padilla's own memoirs *op. cit.*, and Jorge Edwards *Persona non grata*, *versión completa*, Barcelona, Seix Barral, 1982.

42 The most pungent analysis of the reasons of why intellectuals were attracted to the Revolution is Mike González, 'The culture of the heroic guerrilla', *Bulletin of Latin American Research*, Vol. 3, 1964. Castro's speech after the Congress of Intellectuals in 1968 is revealing. 'Where did the death of Che Guevara have its most profound impact? . . . among the intellectual workers. . . . not organisations or parties.' *Bohemia*, 19(1), 1968.

43 The classic denunciation of successor elites is Frantz Fanon, *The Wretched of the Earth*, Harmondsworth, Penguin Books, 1980, where (p. 37) they are described as 'the spoilt children of yesterday's colonialism and today's national governments looting the new nations' resources'.

44 Two key figures here were René Dumont, an agronomist who advised Castro on agrarian reform. See his *Réforme agraire à Cuba*, Paris, Editions Tiers Monde, 1962. (He was to be attacked by Castro for criticising the 10 million ton harvest) and André Voisin, a French cattle geneticist who fired Castro's enthusiasm for cattle breeding. Economists included Brian Pollitt and Dudley Seers from Britain, Charles Bettleheim and Michel Gutelman from France and Ernest Mandel from Belgium. The moral incentives debate can be followed in B. Silverman (ed.), *Man and Socialism in Cuba*, New York, Atheneum, 1971 and Robert M. Bernardo, *The Theory of Moral Incentives in Cuba*, University of Alabama Press, 1971.

45 This documentary was banned in France. It must not be forgotten that the Algerian war did not finish until 1962. Thus France was the object of strong anti-colonialist propaganda for the first three years of the Revolution from Cuba.

46 Although there is an interesting exception – it was through Castro's personal intervention that the Lezama Lima's *Paradiso*, with its notorious chapter 8 was published. Film was the most dynamic form of cultural expression. For this see Michael Chanan, *The Cuban Image: Cinema and Cultural Politics in Cuba*, London, BFI, 1985, and Paulo Antonio Paranagua (ed.) *Le Cinema Cubain*, Paris, Centre Georges Pompidou, 1990. The latter is a vade-mecum for Cuban film and European influences with an invaluable chronology of Cuban culture and politics. The issue of film censorship had been brought up by the film P.M. – see Miller, *Intellectuals*, *op. cit.* It was also to be raised by the controversy over whether *La Dolce Vita* should be shown – see M. Halperin's chapter in

Ronald Radosh (ed.) *The New Cuba: Paradoxes and Potentials*, New York, William Morrow, 1976. For Cuban poster art, see Susan Sontag's introduction to *The Art of Revolution*, New York, McGraw-Hill, 1970. In 1967 the Parisian Salon de Mai exhibition of avant garde art was shown in Havana, the first time in the Western hemisphere, a deliberate snub to the Russian concept of socialist realism. For the literary background and literary politics see Lourdes Casal, 'Literature and Society', in Carmelo Mesa-Lago (ed.), *Revolutionary Change in Cuba*, Pittsburgh, Pittsburgh University Press, 1971; Seymour Menton, *Prose Fiction of the Cuban Revolution*, Austin, Texas University 1975 and the collection *Literatura y Arte Nuevo en Cuba*, M. Barnet and others, Barcelona, Estela, 1971. See also the articles 'Writer and State in Cuba', *Cuban Studies* (1989).

47   See Hans Magnus Enzensberger, 'Tourists of the Revolution', in *Dreamers of the Absolute*, London, Radius, 1988. And more particularly Paul Hollander, *Political Pilgrims*, New York, Oxford University Press, 1987, which deals with China, Cuba, Russia and Vietnam.

48   One of the best analyses, sympathetic but critical, is Janette Habel, *Cuba: The Revolution in Peril*, with Foreword by F. Maspero, Verso, London, 1991, who writes from long experience since being one of the first youthful French enthusiasts to visit and work in Cuba in the 1960s. Maspero was one of the leading publishers of pro-Cuban books in France.

49   At the governmental level the 'Special Relationship' may have some validity, but what does it mean to blacks, native Americans, Hispanics – to say nothing of Irish Americans and other hyphenates? Very little, I suspect. There can be no doubt that the idea was a reality during the missile crisis of 1962 when Macmillan and Kennedy were in constant communication. See Harold Macmillan's, Memoirs, Vol. 6, *At the End of the Day*, 1961–63, Basingstoke, Macmillan, chapter 7, 'On the Brink' pp. 179–220, and Alistair Horne, *Macmillan, Vol. II, 1957–86*, Basingstoke, Macmillan, 1989.

50   For this see *Inter-American Economic Affairs*, Vol. XIV, No. 1, summer 1960.

51   Although the French had been active in the River Plate in the mid-nineteenth century (especially in Uruguay), it was not until the French Intervention in Mexico in the 1860s and Napoleon III's concept of Panlatinism (the term 'Latin America' was a French invention) at a time when the Monroe Doctrine was inoperative during the US Civil War that French interest increased. For contemporary French interest in the Caribbean see Helen Hintjen's 'France in the Caribbean', in Sutton, *op. cit.*

52   For Valladares see *Beyond all Hope: the Prison Memoirs of Armando Valladares*, London, Hamish Hamilton, 1986. Another person to be imprisoned was Pierre Golendorf, a communist party militant who went to work in Cuba but who was later to be imprisoned as a CIA agent. See his *Sept ans à Cuba: 38 mois dans les Prisons de Fidel Castro*, Paris, Belfort, 1976 and also P. Golendorf (ed.) *Valladares, Prisoniero de Castro*, Barcelona, Planeta, 1982. For another case see Jorge Valls, *Donde estoy no hay luz y está enrejado*, Madrid, Playa, 1984.

53   The keyword for this and for an understanding of Cuban history generally, is M. Moreno Fraginals, *El Ingenio*, 3 vols., Havana, Editorial Social, 1978 – the first volume has been translated by Cedric Belfridge as *The Sugar Mill: the socio-economic complex of sugar in Cuba 1760–1860*, New York, London, Monthly Review Press, 1976.

54   For an overview, see A. Hennessy 'Spain and Cuba: an enduring relationship' in Howard, W. (ed.) *The Latin-American Connection: Implications for US*

Foreign Policy, Boulder, Westview, 1986. The life's work of Emilio Roig de Leuchsenring was devoted to combating the US view of the war of 1898 and US Intervention, especially in his campaign to rename the usually designated 'Spanish American War' of 1898 the 'Guerra Hispano-Cubanoamericana'. See *Revaloración de la Historia de Cuba por los Congresos Nacionales de Historia*, La Habana, Oficina del Historiador de la Ciudad, 1961.

55   The best account of the crisis years of the 1890s is by Louis A. Pérez, *Cuba Between Empires, 1878–1902*, Pittsburgh, University of Pittsburgh Press, 1983.

56   For a general discussion see A. Hennessy, 'Cuba' in M. Falcoff and F.B. Pike, *The Spanish Civil War, 1936–9: American Hemisphere Perspectives*, Lincoln, University of Nebraska Press, 1982. An interesting collection of testimonies is *Cuba y la Defensa de la República Española*, La Habana, Editora Política, 1951. See *Bohemia*, 26 January 1968, '31 años después' on the reunion of Cuban and other writers who had been at the Congress of Intellectuals in Valencia in 1937 and were at the Congress in Havana in 1968.

57   Stuart Hall and Norm Fruchter, *New Left Review*, 7(1), 1961.

58   See Peter Binns and Mike González, *Cuba, Castro and Socialism* (International Socialism 8, Spring 1980).

59   A useful collection of essays on the thinkers influencing the New Left (Guevara, Sartre, Marcuse, Fanon, Black Power, R.D. Laing) is Maurice Cranston (ed.) *The New Left*, London, Bodley Head, 1970. For the US see Richard E. Welch, *Responses to Revolution: the United States and the Cuban Revolution, 1959–61*, Chapel Hill, University of North Carolina Press, 1985 and Paul Lyons 'The New Left and the Cuban Revolution' in Radosh, *op. cit.* On Britain see *Out of Apathy: Voices of the New Left 30 Years On* (ed.) by Oxford University Socialist Discussion Group, London, Verso, 1989, especially Stuart Hall, 'The 'First' New Left: Life and Times'.

60   See Kenneth Devlin, 'The Challenge of Euro-Communism', *Problems of Communism*, Jan–February 1977, and Eusebio Mujal-Leon, 'The PCE in Spanish Politics', *Problems of Communism*, July–August 1978. The 'frente de liberación popular' founded in the mid-1950s came under some Castroist influence but its ideological heterogeneity, consisting of Trotskyism, French/Italian left socialism and left-wing Christian democracy influenced by Third World ideologies, led to its break up in the late-1960s. For the complexities of university 'groupuscules' see J.M. Maravall, *Dictatorship and Political Dissent: Workers and Students in Franco's Spain*, London, Tavistock, 1978.

61   For a succinct contrast between the New Left and the Old Left see David Caute, *The Year of the Barricades: '68*, London, Paladin, 1988. This is particularly good in showing the interaction between leftist politics and the counter-culture. An overview is A. Hennessy, 'Apothesis of the Innocents', *International Affairs*, July 1971. For Britain see also the collection of Bernard Crick and William A. Robson (eds), *Protest and Discontent*, Harmondsworth, Penguin, 1970. Richard Lowenthal, 'Reason and Unreason', *Encounter*, Vol. 33, November 1969, is very suggestive.

62   Robin Blackburn and Alexander Cockburn, *Student Power: problems, diagnosis, action*, Harmondsworth, Penguin, 1969.

63   A useful wide-ranging overview (although excluding Latin-America) is Christopher Driver, *The Exploding University*, London, Hodder and Stoughton, 1971. For the US Christopher Jenks and David Riesman, *The Academic Revolution*, New York, Doubleday, 1969. An interesting collection of dissentient

academics is Theodore Roszack (ed.), *The Dissenting Academy*, Harmondsworth, Penguin, 1969.

64   Quoted in Hennessy, 'Apotheosis', *op. cit.*

65   For Che Guevara a useful collection has been edited by John Gerassi, *Venceremos: the Speeches and Writings of Che Guevara*, London, Weidenfeld and Nicholson, 1965.

66   See H. Matthews, *The Cuban Story*, New York, Braziller, 1961 and his *Castro: a Political Biography*, London, Allen Lane, 1969. For another biography by a veteran journalist see Tad Szulc, *Fidel: a Critical Portrait*, London, Hutchinson, 1986.

67   An interesting comparative analysis is in Alan Knight, *Bulletin of Latin American Research*, 9, 1990. See also Brian Meeks, *Caribbean Revolutions and Revolutionary Theory*, University of Warwick Caribbean Studies, Basingstoke, Macmillan Press Ltd, 1993.

68   J. Servan-Schreiber, *Le Défi Américain*, Paris, Denoel, 1967.

69   For this see Hennessy, *Intellectuals*, *op. cit.*

70   For Franqui see Miller, *Intellectuals*, *op. cit.* For Casa see Judith Weiss, *Casa de las Americas: a Cultural Journal of the Cuban Revolution*, Chapel Hill, University of North Carolina, 1977 and Susan Frenk, 'Two Cultural Journals of the 1960s: Casa de las Americas and Mundo Nuevo', *Bulletin of Latin American Research*, vol. 3, 1984. Among many of Franqui's writings see his *Diary of the Cuban Revolution*, New York, Viking Press, 1980; *Family Portrait with Fidel*, London, Cape, 1980 and *Vida, aventuras y desastres de un hombre llamado Castro*, Barcelona, Planeta, 1988.

71   Régis Debray, *Teachers, Writers, Celebrities*, Introduction by F. Mulhern, Translated by D. Macy, London, Verso, 1970. Richard Hofstadter '*Anti-Intellectualism in American Life*', New York, Random House, 1962, is the key study for the fluctuations in the influence of intellectuals but see also Christopher Lasch, *op. cit.* In Spain the majority of liberal and leftist intellectuals were scattered in a diaspora in Europe and throughout the Americas which bears comparison with that of Germany in the 1930s. Few went to Cuba – Juan Rámon Jimenez did so briefly before passing on to Puerto Rico. For exiled intellectuals in Cuba see Consuelo Naranjo Olorio, *Cuba, otro escenario de lucha: la Guerra Civil y el exilio Republicano Español*, Madrid, CSIC, 1988.

72   Arnold Wesker's comment on his three months in Cuba directing his play in 1968 was 'It was just marvellous, I've never known anything like it' . . . quoted in Caute *op. cit.*, p. 31. For David Mercer's interview see *Bohemia, op. cit.*

73   See Juan Goytisolo, *Pueblo en Marcha*, Paris, Libreria Española, 1963, based on a ten weeks' visit. His family had been millowners in Cuba, and reading correspondence about his grandfather's slaves roused his social conscience. He was later to become disillusioned.

74   C. Wright Mills, *Listen Yankee*, New York, Ballantine Books, 1960.

75   J.P. Sartre, *Sartre on Cuba*, New York, Ballantine Books, 1961. For Sartre, Castro was the embodiment of the Nietzschean superman. For Simone de Beauvoir's account of the visit see her *Force of Circumstance*, New York, Putnam, 1965, pp. 500–5.

76   The original method by which the party was established can be traced in the issues of *Cuba Socialista*. See unpublished paper by A. Hennessy, 'Castro's New Party', (1963).

77   This was the title of an article by Debray, 'Latin America: the long March' *New Left Review*, vol. 33, Sep–Oct, 1965.

78 There is a spirited account of this in Andrew Salkey, *Havana Journal*, Harmondsworth, Penguin, 1971. For the resolutions of the Congress see *Cultural Congress of Havana*, Havana, January 1968, also the weekly copies of *Bohemia*, Jan–Feb, 1968. See issue of 19 Jan for Castro's speech at the closure of the Congress. Within four months of this spirited and oblique critique of the Soviets he was to support the Warsaw Pact's suppression of the Czech dissidents, illustrating the constraints under which the Cubans were then operating.

79 The Tlatelolco massacres before the Olympic games of 1968 involved the slaughter of some hundreds of demonstrators, most of whom were students. Cuba could not afford to offend the only Latin American state which had never submitted to the US blockade. See E. Poniatowska, *Massacre in Mexico*, New York, Viking, 1975.

80 For the blistering attack on the bearers of a new colonialism see Castro's speech in *Granma*, 9 May 1971, condemning those foreign intellectuals who had previously supported the Revolution. These included Mario Vargas Llosa, Carlos Fuentes, Octavio Paz, Jorge Semprún, Juan Goytisolo, J.P. Sartre, Simone de Beauvoir, Alberto Moravia and Susan Sontag among many others. The most striking figure to stand by Cuba was Gabriel García Marquéz. Oscar Lewis's oral history project was to be one casualty of the hardening of the line, see *Living the Revolution: an Oral History of the Cuban Revolution*, Urbana, University of Illinois Press, 1977, vol. 1 Introduction, together with Maurice Halperin's critique of Lewis's, 'naiveté', 'The Case of Oscar Lewis', *The Taming of Fidel Castro*, Los Angeles, University of California Press, 1981. Halperin had taught in Moscow before teaching at Havana University for six years. For the Padilla Affair see the special issue of *Index on Censorship*, 1972, 2. An excellent discussion is Lourdes Casal, 'Literature and Society', in C. Mesa-Lago (ed.) *Revolutionary Change in Cuba*, Pittsburg University Press 1971.

81 See N. Miller, 'Intellectuals and the Cuban Revolution' in Hennessy, *Intellectuals, op. cit.*

82 See R. Dumont, *Is Cuba Socialist?* and K.S. Karol, *Guerrillas in Power*, New York, Hill and Wang, 1970.

83 From Hennessy, *op. cit.*, p. 25.

84 From a large literature see Carmelo Mesa-Lago and June Belkin (eds), *Cuba in Africa*, Pittsburgh, University of Pittsburgh, 1982.

85 Communist states feel uneasy tolerating guerrillas as they can easily elude centralised control. This was what effectively destroyed Alberto Bayó's attempts during the Spanish Civil War to persuade the Republican Government to adopt a guerrilla strategy as this would have removed control fron the communist dominated International Brigades. Bayó's ideas, frustrated in Spain, were to find expression in Cuba where his teachings passed on to Castro in Mexico were to be put into practice in the Sierra Maestra.

86 See Georges Fauriol and Eva Loser, *Cuba: the International Dimension*, New Brunswick, Transaction Publishers, 1990, pp. 147–49. Rhodesia provided one example of Cuban restraint, others were the low-key treatment of the Northern Ireland problem in the Cuban press, and the restrained response to the 'spy' incident and the ignominious expulsion of the Cuban Ambassador.

87 Jorge Domínguez, *To Make a World Safe for Revolution: Cuba's Foreign Policy*, Cambridge, Mass., Harvard University Press, 1989, p. 201.

88 Anthony J. Payne, *Politics in Jamaica*, London, C. Hurst, 1988, Chap. 9, and Evelyne and John Stephens, *Democratic Socialism in Jamaica: the political*

movement and social transformation in dependent capitalism, Basingstoke, Macmillan, 1986.

89   David Thomas 'The United States factor in British relations with Latin America', in Victor Bulmer Thomas, (ed.) *Britain and Latin America: a changing relationship*, Cambridge, Cambridge University Press, 1989, p. 78.

90   *Ibid*. See J.R. Sargent, *Report of the tripartite economic survey of the Eastern Caribbean*, London, HMSO, 1967 for early plans for an airport. The first military planes to use the airport were American. Barbados, hostile to the Cuban presence in Grenada had nevertheless previously granted landing facilities to Cuban planes (old British Britannias) to ferry troops to Angola – as did Burnham's Guyana with which Cuba had a curious relationship given the way Cheddi Jagan, Burnham's inveterate opponent, had close Moscow links. An excellent overview is the collection of essays in Barry Levine (ed.), *The New Cuban Presence in the Caribbean*, Boulder, Westview, 1983.

91   Bulmer-Thomas, *op. cit.* p. 79.

92   See Brian Meeks, *op. cit.* There was no dominant Nicaraguan personality, equivalent to Castro, nor an ideological mentor with a resonance throughout Latin America. Whatever his virtues, Sandino was no Martí.

93   A useful overview is Jean Stubbs, *Cuba or the Test of Time*, London, Latin America Bureau, 1989.

94   The most articulate exile in Europe and arguably the greatest living Cuban writer is Enrique Cabrera Infante, now a British citizen writing in English as well as Spanish. For his critique of the Revolution's cultural policy, 'Bites from the Bearded Crocodile' in *London Review of Books*, Anthology 1, London, Junction Books, 1981. Carlos Franqui, a key figure in the early cultural policy of the Revolution had been living in Italy since the early 1970s. Many exiles came to Spain and then went to the US, for example Carlos Alberto Montaner. In France writers include Juan Alcocha, and the playwright Triana, two of whose plays have been translated and shown in England by the R.S.C.

95   Vicente Romano, *Cuba en el Corazón: Testimonios de un Desarraigo*, Prologo de Jesus Ibañez, Barcelona, Anthropos, 1989. Although only based on nine interviews ranging from a student of 22 to a gynaecologist of 67 (Marta Fayde, author of *Ecoute Fidel*, they all reveal a deep sense of nostalgia for Cuba and are disillusioned with conditions in Spain and the reception they received. Bitterness was expressed about the rich, and intellectual exiles (Valladares being described as a 'millionaire'). Prominent among writers has been Carlos Alberto Montaner and César Leante – see his *Fidel Castro: el fin de un Mito*, Madrid, Editorial Pliegos, 1991. There may be as many as a quarter of a million Cubans claiming Spanish citizenship but Cuba does not recognise dual nationality. The book analyses four main apolitical organisations which cater for exiles' needs. Three are primarily social centres – the *Centro Cubano de Madrid* (1966), Sor Isabel – a Cuban nun (1961) who runs her own Centre providing meals etc., and *La Casa de Cuba: Comité pro Reconciliación de la Familia Cubana* – the only one to enjoy good relations with the Cuban embassy in Madrid. Finally, the International Rescue Committee (*Rescate*) – a New York-based organisation with world-wide links, not confined to Cubans – is committed to aid anyone suffering from the loss of liberty. The privileged position of Cubans in the US may be contrasted with the fate of Haitians wishing to become exiles there. For a revealing insight of the US-exile phenomenon see the documentary Miami-Havana directed by Estella Bravo. There is an exile organisation based in London (*La Sociedad de los Amigos del Pais*)

which is analysing the form which a free market economy might take in Cuba if the regime collapses. They are looking for examples, not very happily, in Eastern Europe.

96 Julie Feinsilver, *Cuba as a World Medical Power*, Cambridge, Mass., Harvard University Press, 1970.

97 For this disturbing expression of North-South asymmetrical exploitation see *Hemisphere*, Winter 1992, IV.4.

CHAPTER 2

Western European influences on Cuban revolutionary thought

Antoni Kapcia

What makes and shapes a revolution is, by definition, no simple matter for analysis. A revolution is *per se* a unique result of a necessarily complex set of factors and processes. In the case of the Cuban Revolution of 1959 that complexity is, if anything, even more baffling – something which the debate surrounding its origins has tended to confirm rather than clarify. For pre-1959 Cuba was, superficially, a society with social cleavages apparently no deeper and economic difficulties no more marked than ten or twenty years earlier.[1] Academic consensus has therefore focused on the purely political factors and the more 'accidental' elements of personality, 'charisma', judgement, etc. Much of this literature – still, surprisingly in evidence – has tended to ignore one fundamental element: the undeniable popular support for, and participation in, the post-1959 radicalisation, a support barely explained by the political skills and charisma of Fidel Castro.[2]

For the 'cement' for the early popularity must be sought elsewhere than in personality. Military success, the leadership's political skills, the social conflicts and crisis of the last months of Batista, the collapse of the *Batistato* and with it the whole political system, the immediate and sustained improvements in social benefits were all undeniably major factors in the completeness of the victory and its consolidation. Yet they cannot explain alone the speed with which the rebel movement gained legitimacy and then engineered a successful politicisation which often proved more radical in its objectives than the leadership itself. An analysis of that radicalisation process must necessarily focus also on the existence and development of an ideological base for both that popularity and the politicisation.

In this sense, any discussion of the ideology of a collective process has to go beyond the leadership's declared or implicit orientation, and our own perceptions must equally go beyond the assumptions often made about ideology generally and certainly about the Cuban case in particular. For, since the formal adoption, in 1961, of Marxism-Leninism, the ideological pattern of the Cuban Revolution has perhaps seemed to many to be a closed book. Yet such a perception makes a number of assumptions, for example, that an ideology is a given, a static, unchanging, factor; that a formal adoption, at an official, leadership, level is the sole or main determinant of a process's ideological orientation (or indeed that, in the Cuban case, this was adopted by the leadership alone); that, once adopted, the new ideology necessarily rejected or ignored the process of the preceding two years, or, more significantly, the preceding two hundred; and, most familiarly in the studies on the Revolution, that those initial years were, anyway, somehow 'ideology-free' and that 1961 was the first occasion on which the issue was clearly broached.

A revolution is, however, by definition a process that involves at least a degree of popular involvement, achieved either by the extent of participation (in the insurrection or the subsequent consolidation), by the extent of the resulting benefits, or by the extent to which the 'vanguard' shares an ideological perception with the supporting population. In Cuba's case, the first two aspects are already well recognised, less so is the third. Yet that third element is undeniably a vital key to unlocking the otherwise puzzling radicalisation, for the shared ideological perspective that became evident in the early years was the cement for a relationship that, in the event, lacked clear formal channels or mechanisms of mobilisation or 'ideologisation'. What is essential, therefore, is to examine the extent to which the majority of the politicised Cuban population, in 1959, perceived the need for and desirability of radical change and also perceived the 26th July Movement as representing an acceptable possibility of attaining that goal. In other words, was there a generalised political culture of 'dissidence' capable of supporting the rebellion from 1953 and then willing to respond positively to the rebel vanguard's radicalisation after 1959? Was there a political culture capable of spawning a popular ideology of revolution at the 'revolutionary moment'?

What then is an ideology?[3] It is a 'system' of 'signs' – ideas, values, symbols and myths – shared by a given social group, which identifies itself consistently as distinct from other such groups and which uses this 'system' to interpret its immediate social and historical environment, as it has been, is and should be in the future. It is, therefore, implicitly, a guide for action towards the achievement of that identified future environment. Evidently, such an ideology must be both flexible (to adjust to new circumstances imposed by the environment) and consistent, in its relationship with the existing political culture within which it has been created. In this sense any ideology is by definition both conservative (conserving what is 'best' or 'natural' in the existing culture) and radical (in its desire to create an alternative to the present). It posits using the present to change the present. That contradiction is essential to an ideology's success in maintaining more than just minority support; for the 'base' dimension of an ideology can be simultaneously the firmest and the most volatile element, especially as many ideologies begin their existence as impositions from above, i.e. not 'organic' (in the Gramscian sense of the term), even if they then develop an ambiguous relationship in their support and direction.

Thus ideologies can be either a) *hegemonic*, whereby a dominant group persuades subordinate groups to consent to their own subordination, inculcating belief-systems which either posit the correctness of that relationship or disguise it and create the 'false consciousness' of autonomy, or b) *dissident*, whereby a subjugated group seeks to define and defend itself and its identity against attempts at total subordination, denial or substitution.[4] The success of the latter depends on the existence of a certain 'space' in society or the political system, i.e. on the relative inability of the dominant group to impose its will totally.

The elements that compose an ideology are, of course, necessarily many, varied and complex, incorporating ideas, political traditions, popularly accepted values, collective experience, popular myths and symbols. Certainly an ideology is not a composite of ideas or intellectual influences alone. Indeed, these will become the more acceptable and powerfully motivating the more the purveyors of such ideas and influences are perceived to be articulators or leaders of a wider movement, the greater the level of political awareness, social communication or education, or the more such ideas coincide with the needs of the particular social or political circumstance. Perhaps the most powerful element is, however, the myth, precisely because of its 'organic', collectively accepted, but essentially unarticulated nature. Myths have power because they survive but are inherently flexible. Therefore both myths and ideas have a potential to mobilise and galvanise in a given conjuncture.

Such was Cuba in the 1950s, with a hegemonic vacuum created by the degeneration of the traditional and the newer hegemonies (Spanish colonialism and American neo-colonialism), the progressive degeneration of the state, the political system and the social fabric in the face of an underlying dependence, impotence and corruption, and the underlying economic crisis from 1929–33.[5] The gradual disintegration of the traditional planter elite in the face of competition and official pressure or neglect, together with the lack of social cohesion in a society until recently divided by slavery, without clear mechanisms of social control (such as a strong, deep-rooted, Church), contributed to this vacuum. In such conditions, an alternative, dissident, ideology was therefore able to challenge, mobilise and eventually overthrow the existing order. The problem with this ideology, however, was its disparate, or submerged, nature; for fifty years of neo-colonial 'cultural invasion',[6] of first open, then subtle, domination by the US, of the disaggregating effect of the post-1934 restructuring and the quota system,[7] and, above all, of the populist experiments of the 1934–52 period,[8] had all fragmented the once vibrant, identifiable and always potentially radical, nationalist tradition. That dissident constituency, so significant in the 1895–1934 period, had simply disappeared as a public force, submerged under the weight of prosperity, cultural ambivalence, apparent economic stabilisation and, eventually, dictatorship.[9] It had not, however, been destroyed, being sustained in a variety of ways not evident until galvanised by the open challenge posed by the 26th July rebels, and even then, not fully until the victorious revolution began to mobilise its assault on the existing structure, providing channels and opportunities for articulation and participation.

Inevitably, this 'reservoir' of popular dissidence was not only difficult to perceive at the time, but also difficult to identify and 'deconstruct' today. Firstly, any ideology is greater and more complex than the sum of its parts, being determined by the dynamic relationship between its component elements; secondly, those 'parts' are themselves necessarily complex, contradictory and often only vaguely discernible. Furthermore, the reality in Cuba of a political culture, even more exaggerated in its ambiguity than elsewhere in Latin America (given the complexity of the relationship with the US) inevitably meant the complication of otherwise clear political phenomena. The experience of an historically 'extended' colonialism had helped to radicalise the nationalist constituency but also to weaken it socially and undermine its self-confidence.[10]

This latter clearly helps explain the uncertainty in many of the rebel leaders of 1895–8 and of the new Cuba which succeeded the American occupation, about the right and the competence of Cuba to be fully independent.[11] The subsequent process of 'Americanisation' (in all senses), from an inherently more dynamic metropolis than Spain had been, deepened the contradiction, further weakening confidence but also radicalising more extensively.

However, the later demoralisation of the 1933–4 experience, and the distractionism engineered by the Batista years (1934–44) and the Auténtico project (1944–52), changed the pattern.[12] Coherent radicalisation was 'frozen', and collective self-confidence was further undermined, by confusion, resignation and the weight of entrenched corruption. Yet the ideological 'reservoir' did survive, at two levels: in the ranks of the petty bourgeoisie (represented above all by the politicised Havana students) and at the popular level. The two levels would be fused progressively by a series of factors – the Moncada assault (coinciding with the significantly symbolic centenary of Martí's birth),[13] the rebels' almost unique determination to act in 1956, the growing polarisation of 1956–8, the growing social effects of deepening economic crisis and intensifying labour conflict, the popularity of victory, and the determination after 1959 to pursue a social revolution that both implicitly and explicitly posed an alternative to the now-rejected system. What had resulted, ideologically, was a symbiosis between the popular political culture (of radical *cubanismo*) and the ethos of a rebel group which, having grown out of the same culture, could legitimise its revolt and pose a viable alternative. For the underlying ideological objective from 1958 was a genuine, 'naturally' Cuban political and economic independence, reinforced by a society and a model of development that viably reflected Cubans' perceived needs, values and myths (enshrined in the 'codes' of *cubanismo*). One of the critical skills displayed by the new leadership was, indeed, its capacity to articulate those 'codes', both disarticulated and unarticulated since 1933.

What then were the components of this *cubanista* canon? First and foremost was nationalism, a concept as vague and flexible, in the 1950s, as it had once been powerful and positive. By the time of the second *Batistato* (1952–58), it had become obfuscated sufficiently to be either an incoherent and often negative resentment, or a superficial stylised form of 'official' politics (represented above all by the conversion of the 'Apostle' myth into an anodyne *Martianismo*.[14] None the less, between the 1890s and 1933, it had displayed a clearly radical (i.e. often anti-elite, anti-capitalist, or anti-imperialist) character, and therefore had possessed a dimension which took it beyond a narrow chauvinism.

The second was a collectivism which, born out of the independence rebellions of 1868–78 and 1895–98 and the early anarchosyndicalist and socialist trade unions of the nineteenth century, had continued through the post-1920s unionisation, been radicalised by the 1933–4 experience and the impact of Marxist perspectives (at both intellectual and popular level, not least via the influential Communist Party), but had been rescued and maintained in the years of fragmentation by the often depoliticised unions and by the essential communalism of both Afro-Cuban religions and societies, and the Protestant sects.[15] This collectivism also implied a faith in egalitarianism and participation.

There was also an identifiable moralism, born out of the values of the pre-1898 dissidence (especially those articulated by Martí) but reinforced by the subsequent rejection of a system increasingly perceived as inherently corrupt. This moralism, directed against both corruption and 'betrayal', became powerful enough in the 1940s to launch the Ortodoxo Party[16] towards probable election in 1952.[17] It also spawned a number of side issues, most notably the persistent, underlying, faith in agrarianism as the 'natural' destiny for a truly independent Cuba.[18]

Another identifiable component was generationalism, a faith in both the march of history towards a better future and the redemptive ability of succeeding generations (by definition young and fresh) to reject the failures and betrayals of the present and rescue the preceding, 'heroic', generations' lost ideal of a 'new Cuba'. This myth, so powerful in its contradictory traditionalism and radicalism, implied an accompanying historicism, an awareness of the historical roots of current struggles or values and of the historical inevitability of progress, a perspective that always contrasted the 'heroic' past and an essentially millenarian vision of the future with the decidedly unheroic present.

The concept of struggle (*lucha*) was also therefore essential, offering its 'martyrology' of the self-sacrificing 'heroes' of the past and an implicit approval of the activists of the present or the future, and a myth of a people in permanent, collective, struggle for the supreme national goal, the full realisation of free, 'natural', nationhood. This meant a clear popular respect for those whose activism (however unsuccessful) proved their commitment. This was, in turn, partly contradicted by the element of 'intellectualism', the often remarkable persistence of popular respect for intellectuals, culture and the socially liberating value of education.

This, then, was the identifiable 'reservoir' of the 1950s: a dissident, but incoherent, political culture, confirmed by the actions and popularity of a rebellion that proved to be 'organic' in the years of insurrection and in the post-victory mobilisation. For the experience after 1959 simply continued the 'natural' process of ideological formation, reinforcing especially the elements of nationalism (increasingly broadened to an internationalist dimension), the values of collectivism or co-operativism and the beliefs in participation, agrarianism, of culture, education and a political intellectualism. All of this became concretized most coherently in the concept of the 'New Man', the myth which merged the existing *cubanista* tradition, the new experience after 1959 and the influence of Marxism, most clearly articulated by Guevara.

Evidently this is more than a simple 'naming of parts'. For, while the component elements of the *cubanista* political culture (and ideology) may be identifiable at a given moment, they were, by definition, changeable and often contradictory. It is, therefore, an essentially problematic task to identify, in turn, the various roots of this culture.

However, one can say, with some degree of certainty that this *cubanismo* was above all a necessary synthesis of the empirical and the intellectual/theoretical, of the interaction between the collective experience since at least the early nineteenth century and the intellectual influences which, in turn, confirmed, reinforced, explained and directed that experience at given points. Space clearly allows little opportunity here to discuss that empirical formation; of more immediate concern is the specific question of the intellectual framework and, within that, the contribution of discernible ideas, values and influences. This then allows an easier identification of the specific contribution of the European intellectual heritage, a task which, in a wider analysis, is perhaps more difficult but which, in this necessarily limited analysis, runs the risk of exaggeration and disproportion, of the tendency to ignore the broader social, political and economic context, and to consider these 'disembodied' influences in isolation, and even as significant on their own and in the absolute.

With these caveats, we can then divide the intellectual roots into three. Firstly, and, in the end, most powerfully and significantly, was the indigenous Cuban tradition, in which successive generations of intellectuals, political leaders and activists sought inspiration from and were influenced by the perspectives of their predecessors, often without any clear interference from non-Cuban terms of reference. In this respect Cuba presents a remarkable case of a self-generating ideological-intellectual tradition, clearly the result of its unique isolation, separated by a confining and negating colonialism from a hemispheric context that was increasingly open to external intellectual pressures.

The second intellectual root is what can be termed the 'Americanist' perspective – by which Cubans related their struggle and aspirations to the immediate regional context or to the ideas and values of a perceived shared cultural heritage, as distinct from their European roots. In this, the impact of the 1776 American Revolution and the later Latin American independence movements clearly gave them a perspective for a possible separatism. The impact later of both liberalism and annexationism in the US helped create the terms of reference of a sense of distinctiveness (especially with the growing commercial and political connections between the Cuban elite and the US and the reality of North American exile for many political activists). It was in the twentieth century that the Latin American context began to exercise, again, a parallel influence – with *arielismo*,[19] the intellectual ferment in Argentina,[20] the upheaval in Mexico,[21] the *Aprista* perspective,[22] the populist experience (especially in Mexico and Argentina), and finally the revolutions in Bolivia (1952) and Guatemala (1954). After 1902, the most obvious North American contribution to a radical *cubanista* ideology was the role played by Roosevelt's 'New Deal' politics in inspiring some of the rebels of 1933.

The third root was the European. It seems initially inconceivable that, in a revolutionary process as unique, nationalist and 'Third Worldist' as the Cuban there should be any identifiable European influences (especially Western European – given the post-1960 orientation towards and reliance on Eastern European models and ideas). Indeed, it is true that overall the European roots cannot compare with either Cuba's indigenous radical tradition or the wider Latin American environment. Moreover, given the relatively limited role of 'ideas' *per se* (i.e., outside their specific social and historical context), one would expect predominantly intellectual influences from Europe to be peripheral at best.

Yet to ignore the Western European dimension is to ignore a tradition which often played a significant part in the process of ideological formation. Most obviously, for example, Cuba remained formally tied to, and dominated by, Spain long after other Latin American societies had gained formal independence. Much, therefore, of the intellectual and philosophical terms of reference for Cuban political traditions can be attributed to the Spanish link, including, paradoxically, the formulation of a separatist concept. Indeed this is the irony of cultural colonialism: that the metropolis so determines the intellectual framework for the colonised that rejection of the former will inevitably be couched in its imposed terms. Ambivalence then becomes a natural contradiction of the colonised mentality.

This explains in large part the 'double-track' followed by Cuban radicals: seeking answers both in a strong and coherent indigenous tradition and in external models and inspiration, partly out of a sense of inferiority but also because this radicalism was essentially more open than the nationalism of much of the rest of contemporary Latin America. It was therefore simultaneously both exclusivist and internationalist, a contradiction which allowed for a deeper intellectual penetration by Europe than in other Latin American societies, where the break with Spain or Portugal tended to have left few roots at the popular level (especially in the more Indian or slave-based societies), other than the often superficial residual religious syncretism, and where the new elites tended to confirm their dependence by turning to non-Iberian European models to legitimise their rule, aspirations and policies. In Cuba, the persistence of colonialism until the eve of the twentieth century inevitably meant a deeper Europeanism in the social fabric, given the level of education, political awareness and general social development that had been achieved by the 1890s. It also meant, however, that, because of the implicit rejection of Europe in the independence struggle, there was a greater inherent attraction towards the US than elsewhere in the continent. Yet overall it was clear that by 1898 Cuba was closer to the Western European intellectual tradition than it might have been with an earlier independence.

The fact that the European connection was Spanish meant very particular intellectual developments, not least because nineteenth-century Spain (ridden by political and intellectual crises) was increasingly unable to exercise a clear intellectual hegemony in the colony. Indeed, the constant political changes in Spain usually confused the political direction of dissidence in Cuba, one moment encouraged by liberalism only to be repressed by the inevitable reaction. The political pressure applied by Spain after the early Cuban flirtation with separatism, but especially after the defeated rebellion of 1868–78, stifled the natural development of political discourse in Cuba, which now became distorted and frustrated by an anachronistic colonialism and the persistence of the essentially conservative institution of slavery.[23] The reimposed 'Hispanisation' after 1879 also predictably increased the attraction of the US, the more inherently appealing hegemonic alternative, both effects naturally weakening the ability of Cuban radicalism to generate the self-confidence so essential to clear nationalist criteria.

The earliest identifiable European contribution to the evolution of *cubanismo* must predictably be the impact of the European – predominantly French, British and Spanish – Enlightenment and of its liberal sequels. At one level this was manifested in the aspiration, amongst *ilustrado* sectors of the *criollo* elite, for greater self-determination, which, as elsewhere, expressed itself in an interest (via the *Sociedad Económica del País* of 1793) in the promotion of education, trade, and 'proper' (and 'scientific') government. The liberalism implicit in, and diffused by the impact of, the French Revolution inevitably had a broader and deeper effect, inspiring, for instance – together with the example of Saint Domingue – sections of the slave population, and also the early workers' movement, the *mutualidades* of the 1820s. Amongst the elite, of course, as elsewhere, the Revolution's attraction was reinforced, or often complicated, by the influence of freemasonry, of decidedly European pedigree, given its introduction by the English occupation of Havana in 1762 (an occupation that also introduced the concepts of free trade, entrepreneurship and landownership). Freemasonry specifically proposed reform, progress and rationalism, yet also introduced an element of 'moralism', of longer-term significance, expressed through the belief in natural harmony and justice, but also in its moral challenge to a corrupt, powerful and established colonial Spanish Church. It seems most likely that the progressive ideas of four of the principal leaders of the 1895–8 independence movement – Gómez, Maceo, García and Martí – were inspired in part by their adherence to freemasonry.

The liberalism thus introduced was necessarily limited socially. None the less, it did create (within a small, cohesive, intellectually self-sustaining bourgeois circle) a coherent body of ideas available for the later Cuban bourgeoisie as it evolved politically. It also founded a tradition of respect for education, seen as the most immediate means of perpetuating the circle's influence. The influences that acted upon this group therefore clearly merit attention, as does the simple, but fundamental, fact that so many of this circle and of Cuba's leading political actors in this critical period studied or taught in the same place – the Seminary of San Carlos y San Ambrosio in Havana, which, given its ecclesiastical immunity, played a vital role in disseminating ideas of rationalism, scientific enquiry, social responsibility, and, ultimately, the correctness and justice of a Cuban separatism.[24]

The principal exponents of this newer thinking were, without doubt, Felix Varela, José de la Luz y Caballero, José Agustín Caballero and Saco. The cleric, Varela, was perhaps the most outstanding, 'cubanising' the relevance of those European ideas he absorbed (abolition, social reform and the morality of separation from an inherently unnatural colonial relationship), and helping establish the study of political science in Cuba. That sense of the 'unnaturalness' of Cuba's position was reinforced by Caballero's interpretation of Locke's rationalism, Etienne Bonnot de Condillac's materialism, and Baconian and Newtonian science, all combining to prepare the ground intellectually for the impact of the new European capitalism.[25] The same rationalisation of a more 'natural' Cuban separatism (albeit an essentially 'white' nation) imbued the thinking of Luz y Caballero, whose faith in the guidance of an enlightened, European-style bourgeoisie, appealed directly to one of the later protagonists of independence, Manuel Sanguily.

This intellectual ferment, however, predated the Spanish reaction (to French liberalism), which then imposed an intellectual strait-jacket on Cuba, petrifying, within a group that now preferred the protection of exclusivity, essentially eighteenth-century notions and values, of morality, respect for the natural order and a sort of physiocratic agrarianism. Indeed, the ideas of the late nineteenth-century radicals show a peculiar persistence of earlier, often essentially Romantic, values alongside the most modern. Yet, one notion of clear later significance was the implicit social dimension to independence, albeit one, at this early stage, referring to an 'iniquitous' and irrational slavery – a clear case of European social thought being interpreted particularly for the Cuban case. However, this same ideological ossification subsequently minimised the discernible impact of the otherwise seminal 1848 bourgeois nationalist revolts in Europe, which, in the context of a still colonial Cuba, might have been significant. By then, however, Spain's intellectual stranglehold and its own intellectual isolation from the Europe of 1848 meant the exclusion of such influences.

For, from the 1840s, especially after the fright of the slave revolts of 1843–4, Cuba became isolated from the major European intellectual currents; any that did penetrate only filtered in through the often distorting medium of Spain.[26] This became particularly evident after the 1860s as an ascendant Spanish liberalism not only tolerated but in some cases encouraged the development of a separate 'Cubanist' identity, although always clearly within the Spanish orbit. Certainly the rise of the Cuban Reformista party, after 1862, was directly stimulated by Spanish political developments.

Of longer-term significance was the increase in Spanish immigration of the late-nineteenth-century, attributable both to the colonial authorities' encouragement of non-African migration (to counterbalance and reduce the rebellious potential of an 'African' Cuba), and to the mass flight from the poverty and economic changes of Galicia, Asturias, Extremadura and Andalucia, or the cultural repression of Catalonia and the Basque country, to Spain's major remaining imperial possession.[27] This social change had profound, often contradictory, effects. On the one hand, the often transitory nature of much of the migration[28] impeded the emergence of a clear Cubanist identity, and the widespread network of thriving immigrant cultural centres – the Centros Gallegos, Centros Asturianos, Centros Vascos, etc. – reinforced by the overwhelming preponderance in the clergy of Spanish-born priests, helped maintain the immigrants' Spanish, rather than Cuban, identity.[29] On the other hand, those same centres were fundamental to the radicalisation, if not the 'nationalisation', of significant parts of Cuban labour; for many became foci of political agitation, education and organisation for the many immigrants who were already politically aware.[30] This late migration had a further, less tangible, effect, for many of the next generation of Cuban radicals, including the separatists, were of Spanish parentage – a factor that continued to be the case up to the 1950s. Therefore, although such radicalism proposed the rejection of the peninsular heritage, the impact of that same heritage was already considerable.

The deepest political influence of these Spanish immigrants was undoubtedly the impact of anarchosyndicalist ideas and activities, especially through Catalan activists and above all in the tobacco unions – where conditions, agglomeration and, not least, the much defended practice of paid readers during work hours, all contributed to make the tobacco labour force the most politically aware and active in Cuba.[31] Indeed, until sugar modernisation, the tobacco industry boasted the only real Cuban proletariat, radically changing the political perspectives of the hitherto *mutualista* unions, which, from the 1860s, began to act more as industrial unions, and to produce more openly polemical literature to express that (notably 'La Aurora' between 1865 and 1868).

Anarchosyndicalism was, then, basic to the formation of a radical Cubanist perspective and ideology, introducing, at a popular level, the concepts of collectivism, radical moralism (i.e. against the inherent 'immorality' of the capitalist system itself), the respect and need for action and commitment, and for a voluntarist and 'spontaneous' approach (without a mediating or 'leading' party). This was in addition to the implicit, and often visionary, almost millenarian belief in the need for an essentially democratic, participatory and egalitarian 'renewal', (manifested in the contemporary journals – *Germinal*, *La Nueva Aurora* and *El Hombre Nuevo*). Although many of the early Cuban anarchosyndicalists were intellectuals, the movement's genuinely popular base, which rapidly created its own 'organic' intellectuals, remained a vital factor in the continuing current of radicalism. Indeed, the founding 1925 congress of the CNOC was patently anarchosyndicalist in perspective, and Fabio Grobart (one of the founders of the Communist Party) later admitted the continuing anarchosyndicalist influence on Party members and union activists, which persisted well into the 1930s, even after the Communist ascendancy in the CNOC.[32]

This current was parallelled by the impact of socialist ideas – again largely associated with the radicalised, and often émigré, intellectual elite.

Given a restrictive colonialism, emigration was naturally the most likely method of contact with such influences, and it is significant that so many early Cuban socialists developed their new ideas through their experiences in France, where intellectual and worker radicalism was gaining ground, and where, in 1871, the Paris Commune stimulated and politicised so many, participant and observer alike. The contact with the ideas of Marx, or with Proudhon and other French radicals (especially in the 1890s, with the Second International), created a body of values and perspectives to challenge the stultifying reaction that Spain's decrepit colonialism increasingly represented. The significance of this new radicalism in Cuba was that it represented the first genuine fusion of the intellectual and popular currents of dissidence. Until the 1890s, however, socialism was more influential in intellectual circles and still often imbued with anarchist ideas. Only after the London Congress of the Second International, in 1896, did the socialist and anarchist positions became more clearly demarcated.[33]

Among the most influential socialists in late nineteenth-century Cuba were Enrique Roig y San Martín, Paul Lafargue and the poet Diego Vicente Tejera, all profoundly politicised by either their European experience or European intellectual and political currents. Roig and Tejera were the most active within Cuba. The former, after working as a reader in the tobacco industry, edited the *El Obrero* newspaper in 1882 and *El Productor* in 1887, directed the Centro de Instrucción y Recreo in Santiago de las Vegas and founded the Alianza Obrera in 1888. The latter, initially persuaded by the moralistic anarchism and Utopianism of Blanc, Sorel and Proudhon, gravitated eventually, via freemasonry, towards a more socialist perspective, albeit one more akin to the radical republicanism of the late nineteenth-century Barcelona where he was based.[34]

After a programme of political education among the Cuban tobacco workers of Key West, between 1897 and 1899, Tejera founded the Cuban Socialist Party (later the Partido Obrero and then Partido Popular), which went on to a briefly successful electoralism in Havana (1899). Based in the traditional tobacco and typographical industries, and on Tejera's personality, the Party tended towards reformism, suffering inevitable defections. Yet its role in the development of Cuban radicalism was fundamental, as Tejera espoused a significantly 'Cuban' interpretation of socialist values, stressing both the agrarian and the moral dimensions – both clearly with a Cuban nationalist, but also a European anarchist, pedigree.

Lafargue's influence was more indirect, but none the less significant. Based in Paris, and married to Marx's daughter, Laura, he was fully active in the Second International of 1889, and his impact was critical – both via Tejera (in Paris between 1888 and 1893) and by the publication of his 'Socialism and the Intellectuals' in 1900 – on the evolving worker-intellectual consensus that characterised the effervescence of radical activity in

Cuba, between the 1880s and 1915, in which the Congreso Regional Obrero in Havana of 1892 was the seminal event.[35]

That consensus was, curiously, stimulated by the emigration of the tobacco-refining industry after the 1850s tobacco crisis, as both Cuban and American entrepreneurs shifted production to Florida to circumvent the trade restrictions on imports of unprocessed tobacco. As a result, a significant part of the tobacco labour force also migrated.[36] This movement presented the developing political perspective with a series of contradictory challenges. On the one hand, it both removed – from a clearly 'Europeanist' environment – the most politicised element of the Cuban proletariat, and succeeded in maintaining – amongst a remarkably cohesive social group in the predominantly Cuban enclaves of Florida – an anarchosyndicalist perspective, which might otherwise have been under greater pressure from socialism. Yet it also removed from Cuba a part of the newly-emerging worker-intellectual consensus, so that indigenous popular radicalism tended to lose some of its coherence and direction – although not its force, as was proven both by the clearly social dimension to the *mambí* struggle after 1895[37] and the emergence of a new militancy in the rail, dock and sugar sectors, filling the vacuum left by the tobacco workers. The survival in Florida of a powerful anarchosyndicalist, essentially internationalist, vision thereafter impeded the development of a traditionally nationalist movement amongst the émigré working class, which tended to remain hostile to the bourgeois nationalism of the political émigrés of New Orleans, New Jersey and New York. An émigré community which seemed still cast in the mould of either Romantic nationalism or, equally objectionable to the radicals, of the more recent elitist positivism.

Therefore, the fusion of the two currents, in the late-1880s and early-1890s, thanks especially to the efforts of José Martí, the synthesis of a vibrant internationalist radicalism and a profoundly moral, socially conscious, nationalism, was critical to the emergence of a movement that was both popular and, in its anti-imperialism and social dimension, unprecedentedly ideological. Indeed, the participation of leading Key West radicals (Carlos Baliño, Carlos Borrega and Francisco Camellón) in the founding of Martí's Cuban Revolutionary Party (PRC) and the resulting attraction of anarchists and socialists to its ranks caused some considerable concern to the East Coast émigrés.[38] The case of the prominent trade unionist, Enrique Creci, illustrated this new ideological dimension, with his perspective of Cuban independence as a natural step in the process of international liberation.[39] This new synthesis was fundamental to both the success of the 1895–8 struggle, and its frustration by an elite and the American occupation authorities, increasingly wary of the inherent radicalism of an independence movement. This movement, subsequently denied the leadership of both Martí and the popular mulatto leader Antonio Maceo, threatened to follow the direction of the radicals in the leadership – notably Baliño and Tejera – with Martí's 'moral' heirs (Enrique José Varona and Bartolomé Masó) exercising only a marginal influence at the time. Baliño's role within the radical movement was a clear indication of the remarkable development of what was, for Latin America, a politically sophisticated labour force. For his socialism, clearly influenced by Marx and Engels, especially while in exile in the US, helped synthesise the established anarchosyndicalism of the Cuban unions with the newer, 'scientific', currents from Europe, not least with his emphasis on the moral and cultural dimension of the revolutionary struggle (as in his *Verdades socialistas* of 1905). Although more important as political leader than as union organiser, with even that influence declining after his return to the US (1910–17), his prestige as both a radical and a PRC leader helped politicise an increasingly unionised working class and also to counter the intellectual influence of the new positivist philosophy.

For the positivist message – of a fluid process of orderly development, founded on scientific progress and guaranteed by 'natural' hierarchies – was understandably comforting to a bourgeoisie which, while it rejected a patently unacceptable colonialism, was appalled by the prospect of popular, and possibly racial, revolt and all too aware of the fragility of its social, political and economic domination, undermined by social changes, steady 'Americanisation' and popular radicalism. Here, the Cuban elite mirrored its contemporary Latin American counterparts, whose 'progressive conservatism' was immediately attracted by the 'order and progress' message that the ideas of Comte, Bergson and Spencer had come to imply in the region, justifying their authoritarianism, their contempt for the indigenous, or imported (i.e. non-European), labour forces, but also their faith in the essentially progressive nature of the economic system in which they aspired to share. The difference in Cuba was the bourgeoisie's dilemma – between an often 'progressive' desire for separation but an awareness of its inability to rule alone. It was, therefore, paradoxically, a European concept which confirmed the pro-Americanism of a Cuban elite which, whether loyalist (to Spain) or separatist, now came to consider annexation to the US as Cuba's only viable path.

Among the leading Cuban intellectuals influenced by positivism, although scarcely the most representative, was Enrique José Varona.[40] Rejecting the inherent idealism and 'religiosity' of Comtean and Spencerean positivism, he none the less based his thought on this perspective, albeit in a unique and highly influential manner.[41] Spanning two phases of Cuban history, he shared both the optimism of his class (in his essential faith in history as inevitable progress and even in his somewhat reluctant acceptance of the need for a new social order) and the scepticism of the new, rapidly disillusioned, Republic. That optimism and faith in science inspired his university reforms during the US occupation, reforms guided by principles of practicality, co-operation and social responsibility and reforms which, together with his universally accepted image of honesty and 'unsullied' patriotism (given his association with the 1895 generation) made him the natural 'mentor' of the 1920s generation of student dissidents. This positivism, so significant in persuading sections of the émigré and domestic elite to join the independence struggle, had found little echo in the vision of Martí, whose intellectual universe, equally European, had been determined by his contact, while in enforced exile in Spain, with the ideas of Krausism. The latter's perspective of a spiritual harmonising (of the essentially unharmonious), of balance and of the pre-eminence of the natural, all appealed to a Cuban whose experience had brutally been one of disharmony and discord, and whose homeland was held back, apparently, by the artificial (unnatural) divisions of race and class, culture and education. This vision of harmony unquestionably drove him towards the determination to unify the discordant elements of the Cuban community into an independence movement whose ultimate goal was the creation of a free, equal and essentially moral, society.[42] While the ideas of Krausism seem not to have influenced other Cubans directly (although the similar belief in history as progress imbued both the positivist and Hegelian or Marxian wings of the movement), the vision so eloquently articulated and embodied by Martí remained an influential guide to action and perspective after his death.

Therefore a catalogue of Martí's ideas does have some value here, not least in confirming the European roots of much of his *ideario*, however much this may miss both the complexity and the evolution of his thought. For, although his vision of a free Cuba had firmly Cuban roots, in that peculiarly introverted, self-perpetuating, intellectual circle (Martí's mentor was Rafael Mendive, himself a disciple of Luz y Caballero), his long and varied experience of exile gave him a breadth of vision that few others of his generation shared. Martí's ideas flowed from the awareness of the strengths and weaknesses of independent Latin America (decreasingly relevant to many US-oriented Cubans), through the appreciation-fear of the *Coloso del Norte*, to the acceptance of some of the most recent European ideas – including, besides Krausism, a respect for European freemasonry, liberalism (and the Hugoist social liberal version), the scientific, educational and progressive emphasis of positivism, the belief in the creative effects of cultural cross-fertilisation (from Spanish *modernismo*), and, with his growing awareness of indigenous Latin American qualities, Romanticism's faith in the essential values of a pre-Columbian continent distorted by an unnatural colonialism. A variety of influences thus persuaded him of the immorality of Sarmiento's preference in his *civilización/barbarie* dichotomy, an inherently Eurocentric and expansionist ethos.[43]

Martí was probably the first Cuban intellectual of his age to see Cuba's situation within a Latin American dimension, a significant contribution to the nationalist debate at a time when other radicals were also beginning to interpret the political struggle in global, even internationalist, terms. Intellectually and politically, Martí's impact was therefore considerable, for, in a sense, he ended one long chapter of often confused, distracted, development and opened a new one, establishing a new tradition, which emphasised the moral, the social and the Americanist dimensions of the national struggle. This new direction, of course, coincided with the overwhelming pressure resulting from the four-year occupation by the US and its consequent and deliberate 'Americanisation', which further weakened the Western European intellectual links. Europe's next appearance on the Cuban intellectual horizon was in the form of the ideas and example of the 1917 Soviet revolution.

The period between independence (1902) and the final, successful, insurrection in the 1950s, saw, therefore, a partial alienation from Europe, a process reinforced by the separation of Church and State, which removed a potentially significant Europeanising influence from the education system. Two intellectual directions were now followed in Cuba: towards the US (both by the 'accommodationist' camp and, later, by those encouraged by Roosevelt's New Deal vision in the 1930s), and inwards, towards Cuba itself. In part this latter direction was a natural response to the widespread demoralisation after 1898, but it also in part reflected a determination to create in Cuba something distinctly Cuban, different from both the now rejected Europe and from the newly-hegemonic US. While this may not have been universally true of the intellectual elite, it was certainly the case in the popular base of the nationalist movement, so evidently strong and coherent within the *mambí* tradition, and now fiercely maintaining a collective *cubanismo* by a variety of means – trade unions, black cultural associations, clubs and sects, etc. The divide between the 'cosmopolitan' West, centred on Havana, and the more *cubanista* East (Oriente), so evident throughout the two independence wars, became even more pronounced. It is not unreasonable to suggest that it was increasingly the East which kept a popular *cubanismo* alive. Indeed, the reality of both wars was that 'victory' was achieved not by a people united across classes and regions but largely by a rural (often black) guerrilla struggle in the East, a struggle from which large sectors of Western, urban, Cuba remained aloof.

When one considers this factor, together with the continuation of the radical (anarchist or socialist) tradition among the organised working class, it is clear that the post-1898 Americanisation process, while it helped demoralise and fragment the intellectual tradition – a process confirmed by the reality of economic and social disaggregation and the degeneration of public politics – did not fragment and divide quite as much as is often maintained. The divisions over the issues of national sovereignty were real enough, between the pro-Platt lobby and the various anti-Platt alliances (Cisneros Betancourt's Junta Patriótica de la Habana (1906) and the Liga Antiplatista of 1909), but also between a bourgeois nationalism (at times opposing the divisiveness of radicalism) and the growing popular radical perspective.[44] Yet, at one level, both the European influence and the 'protectorate' itself had a double effect, both dividing the fragile unity of 1892–8 and cementing a basic radicalism that would emerge later.

At a popular level, many activists' ideological distaste for any wider anti-Spanish sentiment after 1892 was compounded by the increase, after independence, in Spanish immigration and by the privileges, status and commercial power retained by the residual Spanish elite, as guaranteed by both the Treaty of Paris and the US occupation.[45]

At the level of the bourgeoisie, however, which of course determined much of the historiography of and about the period, the separation from Europe was a fact. Thereafter, for a while, if European influences did enter Cuba either they would come via Latin America (as was the case with the Córdoba University Reform movement of 1918 and the emergence of the heterodox radicalism of APRA and Aprismo), or they would be purely cultural.[46] Indeed, the perception began to develop among an intellectual elite which partly rejected its own roots that, while Cuba offered little, the North American ethos was decidedly uncultured, and therefore that escape to a European model was the only correct direction to maintain cultural standards. Hence writers and artists began to look to Paris, especially, for their inspiration, and the Eurocentric patterns of the *vanguardismo* of the 1920s and 1930s, of the 'Orígenes' group of the 1940s, and even to an extent of the *negrismo* of the 1930s, indicated this imitative tendency.[47]

None the less, alongside this withdrawal from a Cubanist or Americanist definition must be set the more positive tendency among many intellectuals to continue the confidently eclectic tradition that Martí had epitomised, based on an ideologically internationalist perspective, a faith in the value of syncretism or synthesis, or a simple recognition of what Europe had to offer for a Cuba that was potentially radical but repressed. Thus the 'Revista de Avance' *vanguardismo* reflected a positive *cubanismo*, a radical perspective, and a tradition that not only looked back to Varela and Martí, but also forward to a radical, free, Cuba, with many of its exponents playing a valuable role in the radicalisation process – continuing the tradition, alongside the 'evasion' of the '*poesía pura*' school of the 1920s–1930s and, later, of 'Orígenes', of the openly committed and influential intellectual radical.[48]

As, however, the carefully constructed neo-colonial edifice began to disintegrate after 1920, the political attraction of Europe re-emerged. At one level, represented by those sectors of the essentially conservative elite who began to question the stability and usefulness of the American connection, one idea that especially appealed was a successor to the old positivism, namely corporatism, especially the variety currently evident in Primo de Rivera's Spain. In the spread of this perspective among the Cuban bourgeoisie, the role of the Church was fundamental. Still largely staffed by Spanish priests and nuns, Cuba's private schools helped to maintain a reactionary elitism but often with a paradoxically 'progressive' stamp – especially in the 'social' teaching of the (often Basque) Franciscans and the Jesuits – which resulted in the emergence of Catholic Action thinking (in the Agrupación Católica Universitaria).[49] It was this corporatism, combining conservative radicalism, elitist rebellion and safe nationalism, which inspired those who gravitated, after 1930, towards the ABC terrorist movement, so influential in the movement to overthrow Machado in 1933. Their vision of a Cuba both nationalist (with Cuban control of resources and land) and hierarchical, satisfied an elite weakened already by the neo-colonial arrangement but now devastated by the Depression and fearful of a more radical Cuba emerging, even if the latter coincided with some of that elite. One can thus justifiably talk of the corporatist contribution to the development of a *cubanista* perspective. Moreover, the contribution of ABC members to both Batista's populism and to the formation of the Auténtico Party also aided the dissident debate.

Spain also provided the next European impulse, in the form of the Spanish Civil War. For Cuba was the Latin American country most clearly involved in that conflict, sending the greatest number of volunteers (almost all Republicans).[50] There were three principal reasons. Firstly, so many Cubans were of Spanish origin or parentage. A fact which, despite some expressions of uncharacteristically anti-Spanish sentiment (even rioting) between 1933 and 1936 – arising partly out of the atmosphere of the 1933 nationalist labour legislation and the refusal of some immigrants to adopt Cuban nationality – which even led to some migrants returning, helped create a widespread interest in, and affinity with, the popular struggle in the *madre patria*.[51] Secondly, the Spanish Second Republic had already aroused great interest on the Cuban left, inspiring many in the anti-Machado struggle. The third factor was the demoralisation and disorientation on the left occasioned by the frustration of the 1933 revolution, the defeat of the 1935 general strike and the move of the Communist Party away from an openly revolutionary position, and towards collaboration with Batista, after the Auténticos had rejected their advances.[52] Hence, as elsewhere, Spain struck a chord in Cuba (still that part of Latin America closest to the old metropolis), inspiring an unprecedented commitment.

Initially, the Nationalist argument tended to hold sway in Cuba, backed by the weight of the conservative press (especially *Diario de la Marina* and *El País*), by commercial interests, by the influence of a predominantly conservative, often reactionary, Spanish clergy, and by the efforts of the Centro Español and the authoritarian sympathies of Batista and his ex-ABC allies. Rapidly, however, the left, regrouping after its defeats, rallied to the Republic and the pro-Republican cause gained ground, particularly as Batista, now in alliance with the Communists, adjusted his position, giving active support to the beleaguered Loyalists – as did the propaganda efforts of the Instituto Hispano-Cubano. As a result, an estimated 80 per cent of the Cuban population expressed sympathies for the Republic.[53]

The actual experience of that Civil War also fed back into the Cuban political system. For some who sided with the Republic, it confirmed their radicalism. For example, those intellectuals who participated in the Second International Conference for the Defence of Culture in Madrid in July 1937 (Alejo Carpentier, Nicolás Guillén, Juan Marinello, Félix Pita Rodríguez and Leonardo Fernández Sánchez [out of sixteen Latin Americans]) returned affected by their experience and by their contact with European political and intellectual trends. It was an experience which often strengthened their desire for a cultural nationalism (although, paradoxically, often increasingly expressed in Eurocentric terms), and their adherence to the 'commitment' strand of intellectual life in Cuba.[54] However, it also disillusioned a significant number of the participants, whose subsequent anti-communism was often channelled into the notorious 'action groups' which dominated student politics and a good part of populist politics in the 1940s.[55] Significantly, few Spanish Republican exiles sought refuge in Cuba, since the US effectively vetoed their entry, leaving many with Mexico as the only alternative.[56]

The Civil War thus had a complex effect in Cuba. On the one hand, the newly anti-communist elements clearly helped create a climate suspicious of the hitherto reputable Marxist alternative, yet those same elements, via the 'action groups' also helped create a climate in which action, often armed, was both acceptable and even laudable, a climate in which many of the 26th July rebels were formed politically. On the other hand, the Communist Party itself continued to flourish, albeit differently. In the 1920s it had boasted a significant intellectual base and its role in the militancy of the unions was unquestionable. Its foundation by, among others, Baliño, also gave it a Europeanist socialist orientation. By the 1940s, however, that intellectual attraction had faded; many were still active, and some were notable in the ranks of the leadership (Guillén, Marinello and Carlos Rafael Rodríguez). But the Ala Izquierda Estudiantil was, in 1931–3, really the last natural attraction of the communist perspective for the student activists. The concentration on the Party's union base (the Party-led *Confederación de Trabajadores Cubanos*, CTC, numbered about half a million members in 1934), meant that some intellectuals felt less comfortable inside than outside the Party. Raúl Roa and, earlier, Antonio Guiteras (himself inspired very much by nineteenth-century French radicals) were examples of this independent stream.[57]

None the less, within student circles, in Havana and Santiago, the role of an openly Marxist perspective was considerably reduced from the 'high' of the 1920s and 1930s. As ever, Santiago perhaps displayed more radical tendencies than Havana, given its traditions and the fact that much of the action, political and intellectual, of 1933–4 took place in the West, while the Oriente base of the rebellion was more union-based. What intellectual influences were discernible within that environment were either the indigenous Cuban tradition, fostered by people such as Roa, the attraction of the wider Latin American context (especially Mexico and Argentina) or, less so, Europe. Yet, by definition, more open to outside ideas than most other groups in Cuba, the students did at least provide a fertile ground for such imports, although few major influences were detectable at the time. This reflected a number of factors: the social fragmentation and political disorientation of the petty bourgeoisie; the divergent attractions of the US, Latin America, Cuba and Europe; the state of political discourse and activity in Cuba, but also the dearth of new ideas from Europe itself. Interestingly, the one European concept that seems to have found any echo in the cultural elite of Cuba at the time, in the 1950s, was existentialism, with its obvious attraction for a minority which felt itself alienated within an alienated culture, and sought both expression and recognition abroad.

In one sense, the post-1933 period did see an emerging, albeit negative, national consciousness. For the encouragement to 'Cubanise' both the workforce and the first- or second-generation Spanish immigrant population (the latter being hitherto entitled to take their father's nationality), and the partial 're-Cubanisation' of the economy, did help to reinforce an awareness of a distinct identity. However, the nationalism evident in the political system was simultaneously losing its radicalism, especially with its populist manipulation by both Batista and the Auténticos.[58]

In the post-War years, perhaps the only important European political influence was the new social ideas of Catholicism. Once again, the Spanish link was significant, given the continuing preponderance of Spaniards in the clergy (by 1959 about two-thirds of the total), and more particularly their concentration in private schools (1,167 out of 1,872 priests, brothers and nuns).[59] For, just as the absence of Catholic priests among the working class (especially in rural areas) was critical to the development of certain political and religious ideas and practices, so too the domination of (Spanish) religious orders in middle-class education guaranteed continuity both of a particular perspective and a social division in Cuba.[60] That perspective was predictably conservative, given that the Cuban church of the 1930s and 1940s reflected the predominant conservatism of the contemporary Spanish church. Even into the 1940s the essentially corporatist sympathies of the clergy were evident, not least in the Jesuit educational institutions. Interestingly, even Fidel Castro admitted later the significance of his Jesuit education, for, despite their overwhelmingly right-wing orientation (and open admiration for Primo de Rivera and Franco), they inculcated in their pupils a sense of elite discipline, but also a respect for human dignity.[61] The complexities of such social teaching, however, did not detract from the fact that, overall, the new anti-communist climate was maintained, through the influence of a clergy whose social base may have been always somewhat limited, but whose influence in certain sectors was perhaps stronger than in other parts of contemporary Latin America. Paradoxically, therefore, the church as an institution may have been increasingly irrelevant, but Catholicism as an ideology was not, contributing significantly to the development of a *cubanista* political culture.

Overall, the most influential aspect of this contribution was the essentially communitarian Thomist ethos of the Catholic, rather than Protestant, version of Christianity, which undoubtedly added to the collectivist tradition of the ideology, as did its openly moralistic emphasis. Thus the persistence of a 'Catholic Action' concept of social responsibility merged with the residual radicalism and collectivism of the Cuban environment to create a disparate movement of Catholic liberals or radicals, usually among students. One example of this was the creation of the *Movimiento Nacional Revolucionario* (MNR) of the 1950s, which, while retaining vestiges of a corporatist conservatism, none the less helped to stimulate the social awareness and the activist tendencies of those students drawn to it.[62] This combination of radicalism and conservatism was, of course, representative of many of the roots of the Revolution, and possibly helps account for the early anti-communism of a part of the vanguard of the 1959–62 period, given that a number of MNR activists moved, after the defeat of the MNR conspiracy in 1954, towards the 26th July Movement. Like the influence of the Jesuits, the MNR and other expressions of Europeanist intellectual or moral perspectives were sources of both radical and essentially conservative inspiration, occasionally within the same person. The political confusion and contradictions of this period in Cuban development are perhaps unsurprising, given the prevailing social fragmentation, demoralisation and vulnerability (if not willing openness) to external pressures and influences. For, to an extent, it was only with the emergence of the 26th July Movement after 1956 that a sense of confidence returned to Cuban radicalism. Before that, since the defeats of 1933–5 (or, if we consider Spain to be a 'moral' extension of the Cuban left, 1933–9), Cuban radicals and nationalists had been obliged to resign themselves to the reality of a Cuba which lived on US beneficence (the annual sugar quota), on endemic corruption and on an inability to realise the high ideals of the independence generation. The faith in the ability of Cubans to solve their own problems in a Cuban way had, quite simply, declined. It was only the 'subjectivist' action of Moncada (1953) and of the *Granma* (1956), both actions carried out – against all objective odds – by a recognisably *martianista* generation at a time of renewed interest in Martí, which gave force to the dormant confidence and radicalism of a *cubanista* perspective.

After 1959 the hitherto closed or confused world that, in part, the *cubanista* tradition represented, opened up fully to a range of influences and factors that now began to develop the existing ideology in many ways, to an extent and at a speed unprecedented in Cuba's history. Most fundamentally, the actual collective experience of revolution reinforced the inherent communalism of that tradition – in the mobilisations of the 1960s, whether for defence, for social change or for production, in the various organs of the process, and in the whole ambience of the years after 1959. The unions (after 1961 less significant in determining direction, but none the less contributing to the collectivisation of the political culture), the FMC, the CDRs, the Pioneros, ANAP, and other organisations, created an environment where, in the years of 'siege', the concept of collective *lucha* became for many a daily reality.[63]

Fundamental to this early process of radicalisation was the very lack of political structure which characterised the first decade of revolution. For ten months of 1959 there was no clear, nationally organised and popular structure within which to mobilise, politicise and participate. The 26th July Movement remained small, with its national co-ordination and direction weakened by political differences, while the PSP, which possessed the co-ordination and direction, remained more marginal than it preferred. It was only in October 1959, with the establishment of both the Rebel Army and the *milicias*, that any large-scale national instrument for mobilisation existed. Thereafter, it was only in 1961 that the 'united party' was established, and even then, in March 1962, it was downgraded and many of its activists (mostly ex-PSP) were removed.[64] The creation of the Party (in whatever form) was therefore of little consequence in the process of active, daily popular politicisation, a process which, in these almost anti-institutional circumstances, meant an inevitable recourse to existing political traditions and also exaggerated the contribution both of individual leaders and of the actual collective experience of revolution to the uniqueness of what was proving to be a collective learning process.

Education therefore played a fundamental role in this radicalisation, by both its extension to hitherto untouched areas and sectors and the new emphasis on a relevant curriculum and participation. The literacy campaign of 1961 was unquestionably seminal in this process.[65]

The PSP, despite its secondary role, also contributed to the politicisation, both at grass-roots level, through its union activists and through its role in the *Escuelas de Instrucción Revolucionaria* (although never as extensively effective as they might have been), and at leadership level, where in particular Carlos Rafael Rodríguez and Blas Roca (always the closest to the Sierra guerrillas) played a major role in the reformulation of the revolutionary process and ideology, and where Marinello became rector of the University of Havana in 1960.[66]

The intellectuals too, after a decade of alienation, were given a special place, and a special duty, in the development of that process. They were expected to commit their privileged talents to the service of the collective good and to play a leading role in the battle against cultural underdevelopment and cultural imperialism, and in the popularisation of the revolutionary ethos.[67]

It was, therefore, only to be expected that at this embryonic stage of an often complex and confusing process, certain individuals would begin to play a perhaps disproportionate role, by virtue either of their leadership qualities, their political skills or their ability to articulate demands and experiences, or by their participation in a still somewhat restricted vanguard group. Within the wider process of popular 'ideologisation', these individuals therefore became not just emblematic but directive, and the intellectual influences and moral perspectives that motivated them became of direct relevance to the social process. The outstanding example, of course, was the principal leader, Fidel Castro, whose ability to lead, articulate and be popularly identified with the general aspirations of the population and the general direction of the Revolution, made his motivation supremely relevant. Certainly, his own moralistic, activist and historicist position had a wide appeal and meaning, both in setting the political agenda and in reflecting the existing *cubanista* consensus.

Ernesto Che Guevara also made a fundamental contribution to this development, although more indirectly through his influence within the ever more cohesive and committed vanguard that the old 'Sierra' group increasingly represented and through his role in the formulation of the new Cuba's economic, social and foreign policy. For, as the post-1986 'rectification' process once again made clear, Guevara's thoughts on the practical, as well as 'moral', path to socialist transition were not simply an example of the irrelevant 'Utopian idealism' to which the 1970s reformers consigned most of the characteristics of the 1960s, but represented an autonomous perception of the essence of the problems, aspirations and commitment of that decade.[68] Moreover, although the ethos of the 'New Man' came to be associated with Guevara alone, it did in fact represent a convergence of the existing *cubanista* tradition and the ideological dimension which he, among others, introduced. His own intellectual and political motivation was, therefore, as important in its way as Castro's. One of the most widely read of the rebels, Guevara's political evolution manifested a vast range of influences and preferences. The majority of these were, as the revolution progressed after 1959, socialist (usually Soviet) and 'Third Worldist', as he looked to the examples of Vietnam (Giap and Ho Chi Minh), or the ideas of Fanon, Mariátegui and Ponce, to discover a viable but appropriate path to revolutionary transformation for the essentially 'Third Worldist' Cuba.[69] Yet Europe played a significant role in his development in two ways: in the impact, initially through Mariátegui, of the perspective offered by Antonio Gramsci – of the role of consciousness, of relativism, of the nature and duty of the intellectual – and, less tangibly, in the always more Europeanist intellectual environment from which he came, namely the Argentina of the 1940s.

The list of other such influential individuals is inevitably short, given the relatively enclosed nature of not just the revolutionary vanguard but also the leading group within that. Besides Castro and Guevara, one can count Raúl Castro, Osvaldo Dorticós (president from mid-1959), Armando Hart (with overall responsibility, variously, for the Party and education) and Raúl Roa. Certainly, none of the pre-1959 PSP leaders could be counted amongst this group at that stage, however significant their contribution and advice. Of the leading group, perhaps the most obviously 'European' in his intellectual background was Roa. A participant in the events of the 1920s and 1930s, he had, after 1935, withdrawn from active political involvement but had remained perhaps more intellectually open than others of his political, rather than literary, generation.[70] Throughout his personal political development before the Revolution he had absorbed, from Europe, Maritain's social perspective, Croce's historicism, the humanistic vision and concerns of several generations of European thinkers, not least the writers of Spain's Generation of 1898, and the social values of British Fabianism.[71] After 1959, in a period of some political and ideological uncertainty, Roa stood out in his intellectual certainty, his breadth of vision and the respect in which he was held. Appointed as Foreign Minister in the early Revolution, a position of considerable importance and influence, he was (not always to the liking of the PSP leaders who were critical of his past public attitude to the Soviet Union) instrumental in stressing the need for Cuba to develop an independent policy line and role in the world, a 'Third Worldist' perspective and dimension, and a non-Soviet socialist definition. There seems little doubt that the Europeanist dimension of Roa's intellectual background contributed to this independent tendency. Therefore, to a large extent, Cuba's search for a *cubanista* self-definition in the world (itself a totally new experience for the hitherto subservient satellite within the US orbit) was the work of the 'Europeanist' Roa.

In part, this tendency was contradicted by a countervailing European influence: that of the French Communist Party. Outside the Soviet Union, the French Party undoubtedly enjoyed a considerable respect among communists, but one that the Cuban Party previously had not entirely shared. For, in the 1940s' debate between the Browderist line offered by the US Party and the Duclos line of the French, over the question of the right conditions for the development of communist parties outside the USSR, the Cuban communists had largely followed Browder, a line that led to the brief, and profitable, alliance with Batista. To some extent, therefore, when the radicals in and around the 26th July Movement began to define the revolution as communist, but, in so doing, to reject the definition implicit in Escalante's version, a desire for distinctiveness pushed them towards the French Party, the other 'pole' available in the non-Soviet communist world. The fact that the latter was then still displaying strong traces of Stalinism did not diminish the attraction, not least given the fact that the economic model adopted for Cuba at that time was partly based on the Soviet experience of the 1930s.

Alongside this, however, was a growing attraction towards other, heterodox, Marxist perspectives, especially those centred on the North American *Monthly Review* group (Sweezy, Huberman, Baran, etc.) and the development theories of André Gunder Frank. These theoretical positions, with their rejection of the orthodoxies of both East and West, implied an 'exceptionalism' which coincided with the thesis that Guevara was developing to explain both Cuba's experience and the future path to revolution in Latin America, and indeed with the underlying impulse of much of the evolving *cubanismo* from Martí onwards. Confirmation of this influence comes from the tendency in the early-1970s (allowing for an inevitable academic 'lag') to adopt, at times relatively uncritically, the views of Frank, whose works were published as often the most significant Marxist analysis of (Latin American) dependency. However flawed such works may have been, and however much Cuban academics may today question their basic assumptions, there seems little doubt that Frank helped to confirm the growing 'North-South' axis of Cuban revolutionary thought, a contribution whose effects are still being felt in the tenor of Cuban economic historiography.

The move to a more heterodox definition of socialist development in Cuba coincided with, and stimulated, the 'Great Debate' in the 1962–66 period, in which the contribution from Western Europe was often influential.[72] The French economist, Charles Bettelheim, for example, backed the 'economist' view of Cuba's future development – to a large extent the policy adopted after 1970 – while the Belgian, Ernest Mandel, sided with Guevara's theory of value, largely the underlying definition adopted before 1970 (and a major component of the post-1984 reappraisal in 'rectification').[73] Beyond this, the contribution of Dumont and Gutelman, although neither were easy to locate within the contending camps, was significant to a debate that really extended beyond the purely economic to the very definition of the revolution itself.

In the same way, the influence of the unorthodox French Marxist philosopher Régis Debray went beyond Cuba's Latin American focus. For his *Revolution in the revolution?*, published in Havana in 1967, helped to articulate and popularise the *foco* ethos throughout the Latin American left, with its emphasis (merging Marxism and existentialism) on what *is* and not what *should be*. Yet he also, by so doing, helped confirm the revolution's view of its own global definition, for the *foco* ethos clearly fed back into the domestic revolution, now increasingly adopting a 'guerrilla' approach to so many of the problems posed by the triple onslaught on underdevelopment, imperialism and continental and ideological isolation. The view, prevalent after 1962, that Cuba should decide its own criteria, act and think independently, and also represent a vanguard for the Third World, owes much to the experience of the 1959–62 period, to the existing *cubanista* political tradition, to Guevara, but eventually something also to Debray.[74]

By 1967, the *cubanista* definition of the revolution was well established. The intellectual and ideological pre-eminence of the *Pensamiento Crítico* journal (1967–71) confirmed this orientation, with its heterodox, 'Guevarist', approach to Marxism – for example, stressing the younger Marx's thinking rather than the ideological ossification of Marxism which Eastern Europe and the Soviet Union seemed to represent – and its clear affinity with the European New Left.

Isolated from the continent, besieged by the US, yet also, in the eyes of many, neglected by the socialist camp, the revolutionary vanguard tended to fall back on three intellectual and ideological supports. The most important and most obvious was the existing Cuban radical tradition, reinforced by the post-1959 experience, refined by Guevara, but still unmistakeably the basis of much of the revolution's thinking and action, embodied above all in the myth and symbolism of the 'New Man'.

Inspiration was also sought increasingly from the Third World context which, in a sense, Cuba had discovered after 1959. It was at this time that Cubans most openly and genuinely identified with the struggle of North Vietnam, a people which seemed to share many of Cuba's particular problems and experiences.

The third support, albeit much less obvious or significant than the first two, was Western Europe. At one level this was a simple, pragmatic, judgement, since the blockade had made any trading partners welcome and the willingness of most Western European countries to maintain relations made them a vital component in Cuba's survival. Therefore, by the negative process of thinking that tended to characterise moments of the early years of the Revolution, a certain sympathy for and attraction towards those nations and cultures willing to 'help' was inevitable. Moreover, a European 'pole' offered a possibility of ideological, as well as economic or political, leverage *vis-à-vis* both the US and the Soviet Union.

The intellectual 'reopening' to Western Europe was therefore logical, but none the less remarkable given the recent history of 'Americanisation' and the growing autonomy in ideological development. This attraction was proved by a range of factors in the 1960s: the increasing 'Europeanism' of the cultural pages of the revolution's journals (notably *Lunes de Revolución* and *Casa de las Américas*), the decision to bring the controversial avant-garde 'Salon de Mai' exhibition to Havana in 1967, and the choice of participants in the International Cultural Congress in Havana in 1968.[75]

Yet this European re-immersion caused problems and complexities for a process that was decidedly seeking its own criteria and its own defined path. For the self-assertiveness and rejectionism implicit in this path, not least evident in the cultural field, conflicted with the tendency towards a 'pole' which had long mesmerised Cuban intellectuals and helped create and confirm the old sense of cultural inferiority. Alongside, therefore, a consistent rejection of the European ethos of the intellectual as critical conscience and autonomous critic, which led to much soul-searching and even conflict within the Cuban intellectual community in the later 1960s,[76] and alongside the developing, almost aggressive, posture that proclaimed Cuba's right to be its own yardstick, even if 'wrong',[77] this respect for European culture sat uncomfortably, and to an extent revived something of the old deference. This may well explain why Debray, who really did little more than confirm Guevara's ideas and praxis, was welcomed and, more surprisingly, became influential. For the Cubans, welcoming any intellectual support for their position, tended perhaps to create pedestals for those whose background, in other respects, they rejected; although in this particular case, Debray's clearly non-Soviet perspective (and criticism of an increasingly 'loyal' but Stalinist French Communist Party) obviously appealed to a Cuba seeking to differentiate itself from its ally in the world at large and in its domestic praxis.

This much was also true of the Intellectual Congress of 1968, a gathering largely of prominent Cuban, Third World and Western European figures, with the latter conspicuously drawn from the ranks of the heterodox. Ernst Fischer, Bertrand Russell and Jean-Paul Sartre were invited but, unable to attend, sent messages of support. Those who did attend included Jorge Semprún, already expelled from the Spanish Communist Party, Wesker, Milliband, Hobsbawm, Guérin and Axelos. Coinciding with several significant indicators of a rejection of 'orthodoxy' and an adoption of an independent radicalism – the second Escalante affair and 'microfaction' debate,[78] the closure of the *Escuelas de Instrucción Revolucionaria*, and the angry exchanges with the Venezuelan Communist Party[79] – this gathering both confirmed the trend and was indicative of the Cuban attraction towards an independence of thought that Western European radicalism then offered.

Furthermore, the significant number of European films, including the most avant-garde, and the respect evident for the unorthodox in culture – whether the Theatre of the Absurd, Brecht, or abstract art – all confirmed a European dimension to the developing ethos that was new, but also, in a sense, reviving a link lost in the welter of 'Americanisation' and relative isolation after 1902. Moreover, the evident popularisation of these cultural ideas and phenomena indicated an empathy that went beyond the traditional intellectual attraction of an elite. This, perhaps, was especially the case of the cinema, long a genuinely popular medium. After 1959, the move away from the hitherto common North American imports towards either Cuban productions or European films, clearly helped create a different pole of attraction. Certainly ICAIC (the Cuban Institute of Cinematic Arts), which oversaw the development of a revolutionary Cuban cinema, looked as much to European avant-garde film-makers as to the Eastern European 'classics'.

This attraction, therefore, in a sense, reflected two aspects: the residual deference that still needed to be expurgated (and largely was) and the growing confidence of an independent society that was discovering its own definitions and turning to a positive eclecticism. As the 'orthodox' reform movement of the 1970s got under way, it was inevitable that this decidedly heterodox Western European pole of attraction would decline in importance. For a start, the new orthodoxy was in part realised both at Soviet encouragement and thanks to the pressure of those, in the old PSP or otherwise, who perceived Soviet models (political and economic) as directly relevant to Cuba after the disaster of the 1970 harvest. But it also reflected something of the decline of that heterodoxy as a viable and coherent 'model'. The Western European left, for example, had became increasingly disenchanted with the Soviet Union, even with Cuba, and, after May 1968 and the 'Prague Spring', with its new-found but frustrated revolutionary positions. Therefore, not only did the left lose interest in an apparently unrevolutionary Cuba, but Cuban intellectuals also lost interest in an increasingly unrevolutionary European left, in a left that seemed to have lost its independent way and to offer nothing to Cuba or any part of the Third World. It was, if anything, OPEC rather than the Left Bank which offered a relevant path for the South. Indeed, the predominant Western European intellectual contribution during this 'reform' period tended to come from the 'technocratic' or technical sources of aid (from France, Spain and even Britain), in economic advice, in cultural links and in the development of postgraduate social sciences. In a sense, therefore, if the post-1986 'rectification' process targeted those same reforms which, according to Cuban leaders, 'mimetically' transposed an inappropriate Soviet/ Eastern European model to Cuba, as well as those within Cuba who argued for this change, or those who personally, even at times corruptly, benefited from it, then the 'technical' advice which accompanied those reforms must also be to some extent in the firing line. However, given that 'rectification' also necessarily involved a rescuing of many of the characteristic elements of the 1960s – for example, the moral dimension to the economy, the thought of Guevara – then one must also expect something of a reappraisal of those same European currents of thinking which confirmed and helped channel the *cubanista* perspective of the early years. To this extent, therefore, what perhaps seems a sterile historical exercise, of no great relevance to the Cuba of the 1990s may in fact be of some significance in understanding the nature and direction of the Cuban Revolution into the next decade or so.

The impact of Western Europe on the evolving *cubanista* revolutionary ideology has therefore been surprisingly considerable over the last two centuries. Certainly it has long constituted one of the major poles of attraction for Cuban intellectual radicalism and one of the major sources of inspiration for ideological development in Cuba, more so in the early years, and less so after 1902. Yet what input there has been has undeniably left its mark, whether on the quest for independence, the moral imperative or any number of identifiable elements.

That is not to say, of course – as made clear earlier in this chapter – that this focus implies an exaggeration of the role either of the intellectual vanguard or of European ideas in the necessarily complex process of 'ideologisation'. That both were significant is clear from any examination of the history of Cuban radicalism. But their evolution should be set alongside the range of other, often more significant, social, political and economic factors that created the 'tinder' for Cuba's revolution in 1959.

The focus is, however, none the less valid. Firstly, because of the often seminal role played by intellectuals (individually or collectively) in the trajectory of political development in Cuba, either as articulators or leaders (*homo poeta* or *homo faber*). Secondly, its validity lies in the fact that the 1960s did witness a revealing change in Cuban attitudes. After centuries of absorbing an unadulterated 'Europeanism' which reinforced both a sense of inferiority and, paradoxically, the intellectual tools for a *cubanista* perspective, the Cuban urge for independence of definition in 1960 meant a deliberate, and at times irrational, rejection of that 'pole'. Yet, by the late-1960s the process of coming to terms with what revolution and independence actually meant in all aspects of politics, economy and society had created a more confident approach towards the hitherto intimidating, and often imitated, influences. The ideology that had emerged by the 1970s was a complex fusion of Cuban, 'Americanist' and external roots, in which Europe was being tapped consciously and fruitfully to reinforce the clearly indigenous ethos which played such a part in guaranteeing the unity of purpose of both leadership and populace, and the support which the whole process has, by and large, enjoyed through most, if not all, of the years of the Revolution's existence.

Notes

1 The range of opinions on the Revolution's origins has been vast since 1959 – from those who see an inevitability in Cuba's move towards socialism, to those who detect simply a bourgeois or populist rebellion. Certainly, the social indices of the Cuba of 1958 seemed to make Cuba an unlikely candidate for revolution, and Batista's second period did seem to enjoy a brief, if superficial, economic boom.

2 One significant recent example is the Tad Szulc biography, *Fidel. A critical portrait*, London, Hutchinson, 1986.

3 The question of ideology is a vexed and complex issue. Not only is there a lack of consensus on the definition and role of ideology, but also the debate between opposing positions has often been intense, acrimonious and negative, obscuring the often considerable advances made. Given the lack of space for any lengthy exposition, and despite the inherent dangers in any assumptions, it seems appropriate here to simply establish and work within one broad definition.

4 The term 'hegemonic' is used here in the sense in which Antonio Gramsci used it. See, for example, his essay, 'The State and Civil Society', in *Selections from Prison Notebooks*, London, Lawrence and Wishart, 1971, pp. 206 *passim*.

5 Here I refer to the end of Spanish colonialism in 1898 and its effective replacement by the US – between 1898 and 1902 by military occupation and rule, between 1902 and 1934 under the terms of the Platt Amendment and other legal controls, and after 1934, indirectly, through the quota system.

6 The term is Paulo Freire's in *Pedagogy of the Oppressed*, London, Penguin (Harmondsworth), 1972, pp. 121–2.

7 This refers to the 'system' established by both the Jones-Cooligan Act and the Reciprocity Treaty, both of which guaranteed Cuban sugar a preferential share of the US market, but with the reciprocal disadvantage of relatively unrestricted entry of US manufactured goods into Cuba.

8 From 1933 to 1940, Batista dominated Cuban politics through a series of puppet presidents. Then, between 1940 and 1944, he ruled as elected president himself. From 1944 to 1952, the Auténtico Party (PRC) was in office, first under Grau San Martín (1944–48), then under Prío Socarrás. From 1947, the principal opposition force was the equally populist Ortodoxo Party (PPC). See Footnote 16.

9 On 10 March 1952, Batista returned to power in a military coup.

10 Here I refer to the fact that, while in mainland Latin America, the removal of Spain's colonialism by 1826 could be seen as a 'natural' development', given both the rising nationalism and aspirations of the *criollo* elite and the decline of Spain, the survival of Spanish power in Cuba owed as much to negative factors as to any positive Spanish ability to maintain a powerful colonial enterprise, i.e. the American and British preference for continued Spanish control of the strategically important island, rather than a vulnerably independent Cuba.

11 Many of the members of the independence party (Cuban Revolutionary Party – PRC) were adherents of the idea of the annexation of Cuba by the US, as

indeed had been several of the leading separatists since 1810. The first Cuban president, Tomás Estrada Palma (an American citizen), was one such.

12   For a further discussion of the use and failure of populism during this period, see Kapcia, 'Cuban Populism and the Birth of the Myth of Martí', in Abel. C. and Torrents, N. (eds), *José Martí. Revolutionary Democrat*, London, The Athlone Press, 1986.

13   The centenary of Martí's birth was celebrated in 1953; the somewhat disparate youth movement of that period was therefore initially referred to as the 'Generación del Centenario', or the 'Generación del Cincuentenario' in celebration of the 50th anniversary of Cuba's spurious independence. See, for example, Jorge Ibarra, 'La generación del Cincuentenario', in *Aproximaciones a Clio*, Havana, Editorial de Ciencias Sociales, 1979, pp. 151–181.

14   For further discussion of this myth, see Antoni Kapcia, 'Cuban populism', *op. cit.*

15   In particular, this refers to the recruitment of thousands of peasant and working class Cubans to both independence struggles, a factor which clearly determined the character of what were often social rebellions.

16   In 1947, the 'heir-apparent' to Grau within the Auténtico Party, Eddy Chibás, having been passed over in favour of Prío Socarrás, left to form his own party, the *Partido del Pueblo Cubano* (Cuban People's Party), popularly known as the *Ortodoxos*. Although the party was structurally different from its parent party – in that it attracted many of the youth wing of the *Auténticos*, together with the women's section and much of the Oriente base its principal political distinction was its emphasis on corruption.

17   For the presidential elections of 1952, the indications were that the *Ortodoxo* candidate, Agramonte (Chibás had shot himself dramatically in 1951) was favourite to win the vote, against both the *Auténticos* and Batista. The latter pre-empted the result with his coup on 10 March 1952.

18   Martí, certainly, constantly implied a faith in the essential 'purity' of the rural Cuban and the appropriateness of an agrarian-based economy. Thereafter, many of the statements of the radical-nationalist current in Cuba referred to the need for land reform, protection of the peasant and the sugar grower and the importance of the sugar economy.

19   This refers to the intellectual movement which, in Latin America, responded to the publication (in 1900) of *Ariel* by the Uruguayan, Enrique Rodó, an essay which was seen by many as counterposing an essentially spiritual Latin America to a materialist North America.

20   In 1918, in Córdoba (Argentina), the successful University Reform Movement set the agenda for many student movements in the continent (especially in Peru and Cuba), with its call for a more 'applied' Latin American university, seen as the engine for social, economic and political change in Latin America.   '

21   The nationalism and educational radicalism of the Mexican revolution, from 1910, had a clearly inspirational impact throughout Latin America, not least in Cuba.

22   The Aprista movement was set up by the Peruvian Víctor Raúl Haya de la Torre, a student leader, in 1924 (as APRA, the American Revolutionary Popular Alliance). With its unique blend of semi-Marxist radicalism, 'Latinamericanist' nationalism and populist collaborationism, it appealed to a wide range of intellectual opinion outside Peru. One wing of the Cuban student radical movement after 1923 was certainly much influenced by Aprismo, an influence which extended into the later DEU (in the 1933–4 revolution) and the

Auténticos, particularly Chibás (see Footnote 16). Beyond that, *Aprismo* played a significant role in the development of the 'Third Road' current of political thought which characterised many of Latin America's political movements from the 1920s.

23 This peculiar combination of motivations led to the essentially conservative abolitionism of José Antonio Saco in Cuba, whose fear of a 'black' Cuba was paramount in his thinking.

24 In particular, four of the leading intellectuals of mid-nineteenth century Cuba – Varela, Luz y Caballero, Caballero and Saco – all taught in the Seminario, while Carlos Manuel Céspedes, the instigator of the 1868–78 War of Independence, and Cirilo Villaverde, the anti-slavery novelist, both studied there.

25 See Sheldon B. Liss, *Roots of Revolution. Radical Thought in Cuba*, Lincoln and London, University of Nebraska Press, 1987, pp. 8–10, for a fuller discussion of Caballero's intellectual background.

26 Those years saw the various revolts known collectively as the 'Escalera' revolt, a phenomenon which evidently played a large part in convincing the Cuban *criollo* elite of the dangers of relinquishing Spanish protection.

27 According to Alistair Hennessy, 'Cuba', in Mark Falcoff and Frederick, B. Pike, *The Spanish Civil War, 1936–39. American Hemispheric Perspectives*, Lincoln and London, University of Nebraska Press, 1982, p. 105, between 1893 and 1895 224,000 immigrants arrived from Spain, of whom 82,000 remained.

28 In the period 1924–8, 117,254 immigrants (of the 123,798 who arrived) returned to Spain. Hennessy, *op. cit.*, p. 105.

29 The various Centros and clubs played a vital role in this continued 'Hispanisation' of Cuba. The Centros Gallegos, for example, were set up in 1879 (Galicians accounted for 47.68 per cent of Spanish immigrants after 1911), while the Centros Asturianos (set up in 1886) counted 34,000 members by the 1930s, with over 100 branches. There were in addition Catalan, Basque, Castillian and Andalucian Centros. The Spanish priests numbered, in 1919, 426 out of the Cuban total of 667. Hennessy, *op. cit.*, pp. 105–8.

30 Significantly, the Primer Congreso Obrero of 1892 was held in the Centro Gallego in the Prado, Havana, and the 1914 gathering of over fifty groups to establish an anarchosyndicalist confederation was held in the Havana Centro Asturiano.

31 The role of such readers was something which the tobacco workers defended fiercely, against many attempts to ban them, and was even carried on in Florida.

32 Olga Cabrera, *Alfredo López. Maestro del Proletariado Cubano*, Havana, Editorial de Ciencias Sociales, 1985, p. 147. The CNOC was the Confederación Nacional Obrera Cubana.

33 *Ibid.*, p. 138.

34 See Liss, *op. cit.*, pp. 37–45, for a fuller discussion of Tejera.

35 Other significant developments of the period were the *Liga General de Trabajadores Cubanos* (1899), the *Club de Propaganda Socialista* (1904), *Partido Obrero Socialista de Cuba* (1905), and the strikes of 1899, 1902–4, 1906–18.

36 The various studies of Gerald E. Poyo provide excellent analysis and detail of the Florida community at that time.

37 The *mambí* was the name adopted by the (irregular) fighters in both wars of independence.

38   Gerard Poyo, 'José Martí: Architect of social unity in the émigré communities of the United States', in Abel and Torrents, *op. cit.*, p. 22.

39   Olga Cabrera, 'Enrique Creci: un patriota obrero', in *Santiago*, (Revista de la Universidad de Oriente), Diciembre de 1979, No. 36, pp. 121–150.

40   Other prominent positivists were Andres Poey, Manuel Sanguily and Enrique Pineiro.

41   Pablo Guardarrama and Edel Tussel Oropeza, *El pensamiento filosófico de Enrique José Varona*, Havana, Editorial de Ciencias Sociales, 1987, pp. 41–73 *passim*.

42   For the best study of Martí's intellectual and philosophical background, see Peter Turton, *José Martí: Architect of Cuba's Freedom*, London, Zed Books, 1986.

43   I refer here to the debate initiated by the Argentinian Domingo Sarmiento, in his book, *Civilización y barbarie: Vida de Juan Facundo Quiroga* (1845).

44   The Platt Amendment was the legal device by which US control over Cuban affairs was ensured after the end of the military occupation in 1901. Originally an amendment to the Army Appropriations Bill in the US Senate, it was then imposed on the Cuban Constitutional Convention, which was forced to incorporate it into the new Cuban Constitution.

45   Between 1902 and 1919, over 400,000 Spanish immigrants entered Cuba, making the Spanish-born population by 1930 16 per cent of the total and making Cuba the most Spanish of Latin American countries; by 1919 only 14 per cent of these migrants had taken Cuban nationality. Hennessy, *op. cit.*, p. 105.

46   Here I refer to the fact that Haya de la Torre specifically conceived of his philosophy as being a fusion of Einstein's theories, Marxism and indigenous nationalism.

47   This *vanguardismo* ranged from the avant-garde work of the 1920s, in the *Revista de Avance* (1927–30), through the experience of the *negrista* movement (of Carpentier, Guillén and others), to the positions adopted later by *Ciclón* magazine. Despite their overt 'Cubanism', all of these movements looked to the European avant-garde for inspiration. The movement around the *Orígenes* magazine was, in turn, clearly inspired by Europe, and especially the work of the Spanish poet, Juan Ramón Jiménez. See Benigno Sánchez-Eppler, *Habits of Poetry; Habits of Resurrection*, London, Tamesis Books, 1986.

48   The immediate roots of this commitment strand were to be found in the *Protesta de los Trece* (1923) and the *Grupo Minorista*, which partly emerged from that event. See Ann Wright, 'Intellectuals of an Unheroic Period of Cuban History, 1913–1923. The 'Cuba Contemporánea' Group', *Bulletin of Latin American Research*, Vol. 7, No. 1, 1988, pp. 109–122.

49   John Kirk, *Between God and the Party. Religion and Politics in Revolutionary Cuba*, Tampa, University of South Florida Press, 1989, p. 40.

50   The number was as high as 850 (Hennessy, *op. cit.*, p. 132), but some estimates go even higher. Of all the Cuban groups that provided volunteers, besides the Communist Party, Guiteras's Joven Cuba was particularly outstanding.

51   The 1933 law stipulated that the workforce of Cuban enterprises be minimally 50 per cent Cuban; it was a law directed principally against the 'threat' of cheap Haitian and Jamaican labour in the canefields of Oriente and its execution produced considerable hardship for the latter.

52   In 1937 Batista allowed the Communist Party to form itself legally as the *Partido Unión Revolucionaria*; it in turn altered its public attitude to Batista.

By 1940, with over 23,000 members, the PUR had become part of Batista's electoral coalition, the *Coalición Democrática Socialista*, winning a large number of seats in both the Constituent Assembly and the Congress, and, in 1942, gaining two posts in Batista's cabinet. At the same time, the newly created CTC (*Confederación de Trabajadores Cubanos*), replacing the CNOC, was dominated, with Batista's approval, by the Communist Lazaro Peña.

53 Hennessy, *op. cit.*, p. 110.

54 In some ways, ever since Martí and Julián del Casal, Martí's fellow *modernista* poet, Cuban literature had witnessed a division, often clear, between those who saw their role as one of political commitment and those who remained faithful to 'art for art's sake'. The experience of Spain had mixed effects on the nature and self-belief of Cuban culture. While some returned disillusioned, others found there a taste of political relevance which was increasingly denied them in Cuba.

55 The *bonches* were the gangs which evolved from the 'action groups' of the 1930–35 period, mostly losing their ideological or even political *raison d'être* or identity. Reinforced by returning Republican volunteers, they became a major force in domestic Cuban politics, aiding the *Auténtico* government of Grau to eliminate the Communists from both the CTC and the university and finally being rewarded by both Grau and Prío with sinecures in local government, the police and the bureaucracy. Student politics from 1940 to 1949 was dominated by the *bonches*, and, after Batista's coup in 1952, many of their leaders sided with the new regime.

56 Hennessy, *op. cit.*, p. 134.

57 Guiteras was one of the most significant protagonists of the 1933–35 unrest. A largely unaffiliated radical, he was a student leader who became Grau's Minister of the Interior in 1933–4 and the focus of revolutionary resistance to the rightward shift after Batista's 1934 coup. Always one of the most popular of the 1933 leaders, his following in the police and army, as well as the student body, was remarkable, and contributed to his leadership of the 1935 general strike, after which he was killed.

58 See Kapcia, 'Martí', *op. cit.*

59 Kirk, *op. cit.*, p. 97. Of these, only 556 were Cuban.

60 *Ibid.*, p. 97. Kirk gives a figure of 65,000 Cuban students in 212 Catholic schools in 1959.

61 Frei Betto, *Fidel y la Religión*, Havana, Oficina de Publicaciones del Consejo de Estado, 1985, pp. 145–155.

62 The MNR included in its ranks the later 26th July activists Faure Chomón, Faustino Pérez, Armando Hart and Vilma Espín, plus Fructuoso Rodríguez and Joe Westbrook.

63 The FMC is the *Federación de Mujeres Cubanas*; the CDRs are the *Comités de Defensa de la Revolución*; the *Pioneros* is the organisation for children below the age for the *Unión de la Juventud Comunista*; ANAP is the *Asociación Nacional de Agricultores Pequeños*, the private (small) farmers' body.

64 This was the so-called 'Escalante Affair'. In 1961 Aníbal Escalante, a leading PSP activist, was given the task of merging the three revolutionary parties (the PSP, the 26th July Movement and the *Directorio Revolucionario Estudiantil*) into an embryonic 'single party', the *Organizaciones Revolucionarias Integradas* (ORI). When, in March 1962, he announced a national directorate for the ORI which included 10 from the PSP, a figure equal to the 26th July Movement's representation, he was removed, denounced and effectively 'exiled' (in a

diplomatic capacity) to Eastern Europe. The ORI was shortly after replaced by the PURS (*Partido Unido de la Revolución Socialista*), which, in turn, gave way in 1965 to the Cuban Communist Party (PCC).

65 See especially Richard R. Fagen, *The Transformation of Political Culture in Cuba*, Stanford, Cal., Stanford University Press, 1969, pp. 33–68.

66 *Ibid.*, pp. 104–137.

67 For a fuller discussion of the new role and problems of the intellectuals, see Kapcia, 'Culture and Ideology in post-Revolutionary Cuba', *Red Letters* (London), No. 15, Summer/Autumn 1983, pp. 11–23. Also in *Caribbean Societies*, University of London, Institute of Commonwealth Studies, Collected Seminar Papers No. 29, pp. 113–121.

68 This refers to the process of 'rectification of past errors and negative tendencies', officially initiated in February 1986, but in fact intimated as early as 1984. The significance of the process here is that, given the process's response to perceived problems created by the 1970–84 'reformers', this has meant a reappraisal of and renewed interest in the economic ideas of Guevara. See especially Carlos Tablada, *Che Guevara. Economics and Politics in the Transition to Socialism*, Sydney, Pathfinder/Pacific and Asia, 1989, and Fernando Martínez Heredia, *El Che y el Socialismo*, Mexico, Editorial Nuestro Tiempo/Centro de Estudios sobre América, 1989.

69 The influence of the two Latin Americans, José Carlos Mariátegui (Peru) and Aníbal Ponce (Argentina), was particularly marked, Mariátegui (in addition to interpreting and introducing Gramsci) writing of the role of culture in revolutionary transformation, and Ponce of the revolutionary approach to education (an approach which partly inspired the Cuban reforms after 1959) and of 'socialist humanism'.

70 I make this point because, after the disillusionment of the post-1934 period, many of Roa's cultural generation preferred to 'retreat' either from political commitment or from external terms of reference.

71 For a fuller discussion of Roa's intellectual background, see Liss, *op. cit.*, pp. 119–132.

72 The 'Great Debate' was the name given to the four years of open discussion and argument, in the media and in meetings, over Cuba's future economic direction (e.g. between an industrial or an agrarian pattern, between command planning or some market mechanisms, between material or moral incentives, etc.).

73 See especially Tablada, *op. cit.*

74 October 1962 (i.e. the missile crisis and the Soviet decision to agree to US demands) was something of a watershed in Cuba's perception of its path to revolution and its definition of socialism.

75 *Lunes de Revolución* was the Monday cultural supplement of the 26th July Movement's newspaper, *Revolución*, between 1959 and 1961. Edited by some of the leading younger cultural figures of Cuba, it rapidly became a standard bearer for radical artistic ideas and sold in runs of hundreds of thousands. *Casa de las Américas* was set up in 1959 and soon became one of the most prestigious cultural magazines in Latin America, sponsoring a series of annual prizes and giving the opportunity for publication to a wide range of Latin American writers over the thirty-three years of its existence to date.

76 I refer especially to the *caso Padilla* of 1970–71. For a discussion of the affair see 'Cuba: Revolution and the Intellectual. The Strange Case of Heberto Padilla', *Index on Censorship*, Vol. 1, No. 2, Summer 1972, pp. 65–88, and

Kapcia, 'Culture and Ideology', *op. cit.*

77 This refers to Castro's comment that Cuba now at least had the right to make its own mistakes, a view intellectualised by Edmundo Desnoes in his collection of essays, *Punto de vista*, Havana, Instituto del Libro, 1967.

78 In 1968, the political battles evident in 1962 emerged again. Escalante, after returning from Eastern Europe, had apparently begun manoeuvering to form a 'microfaction' within the PCC to alter the Revolution's current economic and foreign (i.e. revolutionary) policies. On this occasion, he was tried and sentenced to 30 years in prison.

79 In 1967, there was a bitter public exchange of views between the hitherto pro-Cuban and insurrectionary Venezuelan Communist Party (who accused Cuba of meddling in internal Venezuelan affairs) and Fidel Castro, who accused the Venezuelans of being 'armchair revolutionaries'.

CHAPTER 3

Economic relations between Western Europe and Cuba since 1959

José Luís Rodríguez

The role of the foreign sector in the economic development of Cuba[1]

In the Cuban view socialism as a system is the essential premiss for a successful development strategy. Internally, the nationalisation of the means of production laid the necessary foundations for the creation of a single socio-economic centre through which the economy could be harmonised and planned. Externally, the integration of the Cuban economy into the international socialist division of labour has been a crucial factor in recent economic development.

From the beginning of the Revolution, development was conceived as a process in which economic and social improvements would inter-relate and complement each other. In this way resources could be managed to meet basic social needs. Such a perception of the development process involving the satisfying of these needs is crucial to the creation of a socialist society. However, there have been errors, which although they may have slowed down progress, have not jeopardised the prospects for a better society.

Amongst the most complex factors in our economic development strategy has been the foreign sector of the economy. Until 1958 the Cuban economy was characterised by its high level of external dependency: not only did the US take 71 per cent of imports and provide 72 per cent of exports but all strategic decisions affecting the economy were taken in the US.[2] After 1959 development strategy would be constrained by this external dependency. The effects of this were to be graphically illustrated once a process of industrialisation started and after the US instituted the blockade in 1960.

To meet the demand for industrial goods an accelerated industrialisation strategy was adopted between 1961 and 1963, accompanied at the same time by a diversification of agricultural production. This policy, however, foundered on the tension created by the balance of payments problem and so the strategy was modified.

Between 1964 and 1975 priority was given to the accumulation of capital to promote industrialisation. This was to be achieved by sugar exports to socialist countries. Only from 1976 did Cuba have the minimum conditions needed to implement a gradual process of industrialisation within the international division of labour. As a result of this development strategy considerable improvements have been made over the past 30 years.

Indeed, the rate of economic growth was 4.3 per cent for the period 1959–1989, which represented a growth of 2.8 per cent per capita.[3] On the other hand, industrial production increased at an annual average rate of 2.9 per cent per capita between 1962 and 1989, while the rate for buildings was 6.0 per cent, and that of agricultural production 0.9 per cent. In order to reach these growth rates, the country invested 63,250 million pesos from 1959 to 1989, with an average annual growth of 2 per cent as regards labour productivity.

The transformation this achieved reflected the progress made by the country in the creation of the necessary conditions to carry out gradual industrialisation once infrastructural problems, both economic and social, had been overcome. Such economic results were also accompanied by positive transformations in the social realm, especially with regard to public health and education.

In this development process the foreign sector of the economy has undoubtedly played an essential role. The importance of such a sector can be first appreciated by looking at the index of the Cuban economic liberalisation, which from 22.4 per cent in 1959 went up to 50.8 per cent in 1989.[4] The dynamics of foreign trade reveal an average growth of 7.3 per cent between 1959 and 1989, with an increase of 6.6 per cent of exports and of 7.9 per cent of imports; this reflects the adverse balance of payments during these years, which are a consequence of the tensions generated by any development process. The adverse balance in this period reached 21,508.3 million pesos, 70 per cent of which was underwritten by the socialist countries which granted important credits to Cuba so that it could meet its debts.[5]

The record of the exchange terms, on the other hand, seems to point to a worsening during the 1960s, with a recovery during the 1970s and again a worsening during the 1980s. Generally speaking, it is estimated that at the end of the last decade, this record was lower than at any time other than the period 1935–40, and that between 1981 and 1990 its development cost the Cuban economy 15,000 million pesos.[6] Nevertheless, sugar and its by-products still dominated exports (Table 3.1).

With regard to imports (Table 3.2), their breakdown reflects up to 1989 a transformation process, characteristic of an economy integrated within an international division of labour, with a high sensitivity to the external provision of intermediate goods.

Table 3.1   Commercial breakdown of exports (in percentages at current prices)

	1958	1989
	%	%
Sugar industry products	80.6	73.2
Mining products	3.8	9.2
Tobacco industry products	6.7	1.6
Fishing products	0.8	2.4
Farming products	1.9	3.9
Other products	6.2	9.7

Source: CEE, *Anuario Estadístico de Cuba*, 1989, p.260.

Table 3.2   Commercial breakdown of imports (in percentages at current prices)

	1958	1989
	%	%
Consumer goods	39.1	10.8
Intermediate goods	34.1	66.4
Capital goods	26.8	22.8

Source: CEE, *Anuario Estadístico de Cuba*, 1989, p.261.

The most significant change in foreign trade during the period examined (Table 3.3) has been its new geographical orientation, reflecting the high level of Cuba's integration within the international socialist division of labour.

This geographical reorientation has been deeply influenced by the effects of the US economic blockade, which has markedly limited exchanges with non-socialist countries.[7] Commercial relations with socialist countries guaranteed a steady market and fair prices for exports, at the same time as they ensured the provision of the basic goods necessary to Cuba's development.

Undoubtedly, it was the Soviet Union which occupied pride of place in these relations. During the period extending from 1959 to 1989 commercial exchange with the USSR represented 63 per cent of the total. Thanks to the credits received Cuba managed to meet an adverse balance of 13,802 million pesos and made a profit in exchange terms ratio of 136.2 per cent between 1963 and 1982.[8]

Table 3.3 Geographical orientation of foreign trade (percentages at current prices)

	1958	1989[1]
	%	%
Socialist countries	1.5	83.1
Exports	2.9	79.9
Imports	0.3	85.3
Capitalist developed countries	88.9	9.9
Exports	91.1	13.1
Imports	86.7	7.8
Underdeveloped countries	9.6	7.0
Exports	6.0	7.0
Imports	13.0	6.9

Note: (1): The author's estimated data.
Source: CEE, *Anuario Estadístico de Cuba*, 1988, 145; 1989, 251, 255, 259; BNC, *Informe Económico*, Junio 1990, 14.

From the point of view of international financial flows, Cuba has also obtained important resources from the socialist countries, especially from the USSR, in advantageous conditions. From the point of view of assistance towards development, Cuba obtained approximately 6608 million pesos from the USSR between 1960 and 1990, 80 per cent of which was directed towards the country's industrial development.[9]

The remaining socialist countries also granted Cuba development credits estimated at 267 million dollars for the 1960s.[10] These financial facilities were specifically complemented by the USSR from 1976 with the payment of preferential prices for Cuba's most important exports. The re-financing processes undertaken with the USSR enabling Cuba to postpone payment of the credit service in 1972 and 1984 under advantageous conditions, were also significant.[11]

Financing credit granted to Cuba by market economies, was linked to favourable international trends and played a complementary role in economic development. These credits were mainly granted on commercial terms during the 1970s, and the amount is estimated to have been in the order of 4250 to 4650 million dollars during that period.[12] As a result of these credits Cuba's external debt rose, in terms of freely convertible currency, from 291.0 million pesos in 1969 to 7000 millions in 1990.[13] The increase of debt has been linked to the hardening of credit repayment terms rather than to any significant new credits.

After 1982 and until 1985, the credit repayment terms were re-negotiated in conditions which were marginally more rigorous than the international average. However, Cuba was compelled to suspend its payments from July 1986. As a consequence, the external financial flows have been reduced almost to nothing if one excludes the current credits for foreign trade.[14]

Thus after 1959, the external sector continued to play an increasingly important role in the economic development of Cuba, especially due to Cuba's integration in the international socialist division of labour. None the less, the external economic links with other world areas, and with Western Europe in particular, must not be underestimated.

The role of Western Europe's relations in the economic development of Cuba

Economic relations and commercial exchange with Western Europe before 1959 were dependent on the dominant position of the US in the Cuban economy.[15] With the success of the Revolution, trade with Western Europe was reactivated as part of the diversification of foreign trade links (Table 3.4).

The development of commercial relations with Western Europe went through different phases during these years. After a slow expansion in the 1960s, they reached their highest levels in the mid-1970s, going back to very low volumes after 1985, though a slight recovery can be noted after 1988. Cuban exports to Europe represented almost 15 per cent of the total in 1975, and imports reached a significantly high level, covering approximately 27 per cent of the total in that year. In general terms, the average annual growth of commercial exchange between 1958 and 1989 reached 5.3 per cent with regard to exports and 5.6 per cent in relation to imports for this period.[16]

Table 3.4   Proportion of Cuban foreign trade with Western Europe (in percentages)

	1958	1975	1989
Total exchange	14.8	21.1	8.5
Exports	15.7	14.9	10.5
Imports	14.0	26.9	7.2

Source: CEE, *Anuario Estadístico de Cuba*, 1988, 410–12, 418–19, 422–23; and *Anuario*, 1989, 249, 253, 257.

Several factors contributed to this trend. During the 1960s, trade with Europe and Japan represented for Cuba an alternative to the US blockade and a necessary complement to trade with socialist countries. In this respect, the decision of Western Europe not to join the US blockade, the dynamics of international competitiveness, the slight progress of the Cuban economy itself, and finally, Cuba's international financial solvency, all played a significant role.

The commercial expansion between Cuba and Europe during the 1970s was due to: i) the positive results achieved during the previous decade, ii) the rapid expansion of the Cuban economy, iii) the advantageous international price of some commodities during these years – including sugar, iv) the positive effects of East-West *détente*, and v) the increased availability of international credit.

This positive trend came to an end during the 1980s, giving way to a contraction of the commercial links between Cuba and Europe from the moment in which the 1982 debt crisis started. From that crisis onwards, Cuba was no longer able to export sugar to the EEC, whose member countries became rivals in the international sugar market. Added to this the US blockade against Cuba hardened, finding some support from a group of European countries as the protectionist position of Europe became stronger.[17] Foreign trade between Cuba and Western Europe then developed mainly with a group of countries amongst which Spain was in the lead (Table 3.5).[18]

The average commercial exchange with the most significant group of European countries that have traded with Cuba in the last 30 years is shown in Table 3.6. As this table shows, Spain had the highest exchange average from 1959 to 1988, and until 1975 it was the sole European country to bring a favourable balance to Cuba's trade balance – on average 14 million pesos per annum. On the other hand, commercial exchange increased between

Table 3.5 Proportion of Cuban trade with selected Western European countries (in percentages)

	1950	1975	1989
UK	3.9	2.3	1.4
FRG (Federal Republic of Germany)	2.1	2.4	1.1
Spain	2.0	6.2	2.0
France	1.0	2.0	0.7
Italy	0.7	1.9	0.7

Source: CEE, *Anuario Estadístico de Cuba*, 1989, pp. 248–49.

Table 3.6   Cuba's annual average commercial exchange with selected Western European countries (in million pesos at current prices)

	1959–1975			1976–1988		
	Exports	Imports	Balance	Exports	Imports	Balance
UK	11.983	28.692	–16.709	22.997	77.369	–54.372
FRG	4.142	31.067	–26.925	26.792	74.188	–47.396
Spain	51.560	37.639	13.929	81.898	136.012	–54.114
France	9.030	33.902	–24.872	41.801	68.078	–26.277
Italy	10.298	26.130	–15.832	26.869	41.426	–14.557

Sources: Calculations based on CEE, *Anuario Estadístico de Cuba*, 1980, 168–70; 1983, 297, 301; 1988, 419, 423.

1976 and 1988, but the balance became more adverse, especially in the case of Spain, the UK and France.

Of course, it needs to be stressed that the worsening of the exchange terms affects these figures. As regards trade with developed capitalist countries between 1963 and 1975 this relation showed a slight improvement of 7.4 per cent, but from 1975 to 1982 there was a worsening of 55.4 per cent.[19]

In general, between 1959 and 1988, the chief commercial partners of Cuba within Western Europe have granted credits so as to enable her to meet adverse balances. The estimated value of these credits was: 974.2 million pesos in the case of the UK; 1046.9 millions for the FRG; 480.6 millions in the case of Spain; 739.6 millions for France; and 442.6 millions in the case of Italy. Such credits represent around 19.5 per cent of the total commercial deficit during these years.

The trade breakdown of Cuba's commerce with Western Europe has also undergone some changes. From the point of view of exports, the quantity of the different products within the total exported to the most important Cuban commercial counterparts in Western Europe has changed (Table 3.7). The tendency to note here is a replacement of sugar exports by seafood and tobacco with regard to Spain; a concentration on seafood and tobacco in the case of France, and on nickel in the case of the FRG, with a greater diversity of exports for the remaining countries.

One factor which undoubtedly compensates for the decrease of exports in the last years is the growth of tourist services. In effect, the tourists that came from the FRG to Cuba in 1989 represented 16.9 per cent of the total; those coming from Spain, 9.9 per cent; and those from Italy, 6.3 per cent. Western Europe has become the area that generates the largest number

Table 3.7   Selected sample of Cuban exports from various Western European countries (in percentages)

	1958	1975	1988
Sugar			
Spain	33.1	82.0	0
Honey products			
UK	5.3	12.0	0
Fresh and frozen fish			
Spain	0	0.6	0
Italy	0	13.2	0
Fresh and frozen seafood			
France	0	53.4	61.6
Spain	0	2.9	24.1
Cigars			
Spain	27.4	2.8	27.4
UK	3.7	11.0	15.5
France	11.1	18.6	13.8
Leaf tobacco			
Spain	14.3	6.7	30.0
France	0	1.9	3.0
Sinter of nickel plus cobalt			
Italy	0	8.7	14.1[1]
FRG	0	23.2	33.5[1]

Notes: [1] Corresponds to 1987.
Sources: CEE, *Anuario Estadístico de Cuba*, 1988, pp. 418–19, pp. 464–75.

of tourists for the country, representing 87.1 per cent of Cuba's visitors, which amounted to 275,618 in 1989.[20] The trade breakdown of Cuban imports from Western Europe reveals the importance of such supplies as a complement to the imports from socialist countries during the last years. Market economies have been significant providers of whole plants, chemical products, means of transport, raw pharmaceutical materials, drugs, and also building equipment. The significance of such imports within the total was most important in the 1970s; for several years the supplies of chemical products, manufactures, and means of transport were mostly provided by the West.[21] In the case of whole plants, Western Europe has remained the most important supplier over the years (Table 3.8).

From a financial point of view, Cuba received important credits from

Western Europe, more specifically during the 1970s (Table 3.9). The credits granted by Western Europe in freely convertible currency represented approximately between 63 per cent and 69 per cent of the total obtained by Cuba in the 1970s.

Access to these important financial resources was made easier due to several factors, amongst which it is worth highlighting: i) the positive economic performance of the country,[22] ii) rising sugar prices, iii) the growth of the international financial market, iv) Cuban solvency. All these factors must be considered within the framework of a relaxation of international tensions in general, and between Cuba and the US in particular.

The servicing of credit was maintained without great difficulties until the summer of 1982, when 36 per cent of debts had to be renegotiated. The European creditors, assembled at the Paris Club, played a central role in the three renegotiation processes between 1982 to 1985. Cuba's most pressing debt, amounting to 380 million pesos – approximately 10.5 per cent of the total – was with Spain.[23] Next came, in order of importance, France, Italy and the UK which represented overall around 11 per cent of the total. The

Table 3.8   Sample of Western European countries supplying complete plants to Cuba (in percentages)

	1975	1980	1988
Selected countries of Western Europe	42.5	7.5	11.4

Source: CEE, *Anuario Estadístico de Cuba*, 1988, pp. 489–91.

Table 3.9   Main credits granted to Cuba by Western European countries (in million dollars)

	Amount	Date
Euromarket	617	From 1973 to 1978
Spain	900	1974
UK	988	1974 and 1975
France	350	1975
Sweden	33	From 1973 to 1975
Italy	35	1975
Switzerland	15	–
TOTAL	2,938	

Sources: Morris H. Morley, *Imperial State and Revolution*, New York, Cambridge University Press, 1987, p. 271; see Mesa-Lago, *The Economy of Socialist Cuba*, Albuquerque, University of Mexico Press, 1981, p. 104.

results of the renegotiation processes were positive for Cuba, with the main creditors assuming constructive positions during these negotiations until 1985.[24] However, the liquidity crisis that the Cuban economy had to face in 1986 made it necessary to ask the creditors for a rescheduling of the payments; a petition which did not meet with the creditors' approval.[25] Thus, the European creditors, joining the countries of other areas, adopted a strict position, drastically reducing the possibilities of finding an acceptable solution for Cuba in relation to the payment of her debt. However, the search for more flexible solutions for the renegotiation of the external debt was agreed by the IV Congress of the Cuban Communist Party.[26] The available data about the evolution of this problem during 1991 suggest that Cuba is exploring possible solutions with some British businessmen in order to renegotiate the debts by means of joint ventures, or as a discountable part of the Cuban exports. Nevertheless, such an adverse situation did not prevent the Cuban government from signing an agreement in 1986 for a clearing payment concerning the nationalisation of some Spanish properties in Cuba.[27]

Prospects for future economic relations between Cuba and Western Europe

Economic relations with Western Europe have played a significant role since 1959 in various ways. On the one hand, the main European countries withstood American pressures to join the blockade against Cuba, adopting an independent position for different reasons.[28] This enabled the country to have access to those supplies that were needed to guarantee its survival at a crucial moment. The commercial and credit flows that came from Western Europe complemented those supplies provided by socialist countries, and helped sustain the ongoing process of economic development. This trend offers some possibilities for the recovery of the economic links with Western Europe.

An analysis of the prospects for the Cuban economy at present could begin with an assessment of those factors which favour development and of the restrictions which the country faces to achieve this.[29] Amongst those factors that have a positive influence on Cuba's development would be:

- The technical and professional level of labour resources.
- The industrial production capacity created.
- The infrastructure development level reached.
- The satisfaction of social needs.
- The people's solidarity and majority political support for the government and its economic and social programmes.

The fundamental restrictions which Cuba has to face could be summarised as follows:

• The adverse foreign financial balance, basically related to the trade balance deficit and the external debt service.
• The effects of the economic blockade by the US.
• The effects of the changes that the economic policies of Eastern Europe and the former USSR are currently undergoing.
• The adverse internal financial balance and the inflation pressures it entails.
• The low efficiency of the country's economic administration.

An analysis of the factors that influence the current development of Cuba shows that the necessary conditions have been created to enable the country to overcome the structural and economic limitations that have slowed down its progress up to the present. In effect, the high technical and professional level of the available labour resources makes it possible to engage in production with a high value-added potential – including some sectors of advanced technology – for which the necessary industrial installations are already available.

These elements are complemented by an energy and distribution network infrastructure (which is being speedily completed) within the agricultural sector. Such an infrastructure guarantees the necessary conditions for more efficient economic performance. Likewise, the level reached with regard to the satisfaction of social needs, added to the solidarity and political support of the people, is a positive factor. Provided the potential is appropriately developed it should be possible to overcome the limitations placed on the country's development.

To face the adverse external financial balance the country has begun to create the necessary conditions to earn freely convertible currency – assuming that the external credit situation will not suffer essential changes in the short run, and that the US economic blockade against Cuba will continue.

Resources have been concentrated within those sectors characterised by high rates of recovery of investments such as tourism, and in a combined policy of expansion of exports and contraction of imports in freely convertible currency.

In relation to tourism, the number of tourists reached in 1991 was 400 thousand. They contributed an income of more than 300 million dollars.[30] According to different sources, it is hoped that, by the end of the century, the figure will rise to 1.5 million tourists, who will contribute an approximate income of 1000 million dollars. With regard to the exports expansion policy, Cuba plans to increase traditional exports such as nickel, citrus and sugar – including its by-products – as well as biotechnological products[31] and electric components.[32]

Apart from this the changes that are taking place in relation to the economic policies of Eastern Europe and the former USSR have, in the short run, a restrictive effect on the economic development of the country. Indeed, such changes entail a modification of the preferential pattern on which their structure was based in the past and the adoption of a trade policy based on world market prices.

Nevertheless, it needs to be borne in mind that the impact of the most radical changes occurring in Eastern Europe will only affect 15 per cent of the Cuban foreign trade. In the case of the USSR, which represented 70 per cent of this trade, the process of change will not produce such an abrupt break, at least in the short run.[33] The major difficulties may derive from those internal economic difficulties which the former USSR has been facing since 1990 and which have been having negative repercussions on Cuba since the summer of 1990. Despite these difficulties, there is still a reasonable basis enabling Cuba to maintain its traditional exports to the states of the former USSR, which is estimated to be 2 million dollars per annum.[34] New export products such as pharmaceutical and medical products with a biotechnological base should offer good possibilities.

Measures have also been taken to expand import substitution, especially in the area of food products and spare parts for machinery and consumer durables.[35] It is also hoped this will stimulate a savings policy amongst the people, and reduce public expenditure. Finally, the restructuring of the economic administrative system through an adequate combination of material and moral stimuli – on which Cuba is presently working – should improve economic efficiency within the country.

To sum up, the fundamental strategy that characterises, in the short run, the development of Cuban society comprises the implementation of a food programme and of a further programme for the acquisition of freely convertible currency, all this within the framework of a long-term selective scheme of industrialisation.

A balance sheet for future economic relations with Western Europe

Positive factors

1) New policies are being implemented with a view to overcoming obstacles to the renegotiation of the external debt. Some acceptable solutions have been reached so creating the prerequisites for improving Cuba's external relations.

2) A policy of encouraging foreign investments which will benefit all

parties, especially in the tourist sector where Spanish investment is already significant. By the end of 1991 some 50 joint ventures in different areas had been established with a further 200 proposals under consideration.[36]

3) The promotion and diversification of the exports policy, as well as a greater flexibility in the administration of foreign trade, which put Cuba in a more favourable position for future negotiations with Western Europe.

4) The disappearance of Cuba's traditional markets in Eastern Europe and the former USSR, the continuation of the US blockade and the geographical distance of Japan, underlines the increasing importance of Western Europe to Cuba's immediate economic and commercial future.

Negative factors

1) The attempt by some European powers to obtain political concessions in return for economic co-operation. Not only is this unacceptable *vis-à-vis* national sovereignty but it does not augur well for future developments.

2) The intransigence of some European creditors who refuse to grant the slightest financial facility to Cuba, unaware of the tremendous economic repercussions that the collapse of the Soviet bloc (and especially the CMEA) has had on Cuba.

3) The double protectionist policy that the EC has been applying to Cuba, both as an underdeveloped country (Cuba is not a member of Lomé) and as a socialist state. This policy does not show any sign of being modified in the immediate future.

Nevertheless, considering these factors we believe there is cause for optimism and that we are justified in hoping for an improvement in the future economic relations between Cuba and Western Europe.

*Edited from the original text and from the translation by Conchita Diéz Medrano.

Notes

1   With regard to this point I have based my argument on my book *Estrategía del desarrollo económico en Cuba*, La Habana, Ed. Ciencias Sociales, 1990, capítulo 4.

2   See J.L. Rodríguez, 'La economía neocolonial cubana', *Cuba Socialista*, No. 37, 1989, 122.

3   Estimated in terms of the gross material product at constant prices in 1965. See

J.L. Rodríguez, *Estrategía*, statistical appendix no. 2, and CEE, *La Economía Cubana en 1989*, pp. 3, 10, 24–25.

4   This index has been calculated from the relation between the volume of foreign trade and the value of the overall social product at current prices. See *Estrategía*, pp. 282, 290; BNC., *Informe Económico*, La Habana, Junio 1990, p. 14, and CEE., *Anuario Estadístico de Cuba*, 1988, p. 989. However, this coefficient has a limited value in the analysis, for if one considers it at constant prices, the sensibility to external factors does not seem to vary significantly in the last 30 years. On this point, see A. Zimbalist's essay included in this book.

5   See CEE, *Anuario Estadístico de Cuba*, 1988, p. 410 and BNC, *Informe Económico*, p. 14.

6   See Miguel de Figueras, *Análisis de las políticas de industrialización en Cuba en el período revolucionario y proyecciones futuras*, CIEI: Universidad de La Habana, 1990, pp. 12–13, and his *Proyectos idóneos para dinamizar la cooperación productiva y tecnológica de Cuba con otros países de América Latina y el Caribe*, CECE, 1991, p. 16.

7   The Cuban government has pointed out on several occasions that a participation of non-socialist countries in the commercial exchange ranging from 20 to 25 per cent is to be considered acceptable.

8   See J.L. Rodríguez, 'Economic Relations Between Cuba and Eastern Europe: Present Situation and Possible Developments', in H. Michael Erisman and John M. Kirk (eds) *Cuban Foreign Policy Confronts a New International Order*, Boulder and London: Lynne Rienner, 1991, as well as the author's estimates for 1989–90.

9   Around 15 per cent of the gross industrial production of Cuba is carried out in companies created with Soviet collaboration. See V. Alvarez, 'Colaboración soviética. Influencia en el desarrollo industrial cubano', *Colaboración Internacional*, No. 1, 1989, p. 15.

10   The calculation in dollars does not necessarily mean that the credit has been granted in this currency. See Eric Baklanoff, 'International Economic Relations', in C. Mesa-Lago (eds), *Revolutionary Change in Cuba*, Pittsburgh, 1971.

11   See Fidel Castro, *La Revolución de Octubre y la Revolución Cubana. Discurso 1959–1977*, La Habana, Ediciones del DOR del CC del PCC, 1977, pp. 220–33, and BNC, *Informe Económico*, Febrero, 1985, p. 3. According to Soviet sources, the Cuban debt to the USSR reached approximately 17,212 million pesos in 1989, even though its increase during the last decade is estimated to be higher than 60 per cent owing to the worsening of the exchange terms relation between Cuba and the USSR. See José Luís Rodríguez, *ibid*.

12   See Morris H. Morley, *Imperial State and Revolution*, New York, C.U.P., 1987, p. 271, and Carmelo Mesa-Lago, *The Economy of Socialist Cuba*, Alburquerque, University of New Mexico Press, 1981, p. 104.

13   See BNC, *Informe Económico*, La Habana, agosto 1982, p. 12, and *Cuba Business*, Vol. 5(3), 1991, p. 14.

14   See A.R.M. Ritter, 'El problema de la deuda de Cuba en monedas convertibles', *Revista de la CEPAL*, No. 36, diciembre, 1988.

15   During the colonial period the geographical orientation of Cuba's foreign trade was much more balanced. However, the American predominance was first felt in the 1820s, and then became fully dominant during the first decades of the present century.

16   The data concerning this particular point were collected from CEE's *Anuario*

Estadístico de Cuba, 1988 and 1989, Capítulo XI, unless otherwise indicated.

17 I am referring here to the agreements reached by the USA with France in 1981, Italy in 1982, Japan and Holland in 1983, and the FRG in 1984, through which these countries guarantee that the stainless steel they export does not contain nickel coming from Cuba. See J.L. Rodríguez, *Crítica a nuestros críticos*, La Habana, Ed. Ciencias Sociales, 1988, p. 91.

18 An analysis of the economic relations between Cuba and Spain can be found in Alberto Recarte, *Cuba: economía y poder 1959–1980*, Madrid, Ed. Alianza, 1980, capítulo 6, and in Enrique Palazuelos, *La economía de Cuba – (II) Las relaciones económicas entre Cuba y Espana*, Madrid, Fundación Banco Exterior, 1986.

19 As a whole, this indicator shows a worsening of 41.4 per cent from 1975 to 1988. See UNCTAD, *Handbook of international trade and development statistics 1989*, New York, 1990, p. 542, and J.L. Rodríguez, *ibid.*, p. 51.

20 See CEE, *Anuario Estadístico de Cuba*, 1989, p. 396.

21 See Carmelo Mesa-Lago, *The Economy of Socialist Cuba*, p. 98, and Gareth Jenkins' essay included in this book.

22 The annual average economic growth rate was 7.7 per cent between 1971 and 1975, an average calculated in terms of the total material product. Such an average has been the highest achieved during the last 30 years. See J.L. Rodríguez, *Estrategías del desarrollo económico en Cuba*, p. 142.

23 See Enrique Palazuelos, p. 151. In 1991 the debt to Spain reached 1,235 million US dollars according to *ABC*. See *ANSA*, Madrid, 5 Enero 1992.

24 See the results of the renegociation processes in A.R.M. Ritter, pp. 129–30.

25 See Chapter 10 in this book by Gareth Jenkins.

26 With regard to this subject, I quote what was then pointed out: 'One of the most complex problems that we have to face at this crucial moment when we are to stimulate our foreign economic relations is our need to explore solutions to the debt contracted by Cuba, especially with regard to several Latin American countries and other creditors that have demonstrated a willingness to find acceptable solutions for all the interested parties. In this respect, Cuba would be willing to consider flexible renegotiations involving new ways of payment, as long as these are reasonable and acceptable solutions for both creditors and debtors.' See 'Resolución sobre el desarrollo económico del país', *Granma*, 17-X-91, 3.

27 Similar agreements were signed with France and Switzerland in 1967. See J. Domínguez, *To Make a World Safe for Revolution*, Cambridge, Massachusetts, Harvard University Press, 1989, pp. 190–91.

28 One may assume that, especially in the 1960s, strong political motivations were involved in the case of France and Spain, while for other countries the economic advantages of some significance were at the forefront at a moment of challenge to North American hegemony. See Morris H. Morley, chapters 5 and 6.

29 See J.L. Rodríguez and Mario Fernández, *El desarrollo económico de la Revolución Cubana: estrategia y política económica: 1959–89*, Canada: Halifax, 1989, pp. 13–20. Paper delivered at the seminar 'Thirty Years of the Cuban Revolution: An Assessment', November 1–4, 1989.

30 See IPS, *Resumen anual económico Cuba 1991*, enero 1992, p. 10, and Ramón Martín, 'Risas . . pero espinas también', in *Tribuna del Economista*, No. 7, diciembre 1989, p. 12.

31 The sale to Brazil of 10 million doses of the vaccine against meningitis B in the

form of a barter, already reached in 1989 a value of 100 million dollars. See IPS, *Economic Press Service, Boletín Quincenal sobre Cuba,* No. 32, 31 de octubre de 1989, p. 724. In 1991 these sales turned around 82 million dollars, according to Brazilian sources.

32   Non-traditional exports increased at an average annual rate of 18.8 per cent between 1981 and 1985. See Andrew Zimbalist and Claes Brundenius, *The Cuban Economy,* Baltimore and London: The Johns Hopkins University Press, 1989, p. 147.

33   The results of the negotiations that led to these signed agreements concerning the commercial exchange for 1990 and 1991, as well as the predictions for the next years, seem to reinforce this appraisal. In effect, several agreements were signed for 1992 with the Ukraine, Kazakhstan, Russia, Kyrgyzstan and Tajikistan according to the world market conditions.

34   See 'Azúcar que sabe amargo o respuesta a Andrei Kortunov', *América Latina,* URSS, No. 4(90), p. 32.

35   Basically, the Food Programme envisages a speedy development of meat, vegetable, and rice production, as well as a considerable increase of the production of milk, eggs, pork, poultry and fish. Also, and for different reasons, sugar cane activity and sugar production are given priority. Apart from the calorific value of sugar and its importance as the main export of the country, there is a varied range of sugar by-products which includes more than 25 animal food products which contribute to the plans above mentioned. Amongst the fundamental goals of such a programme there is, on the one hand, the production, by the end of the next five-year period, of 100 thousand tonnes of pork per year, 172,500 tonnes of poultry meat, 3,250 million eggs; on the other hand, it aims at self-sufficiency with regard to both rice production and milk products. See also IPS, *Economic Press Service, Boletín Quincenal sobre Cuba,* No. 7, 15 de abril de 1990, pp. 3–5.

36   IPS, January 1992, p. 10.

CHAPTER 4

Perspectives on Cuban development and prospects for the 1990s

Andrew Zimbalist

Introduction

Cuba has long been accustomed to being the only centrally-planned social-ist country in the Western Hemisphere. As Cuba enters the 1990s, it is confronting the prospect of being the only centrally-planned socialist coun-try in the world. To be sure, Cuba still has company in China and North Korea, but Cuba's erstwhile trading partners in the CMEA, with whom Cuba conducted over 85 per cent of its trade in the last years of the 1980s have all moved away from socialism and central planning. Heightened uncertainty as well as the loss of trade preferences face the Cuban economy in the 1990s.

Trade and the Cuban economy

As is true for all small economies, international trade is very important for Cuba. Socialist Cuba's reliance on trade, however, has often been over-stated. First, it is important to note that before the Revolution the Cuban economy had an above average (and rising) dependence on trade for a country of its size and per capita income (Table 4.1).[1]

Second, the comparison of the pre- and post-1959 periods has often been made without making the necessary accounting adjustments to render the figures commensurable. Mesa-Lago, for instance, has compared the pre- and post-revolutionary periods' import shares without adjusting for the fact that Gross Domestic Product (from the Western national income accounting system) is much larger than Gross Material Product (from the CMEA system).[2] As can be appreciated from Table 4.1, when the unadjusted import share is used, it appears that Cuba's import dependence has grown mark-edly during the revolutionary years. The adjusted share, however, suggests similar levels of trade dependence in the 1950s and 1980s. In fact, the adjusted share in the 1980s is slightly below that in the 1950s and this is so

Table 4.1 Estimates of Cuban imports as a share of national income (in percentages)

	Unadjusted share*	Adjusted share**
1952–58	32.8	32.8
1962–69	25.1	16.8
1970–79	33.9	22.7
1980–87	46.8	31.3

* Pre-1959 is as a share of GDP. Post-1959 is as a share of '*ingreso nacional disponible*', which is essentially GDP minus non-material services (NMS) and depreciation. NMS has been estimated by Zimbalist and Brundenius to equal 26.5 per cent of GDP in Cuba in 1981 (1989, p. 43).
** Post-1959 based on estimated GDP, including NMS and depreciation (estimated at 10 per cent of GDP). It, however, does not adjust for the fact that imports are measured in current prices and GDP is largely in constant prices.

Sources: Ismael Zuaznabar, *La economía cubana en la década del 50*, Habana: Editorial de Ciencias Sociales, 1986, Ch. 7; Claes Brundenius, *Revolutionary Cuba: The Challenge of Growth with Equity*, 1984, p. 32; *Anuario Estadístico de Cuba, 1987*, p. 102; Banco Nacional de Cuba, *Memorias, 1955–56*, p. 119 and *Memorias, 1957–58*, p. 183. Andrew Zimbalist and Claes Brundenius, *The Cuban Economy: Measurement and Analysis of Socialist Performance*, Baltimore: Johns Hopkins University Press, 1989, Ch. 4.

even though it does not adjust for the upward bias resulting from import values being in current prices while GDP estimates are basically in constant prices. In both the adjusted and unadjusted series, one notes a sharp initial drop in import shares, as Cuba realigned its trading partners during the 1960s, and then a distinct upward trend.

Although higher import shares are associated with trade dependence, higher shares *per se* do not denote economic weakness. To be sure, conventional trade theory would argue that higher import shares are consistent with greater international specialisation and, thus, represent a positive development. To some extent, this is the case for Cuba, but it must also be noted that Cuba's exports did not keep up with its growing imports and this led to growing foreign indebtedness, hardly a salutary development. The primary point here, however, is that Cuba's increasing import share enhanced Cuba's vulnerability to late-1980s' perturbations in its trading relationships. In a similar sense, it can be argued that Cuba's vulnerability to the post-1960 US economic blockade was great and, hence, the costs of this blockade were extremely high.[3]

Trading partners

Despite its overwhelming quantitative importance, trade with the CMEA was never a qualitative replacement for trade lost with the US since 1960. Cuba's 1959 machine park was made in the US and Cuba required then, as it does now, Western technology and parts to keep its economy running. Despite limitations, many imposed by the politics of the US blockade, Western Europe, Canada and Japan have stepped in at crucial junctures with vital products to provide a lifeline for the Cuban economy.[4]

After a recession during 1986–87, the Cuban economy resumed growth (albeit very modest) during 1988–89. The newest impediment to Cuban economic performance emerged not from doctrinal disputes with Gorbachev or Eastern Europe but from supply disruptions resulting from transitional economic policies and socio-political instability within the CMEA.[5] Delays in the shipment of oil, wood, wheat, paper and other goods exacerbated an already severely bottlenecked Cuban economy.[6] With the 1990–91 collapse of the CMEA and dissolution of the USSR, Cuba has put renewed emphasis on developing deeper trade ties with Latin America and China as well as the developed market economies of Western Europe, Canada and Japan.[7]

Further, the US invasion of Panama in late December 1989 has curbed Cuba's use of front companies in Panama's Colon Free Zone to trade in US goods. I estimate that Cuba imported an average of roughly $6 million yearly through these companies during 1986–88.[8] Although it is difficult to predict at this point how much of a crackdown on this activity the US will impose, it is probable that the Cubans will be able to turn to other free trade zones in the Caribbean to re-establish some of this trade. More difficult to replace would be the trade between Cuba and subsidiaries of US companies based in third countries. This trade has been allowed since 1975 and amounted to an annual average of approximately $250 million during 1982–87.[9] In 1989, however, Senator Connie Mack of Florida introduced an amendment to an appropriations bill to prohibit such trade. The Mack measure failed to carry in 1989, was vetoed by President Bush in 1990 under pressure from OECD countries, but the Senator reintroduced it in 1991. The measure's dubious standing in international law and political pressure from a variety of countries make it unlikely that the Mack proposal will be implemented.

Although it is difficult to believe that the counterproductive US blockade of Cuba will resist the forces of reason indefinitely, as the 1990s begin US/Cuba relations seem to be more tense than ever before. As long as the blockade persists and with the collapse of CMEA the potential role of an economically integrated Western Europe in Cuban economic development will loom large.

Aid and debt

Along with CMEA trade came preferential prices and development aid. Soviet aid to Cuba has been of extraordinary importance in promoting the Cuban economy. The aid has taken the form *inter alia* of payments for Cuban sugar at considerably above world market prices since the mid-1970s, of charges for Soviet petroleum considerably below world prices until 1986, of project aid and balance of payments loans. While the centrality of Soviet aid cannot be denied, its magnitude has been vastly overstated by Western sources. The US CIA has furnished the Western media with faulty estimates that rely on artificially inflated exchange rates, untenable assumptions about opportunity costs and suppression of the facts that Cuba must buy often overpriced, shoddy Soviet goods with the lion's share of Soviet sugar payments.[10] More reasonable estimates would show Soviet aid to Cuba to be at the upper end of foreign aid to Latin American countries, taken as a share of national income. If one also included the implicit aid in the Soviet's repeatedly delaying the repayment date for Cuban debt (around 10 billion roubles), then Soviet aid to Cuba would surpass Western aid to other Latin American economies on a per capita or GDP share basis, with the exception of Puerto Rico. However, before making inferences about the Cuban economy's ability to sustain itself without outside aid, it is well to remember both the tremendous cost of the US blockade and the proportionately extravagant foreign aid programme to other developing countries maintained by the Cubans.[11]

To be sure, overall Soviet price subsidies have diminished in recent years. Since 1976 Cuba's price for Soviet oil has been set equal to the average of the five previous years on the world market. Until 1986, this meant that Cuba was paying below the world price; however between 1986 and 1990 the Cubans paid an average 27.02 pesos per barrel for Soviet oil which was considerably above the world price (measured at official exchange rates). In fact, from 1980 to 1991 the terms of trade with the Soviet Union turned against the Cubans.[12]

Cuba's increasing difficulties with the CMEA had been compounded by shrinking Western markets and growing hard currency debt. Unlike the rest of Latin America, however, the Cuban economy grew strongly during 1980–85. This was not because Cuba avoided building up a sizeable debt during the 1970s. It did. It was because, rather than borrowing money and then squandering it in capital flight or luxury imports, Cuba used the loan capital to invest in productive assets. By 1985–86, however, a combination of external factors interrupted Cuba's growth and saddled the island with an increasingly acute foreign exchange crisis. Cuban hard currency imports in nominal terms were one-third below the 1985 level in 1987 and 1988; in real terms the drop was closer to 50 per cent. Medium- and long-term debt service payments have been irregular since 1986 and no new rescheduling agreement with Cuba's creditors has been reached in the last four years. By the end of 1991, hard currency debt exceeded $7 billion. Together with Cuba's debt to the CMEA, this placed Cuba among Latin America's more heavily indebted nations in per capita terms.

Excepting short-term supplier's credits, new hard currency loans have not been forthcoming since 1985. Instead, Cuba has attempted to lure direct foreign investment, but given the US blockade foreign capital has been reluctant to invest in Cuba except in the tourist sector.[13] Debt relief in the form of rescheduling and fresh loans from Western Europe and Japan will be important ingredients to any prospective recovery.

The domestic economy

Just as it is a mistake when some analysts point to Castro's rectification campaign as the cause of Cuba's economic malaise and ignore the importance of international economic forces, it would be a mistake to ignore the issues of domestic economic planning and management in assessing the prospects for the Cuban economy in the 1990s.

Cuba did not have stable institutions of economic planning until the late-1970s. Indeed, Cuba's first five-year plan did not come until 1976–80. The gradual introduction of Cuba's new planning system, the SDPE (*Sistema de Dirección y Planificacíon de La Economía*), was begun in 1977.[14] The SDPE basically was modelled after the 1965 Soviet reforms. It attempts to 1) put enterprises on a self-financing basis, 2) introduce a profitability criterion with its corresponding incentives, and 3) promote decentralisation, organisational coherence and efficiency. As with the earlier Soviet reform, it has met with the obstacles *inter alia* of bureaucratic resistance, pervasive shortages and an irrational price structure. Possibilities for decentralised decision-making in Cuba have also been constrained by the inadequate supply of skilled managerial and technical labour. Moreover, Cuba confronted additional difficulties in adapting the Soviet-styled reform to Cuban political culture. The Cubans began tinkering with their new system almost from the outset.

A central theme of the SDPE was decentralisation. By putting enterprises on a self-financing scheme and introducing profit-sharing, enterprises were supposed to be exercising increasing autonomy from the centre. This, in turn, was to promote efficiency. Nominal self-financing and profit-sharing by themselves, however, did little, if anything, to enhance the scope of enterprise decision-making. Among other things, in the context of centrally fixed prices, centrally determined investments, and extensive input shortages, these mechanisms did not alter the basic mode of operation of

Cuban planning. With prices centrally set every five or more years, they were not a reliably rational guide to production or allocation choices; nor could they systematically identify, through a profitability index, well-managed enterprises. With shortages commonplace, otherwise efficient enterprises were often thwarted in their production efforts because of non-delivery, untimely delivery, or delivery of improperly specified, poor quality inputs. Bottle-necks and planning imperfections, in turn, necessitated amendments to the plan after the beginning of the year – often raising an enterprise's output target without increasing its supply of raw materials.

Enterprises, behaving rationally in this environment, hoarded inputs, thereby aggravating the shortage problem. Since the behaviour of profits was fickle because of these and other factors, the planning authorities were compelled to limit, on equity grounds alone, the extent of profit retention and distribution, thus weakening the incentive effect. And since profits thrived in certain enterprises despite the absence of properly specified, high quality production, the planner devised new administrative regulations to control this behaviour. In the end, the profitability algorithm became hopelessly complicated and the incentive mechanism debilitated. Since the centre decided upon what investment projects were to be undertaken, the fact that enterprises paid for increasing shares of investment costs out of their bank funds rather than state budget funds (the share of enterprise financed investments in total investment financing in Cuba rose from 1 per cent in 1981 to 30 per cent in 1985) did not imply a substantive decentralisation of capital allocation.[15]

To be sure, in at least one important respect the SDPE represented further centralisation of the planning system. Prior to 1976, the system of material supplies was carried out by consolidated enterprises. Subsequently, most material balances came to be implemented by the central planning board (Juceplan) or the central state committee on technical-material supplies (Ceatm).

The SDPE, then, like the 1965 Soviet economic reforms, did not bring a significant change in underlying centralisation of decision-making in the economic mechanism. There were, however, peripheral changes which accompanied the SDPE, many introduced in an effort to adapt the Soviet centralised model to Cuban conditions, that did increase the flexibility of the system and allow for some decentralisation of decision-making. Among these new policies was the post-1976 system of popular power which controlled the management of locally oriented service and production enterprises. In the mid-1980s, such enterprises amounted to 34 per cent of all Cuban enterprises. The local budgets of Popular Power grew from 21 per cent of the total state budget in 1978, to 26 per cent in 1980, to 30 per cent in 1982 and 33 per cent in 1984. The local budget share in the Soviet Union in 1980 was 17.1 per cent.[16]

Another policy allowed for enterprises to make their own contracts for products which were not in the nomenclatura and were not centrally balanced. There has also been encouragement for the development of 'secondary' (non-plan) production, once the plan is fulfilled. Further, the realisation that there were growing stocks of unused inputs within enterprises led to the practice of 'Resource Fairs' where enterprises traded freely and directly with each other, first organised by the Ceatm in 1979. The Fairs of 1979 and 1980 witnessed the sale of 40 million pesos of inputs. Inventory sales of production inputs by enterprises have continued to grow. In October of 1982 the President of Juceplan reported that some 500 million pesos of such resources had already been identified.[17] In May 1985, at the conclusion of the Fourth Plenary on the SDPE, the judgement was reached that the Ceatm was still allocating too many products and the number should be significantly reduced, allowing enterprises to contract directly with each other for these products.[18] In fact, the degree of centralisation contemplated in the Soviet-designed system was never approached in Cuba, as it was resisted by sectoral and provincial planning bodies.

Other measures of decentralisation were the strengthening of the Cuban Institute of Internal Demand, the introduction of free labour contracting in 1980, and an increasing acceptance of private productive and service activity – most notably housing construction co-operatives and free farmers' markets.[19] There was also some light manufacturing by artisans and enterprises were permitted to use up to 30 per cent of their profits to make input purchases from the private sector. Free farmers' markets were opened in 1980. Sales of fresh vegetables and fruits grew rapidly until the government crack-down on 'abuses' (exorbitant prices, excessive middle-person profits, resource diversion from the state sector, etc.) in February 1982. Sales began to grow again after the promulgation of new regulations (20 per cent sales tax, progressive income tax on private farmer income from 5 to 20 per cent, and the expansion of the state-controlled parallel market to compete with the farmers' markets) in May of 1983. However, new abuses, more serious diversion of resources from state uses, and reported incomes above 50,000 pesos for truckers, wholesalers and some farmers, led to the indefinite closing of these markets in May 1986. Although such free market sales of produce were permitted elsewhere in the Soviet bloc, private plots (except for Poland) tended to be no larger than one-quarter or one-half a hectare. In Cuba, such plots typically range from 20 to over 60 hectares. Although private farmers are required to deliver a share of their output to the state, actual deliveries are often modest relative to output leaving substantial produce to be consumed locally or marketed independently. Castro, for instance, charged that some private farmers delivered no more than 10 per cent of their output to the state.[20] Thus, the potential for economic and political disruption emerging from the private agricultural sector in Cuba *prima facie* was greater than elsewhere in the CMEA.

Nevertheless, these decentralising measures taken together did not alter the key dynamic of Cuban planning. Prior to the beginning of the rectification campaign in April 1986, it was apparent from various government documents and speeches that the need for further decentralisation and greater worker participation was clearly perceived.[21] The documents of the Fourth Plenary evaluating the SDPE, held in May 1985, in particular, laid out a series of decentralising measures that the Cubans intended to carry out. With the severe difficulties concerning foreign exchange earnings that Cuba began to experience around that time, along with the growing excess of uncompleted investment projects, however, resources became too scarce to sustain the momentum toward decentralisation and the state tightened its grip on the economy in order to economise on the use of foreign exchange as well as to bring existing investment projects to successful completion.

Unintended or profligate use of resources in both the private and public spheres came under increasing scrutiny, as did the lack of co-ordination among sectoral ministries of the economy and among state planning institutions (e.g., the State Committee on Finances, the State Price Committee, the National Bank, Juceplan). Together with the difficulties of increasing labour indiscipline (exacerbated by shortages of inputs and consumer goods), enterprise overstaffing and corruption among officials, these problems brought on the rectification campaign in early 1986. Market-oriented decentralisation was put on hold, although some efforts at administrative decentralisation have continued.

Characterising the present period

There is no question but that the rectification campaign brought a halt to the previous trend toward liberalisation and increased emphasis on material incentives. Many prominent interpreters of Cuban reality, however, have exaggerated the nature and meaning of this shift, either by misapprehending the substance of the SDPE or by misconstruing the new policies. Both Jorge Pérez-López and Jorge Domínguez, for instance, claimed that the SDPE itself represented market socialism and the trimestral publication of Radio Martí declared the dissolution of the SDPE with the rectification campaign.[22] Pérez-López also charged that Cuba had suspended worker productivity bonuses.[23] Mesa-Lago wrote that most urban private sector activity had been eliminated.[24] Pérez-López, Domínguez, Mesa-Lago and others have compared the rectification campaign to the late-1960s, a period when there were no individual bonuses, no overtime pay, no unified central plan, no cost accounting, no national budget and little record keeping.[25]

The reality is different. As already noted, the SDPE did not approach market socialism and its basic structure is still intact. Worker productivity bonuses were never as prominent in Cuba as elsewhere in the CMEA, yet they are still very much in evidence. Urban private sector activity has come under increasing regulation but it is still permitted. None of the salient characteristics of the late-1960s economy are present in the rectification campaign, although one can readily observe the strong hand of Fidel Castro in each period.

In my view, the best way to interpret the initiation of the rectification campaign is as a moratorium/retrenchment in the reform cycle of a centrally planned economy (cpe). Periods of liberalisation in cpe's inevitably generate economic, political and social tensions as well as outcomes that are antithetical to the stated goals of socialist society. It is natural, if not inevitable, that liberalisation policies provoke periods of reassessment and retrenchment, as experienced in Hungary and China. Of course, the nature, timing and intensity of the cycle depends on factors peculiar to each country and to the international political and economic climate.

The policies of rectification

A   Balancing material and moral incentives

Material incentives are problematic in centrally planned, shortage-type economies. Not only are there ideological concerns with inequality and attitude, but there are limits to motivating workers and managers with more money if there are not desirable goods available for purchase. These limits, of course, become more severe for cpe's with lower levels of economic development, especially during times of severe foreign exchange constraints. Another difficulty with material incentives at the workplace affects market and planned economies alike: measuring individual contribution to the quantity and quality of output is never straightforward. Each of these problems was pertinent to the Cuban situation in the mid-1980s.

Three types of material incentives for workers are used in Cuba: *normas* or piece-rates; *primas* or bonuses; and, *premios* or profit-sharing. The details of their operation are peripheral to my main concern.[26] It is, however, relevant to note the following.

Normas were applied to 1.2 million workers (37.2 per cent of the labour force) at the end of 1985. Three-quarters of the *normas* were 'elementary', i.e., not determined by a time-and-motion study. Income paid for over-fulfilment of *normas* grew from 121.7 million pesos or 3.9 per cent of worker income on average in 1980 to 274.5 million pesos or 6.0 per cent of worker income in 1985. *Primas* were introduced experimentally in 1979 and then gradually applied throughout the economy in 1980. Varieties of *primas* abound in Cuba, but most involve giving a bonus to a group of workers for increasing exports, saving on raw materials or energy, over-fulfilling quality or quantity targets, or developing new products. The value of *primas* paid out grew steadily from 14 million pesos in 1980 to 90.7 million in 1985, the latter figure still only representing 1.9 per cent of the basic wage. *Premios* were introduced experimentally in 1979. By 1985 total *premio* payments amounted to 71.1 million pesos or 1.6 per cent of the basic wage. Among other things, the extension of *premios* was frustrated by Cuba's system of administered prices, making the meaning of profit or any financial indicator dubious. Taken together, the three material incentives grew rapidly during the early-1980s but still only accounted for 10.6 per cent on average of the basic wage in 1985, considerably below elsewhere in the CMEA.[27]

In addition to the problems mentioned above, it was discovered that often the three incentives overlapped, paying the worker twice or thrice for the same work, e.g., sugar mill workers paid for exceeding their *norma*, working overtime and increasing exports. Hence, to avoid this duplication many *primas*, especially those related to export production, have been curtailed. In other cases, incentives were applied that had little justification, such as mechanics paid five times for repairing the same piece of machinery or radio announcers working on piece-rates. In yet other cases, elementary *normas*, set with the participation of the affected workers, were too low. In 1986, more than one-third of all workers with *normas* produced over 130 per cent of their rate.[28] In these instances, the design of certain incentives and output goals were re-evaluated. Overall, rectification brought a stream-lining of the three incentive systems, but each scheme was maintained.

At the same time, recognising the limitations of material incentives in fostering productivity increases, Castro sought to re-emphasise moral in-centives and voluntary labour. Voluntary labour does indeed seem to have been reinvigorated, but the efficacy of moral incentives at the workplace is more difficult to evaluate. Political exhortations and moral incentives will not successfully motivate workers over a sustained period, especially in the absence of more democratic decision-making practices.

In sum, although rectification has signified an effort to rebalance the importance of moral vs. material incentives, the basic incentive structure of the SDPE has been retained. Hence, comparisons between rectification and the late-1960s are overblown.

B Reducing the scope of private sector activity

The most important policy of rectification regarding private activity was the abolition of the free peasant markets in May of 1986. As noted above, the leadership perceived a plethora of threats from these markets. Private farmers were enriching themselves, thus, among other things, dispiriting the membership on the newly-formed co-operative farms. Castro gave examples of a farmer who made 50,000 pesos from planting a hectare of garlic and of another who hired four workers and owned two trucks and earned 150,000 pesos. Castro claimed that it was virtually impossible to collect taxes effectively on these high peasant incomes. Urban workers and consumers were supposedly not only demoralised by the easy money made by private farmers but also indignant at the astronomical prices they were obliged to pay for fresh produce on these markets. More significantly, the operation of these markets entailed a substantial diversion of resources (use of trucks, shirking at work or leaving early, pilfering of gasoline, insecticides, etc.) away from the state plan and toward the private sector. They also prompted farmers to lower deliveries to the state of exportable produce in order to sell it at better prices on the free markets. With rectification, the state attempted to replace these markets, which accounted for less than 5 per cent of food sales according to official figures, by expanding the state run parallel markets. Also, a new distribution enterprise, Frutas Selectas, was set up and farmers were offered higher prices for sales to the state. To say the least, this new arrangement has created considerable inconvenience for large numbers of consumers who were forced to locate new sources of supply for many food items.[29]

Another significant measure was to regulate the sale of private housing. The 1984 housing law provided for converting all tenants into home owners (it was already the case that over 60 per cent of dwellers owned their homes) within 20 years. The state had already sanctioned private home construction and greatly eased private access to building materials. The result was twofold: a construction boom with private construction accounting for one-third of new houses in the 1980s and a speculation boom with sky-rocketing prices for real estate. To curb the latter and its beneficiaries, the state decreed that all housing sales would have to pass through a state agency that would regulate prices. The 1984 housing law itself was left intact.

Other private sector activity came under tighter state regulation and, thus, the scope of some activities was reduced. The principal new restriction was that private service workers (plumbers, electricians, mechanics, etc.), artisans, street vendors, taxi drivers and so on must be licensed and must receive all materials through a state-issued certificate. That is, the state still recognised that many services can be provided more efficiently by the private sector, but it did not want the success of this sector to be at the expense of diverted resources and pilfered materials. In the spring of 1989, the private advertising section in the popular magazine, *Opina*, which had been curtailed, was reopened. The number of private wage workers and workers for their own account fell from 52.1 thousand in 1985 to 43.2 thousand in 1987 as private non-farm income fell from 102.5 million pesos to 67.8 million pesos, but private non-farm income began to recover in 1988, rising to 80.7 million pesos.[30] Thus, urban private sector activity was reduced, but it was hardly obliterated.

Despite the closing of the peasant markets, private farm income has actually increased from 495.6 million pesos in 1985 to 528.9 million pesos in 1988. Within the private agricultural sector, incomes of workers in producer co-operatives fell from 161.8 million pesos in 1985 to 152.5 million in 1988 while the incomes of individual private farmers expanded from 333.8 million pesos to 376.4 million.[31]

C   Efforts at administrative decentralisation

Although market-oriented decentralisation has for the moment been eschewed, the Cuban government has actively pursued policies aimed at administrative decentralisation. Even though the main architect of the 1975–85 liberalisation policies, Humberto Pérez, was replaced in early 1985 as head of the central planning board, the perception of a torpid, overcentralised system remained and was widespread amongst government economic functionaries and managers. The momentum toward decentralisation, though slowed and redirected, has not been broken.

Several ongoing efforts, such as the formation of production brigades in agricultural and industrial enterprises as well as the formation of and transfer of planning functions to *uniones de empresas* (industrial associations), have continued. Other initiatives are new. In early 1988, following the recommendations of a special commission to study the SDPE, several new procedures were adopted in the planning process.[32] The number of commodities and commodity groups subject to central planning was to be drastically reduced from 2300 to 800.[33] The number of directive indicators to the enterprise was to be cut from an average of 28 to 18.[34] The system of material balances was to be decentralised by 'extending direct ties in order to eliminate intermediaries in the process of elaborating and executing the plan of material and technical supplies'.[35] Concretely, the number of material balances performed by the central state supplies committee, Ceatm, was to be diminished by 382 or by 31 per cent and passed down to the level of the industrial association or the enterprise.[36] Further, according to a February 1989 report of the *Comisión Nacional del Sistema de Dirección de La Economía*, direct supplies contracting was established between enterprises for 518 different products during 1988.[37]

Separately, experiments are being carried out in a variety of sectors that are also intended to promote greater flexibility, enhanced worker participation and more local autonomy. Some initial success has been reported, particularly in the case of 'continuous planning' at the enterprise level. The latter enables the enterprise to draw up a production and input plan based on last year's levels and its expectations for the coming year prior to receiving the plan control figures from the national ministry. Previously, control figures often arrived at the enterprise too late for a serious discussion or for any meaningful amendments to the plan to occur. Not only does 'continuous planning' avoid the last minute rush syndrome, but it allows for some initiative at the enterprise level. It does this, of course, at the expense of a possible loss of co-ordination, but given the failure of the planning authorities to produce a realistic, balanced comprehensive plan in the past it is not clear what if anything is lost by the new method.[38]

Whether these changes lead to improved efficiency is an interesting question to which there is no obvious answer. I remain sceptical that the reforms will alter the behaviour of the system in an appreciable way. None the less, it does seem significant that the efforts at reform are being made because they denote an awareness of the imperative for substantive decentralisation. This awareness, in turn, suggests the eventual return to a course of liberalisation. The timing and extent of such liberalisation, of course, will depend upon political and economic circumstances in Cuba, not the least of which will be the policy preferences and permanence of Fidel Castro.

Why is Cuba different?

Why has Castro not followed the path of marketisation adopted in the Eastern bloc? At one level the answer to this question is obvious. There is little reason a priori for Cuba to be at the same cyclical juncture as the other countries. To be sure, not all the CMEA economies moved at the same pace of reform, nor did they begin with equal degrees of centralisation.[39] With the exception of Yugoslavia, Cuba stood out among its trading partners in Eastern Europe as having the only home-grown revolution. Further, Cuba was among the less developed and smallest of the CMEA economies. Central planning offers many potential advantages in terms of positively gathering and channelling resources for development. The smaller and less complex an economy, the more it lends itself to central planning, and the less likely that central planning will encumber the growth process. Cuba, after all, did not experience the secular growth slow-down of the Soviet Union. On the contrary, the early-1980s were a period of rapid growth for Cuba and between 1970 and 1988 the Cuban annual rate of real growth has been 4.1 per cent versus 1.2 per cent for the rest of Latin America.[40]

What is true, however, as discussed above, is that the Cuban economy stagnated in the second half of the 1980s. In 1986 low sugar prices, plummeting petroleum prices (Cuba's re-export of Soviet petroleum provided roughly 40 per cent of its hard currency earnings during 1983–85), devastation from Hurricane Kate, several consecutive years of intensifying drought, drastic dollar devaluation, the tightening of the US blockade and growing protectionism in Western markets all combined to reduce Cuba's hard currency earnings by $337.1 million, or 27.1 per cent. Cuba responded with a) a programme to promote non-traditional exports and import substitution, b) tighter controls on foreign trade, c) suspension of interest service on the debt, d) an austerity programme to save on foreign exchange, and e) the rectification campaign. On the one hand, the campaign enabled the state to prevent (or, at least, diminish) the diversion of exportable produce to the farmers' markets and of imported materials to the private sector. On the other hand, the campaign signalled a recognition that it would be increasingly difficult to use material incentives to stimulate work effort. The scarcity of hard currency denoted greater shortages of consumer goods and, hence, the absence of a material counterpart to higher peso incomes. Such imbalances are always a problem in shortage-ridden cpe's, but in Cuba during 1986–88 they became particularly acute.

It should also be noted that Castro has not hesitated in the past to be a nonconformist in either economic or political policy. In the late-1960s, for instance, as the Soviet Union was implementing its Liberman reform, Cuba was abolishing cost accounting and material incentives. In the mid- and late-1970s, as Cuba was introducing the Soviet-styled SDPE, the model came under continual criticism in Cuba for being too centralised. At the time, Cuba pioneered in establishing its system of Popular Power with contested local elections and in turning over the management of local enterprises to the newly-elected municipal bodies. Miguel Figueras, Vice-President of Juceplan at the time, commented to the author that between 1977 and 1981 the Cubans were decentralising 15 per cent of the Soviet-styled planning institutions each year.[41] Thus, it was not surprising in early 1986 when Cuban Vice-President, Carlos Rafael Rodríguez, commented favourably upon the early stages of *perestroika* at a CMEA meeting in Bucharest, drawing 'specific attention to what he called the mood of imaginativeness and flexibility now abroad among the Moscow allies, with which he associated the Cuban process'.[42] Castro has also gone against the Soviet grain repeatedly in his political policies.

The rectification campaign, of course, was also motivated by ideological factors. Standard concerns about 'bourgeois' mentality, growing corruption and inequality were joined by the leadership's preoccupation about Cuban youth. Cubans entering the labour force for the first time in the mid-1980s were born after the revolutionary struggle against Batista, after the literacy campaign, after the Bay of Pigs and after the Cuban missile crisis. To many it seemed that they did not have the same emotional commitment to the Revolution and its socialist values. Their formative social years were during a time of ascendancy of material incentives, from 1970 to 1986. The rectification campaign has sought to rebalance material and moral incentives, to transform the incipient materialist ethos and to re-educate Cuban youth. None the less, it is difficult to imagine Castro's exhortations substituting for the historical events listed above or for more democratic institutions.

To argue that the rectification campaign was initially motivated by certain internal economic and ideological problems is not to say that the campaign is sustained solely or chiefly by these same problems. Indeed, it appears that Castro's commitment to his course has rigidified in the last two years as the world has witnessed the tremendous social and political turmoil unleashed by the revolutionary changes in the former Soviet bloc. Castro no doubt has also observed that the path of market-oriented reform of cpe's offers no guarantees and the performance record so far is very poor. The dilemma is that piecemeal and partial measures of reform do not unlock the logic of central planning. On the contrary, by generating contradictory signals and administrative conflict they may do more harm than good. Hence, early measures engender the necessity of subsequent, more fundamental reform. Enterprise autonomy and cost accounting, for instance, make little sense without scarcity prices. In short, economic reform via market decentralisation threatens economic stability and political power.

In the face of repeated US efforts to assassinate Castro, destabilise Cuba's economy and overthrow the regime, Castro – authoritarian by nature anyway – drew the lesson early on that he needed complete control over the political apparatus to withstand outside aggression. Nothing has happened to change Castro's mind or reduce his paranoia about destabilisation from abroad. With this perspective, Castro's renewed intransigence and socialist dogmatism are better understood.

Conclusion

Cuban scholars are not noted for fashioning consensus, much less unanimity. Yet it is unlikely that a Cubanist could be found who would not agree with the proposition that Cuba in 1992 is amidst the worst crisis of the Revolution. It is perhaps arguable that the material situation on the island in 1969 was as difficult as it is today, but back in 1969 the Revolution was young and the Cuban people for the most part were energetic and hopeful. Cuba was then an increasingly accepted and economically integrated member of the large world socialist community.

The proximate cause of Cuba's present predicament is not hard to identify. Cuba has a small and heavily trade-dependent economy. In the presence of the US embargo, Cuba came to depend on the former Soviet trade bloc (CMEA) for over four-fifths of its imports. Without access to the US market, with access to other markets restricted and with imports from the former CMEA countries reduced by over two-thirds, Cuba's economy and its people are struggling to survive.

The government's response to the crisis has been deliberate but inadequate. A number of reforms initiated prior to 1989 are being continued, others are being accelerated and some new programmes are being put in place.[43] The new emphasis on foreign investment and tourism, structural reforms in the operation of foreign trade, and the impossibility of central planning in the presence of ubiquitous supply uncertainties have combined to transform the nature of Cuba's economic mechanism. Despite the promise of some extension of private enterprise and the market in the service sector, however, the needed and more concerted introduction of a broader market mechanism has not been forthcoming.

Cuban imports from Eastern Europe, which accounted for approximately 15 per cent of total Cuban imports, fell by roughly one-half in 1990 and practically disappeared in 1991. Imports from the former Soviet Union, which accounted for over 70 per cent of Cuba's imports, fell by over 30 per cent in 1990 (measured in current prices), and then dropped precipitously in 1991.[44]

A sense of the magnitude and importance of the reduction in Soviet exports to Cuba is conveyed by the following figures. In 1989, Cuba imported $5.52 billion worth of goods from the Soviet Union, including 13.11 million tons of petroleum (8.5 million tons of which was crude oil).[45] The revised trade agreement for 1991 called for CIS (Commonwealth of Independent States, formerly the Soviet Union) exports of $3.363 billion to Cuba, including 10 million tons of petroleum. As of October 1, 1991, however, the CIS had only exported $1.305 billion worth of goods, or 38.8 per cent of the planned yearly total. At this pace, by year's end CIS exports would have reached $1.74 billion. Even this level, however, appears optimistic since the pace of shipments slowed down in September following the aborted Soviet coup in August, and both political events and economic disorder in the former Soviet republics conspired to further decimate deliveries during the last trimester. Some reports out of Cuba indicated that there were no petroleum shipments the entire month of December.[46] But even assuming the trade pace of the first nine months was maintained and the full $1.74 billion of goods arrived in Cuba during 1991, this would represent only 31.5 per cent of the value of Soviet imports two years earlier![47]

The collapse of the CMEA and the economies of Eastern Europe and the Soviet Union together led to a reduction of Cuba's overall imports of almost 60 per cent, or a drop equal to roughly 20 per cent of Cuba's GDP.

Further, since most of the would-be imports are raw materials and intermediate goods, their absence can have a multiplicatively downward effect on production.

For some imports, however, the reduction in domestic output is minimal. For instance, some of the reduced oil imports resulted in more careful use of electricity in the household. Here all that is lost is the value-added from domestic electricity generation – considerably less than the value of lost imports. Overall, we can estimate that an import fall of between 50 and 60 per cent would result in a GDP drop on the order of 30 to 35 per cent between 1989 and 1991.

Conditions are likely to deteriorate further in 1992. Although Soviet aid to Cuba *per se* ceased in 1990, the 1991 trade agreement called for Cuba to receive 22 cents per pound of raw sugar and for Cuba to pay the world market oil price.[48] Whether the 13 cents differential between the spot market and CIS prices is termed aid or not is subject to interpretation. Less than 20 per cent of world sugar sells on the spot market with the rest sold on the basis of preferential medium-term contracts, most with prices considerably above those on the spot market. The US, for instance, buys raw sugar from the Caribbean Basin countries at nearly 22 cents per pound, and the price paid in the European Community is similar. Whether or not the differential is considered to be aid, it is almost certain that any Cuban sugar sold to the former Soviet republics in 1992 will be at a price much closer to the spot market than the 1991 preferential price. Thus, it is likely that instead of receiving roughly 8.3 million tons of oil for the 4 million-odd tons of sugar sold to the Soviet Union in 1991, Cuba can look forward to receiving in the region of 6 million tons of oil (from Russian, Kazakhstan, South American and Middle East producers) for the same 4 million tons of sugar in 1992. Meanwhile, present petroleum and other input shortages can be expected to lower the 1991–92 *zafra* below the already reduced 1990–91 level.[49]

All told, it seems that without new oil Cuba's various export projects do not promise to bring in much more than a billion dollars in additional revenue annually in the coming years. The loss of CMEA trade is far in excess of this and the 1992 reduction of CIS oil deliveries, along with the expected smaller sugar harvest, lower sugar prices and the tightening US blockade, make it unlikely that Cuba will reverse its declining economic fortunes this year. None the less, Cuba has already taken its biggest 'hit', with its GDP in 1991 up to 35 per cent below what it was in 1989. While an additional drop of up to 7 to 12 per cent is possible for 1992, with the reconstruction of some of its lost Soviet trade with the new republics and the realisation of its modest growth potential in some new export products the economy may bottom out in 1992 and begin a slow road to recovery. Of course, to the extent that significant quantities of oil are discovered off the northern coast recovery will come more rapidly and robustly.

Eventually, however, Cuba will only succeed economically if it makes its economic mechanism more agile, flexible and efficient. This will require greater decentralisation and a broader engagement of the market mechanism. Ultimately, it is the political challenge of democratisation that will determine the long-run viability of Cuban socialism.

Notes

1 The import share averaged 31.7 per cent during 1952–56 and then rose to 34.0 per cent in 1957 and 36.6 per cent in 1958.

2 Carmelo Mesa-Lago, *The Economy of Socialist Cuba*, Albuquerque, University of New Mexico Press, 1981, p. 79. Gross Material Product is '*ingreso nacional disponible*' plus depreciation. It does not include non-material services and, hence, is at least 25 per cent below GDP.

3 In 1982, the Cuban National Bank estimated that through 1980 the blockade had cost Cuba some $10 billion. Recently, the Cubans have published updated estimates, suggesting an ongoing cost of nearly $500 million per year during the 1980s. See Banco Nacional, *Informe Económico, 1982* and Latin American Regional Reports' *Caribbean Report*, May 12, 1988.

4 The details here are provided in the excellent case studies in this volume.

5 Soviet oil deliveries to Cuba actually rose from 7.37 million metric tons in 1986, to 7.85 million in 1987 and to 8.50 million in 1988. Total Cuban imports from the Soviet Union in value terms remained basically flat at around 5.4 billion pesos between 1986 and 1988 (*Resumen estadístico del comercio exterior*, 1986–88, p. 12, 1990).

6 This point is elaborated in Zimbalist, 'Teetering on the Brink: The Post-CMEA Economic and Political Crisis in Cuba', *Journal of Latin American Studies*, May 1992. A related problem for Cuba has been that it has been in arrears in its contracted sugar deliveries to the CMEA. This necessitated borrowing from European sugar brokers in 1988–89 and paying them back in 1989–90 which has prevented Cuba from taking full advantage of the higher market prices for sugar in 1989–90. Cuba, then, has not reaped the expected benefit from its large 1989 *zafra* of over eight million tons.

7 Trade with China equalled 176 million pesos in 1988, 420 million in 1989 and was approximately 500 million in 1990.

8 Based on data presented in Ministerio del Comercio Exterior, *Resumen estadístico del comercio exterior*, 1986–88, septiembre 1989.

9 Estimate from study by SAIS, *Opportunities for US-Cuban Trade*, Washington D.C., June 1988, p. 14. Morley estimates this trade at $89.4 million in 1979, $303.2 million in 1980 and $73.8 million in 1981 (p. 339).

10 For a full discussion of the problems with the CIA's estimates of Soviet aid to Cuba, see Zimbalist and Brundenius, *op. cit.*, Ch. 9.

11 On Cuba's ability to sustain itself without foreign aid see, for instance, Lawrence Theriot, *Cuba Faces the Economic Realities of the 1980s*, Washington D.C., US Department of Commerce, 1982. Details on Cuba's foreign aid programs can be obtained from Zimbalist and Brundenius, *op. cit.*, Ch. 9 and Julie Feinsilver, *Cuba as a World Medical Power*, Cambridge, Harvard University Press, 1990.

12 For different estimates of the extent of this deterioration, see J.L. Rodríguez, 'Thirty Years of Economic Relations', *Cuba Business*, Vol. 3, No. 6, December 1989, p. 6.

13 See the discussion of this point in Gareth Jenkins' piece in this collection. Also see Zimbalist 1992, *op. cit.*

14 The adoption of the SDPE occurred in 1976, but this year was designated as a year of study and preparation. The gradual implementation of the system began in 1977. Since mid-1986, it is more commonly referred to as simply the SDE.

15 Banco Nacional de Cuba, *Informe Económico*, March 1986, p. 6.

16 Nelson Mata, 'Los gastos de presupuesto de los Organos Locales de Poder Popular', *Finanzas y Crédito*, No. 5, 1986, p. 56.

17 *Granma*, October 5, 1982, p. 2. Additional data through 1984 and analysis is provided in Oscar U-Echevarría *et. al.*, 'Consideraciones metodológi cas para el cálculo de la demanda de piezas de respuesto', *Cuba: Economía Planificada*, 1, No. 2, 1986, pp. 110–139.

18 Juceplan, Dictamenes de La IV Plenaria (1985), p. 25.

19 This system was actually begun on an experimental basis in 1979 in the province of Pinar del Rio, and was not implemented until 1986 in Havana. The Soviet Union, of course, has had this system for many years.

20 Carmelo Mesa-Lago, 'The Cuban Economy in the 1980s', in Sergio Roca (ed.) *Socialist Cuba: Past Interpretations and Future Challenges*, Boulder, Westview Press, 1988.

21 The rectification campaign is the name given to the current period of re-evaluating the balance of material and moral incentives, redressing the perceived excesses connected to materials incentives and private sector activity, and addressing other problems of economic and political management.

22 Staff of Radio José Martí's, *Cuba Quarterly Situation Report*, 1986, Vol. 3, No. 3, sec III, p. 13. Pérez López, 'Cuban Economy in the 1980s', *Problems of Communism*, Sept–Oct 1986, p. 34. Domínguez, 'Blaming Itself, Not Himself: Cuba's Political Regime After the Third Party Congress', in Roca, *op. cit.*, 1988. Also see the essay by Rhoda Rabkin, 'Cuba: The Aging of a Revolution', in Roca, who asserts that there was 'managerial autonomy' prior to the Rectification Campaign (p.35).

23 Pérez-López, *op. cit.*, p. 16.

24 Mesa-Lago, *op. cit.*, pp. 74–80.

25 See sources in earlier footnotes; also see, *inter alia*, Dóminguez, 'Cuba: Charismatic Communism', *Problems of Communism*, Sept–Oct 1985; Joseph Treaster, 'Castro Recoils at a Hint of Wealth', *New York Times*, February 8, 1987, p. III-1.

26 For a full discussion of these incentives and their evolution over time, see Zimbalist, 'Incentives and Planning in Cuba', *Latin American Research Review*, 24, 1, January 1989.

27 In the mid-1970s, for instance, the variable part of the basic wage ranged from 15.2 per cent in Hungary to 55.2 per cent in the German Democratic Republic, with Bulgaria at 39.8 per cent, Poland at 31.7 per cent, the USSR at 36.4 per cent, and Czechoslovakia at 43.8 per cent. José Acosta, *Teoría y práctica de los mecanismos de dirección de la economía*, Havana, Editorial de Ciencias Sociales, 1982, p. 291.

28 *Granma*, 14 January 1987, p. 5.

29 Preliminary figures for non-sugar agriculture in 1989 also suggest a negative impact on production.

30 Indications are that it continued to increase in the first half of 1989 when total private sector incomes increased 4.7 per cent. *Anuario Estadístico de Cuba*, 1987, p. 193; Comite Estatal de Estadísticas, Balance de Ingresos y Ingresos Monetarios de La Población, July 1989, p. 21 and August, 1989, p. 3.

31 *Ibid.*, July 1989, p. 21.

32 The new planning procedures are published in two volumes, entitled *Decisiones Adoptadas Sobre Algunos Elementos del Sistema de Dirección de La Economía*, Habana, Juceplan, March 1988. An abridged version is published in *Cuba: Economía Planificada* (the journal of Juceplan) Vol. 3, No. 3, 1988 and Vol. 4, No. 1, 1989.

33 *Ibid.*, Vol. 1, p. 8.

34 *Ibid.*, p. 9.

35 My translation, *ibid.*, p. 7.

36 *Ibid.*, p. 35.

37 Balance de las tareas para el perfeccionamiento del sistema de dirección de la economía, p. 10.

38 Since September 1988 the Grupo Central has been replaced by a smaller body, the Executive Committee of the Council of Ministers, as the primary state organ responsible for orienting the economic plan. It is not apparent what, if any, influence this has had on the degree of centralisation or decentralisation in the planning process. The Executive Committee reports meeting biweekly to discuss a broad range of sectoral and administrative issues, usually with representatives from enterprises or administrative bodies in the affected areas. *Granma*, September 25, 1989, pp. 2–5.

39 China, of course, is not in the CMEA and has taken, since June 1989, a rather sharp turn against reform.

40 The Cuban growth estimate is from Zimbalist and Brundenius, *op. cit.*, Ch. 5. The figure for Latin America is from the Inter-American Development Bank, *Economic and Social Progress in Latin America*, Washington D.C., 1988, p. 20.

41 Conversation with Zimbalist, Havana, Cuba, January 1985.

42 The Economist Intelligence Unit, *Country Report: Analysis of Economic and Political Trends for Cuba, Dominican Republic, Haiti, Puerto Rico*, No. 4, 1986, p. 10.

43 For a full discussion of these reforms, see A. Zimbalist, 'Industrial Reform and the Cuban Economy', in I. Jeffries (ed.) *Industrial Reform in Socialist Countries*, London, Edward Elgar, 1992, and, A. Zimbalist and W. Smith, 'Reform in Cuba', in Kim and Zacek (eds) *Reform in Communist Systems: Comparative perspectives*, Washington, D.C., Washington Institute, 1991.

44 The 1990 figure for Soviet trade is from *Cuba Business*, October 1991, p. 2, and for trade with Eastern Europe it is estimated based on proportions in import reduction reported in Elena C. Alvárez, 'Algunos efectos en la Economía cubana de los cambios en la coyuntura internacional', *Instituto de Investigaciones Económicas*, Habana, Cuba, Junio de 1991, p. 7. Also see the opening speech of Fidel Castro at the Fourth Party Congress, 10 October 1991, reprinted in FBIS, *Daily Report Supplement: Latin America*, 14 October, 1991.

45 These figures and others, unless otherwise noted, are from the *Anuario Estadístico de Cuba, 1989* published by the Comite Estatal de Estadísticas and the *Resumen Estadístico del Comercio Exterior, 1986–88*, published by the Ministerio de Comercio Exterior.

46 Reconstructing estimates from Castro's speeches during December 1991 and

other sources suggests that Cuba received around 8.3 million tons of petroleum from the former Soviet Union in 1991. Of course, the bulk of this arrived to Cuba via triangular trade wherein the former Soviet Union sent oil (contracted with South American oil exporters) to Western Europe and Japan and Venezuela, Colombia and Ecuador (contracted with the former Soviet Union) sent oil to Cuba. For 1992 Cuba has signed a pact with Russia to exchange 2.5 tons of raw sugar for 4.5 tons of petroleum. This exchange ratio implies a price about 10 per cent above the spot market sugar prices (with benchmark crude at around $18 a barrel and spot sugar at around 9 cents a pound). Cuba has signed additional agreements with Kazakhstan and St Petersburg to exchange sugar, citrus and medical products for oil.

47   In his speech to the National Assembly of People's Power on 27 December, 1991, Castro stated that as of 21 December, 1991 only $1.673 billion of goods had arrived from the former Soviet Union (*Granma International*, 12 January, 1992, p. 4). There is, however, some ambiguity as to whether Castro's figures refer only to goods that were scheduled for delivery in 1991 or whether they also include goods scheduled for delivery in 1990 but were delivered with a delay in 1991. The numbers cited are in current prices and it is likely that in constant prices the fall off would be a bit less sharp. This is because the price Cuba paid for Soviet oil fell approximately $7 a barrel between 1989 and 1991.

48   There was also a year-end credit clearing accord, but it is unclear how this worked out.

49   Cuba has also shifted some sugar cane land to the production of root crops and vegetables. Prior to 1990, Cuba could sell virtually all the sugar it desired to the Soviet Union at a stable, preferential price. Now that is no longer the case and the Cubans seem to have reformulated their traditional goal of maximising yearly cane production. Expectations for this year's harvest are 6.5 to 7.0 million tons.

CHAPTER 5

Cuba's international sugar trade

Gerry Hagelberg and Tony Hannah

Scarcely any of the historical sugar islands of the world still depend on sugar as much as Cuba. In the thirty years following the Cuban Revolution, sugar production grew by 40 per cent. At the start of the 1990s, sugar cane occupied 45 per cent of Cuba's arable land. Next to commerce, the growing and processing of sugar cane constituted the largest single branch of the Cuban economy in 1989, alone contributing 10 per cent to the global social product. Put in another way, Cuba turned out three-quarters of a tonne of sugar per head of population that year. Not counting private cane growers, Cuba's sugar industry in 1988 employed 235,000 people on the agricultural side – better than one out of every three workers in the state farm sector – plus some 140,000 people on the industrial side – nearly one in five of the country's industrial labour force. As in pre-Revolutionary days, sugar remained the mainstay of Cuba's foreign trade and the principal earner of foreign exchange, accounting for almost three-quarters of total merchandise exports. Although its share of world output fell from around 12 per cent to under 8 per cent, Cuba was still the biggest sugar exporter in the world. Notwithstanding an extremely high level of per caput consumption, domestic offtake absorbed only 10 per cent of the industry's output in 1985–89.[1]

Before and since the Revolution, Cuba's sugar production and exports have fluctuated widely from year to year, and underlying trends are only revealed over longer periods. In contrast to earlier times, however, the annual swings in production and exports after 1960 did not reflect external marketing constraints. For the duration of Cuba's special trade ties with Eastern Europe and the former Soviet Union, supply rather than demand regulated the overall volume of exports (Table 5.1).

Higher than normal exports in 1960–61 lowered stocks to a level where the annual volume of sales thereafter was almost entirely governed by the size of the current crop. Between 1950 and 1961, year-end stocks on average amounted to about a fifth of annual exports and except in 1950–51 never dropped to less than 10 per cent of the following year's sales. After 1961, in contrast, year-end stocks averaged just under 8 per cent of annual

Table 5.1   Cuban sugar production, exports and consumption, five-year averages (1,000 tonnes, raw value)

Period	Production	Index	Exports	Index	Consumption	Index
1955–59	5,409.5	100	5,185.8	100	279.0	100
1960–64	5,211.5	96	4,975.1	96	390.8	140
1965–69	5,310.7	98	4,969.0	96	596.3	214
1970–74	5,993.0	111	5,369.1	104	538.5	193
1975–79	6,859.5	127	6,449.2	124	524.2	188
1980–84	7,509.9	139	6,961.3	134	627.4	225
1985–89	7,582.4	140	6,899.1	133	779.9	280

Sources: Production, basis 96°, crop ending in year indicated: Junta Central de Planificación, *Boletín Estadístico*, 1970; Comité Estatal de Estadísticas, *Anuario Estadístico de Cuba*, various years. Exports and consumption, raw value, calendar year: International Sugar Organisation.

exports. Areas of mature cane left standing from one season to the next – the other cushion that existed in the 1950s to buffer yield fluctuations – were also reduced.

Overall, production and exports in the 1960s were somewhat smaller than in the previous decade. The decline was actually greater than the figures suggest because before the Revolution, Cuba used surplus sugar cane to make high-test molasses when markets for sugar were restricted. Inclusion of the sugar equivalent of high-test molasses produced and exported in 1955–59 would increase the averages for that period by over 300,000 tonnes (Hagelberg, 1974:132). Less than 20,000 tonnes of high-test molasses, in sugar terms, were produced in 1960 and none thereafter.

The jump in production in 1970–74 was mainly due to the exceptional harvest of 1969/70, climax of a plan to reach ten million tonnes and not equalled before or since. Taken together, the 15 crops from 1960 to 1974 averaged 5.5 million tonnes, not very different from the average outturn in the 1950s. The pace distinctly quickened in the second half of the 1970s. But subsequent crops again mark a plateau from which further growth evidently became inherently more difficult. The increase in output programmed for 1986–90 in Cuba's Third Five-Year Plan, which would have boosted export availabilities, proved elusive.

Production was expanded by devoting more land to cane as well as from higher yields. The area under cane grew by 23 per cent from 1.44 million hectares in 1970–74 to 1.77 million hectares in 1985–89. The area harvested increased by 10 per cent from 1.21 million hectares to 1.34 million hectares. Sugar yields have varied, but on average improved by 15 per cent from 4.94 tonnes (raw value) per hectare harvested to 5.67 tonnes.

In land productivity, Cuba lies somewhat below the midpoint of the world range of cane sugar producers (Blume, 1985; Food and Agriculture Organisation, 1990). For more than a century until 1960, the fortunes of the Cuban sugar industry were tied to the nearby US market. In the second half of the 1950s, deliveries to the US absorbed 55 per cent of Cuba's sugar exports and filled 73 per cent of US quota receipts from foreign countries (US Department of Agriculture, 1975). As part of the special relationship between Cuba and the US, the US import duty on Cuban raw sugar was, from 1948, fixed at 0.5 cent per pound, against 0.625 cent for full-duty countries, and only the Philippines enjoyed better tariff treatment. Annual average raw sugar prices in the US market in 1955–59 fluctuated between 5.95 and 6.27 cents per pound, c.i.f. New York duty paid, compared with world market prices ranging between 2.97 and 5.16 cents per pound, f.a.s. Cuba. Deducting duty, insurance and freight, the actual quota premium varied from 0.14 to 2.38 cents per pound (International Sugar Council, 1963:II, 181).

Closure of the US market to Cuba in 1960 ruptured the main artery of the world sugar trade, through which had flowed roughly a fifth of total world sugar exports from the world's largest exporter to its then largest importer. Cancellation of Cuba's US sugar quota resulted in a radical reorientation of the island's sugar exports and changed the map of international sugar movements. The US replaced Cuban sugar by increased domestic production and foreign supplies drawn from all five continents. In turn, the Soviet Union, Eastern Europe, and China replaced the US as the main outlet for Cuban sugar. The exceptional nature of Cuba's trade with the socialist countries, outside the ambit of the free world market, was eventually recognised in the special arrangement provisions introduced in the International Sugar Agreement of 1968 and continued in the Agreement of 1977.[2]

At the outset, however, Soviet dealings with the new government in Havana followed normal business practice. Pent-up demand had already in the 1950s converted the Soviet Union into a fairly substantial net importer of sugar, despite rising domestic production, with Cuba becoming the main foreign supplier in the second half of the decade. During the summer and early autumn of 1959, Cuba sold 500,000 long tons to the Soviet Union – not much more than it had shipped to that country in 1955 – at prices below those quoted at the time on the world market. Dr Raúl Cepero Bonilla, Minister of Commerce of the Revolutionary government, justified the discounts on the ground that the sales broke a declining price tendency and increased buyer interest (Cepero Bonilla, 1959).

With plenty of sugar to sell, the immediate aim of Cuban foreign trade policy at that point was to expand exports to the free world market. Along with the Soviet Union, Japan was singled out as capable of absorbing more

Cuban sugar. To realise this potential, Cuba was advised to conclude bilateral treaties with large importing countries and buy their goods in return (Cepero Bonilla, 1959). The best policy to increase sugar sales was to sign commercial agreements that created long-term purchase commitments, the new government reasoned (Cepero Bonilla, 1960). While a price discount to clinch a large deal was acceptable, a price war to stimulate demand and knock out competitors was considered ineffective.

In line with such thinking, Cuba signed a trade agreement with the Soviet Union in February 1960, which provided for the delivery of 425,000 tons of sugar on top of 575,000 tons already contracted for that year, and of one million tons annually from 1961 to 1964. The additional 425,000 tons to be shipped in 1960 were to be paid for in Soviet merchandise, while the purchases in 1961–64 were to be settled 20 per cent in convertible currency and the rest in goods. Both parties were to value their exports at the world market prices prevailing when contracts were signed. The Soviet Union undertook to use its imports from Cuba for internal consumption and not to export sugar to countries which were customary buyers from Cuba (Cepero Bonilla, 1960).

Volume aside, which merely manifested the growing Soviet appetite for Cuban sugar, this agreement broke new ground in signalling an increasing Soviet export capability (thanks, above all, to the development of Soviet oil production) – underlined by the simultaneous grant of a $100 million credit for the purchase of plant, equipment and materials – and Cuba's willingness to buy Soviet goods. Acceptance of payment in kind was portrayed as the key element. Defending the decision to open Cuba to Soviet products, Cepero Bonilla wrote: 'This decision, and only this decision, made it possible for the Soviet Union to commit itself to purchase five million tons of sugar in five years.' Although reciprocity had not prevented reductions in Cuba's share of the American market, he argued that giving the Soviet Union an outlet for goods surplus to its own requirements would tend to protect the market for Cuban sugar in the USSR beyond the life of the agreement against Soviet inclinations to become self-sufficient in sugar (Cepero Bonilla, 1960).

These arrangements were overtaken by the cancellation in mid-1960 of the unshipped balance of that year's Cuban quota in the US. The Soviet Union immediately took up the affected quantity. Other socialist countries had meanwhile also concluded trade agreements with Cuba. China had bought 50,000 tons of Cuban sugar in January 1960, and committed itself to 500,000 tons annually under a five-year agreement signed in July, payable in Chinese merchandise, except for 20 per cent in pounds sterling in the first year. Another 60,000 tons had been sold to the German Democratic Republic in February 1960 (Anon., 1964).

When, towards the end of 1960, Cuba was excluded altogether from the US market, the socialist countries agreed to buy 4 million tons of Cuban sugar in 1961, of which 2.7 million tons were to go to the Soviet Union and 1 million tons to China (Ménendez Cruz, 1960). In an important departure from previous practice, the price was no longer linked to the world market, but fixed at 4 US cents a pound, f.a.s., roughly 1 cent above ruling world market prices. Not long after, the total volume to be purchased by the socialist countries was increased to 4.86 million tons (Cepero Bonilla, 1962). In response to the rise of world market prices in 1963, the Soviet Union raised its purchase price for Cuban sugar to 6 cents a pound (Anon., 1963a). A new long-term agreement signed by Fidel Castro and Nikita Khrushchev in January 1964 set targets for Cuban sugar exports to the Soviet Union rising from 2.1 million tons in 1965 to 5 million tons yearly in 1968–70, at 6 US cents a pound, f.a.s. Cuban ports, payable in Soviet goods (*Cuba Socialista*, 1964). If the projected growth of Cuban exports smacked of political hyperbole, so did the claim in the agreement's preamble that the Soviet Union was 'capable of producing a sufficient amount of sugar to satisfy the demand of its population and for export,' implying that it could do without Cuban sugar. In the event, Cuba supplied 13 million tons in the years 1965–70, 54 per cent of the total contemplated. And from 1972 on, the Soviet Union became a large, though irregular, buyer in the free world market, in addition to its imports from Cuba.

The wholesale redirection of Cuba's sugar exports did, however, entail major adjustments. Whereas the USSR and China – the one a net importer despite increasing domestic production, the other with a vast population and minimal per caput consumption – could be regarded as potentially sizeable markets for Cuban sugar, Eastern Europe was not an obvious natural outlet. Czechoslovakia and Poland were traditional sugar exporters and remain so to this day (aside from rare lapses into the net importer column). Bulgaria did not become a sugar importer until 1961. East Germany was a net exporter until 1961 and occasionally thereafter. And neither Hungary nor Romania nor Yugoslavia has consistently figured as a deficit area.

Eventually, annual Cuban sugar exports to Article 31 countries were to reach double the average volume of Cuban sales to the US during the 1950s (Table 5.2).

Rising purchases by Article 31 countries, above all the Soviet Union, in fact provided the driving force behind the overall growth of Cuban sugar exports since the Revolution. But with Cuba's supply capacity and its partners' import demand both prone to large asynchronous fluctuations, progress was erratic. The early years of the Cuban Revolution coincided with a period of rapid expansion of the Soviet and Chinese sugar industries. Between 1960 and 1969, their combined output rose by 80 per cent from 7 million to 12.8 million tonnes. Until the early 1970s, Article 31 countries in

Table 5.2   Average annual Cuban sugar exports to Article 31 countries (1,000 tonnes, raw value)

	1960–64	1965–69	1970–74	1975–79	1980–84	1985–89
USSR	1981	1986	1884	3558	3464	3674
Other European CMEA						
Bulgaria	64	180	200	209	291	322
Czechoslovakia	78	228	178	83	141	140
GDR	136	225	294	203	248	306
Hungary	0	10	44	59	37	0
Poland	139	25	32	43	27	70
Romania	0	25	87	23	154	163
Asian CMEA						
Mongolia	0	2	3	3	4	2
Vietnam	7	47	72	95	57	12
Other Article 31 countries						
Albania	6	9	15	16	15	25
China	667	490	390	337	695	778
North Korea	18	71	131	25	20	28
Yugoslavia	31	78	36	68	8	4
All Article 31 countries[a]	3125	3375	3366	4722	5159	5523
Share of total Cuban sugar exports (per cent)						
USSR	39.8	40.0	35.1	55.2	49.8	53.2
Other CMEA[b]	8.3	14.9	17.0	11.1	13.7	14.7
China	13.4	9.9	7.3	5.2	10.0	11.3
All Article 31 countries	62.8	67.9	62.7	73.2	74.1	80.1

[a] May not add up due to rounding. [b] 1989 membership.
Source: International Sugar Organization.

effect laid off a substantial portion of their Cuban sugar receipts in the free world market, considerably enhancing their share of world exports in the process. Only about 800,000 tons – one-sixth of the large volume of Cuban sugar acquired by the socialist countries in 1961 – were said to have been recycled to the free market (Cepero Bonilla, 1962). But at the height of its activity as a free market seller between 1966 and 1971, the Soviet Union alone exported 8.1 million tonnes of sugar, raw value, equivalent to 68 per cent of its imports from Cuba.

What Cuba gained and lost by this traffic is difficult to say. On the one hand, to the extent that sugar went to countries which Cuba could not, with the same efficiency, service directly (as in the case of Soviet shipments to Afghanistan or Chinese sales to Hong Kong), its Article 31 partners arguably acted as distributors. On the other hand, special arrangement exports were transmuted into free market exports which influenced free market prices. At times, cheap white sugar could be had from Article 31 sources at less cost than Cuban raws, depressing free market prices and, by extension, Cuba's earnings from direct free market sales. But unsold Cuban stocks hanging over the free market, had the socialist countries not served as intermediaries, might well have had the same effect.

This trading pattern changed abruptly in 1972, when both China and the Soviet Union for the first time drew heavily on the free world market to supplement their imports from Cuba (Table 5.3). In the same year, Soviet exports to the free world market suddenly fell to a small fraction of their previous level (Chinese free market sales were already in decline). Since the latter 1970s, China more often than not covered the greater part of its import needs from non-Cuban sources, with Australia and Thailand major suppliers, and in recent years again assumed a more prominent role as a re-exporter. Cuba remained the principal source of Soviet sugar imports, but no longer enjoyed a monopoly, while Soviet exports stayed at a modest level of at most 300,000 tonnes in any one year.

In terms of volume, Cuba's sugar trade with the Soviet Union since 1960 clearly divided into two distinct periods. In the first, from 1960 to 1974, Cuban exports averaged 1,950,021 tonnes a year, with a mean deviation of 496,563 tonnes. Annual shipments fluctuated enormously between less than 1 million tonnes in 1963 and more than 3 million tonnes in 1961 and 1970. In 1975–89, exports averaged 3,565,400 tonnes, an increase of 83

Table 5.3 Total sugar exports of selected Article 31 countries as a percentage of imports from Cuba

	1960–64	1965–69	1970–74	1975–79	1980–84	1985–89
USSR	35	62	35	4	6	6
Bulgaria	68	12	6	0	12	21
Czechoslovakia	562	183	148	259	149	159
GDR	174	84	55	38	43	79
Poland	457	1784	869	518	514	248
Romania	–	441	84	253	39	63
China	35	70	29	45	23	45

Source: International Sugar Organization.

per cent over the earlier period, and the mean deviation of 361,774 tonnes shows a much smaller absolute and relative dispersion around the average. Cuba's exports to other Article 31 countries followed a different and less striking pattern. No definite trend is discernible in the 21 years from 1960 to 1980, during which shipments averaged 1,293,896 tonnes a year, with a mean deviation of 221,928 tonnes, a somewhat more stable performance than that in respect of the Soviet Union from 1960 to 1974.

The years 1981–89 marked a new stage; in these nine years, Cuban exports to other Article 31 countries averaged 1,827,544 tonnes, up 41 per cent from the 1960–80 average, with a mean deviation of 246,075 tonnes, a relatively smaller variation than before. Exports to members of the CMEA alone, other than the Soviet Union, averaged just over 1 million tonnes in 1981–89, up 45 per cent from the 1960–80 level of nearly 700,000 tonnes.

As by far the largest market, the Soviet Union absorbed most of the impact of Cuban crop fluctuations. High points in Cuban sugar deliveries to the Soviet Union coincided with unusually large Cuban crops (1961, 1970, 1982), nadirs with abnormally small harvests (1963, 1969, 1972, 1980). But beyond that, Soviet flexibility with regard to Cuban export performance allowed Havana, particularly in earlier years, to give priority to the free market in order to earn more convertible currency and fulfil its export entitlements under the International Sugar Agreements of 1968 and 1977. Only in more recent times was Cuba forced to negotiate postponements, purchase sugar in the free market, and arrange complicated swaps in order to make up for the chronic overcommitment of its export availabilities.

In contrast to Cuba's sugar trade with Article 31 countries, exports to the rest of the world backed and filled without a firm trend in either direction. Three advances into 2-million-tonne terrain in 1970–71, 1974, and 1978–81 turned out to be temporary. Depending on the periods com-

Table 5.4   Share of Cuban sugar in total sugar imports of selected Article 31 countries (per cent)

	1960–64	1965–69	1970–74	1975–79	1980–84	1985–89
USSR	90	99	83	87	56	73
Bulgaria	72	72	76	92	90	75
Czechoslovakia	100	100	100	100	87	86
GDR	83	82	81	99	100	93
Poland	82	100	100	100	39	73
Romania	0	100	97	23	86	97
China	86	100	67	33	44	35

Source: International Sugar Organization.

pared, an increase or decrease can be found. Price, availability, and the existence or not of an International Sugar Agreement with economic provisions, all seem to have had some bearing on the level of exports in absolute or relative terms. Annual shipments in the entire 30-year period of 1960–89 averaged 1,660,466 tonnes, with a mean deviation of 274,509 tonnes. Instability and impermanence characterised the trade with individual market economies. Few countries in this category have an unbroken record of purchases for the whole period since the Revolution. Only three industrialised countries – Canada, Finland, and Japan – figure with some regularity as significant importers of sugar from Cuba, albeit with wide swings. Shipments to Japan, the most important free market outlet for Cuban sugar, ranged between less than 200,000 and more than 1.2 million tonnes. Cuban exports to Western Europe dwindled, as once important markets became part of the EC, with its protectionist sugar regime favouring domestic production and exclusive preferential arrangements with designated African, Caribbean and Pacific countries under the Lomé Convention.

Havana's policy of seeking bilateral agreements produced a number of deals also with non-socialist countries, based to a greater or lesser extent on barter. Between 1959 and 1962, Cuba signed new commercial pacts with ten capitalist countries (Anon., 1963b). Within ten months of the triumph of the Revolution, a trade and payments *modus vivendi* was concluded with Spain to replace a similar agreement dating from 1953. This was followed in November 1963 by a three-year agreement dealing explicitly with sugar, renegotiated and extended for further three-year periods in 1965 and 1970. The second extension was superseded by a new four-year agreement in 1971, which in turn was succeeded by a three-year agreement in 1974 for the period 1975–77. The agreements with Spain commonly specified quantities and prices, both occasionally modified in subsequent annual trade protocols, and established the method of payment which for the greater part was effected by clearing against Spanish exports to Cuba (Recarte, 1980:160–184 and Chapter 8 in this volume). Similarly, an agreement with Morocco, concluded in 1961 and renewed several times thereafter with different terms, provided for the establishment of a clearing account to facilitate the purchase of Cuban sugar, payable partly in convertible currency and partly in Moroccan goods (C. Czarnikow Ltd, 1961–1971). Also in 1961, Cuba entered into a barter arrangement with Chile involving an exchange of sugar for copper, timber and agricultural products. Two years later, Cuba agreed with Uruguay to exchange sugar for rice and beef (León, 1963).

But these agreements did not give Cuba notably more stable, longterm outlets for its sugar, insulated from external events. Spain's import requirements shrank years before its entry into the EC, owing to increased home-grown sugar production, which dissatisfaction with the cost of imports may have helped to encourage. Japan's sugar imports declined altogether after the mid-1970s in the face of protectionist measures that favoured the domestic sugar industry and the use of alternative sweeteners. Cuba now competes against Thailand, as well as Australia and South Africa, on the reduced Japanese market, and the concurrent withdrawal of Brazil points to the freight cost handicap of more distant suppliers. Brazil, on the other hand, replaced Cuba as one of the larger sources of Moroccan imports. Syria, which once obtained the bulk of its imports from Cuba, more recently was supplied mainly by the EC, which also became a strong competitor in Algeria, Egypt, and other Cuban markets.

The twelve countries of the EC together with Algeria, Angola, Canada, Egypt, Finland, Indonesia, Iraq, Japan, Libya, Malaysia, Morocco and Syria in most years accounted for at least 80 per cent of Cuban sugar exports to the free market. Not included are a few more or less regular buyers of smaller quantities and several occasional outlets which in some instances, however, absorbed considerable amounts. Overall, the number of free market destinations and the volume of free market sales indicate that efforts to isolate Cuba after the Revolution had little demonstrable impact on its sugar trade outside the US. By the same token, Cuba had only limited success in developing new outlets for its sugar outside the socialist bloc and failed to enlarge its free market business. Partly because of this and partly because of structural changes in the market itself, Cuba lost its position as the largest supplier of the free world market.

Changing circumstances and interests in time altered Cuba's stance on issues pertaining to the management of the world sugar market. By a historical accident, Fidel Castro's entry into Havana on 1 January 1959 coincided with the coming into force of a new International Sugar Agreement. Although Cuba possessed close to 40 per cent of the basic export tonnages of all member countries, the new authorities had serious doubts concerning the fairness of the Agreement and its usefulness to Cuba. On the eve of the Revolution, Cepero Bonilla (n.d.[1958]:179–80) had denounced the not very different accord of 1953:

> The Agreement did not manage price movements and cannot manage them so long as it does not adequately control supply and demand. Large exporter countries are not in the Agreement, and importer countries, members or not, can practise without hindrance a policy of self-sufficiency in sugar which limits the scope of the world market. ... if the Agreement is not substantially modified, Cuba will continue to fall back in the world market, except when accidental and passing factors emerge. Cuba cannot rely on chance to protect its share of the world market. If the Agreement is radically modified and converted into an effective instrument of market regulation, Cuba can continue to participate. But so long as the importer countries do not give part

of their consumption increases to the exporting member countries and the growth of exports by non-member countries inevitably results in the decline of exports by member countries, Cuba gains nothing from staying in the International Sugar Agreement.

The critique acquired official character when Cepero Bonilla became Minister of Commerce, although Cuba eventually ratified the 1958 Agreement after a visit by the executive director of the International Sugar Council. At a Council meeting in February 1959, Cepero Bonilla took the position that Cuba could produce 8 million tons at a lower cost than most and was restricted too much, while other exporters and high-income importers contributed too little to market stabilisation. The thing to do, he urged, was to prohibit imports from non-members, eliminate production subsidies, and actively promote consumption. Back in Havana, Cepero Bonilla insisted:

> The basic quota assigned by the Agreement does not guarantee . . . sales. The importing . . . members of the Agreement . . . are not required to limit their sugar production, and they can buy from exporting countries that are not members of the International Sugar Agreement. Every time there is an increase of production in importing countries, or in exporting countries that are not members, the demand for sugar in the world market declines and violent price decreases arise. Under these circumstances Cuba's sales decline for lack of markets. In the past, Cuba has been able to export more sugar to the world market at better prices only at those times of a real supply crisis, or because of wars, war threats, or violent drops in production of other countries (Cepero Bonilla, 1959:14–15).

And again:

> The International Sugar Agreement has, among its many faults, the following two: one, it does not guarantee a market, it only assigns export quotas, but the member importing countries are not under the obligation to buy sugar; and two, it authorizes the expansion of sugar production in the importing countries. The quotas indirectly limit production of the member exporting countries, but not that of the member importing countries, which can reduce their sugar requirements in the world market through an increase of internal production, without violating the International Sugar Agreement (Cepero Bonilla, 1960:13–14).

Havana's attitude to price regulation was then based on the idea that it could tolerate low prices in order to discourage competition, since the premium on quota sales to the US would raise the average return to a level other exporters hoped to achieve under an International Sugar Agreement.

'The Revolutionary Government prefers that the price of sugar be at a level that will not stimulate the inefficient productions of other areas, but rejects a price war as inoperative,' Cepero Bonilla (1960:7–9) wrote. 'Cuba does not want high prices for they would stimulate sugar production in other areas.'

The 1958 Agreement collapsed under the burden of trying to adjust to the new trade flows following the exclusion of Cuban sugar from the US market. Amidst the heightened acrimony between Cuba and the US, a UN sugar conference in 1961 ended in failure when no compromise could be found on Cuba's demand for a quota of 6.8 million tonnes, made up of 4.8 million tonnes to socialist countries and 2 million tonnes to the free market (Cepero Bonilla, 1962).

Another UN sugar conference in 1965, inspired to revive the Agreement by the spirit of international economic co-operation adumbrated at the UN Conference on Trade and Development the year before, turned out to have come at an inopportune time for exporting countries to address the issue of quotas. In the subsequent consultations, Cuba showed no urgency to come to a new Agreement, blaming the policies of some importing developed countries with market economies for the deterioration of the market.

Early in 1967, Cuba's attitude evidently underwent a change. The free market sugar price had fallen in 1966 to its lowest point since the Second World War. Cuba's share in world centrifugal sugar production had declined from 12.3 per cent in 1956–58 to 8.4 per cent in 1964–66 and its share of world net exports from 41 per cent to 26 per cent. Although the 1967 crop augured a recovery and there were plans to produce 10 million tonnes in 1970, Cuba's immediate situation dictated a shift in emphasis from volume to value in its free market exports, the main source of hard currency earnings. In the successful negotiations for a new Agreement in 1968, Cuba accepted a basic free market export tonnage of 2,150,000 tonnes, against 2,415,000 tonnes under the 1958 Agreement, as well as some limitations on the possibilities of channelling additional quantities to the free market via re-exports by its socialist trading partners.

Cuban representatives played an active role in the International Sugar Organization during the life of the 1968 Agreement. Raúl León Torras, then Cuba's First Deputy Minister for Foreign Trade, was elected vice-chairman for 1972 and succeeded to the chairmanship in 1973, the year in which a UN conference in Geneva would discuss a successor agreement for 1974–78. At the conference, Leon Torras was elected first vice-chairman as spokesman of the exporting countries, particularly the less developed, and Cuba took the lead in calling for higher prices. Regulation of the world sugar market again lapsed, however, as differences with the importers, especially on the price issue, could not be reconciled. Cuban pronouncements now laid equal stress on the inherently incompatible aims of achieving adequate prices and discouraging the competition, and a working Agreement was seen as more eventually desirable than currently needed. In one of its periodic supply-side conditioned surges, the free market price jumped to over 60 US cents a pound in November 1974, but a year later was again touching 13 cents. Until 1974, Havana was averse to joint international initiatives by exporting countries alone. Cuba stood aloof from a short-lived scheme in 1966 which sought to set a minimum price for sugar exports, on the ground that it did not contribute to achieving UNCTAD commodity agreement objectives. At the time of the 1973 sugar conference, Havana was still reluctant to entertain the idea of unilateral exporter action. But in another reversal, Cuba supported the formation of the Group of Latin American and Caribbean Sugar Exporting Countries (Geplacea) which met for the first time in Mexico in November 1974, and a Cuban official became the first executive secretary of an exporter organisation that proclaimed as its basic goal 'to serve as a flexible consulting and co-ordinating mechanism for common matters related to the production and marketing of sugar.'

At a UN sugar conference in 1977, the last to succeed in negotiating a five-year Agreement with market control functions, Cuba again took the lead in advocating higher prices with a proposal for a range of 15–25 US cents a pound. In response to developments in the world sugar economy, Cuba also sought a larger direct share of the free market and successfully negotiated a basic export tonnage of 2.5 million tonnes, 350,000 tonnes more than its entitlement under the 1968 Agreement and substantially above its previous free market performance. By 1977, expansion of sugar production in the EC was well under way, and with it of white sugar exports from the EC to the free market. While the Soviet Union had virtually disappeared from the free market as a seller after 1971, it had recently announced plans for a large increase of domestic production. This turned out to be a false signal, but at that point Cuba had reason to fear the possibility of eventually finding itself squeezed between expanding supplies from Western Europe and shrinking Soviet requirements, and needed to reassert its position on the free market.

The 1977 Agreement compromised on a price range of 11–21 cents a pound, increased to 13–23 cents in 1980 under pressure from the exporters. In the event, average monthly world market prices exceeded 11 cents for just two-and-a-half years between October 1979 and March 1982, and did not firmly re-enter the range until the summer of 1989. Faced with the choice between an unremunerative free market and a Soviet market still capable of absorbing all the sugar it could supply, Cuba again laid greater stress on special arrangement exports and in the fruitless talks on a new Agreement in 1983/84 was ready to accept a free market quota of 2.35 million tonnes.

As a Third World spokesman, Cuba had long since changed its stance on the price issue from what it was in the early days of the Revolution when Cepero Bonilla said that his country was opposed to world market prices in the four-cent range, because they encouraged marginal production, and that three-cent prices (equivalent to barely 10 cents in 1982 US dollars) would not prove unhealthy for Cuba in the long run. Exactly thirty years later, Fidel Castro, speaking to a Cuban trade union congress on 28 January 1990, dismissed the world market price, then running at over 14 cents a pound, as 'the sugar garbage heap price' (*Granma Weekly Review*, 11 February 1990).

These mutations in Cuba's attitude to the world market were largely influenced by the evolution of its trade relations with the socialist bloc, particularly the Soviet Union, which entered into a new phase when Cuba joined CMEA in 1972. Under an agreement signed at the end of that year, the price paid by the Soviet Union for Cuban sugar, which since 1963 had been kept at 121.23 roubles per tonne, was raised to 200 roubles (Table 5.5).

Further increases followed and a form of indexation was instituted. Referring to the price of 500 roubles per tonne agreed for the period 1975–80, National Bank of Cuba (1975:32) added: 'In accordance with the procedure in force for the establishment of trade prices between both countries, the forementioned price could be modified according to the variations of prices of Cuban imports from that country.' Or as Banco Nacional de Cuba (1982:14) put it: 'The price of sugar exported to the USSR was linked and varied in proportion to the prices that Cuba had to pay for imports from that country, including oil.' Table 5.5 shows the agreement and contract prices in various currencies as reported in official Cuban publications.

The contract prices of Cuban sugar exports to the Soviet Union and other countries published until 1982 (Appendix Table 1, p. 158) broadly agree with the actual unit values calculated from the volume and value of exports given in Cuban statistical yearbooks (Appendix Table 2, p. 160), the differences probably being mainly due to the fact that the unit values include shipments in addition to contracted quantities and encompass white as well as raw sugar exports.

Examination of the contract price and unit value series affords some insight into the pricing of Cuban sugar exports. The contract prices for most of the Article 31 countries (Appendix Table 1) exhibit a pattern of recurring values which, though not altogether consistent, suggest a system of reference prices, characterised already in the earlier years by a certain differentiation between the more developed members of CMEA, on the one side, and Albania, Mongolia, North Korea, and Vietnam, on the other.

In time, a clear stratification emerged, with the prices of exports to the Soviet Union diverging increasingly from the rest. Below the Soviet price level, a second and third tier developed from 1973 on (the first year in

Table 5.5   Prices of Cuban raw sugar exports to the USSR

Years	Pesos/tonne[a]	Roubles/tonne	US cents/lb f.o.b.[b]
1961–62	—	—	4.09
1963–72	134.70[c]	121.23[d]	6.11[e]
1973	219.68	200.00[bf]	12.02
1974	358.97	341.67[dg]	19.64
1975	553.54		
1976	509.18		
1977	497.49	500.00[bh]	c.30.00[h]
1978	608.14	615.61[di]	
1979	602.85		
1980	759.19		
1981	606.09		
1982	658.12	660.00[dj]	

[a] Average contract price. *Anuario Estadístico de Cuba*, various issues. The series on contract prices was not updated beyond 1982 in more recent statistical yearbooks.
[b] National Bank of Cuba (1975).
[c] 1970–72.
[d] Banco Nacional de Cuba (1982).
[e] Note in source: Does not take into account the devaluation of the dollar in 1972.
[f] Price set in agreement, 23 December 1972. Dollar equivalent given as 11.95 cents per pound f.o.b.
[g] Average for 1973–75.
[h] Agreement price for 1975–80.
[i] Average for 1976–80.
[j] Average for 1981–82.

which the marker price of 134.70 pesos per tonne or 6.11 US cents a pound did not cover the lowest free market price notation), made up of the other European CMEA and Asian trading partners, respectively. The run of Soviet contract prices thereafter was not all one way, however. On occasion, the rising trend was interrupted by substantial downward corrections, as shown by the 20 per cent decline from 1980 to 1981. The level of world market prices was evidently not the only factor behind these movements. While the reduction in 1981 followed the direction of world market prices, as did the smaller decline between 1975 and 1977, no such parallel exists to explain the contraction in Soviet unit values ten years later.

Contracts with market economies in the period 1970–82 generally fell within the range of free market prices in the corresponding year – with some exceptions, notably the uniformly low set of contract prices in 1973, the high-priced Spanish contracts in 1976 and 1977, and the low Canadian price in 1979. Taken together with the at times markedly concessional prices for Albania, Mongolia, North Korea and Vietnam, it seems that the system of contract prices did not invariably redound to Cuba's advantage.

The stratification of prices becomes even more striking after 1982 in the unit values of Cuban sugar exports (Appendix Table 2). The price of Cuban exports to China, which up to the mid-1970s was on a par with East European values, completed its descent to the free market level. The unit values of exports to the USSR, on the other hand, climbed to another plane, far above the highest free market notations in these years and also further divorced from the prices paid by other European CMEA members. During 1985–88, the Soviet Union accounted for 54 per cent of the total volume of Cuban sugar exports, but for 81 per cent of the total value. This compares with a Soviet share in the value of Cuban sugar exports of 58 per cent in 1975 and 62 per cent in 1980. In value terms, Cuba's international sugar trade acquired an extraordinary degree of concentration in the course of the 1980s.

Just as Cuban sugar exports to some market economies rested on barter, so part of Cuban sugar sales to socialist countries was settled in convertible currency. Banco Nacional de Cuba (1982:21) reported the following free currency earnings from sugar exports to socialist countries in the period from 1975 to the first half of 1982 (in millions of pesos):

1975	1976	1977	1978	1979	1980	1981	First half 1982
350.1	130.1	177.2	104.7	99.6	—	180.8	303.9

In 1989, Cuba reportedly received 151.1 million pesos in convertible currency for sugar exports to socialist countries (Banco Nacional de Cuba, 1990a:20).[3]

During the 1980s, Cuba was also able to conduct a substantial re-export business in oil and oil products for hard currency. On the other hand, Cuba spent some 207 million pesos in convertible currency in 1984 and 1985 buying sugar on the free market in order to meet its commitments to the Soviet Union, according to informed trade quarters (du Genestoux, 1989). At a time of high oil and low sugar prices on the respective world markets, this allowed Cuba to transmute a much larger sum of clearing pesos into hard currency, as the following balance illustrates (based on du Genestoux, 1989):

Sugar bought on the free market	2.5 million tonnes at 83 pesos/tonne	207.5 million pesos in convertible currency
Sugar sold to USSR	2.5 million tonnes at 612 pesos/tonne	1530 million pesos in clearing currency
Oil bought from USSR	6.7 million tonnes at 200 pesos/tonne	1340 million pesos in clearing currency
Oil resold on the open market	6.7 million tonnes at 170 pesos/tonne	1139 million pesos in convertible currency

A look at what Cuban imports from the Soviet Union cost in Cuban sugar exports to the Soviet Union suggests that the terms of trade became increasingly favourable to Cuba during the 1970s, but overall probably worsened somewhat thereafter as a result of higher energy prices. The list of Cuban imports in Appendix Table 3 (p. 161) is confined, in the main, to staples which can be assumed not to have changed much in quality. Tractors and cane loaders are included because of their relevance to sugar production. Except cane loaders, Soviet deliveries in each of the listed categories exceeded 20 million pesos in the last year for which data are available. Together, the items in Appendix Table 3 represented 64 per cent of Cuban merchandise imports from the Soviet Union in 1987. Crude oil and oil products alone accounted for 47 per cent of Cuban merchandise imports from the Soviet Union in 1987, while sugar constituted 84 per cent of Cuban merchandise exports to the USSR.

Although the benefit cannot be measured exactly, Cuba's trade with the Soviet Union evidently contained a substantial element of resource transfer. The advantage enjoyed by Cuba in its terms of trade with the USSR after the first oil crisis is apparent from how much oil, butter, wheat and cotton 1 tonne of sugar bought under the Cuban-Soviet arrangements, compared with alternative scenarios, although such hypothetical exercises obviously should not be taken too literally (Table 5.6).

Arguably, on principles of international trade theory, an objective assessment of the Cuban-Soviet terms of trade ought to embrace not only the price of Cuban sugar and the prices and quality of Soviet goods supplied in exchange, but also the cost of producing sugar in the Soviet Union. Cuba undoubtedly was a far more efficient sugar producer than the Soviet Union, with roughly double the sugar yield per hectare planted and 50 per cent more daily processing capacity in the typical factory. Unless it were shown that Soviet oil was priced much below its cost of production, a Cuban-Soviet carbohydrate-hydrocarbon exchange, even with some premium over the world sugar price, was defensible on the Ricardian principle of comparative advantage against the charge of being purely a political artefact,

Table 5.6   Purchasing power of sugar in terms of selected commodities based on 1) Cuba-USSR trade practice, 2) US import prices for sugar and world market prices for the other commodities, and 3) world market prices for all.

	1968	1970	1975	1980	1985	1988
Petroleum						
(1)	7.8	7.3	12.4	8.9	5.1	4.5[a]
(2)	12.0	13.0	6.2	3.3	2.3	3.9[a]
(3)	3.4	6.5	5.7	3.1	0.46	1.2[a]
Butter						
(1)	0.12	0.17	0.44	0.68	0.59	0.55
(2)	0.25	0.26	0.45	0.41	0.36	0.32
(3)	0.07	0.13	0.41	0.39	0.07	0.15
Wheat						
(1)	1.7	1.9	3.1	4.7	5.2	10.0
(2)	2.4	3.0	3.3	3.8	3.3	3.4
(3)	0.70	1.5	3.0	3.7	0.66	1.5
Cotton						
(1)	0.19	0.18	0.44	0.69	0.71	0.64
(2)	0.23	0.26	0.42	0.32	0.34	0.35
(3)	0.06	0.13	0.39	0.31	0.07	0.16

[a] 1987.

Sources: (1) Appendix Table 3, p. 161; (2) and (3) calculated from International Financial Statistics 1989. Specifications: Petroleum: (1) Cuban import unit values for crude oil and oil products, c.i.f.; (2) and (3) Venezuela (Tia Juana), assumed weight of barrel: 0.136 tonne. Butter: (1) Cuban import unit values, c.i.f.; (2) and (3) New Zealand. Wheat: (1) Cuban import unit values, c.i.f.; (2) and (3) US Gulf Ports. Cotton: (1) Cuban import unit values, c.i.f.; (2) and (3) Liverpool Index. Sugar: (1) Cuban export unit values, f.o.b.; (2) US Import Price; (3) ISA Daily Price.

devoid of economic logic.

The economic and political changes that began to sweep through the Soviet Union and Eastern Europe in 1989 were greeted in Havana with deep misgivings, at the heart of which lay the fear that mooted reforms towards the adoption of world market prices and convertible currency payments in CMEA trade would spell the end of the preferential arrangements for Cuban sugar. Fidel Castro chose a memorial ceremony on 7 December 1989 for Cubans who had died on foreign missions to comment on 'the current crisis in the socialist camp, from which we can only expect negative economic consequences for our country,' focusing directly on the issue of the terms of trade to justify the banning of certain Soviet magazines in Cuba:

> Some of those publications have already started calling for an end to the fair and equitable trade relations that were established between the USSR and Cuba. . . . They want the USSR to begin practising unequal trade with Cuba by selling its products to us at ever higher prices and buying our agricultural produce and raw materials at ever lower prices, just as the US does with other Third World countries – in short, they want the USSR to join the US blockade against Cuba (*Granma Weekly Review*, 17 December 1989).

This self-contradictory association of revised trade terms with the US blockade could no longer be expected to cut much ice in Eastern Europe and can only have been meant to shame Soviet listeners. Barring a descent from *perestroika* into chaos, there was at that point no sign that the Soviet Union would not continue to be a large sugar importer and be prepared to maintain a special arrangement with Cuba, albeit with gradual modification – dictated, if for no other reason, by reduced Soviet oil availabilities.

In the event, Cuba did not feel the full consequences of the unification of Germany, the disintegration of CMEA and the depressing effect on sugar demand of Eastern Europe's economic difficulties until 1991, when exports to that part of the world slumped to less than 70,000 tonnes. A significant recovery from this level is not in sight.

In contrast, the normal volume of Cuban sugar flowed to the Soviet Union in the final year of the last five-year umbrella trade and credit agreement between the two countries. A new one-year transitional agreement for 1991 by all accounts maintained a preferential price for Cuban sugar, although lower than the previous and denominated in US dollars rather than roubles, and Cuban sugar shipments actually rose by 7 per cent over the year before.

Prospects of a relatively soft landing into a more market-orientated environment were shattered by the breakup of the USSR in the wake of the failed coup in August 1991. This nullified the presumption of a continuing trade flow in roughly the same volume for the foreseeable future, based on the overall sugar supply/demand balance of the Union, and the survival of some kind of central purchasing and distribution mechanism. Suddenly, there were fifteen separate states scattered across two continents, vastly different in size and of nearly every possible configuration of market characteristics: with and without domestic white beet sugar industry; with and without domestic raw sugar refining capability; importer and exporter; high and low per caput consumer.

While in the aggregate the former Soviet republics remain a large potential outlet, Cuban sugar is unlikely to figure to the same extent as before. Though import demand may recover from its current depression, Cuba, with no raw sugar refining facilities, has limited capacity to supply white sugar to the several republics which depend on white sugar imports. More generally, Havana will have to compete against exporters with shorter supply lines and who can offer more attractive financial conditions.

Further in the future looms greater sweetener self-sufficiency in the Commonwealth of Independent States (CIS), with more sugar coming from beet-growing republics as well as corn wet milling industries in major maize regions like Kirghizia. Together, the Ukraine and Russia, respectively in first and fifth place among the world's beet sugar producers, accounted for over 90 per cent of Soviet beet sugar output, and on that scale, only a small gain in efficiency would mean a lot more home-grown sugar. Unlike in the 1960s, there is no huge new market in the offing to which Havana can turn to offset the reduced demand for Cuban sugar in the former socialist bloc. This is a problem that not even rapprochement with Washington would solve, since total US sugar import requirements are now smaller than what Cuba alone supplied in the 1950s. Successful conclusion of the GATT talks on agricultural trade liberalisation and reform of the Common Agricultural Policy of the EC may eventually re-enlarge the international sugar market. But, in essence, Cuba's opportunities to export more sugar at a remunerative price are again contingent on the crop failures and supply shortfalls of other producers – the conditions that frustrated Cepero Bonilla some thirty years ago.

The collapse of the socialist bloc has plunged Cuba's economy and its premier industry into a crisis from which only a miracle could give quick relief. While perhaps only a fifth of the total volume of sugar exports has been lost, the end of premium prices means a savage cut in unit earnings. To gauge the impact on the country's import capacity: in 1989, though socialist bloc premiums lifted the average unit value of 7.1 million tonnes of Cuban sugar exports to all destinations to nearly 550 pesos a tonne (compared with a unit value of 214 pesos a tonne received on shipments to market economies alone), the deficit in the merchandise trade balance reached 2.7 billion pesos, equal to over 250 pesos per inhabitant or 17 per cent of per caput disposable national income. Along with the premiums, the sources of credit to cover such a large trade imbalance are gone.

For Cuba's Minister of Finance, the end of premium sugar prices implies that an industry which contributed heavily to government revenues, is now bound to require a substantial government subsidy in order to operate at normal world market prices and the present exchange rate, exacerbating an already grave fiscal disequilibrium.

Finally, the Cuban sugar industry itself faces retrenchment and rationalisation. How far it can hold its own in the new conditions will depend on its ability constantly to improve its efficiency and international competitiveness.

Future historians may well conclude that the forced redirection of the mainstream of Cuba's sugar trade from the US to the Soviet Union and other socialist countries at the beginning of the 1960s gave the island a historical reprieve in that it substituted an expanding for a shrinking export market. They will be in a position to know whether in the succeeding 30 years Cuba developed a sufficiently robust economy to continue advancing without a large foreign subsidy. If in the end the country sinks into poverty, the question will be whether this was the inevitable fulfilment of the old Cuban saying *Sin azúcar, no hay país* – without sugar, there is no country – or whether things could have been done to avert such a fate.

Appendix Table 1: Average contract prices of Cuban sugar exports (pesos/tonne)

Destination	1970	1971	1972	1973	1974	1975	1976	1977	1978	1979	1980	1981	1982
							Raw sugar						
USSR	134.70	134.70	134.70	219.68	358.97	553.54	509.18	497.49	608.14	602.85	759.19	606.09	658.12
Bulgaria	113.54	134.70	134.70	222.22	361.12	361.11	361.11	381.94	402.78	423.61	444.44	494.86	515.45
Czechoslovakia	134.70	134.70	134.70	134.70	361.12	361.11	361.11	361.11	361.11	361.11	437.93	366.99	460.43
GDR	124.12	134.70	134.70	134.70	361.12	361.11	361.11	361.11	361.11	361.11	437.93	506.41	506.41
Poland	—	—	—	134.70	361.12	361.11	361.11	361.11	—	361.11	437.93	419.22	—
Romania	—	110.42	111.89	112.23	361.12	361.11	317.19	—	361.11	361.11	361.11	492.16	368.34
Albania	—	—	72.75	—	—	—	—	—	—	—	—	—	—
China	—	—	—	—	382.68	502.05	349.37	283.63	225.87	212.35	361.11	424.96	363.66
Mongolia	134.70	66.14	72.75	72.75	134.70	134.60	134.70	134.70	134.70	134.70	134.70	137.40	137.40
North Korea	—	—	—	—	137.64	361.11	361.11	361.11	—	361.11	235.26	368.33	—
Vietnam	—	—	—	—	72.75	72.75	72.75	72.75	150.46	142.14	154.85	215.33	241.44
Yugoslavia	—	—	—	—	232.37	466.57	166.12	—	—	—	—	284.56	—
Canada	76.79	88.96	144.13	149.61	545.20	309.58	228.62	144.46	134.28	139.46	436.91	249.67	204.96
Finland	—	86.82	141.10	169.69	400.14	364.04	194.81	131.20	129.93	171.36	424.93	304.61	182.76
Iraq	63.60	93.22	151.90	—	421.30	385.61	203.40	129.77	134.98	153.99	423.81	288.38	151.47
Japan	86.04	103.27	146.38	158.67	317.91	470.22	184.76	138.19	135.50	168.86	455.12	226.47	146.15
Malaysia	76.78	97.38	135.48	142.72	213.85	—	151.50	—	147.52	200.76	448.89	242.12	233.28
Spain	—	—	—	—	374.12	585.02	420.35	304.70	—	250.53	—	—	—
Sweden	76.77	102.85	139.22	150.35	550.71	284.36	243.06	140.34	—	—	—	—	—
United Kingdom	—	94.58	141.32	183.82	457.02	251.29	210.90	—	—	195.08	—	—	—

Destination	1970	1971	1972	1973	1974	1975	1976	1977	1978	1979	1980	1981	1982
							Refined sugar						
GDR	137.35	147.93	147.93	147.93	431.89	431.89	431.89	431.89	431.89	431.89	523.77	595.41	595.41
Hungary	109.13	132.95	134.84	126.76	431.89	431.89	431.89	431.89	431.89	431.89	523.77	671.44	—
Poland	147.93	147.93	147.93	147.93	431.89	—	—	—	431.89	431.89	—	—	—
Romania	113.54	113.54	—	—	—	—	—	—	—	—	—	—	—
Albania	77.16	85.98	85.98	147.93	161.60	431.89	431.89	254.20	181.11	151.48	161.41	415.00	276.44
North Korea	—	—	—	—	147.93	431.89	431.89	431.89	—	431.89	431.89	431.89	431.89
Yugoslavia	—	—	—	—	287.47	356.37	297.52	—	—	—	—	—	—
Angola	—	—	—	—	—	—	286.56	161.49	146.65	151.49	522.05	397.67	294.32
Egypt	—	—	—	—	—	—	191.16	161.67	146.60	152.32	498.73	368.24	223.74
Spain	120.14	121.49	143.30	143.74	404.68	651.88	—	—	—	250.53	—	277.95	285.06
Sudan	—	—	—	—	—	—	—	161.85	—	—	—	—	—
Suriname	—	—	—	—	—	—	200.66	180.31	—	—	—	399.49	225.67
Syria	—	—	—	—	—	—	247.08	181.03	133.76	—	—	444.13	237.15
Turkey	—	—	—	—	476.65	531.63	—	—	—	—	—	—	—
United Kingdom	—	—	—	—	—	314.33	—	—	—	—	—	—	—

Source: Comité Estatal de Estadísticas, *Anuario Estadístico de Cuba*, various years.

Appendix Table 2: Unit values of Cuban sugar exports (pesos/tonne, basis 96°)

Destination	1965	1970	1975	1980	1981	1982	1983	1984	1985	1986	1987	1988
USSR	134	131	482	743	605	625	873	868	987	867	853	922
Bulgaria	112	110	355	423	474	500	513	446	416	407	461	436
Czechoslovakia	134	132	356	431	362	444	522	499	505	508	507	507
GDR	136	124	359	423	485	500	498	505	500	547	550	549
Hungary	—	100	379	537	657	591	—	—	—	—	673	656
Romania	—	104	357	355	—	—	—	—	—	—	—	—
Vietnam	69	65	147	99	204	247	241	247	255	187	149	133
China	134	133	416	226	377	334	278	288	232	162	139	169
North Korea	116	86	183	356	—	—	—	—	—	—	—	—
Algeria	63	89	416	401	351	197	229	152	97	136	157	172
Angola	—	—	—	461	555	260	253	122	140	149	184	230
Canada	38	71	330	398	283	190	141	115	81	128	127	153
Egypt	57	82	420	363	382	203	206	155	98	158	155	198
Indonesia	—	—	—	227	479	178	—	—	—	—	150	169
Iraq	58	63	297	391	292	217	159	138	113	146	161	237
Japan	50	85	613	354	274	132	134	83	74	122	117	134
Morocco	83	76	383	—	—	—	—	—	—	—	—	—
Spain	140	111	569	—	257	271	—	—	—	—	—	—
All	110	114	458	531	468	488	582	584	616	608	615	587

Source: Calculated from *Anuario Estadístico de Cuba*, various years.

Appendix Table 3: Prices of selected Cuban imports from the Soviet Union in terms of sugar

	1968	1970	1975	1980	1985	1988
One tonne of sugar bought:						
Canned meat, t	0.14	0.14	0.41	0.70	0.64	0.60
Butter, t	0.12	0.17	0.44	0.68	0.59	0.55
Fish, shellfish, t	0.35	0.46	1.2	1.2	1.1	1.0
Wheat, t	1.7	1.9	3.1	4.7	5.2	10.0
Maize, t	2.4	2.1	3.5	5.4	7.3	10.8
Wheat flour, t	1.2	1.4	2.1	3.1	4.6	6.6
Lard, t	0.39	0.50	1.1	1.7	2.0	1.9
Lumber, m^3	2.4	2.1	6.2	6.6	6.5	6.1
Cotton, t	0.19	0.18	0.44	0.69	0.71	0.64
Vegetable oil, t	0.47	0.57	0.95	1.3	1.9	1.8
Fertiliser, t	3.0	3.6	8.0	11.1	11.2	11.2
Tyres, units	2.6	2.3	10.3	9.7	8.6	8.7
Textiles, 1000 m^2	0.63	0.53	1.2	1.7	1.3	1.2
Rolled steel, t	1.0	0.90	2.4	3.6	3.5	3.3
Tin plate, t	0.60	0.59	1.6	2.1	1.5	1.4
Steel pipe, t	0.67	0.61	1.7	2.5	2.0	1.9
Oil, crude, and products, t	7.8	7.3	12.4	8.9	5.1	4.5[a]
Tonnes of sugar required to buy:						
Tractor	18.4	24.7	8.1	4.9	8.0	8.7
Cane loader	10.5	11.4	7.7	4.8	4.7	4.2

[a] 1987.   t tonne

Source: Calculated from *Anuario Estadístico de Cuba*, various years.

Notes

1   Except where otherwise indicated, all data stem from various issues of the *Anuario Estadístico de Cuba* and information compiled by the Economics and Statistics Division of the International Sugar Organization. Sugar statistics should not be interpreted too closely. It is not always clear whether the original data are couched in long tons or metric tons (tonnes). Here, the expression 'tons' is used where we are in doubt. Moreover, raw and white sugars differ in quality; they are converted to a common standard on the basis of their polarisation. This expresses the power of a sucrose solution to rotate a plane of polarised light. Standard raw sugar is defined as measuring 96 sugar degrees by the polariscope. To convert sugars of different polarisation to raw value, the International Sugar Organization employs the formula (2P-100)/92, where P = degrees of polarisation of the sugar in question. In the *Anuario Estadístico de Cuba*, however, physical raw sugars are translated into 96-degree terms by the polarisation ratio, not the ISO formula, at least in respect of production. The polarisation ratio is obtained by dividing the polarisation of a given sugar by 96, the resulting factor then being multiplied by the tonnage produced to get the raw value equivalent. At the average polarisation of Cuban raws reported in recent years (around 98.3 degrees), the polarisation ratio results in a raw value equivalent about 2.5 per cent lower than the ISO formula. Finally, for unknown reasons, exports to Hungary of 88,152 tonnes in 1987–88 recorded in *Anuario Estadístico de Cuba 1988* were not reported to the International Sugar Organization. According to F.O. Licht's International Sugar and Sweetener Report (9 July 1990), Havana had been repaying a Hungarian loan with sugar that was sold on the world market.

2   Article 36 of the International Sugar Agreement of 1968 and Article 31 of the 1977 Agreement, 'Exports by Cuba to socialist countries', comprised Albania, Bulgaria, China, Czechoslovakia, the German Democratic Republic, Hungary, Mongolia, North Korea, Poland, Romania, the USSR, Vietnam, and Yugoslavia.

3   With sugar and final molasses exports to market economies valued at 336.6 million pesos, this adds up to convertible currency earnings of 487.7 million pesos for sugar and allied products in 1989. Banco Nacional de Cuba (1990b:22), however, put total convertible currency sugar exports in 1989 at 645.7 million pesos. Against this, it reported convertible currency sugar imports of 345 million pesos, explaining that an overrun of 169 million pesos in actual over projected sugar purchases 'was essentially to cover increased deliveries to the Soviet Union for additional needs and agreements to speed up deliveries. This, in the final analysis, produced a surplus of domestic and foreign sugar to be exported to other countries.'

CHAPTER 6

Anglo-Cuban commercial relations in the 1960s: A case study of the Leyland Motor company contracts with Cuba

George Lambie

Introduction

As a result of the political and commercial influence of the US in the Caribbean during the inter-war years, Leyland Motors Ltd, like many other British exporters to the region, tended to concentrate its efforts on the British colonies where it enjoyed some of the best markets in the Americas for its products. During the Second World War the economies of the main industrial nations were geared to arms production, and the entire Caribbean, as indeed most of the underdeveloped world, was unable to import its requirements of manufactured products. When the conflict ended demand for industrial goods in these nations was so strong that they often abandoned their traditional suppliers to gain access to the products they had been starved of for four years.

By 1945 British industry, though distorted by the war effort, was in better shape than the industrial sectors of most of the other European powers which had been engaged in the conflict. Before the war Britain's main European competitors in the international market had been Germany, France and Italy, all of which by 1945 were left with much of their industry destroyed or severely weakened.[1] Consequently those British manufacturers who could switch quickly from wartime to peacetime production were able to take advantage of the strong demand in foreign markets for industrial goods ahead of their competitors in Europe. This was especially true for Leyland which disengaged from military vehicle production, and returned to its role as a civilian motor manufacturer only months after the war had ended. In contrast, companies such as Mercedes Benz of Germany and Fiat of Italy, who had suffered great damage to their productive capacity during the war, took several years before they could resume their function as manufacturers and exporters of civilian motor vehicles.

Naturally, after the war US industry emerged as an even more vigorous competitor in the international market than before the conflict, but in the immediate post-war years American motor manufacturers were mainly occupied with filling pent-up demand at home rather than engaging in export drives abroad. Aware of the opportunities open to British exporters at the end of the war, and to avert a balance of payments crisis, the Labour government encouraged British manufacturers to regain their foreign markets by offering cheap credit and priority access to basic inputs, like steel, to those companies which produced for export. By 1948 Britain was producing 42 per cent of all European exports. This was almost ten times the amount being produced by West Germany at that time.[2]

In 1950 after five years of concerted effort to regain its position in foreign markets, British industry was generating 25.5 per cent of world exports of manufactures, which represented a level of export performance which it had not enjoyed since the 1920s. From 1950 onwards, however, as Japanese and much of European industry completed its reconstruction, British manufacturers were no longer able to enjoy a privileged position in international markets and their share of world exports fell dramatically.[3]

Leyland's commercial interests in Cuba before the Revolution

Leyland initiated commercial relations with Cuba in the 1920s and 1930s when the company obtained a number of small orders to supply the British-owned Havana Railways with buses and trucks.[4] By the late-1940s exports of Leyland vehicles to the Commonwealth and other traditional British markets exceeded pre-war levels, and a number of big orders were received from new customers, including Cuba.[5] The Cuban order, however, was exceptional because while Leyland's export drive to Latin America and the British Caribbean was moderately successful, US influence in the non-European Caribbean continued to restrict substantial outside commercial penetration. Leyland's new business with Cuba was secured mainly because of the intervention of the American entrepreneur William Pawley.

Pawley, who owned two bus companies in Florida, had sought in the late-1940s to replace part of his fleet of General Motors buses with Leyland vehicles, which had shorter delivery times and were believed to be more reliable than their American equivalents. But opposition from the Teamsters Union, on the grounds that jobs in the American motor industry would be lost if the order went through, frustrated the deal. Coincidentally, at that time representatives from one of Pawley's companies were acting as public transport consultants to the Cuban government and one of their main recommendations was that the old tramway system in Havana should be dismantled and replaced by a modern bus service. Because Pawley had already begun negotiations with Leyland he suggested to the Cubans that they might like to buy Leyland buses for their new transport network.

Apparently Pawley had had influence in Cuban business circles since the late-1920s, when he had organised and become President of Cuba's first airline the Compañía Nacional Cubana de Aviación Curtiss (this company was merged with Pan American Airways in 1932). His high standing in Cuba, along with his personal friendship with Batista, who, though not in power at that time was still able to influence political and economic decisions, made him a valuable asset for Leyland to have on its side. Both Pawley and Batista took part in the final negotiations with Leyland. During these negotiations it was agreed that Pawley's firm would be responsible for removing the old tramway system in Havana and arranging for the delivery of the buses. After the contract was signed a new private Cuban company, Autobuses Modernos, was set up to run the bus fleet. As a reward for his services, the Cubans offered Pawley the post of president of the new company, which he accepted. Pawley also established a good reputation with Leyland's management who hoped to use his influence in other parts of Latin America – Pawley had served as American Ambassador to Peru and Brazil in the 1940s – to secure further contracts in US dominated markets.[6]

The Cuban order for 620 Leyland Royal Tiger buses, which was signed in 1950, was valued at $10 million, and at that time represented the largest single dollar order ever negotiated by a British company.[7] Another exceptional aspect of the contract was that Leyland was paid out of the bus fares, and had to put its collectors in Cuban depots.[8] This arrangement gave Leyland an intimate knowledge of the Havana bus service, which proved to be an advantage when negotiating for further contracts with the Cubans.

Business as usual: Leyland and the Cuban Revolution

Once established as a principal supplier to the Cuban public transport sector, Leyland continued in subsequent years to receive orders for spare parts, maintenance services and replacement vehicles. And, in 1958, only a few months before Castro's guerrilla army entered Havana, a second large contract, this time for 200 Leyland Olympic series II buses valued at £1.5 million ($6 million), was signed with the newly-formed company Omnibus Metropolitanos S.A. which had recently taken over Autobuses Modernos.[9]

The placing of this order coincided with a controversy over British arms sales to Cuba. In October 1958 the British government authorised the sale of 17 Sea Fury piston-engined fighters to Batista's regime.[10] The planes were to be supplied with a large quantity of air to ground missiles which were clearly for use against the rebels.[11] Not surprisingly Batista's enemies, both in Cuba and abroad, were incensed by this action, especially given that even the US had halted sales of arms to the dictatorship since April of the same year. Castro responded by calling for a boycott of British goods and warned that British property on the island (valued at £11 million) might be confiscated when his guerilla army came to power.[12] Although the Macmillan government refused to accede to threats, export licenses for the planes were withheld until November, and only twelve aircraft were finally sent to Cuba while Batista was in power. The delivery of a number of tanks which had been ordered from British companies was also inexplicably delayed. In mid-December, under pressure from the Labour opposition, and after it was clear that Batista was finished, Macmillan's government finally agreed to stop all arms shipments to the Cuban dictator.[13]

In early January 1959, after the rebels had seized power, the British Embassy in Havana tried to appease Castro further by pointing out that because of London's decision to stop shipping arms to Batista, British companies had lost £5 million worth of sales.[14] The loss to British arms manufacturers was, however, Leyland's gain, as in mid-January Castro called for an end to the boycott of British goods and sanctioned the completion of the bus order.

When Castro came to power the US refused to lift the arms embargo which it had initially imposed on Batista, and as relations began to deteriorate between Washington and Havana the Cubans became anxious to find alternative suppliers of military equipment. Having let Britain off lightly for its complicity with Batista, Castro told the Cuban Ambassador in London to see if Macmillan's government would return the goodwill by replacing the 17 Sea Fury planes ordered by Batista with an equal number of Hawker Hunter Mark V jet fighters.[15] This request, which was made in September 1959 was opportunely timed with the dispatch of the first shipment of Leyland buses to Havana. But after much deliberation, and under duress from Washington which claimed the aircraft would be used against the US, the British Foreign Minister Selwyn Lloyd refused to agree to the Cuban request.[16]

Had the Leyland deal been the only substantial business Cuba was conducting with Britain at that time it may have suffered from this decision, but the Castro government had a far more controversial British contact on which to register its displeasure. In November 1958 the Batista government had ratified a large joint Anglo-Cuban venture to build a shipyard and numerous service facilities at Mariel to the west of Havana.[17] The leading company in the British consortium was the Hawker Siddeley Group which was also the manufacturer of the Sea Fury aircraft which were sent to Batista. This shipyard contract was kept on ice for the first 10 months that Castro was in power, but when Hawker Siddeley and the British government refused to exchange the obsolete Sea Furies for modern jet fighters, the shipyard contract was cancelled by Havana.

However, the apparently innocuous bus contract with Leyland was not affected. In fact the Revolutionary government was anxious to let the deal go ahead because it included, along with the order to supply new vehicles which were badly needed, an undertaking to assist the Cubans to rebuild approximately 300 buses from the 1950 contract which had fallen into disrepair. During the course of the rebuilding programme many Cuban mechanics received invaluable training, and were able to go on to set up an efficient local maintenance and repair service for the city's fleet of Leyland buses. Because of Cuba's worsening relations with the US and declining hard currency earnings, this project, which encouraged maximum use of Cuba's internal resources, caught the attention of the Revolutionary leadership and marked the beginning of a close commercial relationship between Leyland and the Castro government which lasted throughout the 1960s and early 1970s.[18]

At the time of the signing of the 1958 contract between Batista's government and Leyland it was hoped that Havana's bus service would run for several years without further additions or improvements. However, because of the rapid economic and social changes which took place in Cuba during the early years of the Revolution, and the mobilisation of large numbers of people to implement these changes, demand on public transport increased at an unprecedented rate, especially in rural areas where such programmes as the literacy campaign were being carried out. Moreover, with diminishing access to spare parts for the island's fleet of American General Motors buses because of Washington's tightening of the trade embargo, Cuba soon began to experience a shortage of public transport, especially in rural areas.

Havana would perhaps have placed more orders with Leyland to satisfy increasing demand but declining hard currency reserves, and Leyland's inability to provide small vehicles for rural use, obliged the Cuban Transport Ministry to import a number of Hungarian (Icarus) and Czechoslovakian (Skoda) mini-buses. In service these vehicles proved to be unreliable, and spares and service back-up was almost non-existent. As with many of the manufactured products which were imported by Cuba from the Soviet Union and Eastern Europe in the 1960s, these buses were unsuited to local conditions.[19]

By 1963 Cuba's public transport system had begun to break down, and the Revolutionary government made the acquisition of new and reliable vehicles a priority. This decision coincided with an increase in the market price of sugar and a change of economic strategy by the Cuban leadership from a spontaneous attempt to industrialise, to a policy of export-led growth which was partly premised on the availability of imports from capitalist countries. Between 1960 and 1962 Britain's imports of Cuban sugar had been at an all time low but in 1963, after the tensions generated by the missile crisis had subsided, and more Cuban sugar became available in the market, Britain restored its orders to pre-Revolutionary levels.[20]

With sterling earnings assured for the coming year the Cubans invited Leyland personnel to Havana to discuss the island's transport requirements. Resulting from negotiations held in early-December 1963, the Cuban state organisation 'Transimport' signed a contract with Leyland on 6 January 1964 to supply 400 EL2.44 Olympic buses with an option on up to 1000 more between 1965 and 1968.[21] The initial order for 400 buses was valued by the press at £3.6 million ($11 million) with an extra £360,000 ($1 million) for spares.[22] A second smaller order was placed on 28 January for 50 Leyland LERT2/1 Royal Tiger long-distance buses with Metro Cammell Weymann bodies.[23]

Although Leyland vehicles had a good reputation in Cuba, and the company was in a strong negotiating position, they had won the contract against stiff competition from French, West German, Spanish, Japanese, and Czechoslovakian manufacturers, which had also been invited to tender.[24] Leyland's success in securing the contract can be attributed above all to its ability to offer five year credit terms to Cuba backed by the British government's Export Credits Guarantee Department (ECGD). Apparently, before tendering for the contract, Leyland's management had persuaded the British government to give Cuba an official credit rating.[25] Leyland's foreign competitors did not receive the same support from their respective governments, but London's initiative was soon followed by France and Japan who decided to extend credit guarantees to their own companies who were seeking orders from Cuba. Leyland was the first British company to obtain ECGD cover to export to Cuba since Castro came to power.

The decision of Sir Alec Douglas-Home's government to give official support to the Leyland contract with Cuba was an outstanding gesture of commercial pragmatism, and was tantamount to a complete rejection of America's trade embargo policy against Cuba. Because of this decision many British firms followed Leyland into Cuba where they established a reliable market for their products.

Bus deal with Cuba rocks 'special relationship' between Britain and the US

Not surprisingly the Johnson Administration was furious with the British government for allowing, and even encouraging with guaranteed credit, a British company to make such a large and blatant infringement of the American trade embargo on Cuba. The gravity with which the signing of the Leyland contract with Cuba was received in Washington can be gauged from the *New York Times's* leading article of 14 January 1964, in which the author wrote:

> the $11 million sale of 400 buses by a British company is not just another breach in the blockade. The magnitude of the transaction and the liberal credit terms make it a breakthrough. For in granting a five year credit as well as an option to buy an additional 1000 buses, the British are in effect declaring that Castro will not be overthrown by economic pressure. And with Cuban sugar commanding high prices in the world markets, other hard-headed businessmen are just as eager to do business with Cuba (p. 30).[26]

Since mid-1963 State Department officials had known that Leyland had a representative in Havana advising the Castro government on Cuba's transport requirements and looking for new business, but they had not expected that such a large order would be placed with the British company. Shortly after the Leyland contract with Cuba was signed Washington sent a memorandum to its London embassy which expressed 'continuing concern' over the British government's attitude to trade with Cuba, and suggested that Whitehall should be persuaded to withdraw its support of sales of motor vehicles and electrical equipment to Cuba because such goods served to strengthen the economic base of the Castro regime.[27] Officials in Washington were particularly anxious at that time to prevent Cuba from importing motor vehicles, because it was estimated that the number of buses operating in Havana had declined from 1600 in 1961 to 800 in 1963, and that the public transport system was on the brink of collapse.[28] After three years of concerted effort to undermine the transport sector of the Cuban economy by preventing spare parts for American equipment, including General Motors and Ford buses, from reaching Cuba, US officials were appalled by Britain's willingness to come to the rescue of the Castro regime.

Washington also pointed out to the British government that by entering into long-term trading commitments with Cuba, backed by guaranteed credit, Britain was providing the Castro regime with an opportunity to continue importing vital manufactured goods even after the sugar price had fallen and Cuba was again faced with shortages of hard currency. Finally, US Embassy officials in London were instructed to make the Conservative government of Alec Douglas-Home aware of the depth of 'US sensitivity [to] the Cuban problem' and the 'US determination [to] maintain pressure on [the] GOC [government of Cuba]'.[29]

From the moment that the Leyland contract was signed it became clear that disagreements were so profound between Washington and London over the matter of trading with Cuba, that there was little hope for an easy reconciliation. As far as the State Department was concerned Cuba's objective was to export its revolution to Latin America and eventually the rest of the Third World.[30] Based on this premise it believed it was in the interest of all 'free' nations to contribute towards the isolation and destabilisation of the Castro regime. Part of this strategy of containment, it was argued, was the need for an effective trade embargo which prevented Cuba from using commercial links with the market economies to strengthen the Revolution, and thereby improve its capacity to export 'subversion' to the Third World. After US backed counter-revolutionaries failed to overthrow Castro by force of arms in the Bay of Pigs invasion in 1961, the trade embargo became the linchpin of Washington's anti-Cuba policy.

While Washington had found it could persuade most of its fellow members of the Organisation of American States to quarantine Cuba, with the notable exception of Mexico, its European allies were less enthusiastic to follow State Department initiatives. From late-1960, when the US embargo on Cuba began to be implemented, to the beginning of 1963 trade between Cuba and Western Europe had remained suppressed because of Cuba's shortage of hard currency and the Castro government's desire to strengthen its trading links with the Soviet Union and other communist countries. But by 1963, with improving sugar prices on the world market combined with the problems caused by the unsuitability and long delivery times of some Soviet bloc technology, Cuba became anxious to increase its trade with Western Europe.[31] The contract which was signed with Leyland in January 1964 was the first substantive evidence that Cuba wished to reopen its internal market to Western technology, and in subsequent months companies in France, Spain, and later West Germany and Italy, followed in Leyland's footsteps.

Foremost among the British government's arguments for maintaining trade links with Cuba against the wishes of the US, was the claim that as a small island nation Britain had always relied more on trade for its economic survival than America, and could not afford to cease commercial relations with a country because it did not approve of its political system.[32] British exporters, and especially Leyland, could also point to their long tradition of conducting business with socialist countries. Indeed, one of Leyland's first big export orders was negotiated with the Soviet Union in 1924.[33] Moreover, after the Second World War when Leyland returned to the production of vehicles for civilian transport, some of the first foreign customers for its buses were the new socialist states, including Poland and Yugoslavia.[34]

In general, by the early 1960s, many socialist countries, and especially the Soviet Union and Eastern Europe, had become important customers of British manufactures. Between 1950 and 1963 British exports to the Soviet bloc increased from £26 million to £123 million, with the most impressive period of growth taking place during the four years from 1959 to 1963 when exports doubled.[35] After visiting a number of Eastern European countries in July 1964 the British Minister of State, Edward du Cann said:

my view is that all nations of the world, developed and developing, the industrialised West and the Communist controlled economies alike, are economically interdependent . . . no country or group of countries can live in economic isolation, and prosper. If trade can help to remove misunderstanding's between us, if it can facilitate the happy process of *détente* between East and West, so much the better . . . so far as HM Government is concerned we are determined to go on promoting trade and thereby to prove that peaceful co-existence is a reality.[36]

The British government's liberal philosophy on trade with socialist countries was partly a response to a number of economic pressures and trading restrictions which faced British exporters in some of their main markets in the 1950s and 1960s.[37] These were, firstly, the gradual breakdown of the system of imperial preference because of increasing Japanese and American competition in the Commonwealth. Secondly, although Britain began to expand its exports to the Common Market during the above period, its failure to gain membership restricted its access to what was essentially a natural market for British products.[38] Thirdly, the formation of the European Free Trade Association (EFTA) in 1959 did not offer as many new market opportunities as had initially been hoped by British exporters. The British government responded to these problems, which were the main cause of the country's poor balance of payments performance in the 1960s, by encouraging commercial pragmatism in its business community, and vigorously defending the belief that wherever markets and means of payments existed for British products they should be exploited to the full.

Another argument which was frequently put forward by those supporting British trade with Cuba, concerned the apparent double standards of the US on the subject of trading with communist countries, of which the clearest example at the time of the Leyland controversy was the sale of American wheat to the Soviet Union.[39] Washington defended its trade with the Soviet Union by claiming that American farmers produced more wheat than was required for domestic consumption, to which Leyland's Chairman Sir William Black responded 'If America has a surplus of wheat, we have a surplus of buses'.[40]

Britain also disagreed with America's political strategy towards Cuba, which advocated starving the Castro government of Western goods so that it would be increasingly forced to rely on the Soviet Union, which, faced with such an expensive and onerous commitment would be disinclined to support more revolutions in the Americas. The British government felt that this aspect of US policy towards Cuba was ineffective and misguided, and also believed that Cuba's huge imports of goods from the Soviet Union and Eastern Europe not only took away valuable business for the market economies but would also result in the Castro regime becoming inextricably tied to the communist camp. One of the most outspoken members of the Conservative government against American policy towards Cuba was the Foreign Secretary R.A. Butler. In a leading article in *The Times*, which drew mainly from statements that had been made by Butler, the Foreign Secretary was reported to have suggested that US policy towards Cuba represented a self-fulfilling prophecy, and that there was little point in Washington condemning Castro for his socialist policies at home, and his support of revolutionary movements in Latin America, if they themselves were consciously pushing him closer to the Soviet Union.[41] Moreover, Butler felt that Castro was not an 'orthodox communist' but an 'unstable nationalist leader' who had made a pact with the USSR for pragmatic reasons. Based on this analysis of Castro's politics, Butler concluded that the task of Western nations was not to force the Cubans to seek a greater dependency on the Soviet Union, but rather to coax the regime back into the West's sphere of influence.

As well as the general arguments put forward by Britain in support of its trading policy towards Cuba, there were also those arguments which were more specifically directed towards the defence of the Leyland contract. The most important issue emerged over the appropriate definition of strategic and non-strategic goods. Washington took the position that trade in non-strategic goods with communist countries was acceptable, except with Cuba, China, North Vietnam and North Korea, where a total trade embargo was in operation. In line with US policy, Britain's Conservative government had voluntarily added Cuba to NATO's list of socialist countries to which the export of strategic goods was proscribed, but they refused to abandon their diplomatic and non-strategic commercial links with the Castro government, arguing that total embargoes were only acceptable if countries were at war with one another.[42] Some confusion existed over the definition of strategic and non-strategic goods between the US Commerce Department and the British Board of Trade, but neither included buses on their strategic listings.

Having incurred the wrath of the US administration, Leyland was anxious to ensure that it conducted its business with Cuba in strict accordance with the British government's official trading policy. It was therefore dismayed to learn that some American politicians, and in particular Senator Barry Goldwater, claimed that buses could be regarded as strategic equipment, especially in time of war. Leyland officials, however, decided to treat such suggestions with derision, and the company's Managing Director, Donald Stokes, when questioned on the matter said, 'these buses are not strategic war material – you would look damn silly going to war on a bus'.[43] Some commentators in the American press also argued that buses could not be regarded as strategic equipment under any circumstances, and Arthur Hoppe of the *Washington Star* wrote mischievously of the grave peril to the

US of an invasion by, 'bearded cigar-smoking troops in cleverly camouflaged vehicles which say "Victoria" or "Charing Cross" '.[44]

Leyland officials concluded that while they may have offended the US by agreeing to supply buses to Cuba and thereby broken the embargo, they could not be accused of endangering America's security. Once this argument had been accepted by most moderate politicians in the US, Leyland was free to defend its business with Cuba on the grounds of commercial pragmatism, which accorded with the official British government stance on the subject of trading with communist countries.[45] Leyland also pointed out to its critics that the company had been supplying Cuba with buses since long before the Revolution, and it saw no reason why its business should cease because of an embargo, which most European observers regarded as simply an American over-reaction to the Castro regime.[46] Moreover, Leyland personnel who had been in Cuba during the early-1960s before the 1964 bus contract was signed, claimed that some US companies were evading the embargo by transferring their export business with Cuba to foreign subsidiaries.[47] Two notable examples were General Motors which shipped to Havana via Antwerp in Belgium, and Ford which continued trading with Cuba from Mexico. It was felt, therefore, that if the US government could not effectively police its own business community, then it had no right to tell British companies to avoid the Cuban market. Finally, Leyland reminded its American critics that it had bid for the Cuban contract against companies from several other countries.[48] This argument, however, did little to mollify Washington because it confirmed their worst suspicions that Japan and most of Western Europe were poised to open up new business with Cuba. In this context Washington's fear that the Leyland contract set a dangerous precedent for other countries was justified. Indeed, the Leyland deal with Cuba turned out to be nothing less than a green light for other members of the Western Alliance to begin a vigorous sales drive in the Cuban market.[49]

Despite the US administration's anger over the Leyland contract with Cuba, which resulted in an official condemnation of the British government by the State Department and at least one direct telephone call from President Johnson to Prime Minister Douglas-Home to discuss the matter, Washington wanted to avoid any action which could jeopardise its 'special relationship' with Britain. Realising that it could do little to prevent the sale from going ahead the State Department issued a statement saying that although ships carrying the buses to Cuba would be subject to the American black list, no other reprisals would be taken.[50] However, a number of American politicians were eager to circumvent the official US position, and made their own recommendations on how Leyland and the British government should be dealt with for their recalcitrance.[51] And soon after the contract was signed the American press were carrying reports of senators who were in favour of the US government imposing a boycott on British goods sold in America. In response to this suggestion the Washington correspondent of *The Times* concluded that those who supported the idea of a boycott were only a 'frenzied fringe', and that it was realised in 'more responsible quarters' that such actions would 'hurt the alliance more than Cuba'.[52]

Britain, Leyland, and the tightening of the US embargo on Cuba

Although it quickly became clear that most Americans felt that reprisals by the US government against Britain would represent a dangerous precedent which could damage the alliance, the British press remained sensitive to the issue, and in a leading article on 19 February 1964 *The Times* noted under the heading 'Reprisal', that it had been announced in Washington that Britain, along with a number of other countries, was to cease to be a recipient of US military aid (p. 11). This action was the outcome of an amendment which was made by Congress in December 1963 to the Foreign Assistance Act which empowered the President to curtail or eliminate economic and military assistance to countries that failed to take 'appropriate steps' to withdraw their cargo carrying ships and aircraft from trade with Cuba by the arbitrary deadline of 14 February 1964.[53]

This ruling was one in a long series of attempts by the US to persuade its Western allies to curb their transportation links with Castro's Cuba. The first significant initiative to be taken by Washington in pursuit of this objective came in September 1962, after the publication of a study by the US Department of Commerce (Maritime Administration) which revealed the full extent of the involvement of allied shipping in Cuba trade.[54] The study showed that even though Cuba had effectively moved over into the socialist camp by 1962, both politically and economically, three-quarters of its imports were still being carried by shipping from the market economies in the first nine months of that year.[55] Of the 572 calls made at Cuban ports by non-communist ships during this period 110 were made by British vessels. This was only surpassed by Greek ships which made 125 calls.

On the basis of this information, the Kennedy administration decided to launch a diplomatic campaign through its embassies in Europe to encourage the European powers to reduce the numbers of their ships involved in Cuba trade.[56] But only West Germany showed an immediate willingness to accede to US demands, while the other powers requested more time to discuss the matter with their shipowners.[57] Impatient for a wider and more favourable response the State Department informed NATO on 2 October 1962 that it was proposing several new measures to discourage Western vessels calling at Cuban ports. These would include: closing US ports to all the ships of any country if a vessel flying its flag was discovered carrying arms to Cuba; making shipowners engaged in trade with Cuba ineligible to carry US foreign aid cargoes; prohibiting the entry into any American port of ships which on the same voyage were engaged in Soviet-Cuban trade.[58] A few days later, and with the support of some American maritime organisations and the International Longshoreman's Association, it was further proposed that ships engaged in Cuba trade should be blacklisted and banned from US ports.[59] The ILA also accepted the responsibility of policing American ports to ensure that allied shipping which attempted to trade with Cuba as well as the US was identified and included on the blacklist. At this stage Washington had still not passed legislation which would allow action to be taken against shipowners with vessels engaged in Cuba trade, but the creation of a blacklist and the possible threat of retrospective legislation was an effective deterrent which resulted in a decline in the number of ships from the capitalist world calling at Cuban ports. Some of the first countries to withdraw shipping from Cuba trade because of blacklisting were Japan, Norway, Denmark and Liberia.[60] Britain, however, remained adamant, and the Council of the British Chamber of Shipping membership indicated that they would only curb their links with Cuba if they received a direct order to do so from the British government.[61]

Before Washington had time to gauge the response of its other allies it became embroiled in the Cuban missile crisis. During the crisis the US placed a total naval blockade on Cuba which lasted for one month and which excluded all shipping from Cuban ports. When the blockade was lifted on 20 November 1962 it was hoped in Washington that the combined effect of its diplomatic campaign, blacklisting, and the shock of the missile crisis would persuade its European allies to cut back further on their shipping links with the Castro regime. But this was not to be, and by the end of November vessels from capitalist countries were again calling regularly at Cuban ports.[62]

Although US pressure on Western governments before the missile crisis to curb their shipping links with Cuba had resulted in some lasting cutbacks, Washington wanted to make its policy more effective, and especially against the British government which insisted that the US had no legal basis on which it could order British shipowners to stop their vessels from entering Cuban ports. Partly because of Britain's intransigence Washington decided to pass formal legislation to dissuade Western shipowners from carrying Cuba trade, and in February 1963 it was announced that foreign merchant vessels calling at Cuban ports would be denied American government financed cargoes.[63]

Undeterred by Washington's directives British shipowners continued engaging in Cuba trade, and during the first nine months of 1963 more

British-registered ships called at Cuban ports than ships from any other capitalist country.[64] Not only did British shipowners refuse to co-operate with the US because they wished to defend their traditions of free maritime trade, but they also found Cuba trade to be extremely lucrative, especially the contracts to carry Russian crude oil to Havana.

In December 1963 when the US announced that it planned to cease economic and military aid to countries which failed to take 'appropriate steps' to curb their transportation links with Cuba, Britain did not feel this was a particularly serious threat because for 1964 it had been allocated only a very small amount of military aid from the US ($100,000), and its loss would be financially insignificant. But the prospect of being openly disciplined by its principal ally was an embarrassment. When implementing the legislation, policymakers in Washington were clearly aware of this factor and hoped to use its potential to the full. Morley points out that in the period leading up to the February deadline, US officials did not expect Britain to take visibly 'appropriate steps' to curb its transportation links with Cuba as the legislation required, but rather to make 'informal approaches' to British shipowners to dissuade them from engaging in Cuban trade.[65]

On 12 February, only days before the US decision to terminate military aid to Britain, Prime Minister Douglas-Home and the Foreign Secretary R.A. Butler began an official visit to Washington. Heading the agenda for talks with President Johnson was the subject of the 'special relationship' which had existed between Britain and America since the war. But, as *The Times* correspondent in Washington, who was assigned to cover the talks, noted, 'all [was] not well' at that moment between the allies.[66] While the heads of state found that they could agree on most issues concerning the 'special relationship', on the matter of Britain's trade and maritime links with Cuba they remained at loggerheads.[67]

According to Morley, Washington had gathered together a great deal of material relating to British trade with Cuba in preparation for the visit, and had formulated a number of recommendations to put to the Prime Minister (pp. 230–1). These included that the British government should: firstly, discourage British shipping from carrying Cuba trade; secondly, adopt a firm policy of denying Cuba access to any 'critical commodities'; and thirdly, withdraw credit guarantees to British traders doing business with Cuba. Finally, it was suggested that Britain ought be reminded that as Washington's closest ally its handling of its relations with Cuba would 'strongly influence' the response of other Western nations to the Castro regime. Therefore the British should be especially careful not to set precedents favourable to Cuba which could be followed by other market economies (p. 231).

A memorandum to Johnson from Secretary of State Rusk went further and advised the President to suggest to Douglas-Home that he hold up the delivery of the Leyland buses, and obtain guarantees that any further bus sales to Cuba were not supported by official credit guarantees (Morley, p. 231). The memorandum went on to say that these suggestions should be reinforced with the threat 'of possible countermoves against [British] firms [with American operations] trading with Cuba', if they were not heeded.

When presented with these demands and recommendations during his meeting with the President, Douglas-Home responded by pointing to Washington's apparent dual standards towards communist countries, which made it acceptable for the US to sell wheat to the Soviet Union but unacceptable for Britain to sell buses to Cuba.[68] Johnson apparently countered by expressing particular concern over the favourable credit terms which the British government was granting to socialist countries, pointing not only to the five year guarantee which had been given to cover the Leyland deal with Cuba, but also the 12 and 15 year credits which were being offered to Moscow to promote the sale of chemical and other plants.[69] The Prime Minister in his reply noted that it was normal practice for governments to insure national exporting firms against default of payment by their foreign customers, and that the US administration had itself underwritten trade with socialist countries in the past.[70] At a news conference given by Douglas-Home after his meeting with the President he said that he had 'chosen' not to remind his host that US exports to Cuba in 1963 totalled $37 million while British sales to Cuba were only just in excess of $5 million for the same year.[71]

With American and British elections only a few months away it appeared that both leaders were anxious to score political points over Cuba. In the US President Johnson faced the challenge of the extreme right-wing Republican candidate Barry Goldwater, and consequently had to ensure that his administration was seen by his own supporters on the right to be taking a hard line on Cuba so as not to risk losing their support. Douglas-Home, however, faced a more complex, and rather ambiguous political situation in Britain over the issue of trade with Cuba. For the right, US pressure on Britain to curb its trade and shipping links with the Castro regime was seen as a direct challenge to British sovereignty and the principles of free trade and freedom of the seas on which it was perceived the nation's commercial and economic success had been founded. Some right-wing newspapers like the *Daily Express* and the *Daily Mail*, which were already sensitive to Britain's post-war loss of Empire and fading prominence as a world power, saw America's demands as evidence that Britain was no longer regarded as an equal ally in Washington but rather a subordinate partner which could be manipulated to serve the needs of US foreign policy.[72] Hence they felt that Britain had a moral and economic obligation to defend itself against American attempts to erode its status, and the issue of trade with Cuba became a *cause célèbre*.

The liberal and left-wing press also shared the view that Britain should not accede to US pressure over Cuba, but felt that the main issue at stake was not so much the defence of Britain's honour but rather the whole question of US imperialism and its refusal to allow self-determination for countries which fell within its sphere of influence. *The Guardian* also drew its readers' attention to the illegality, both in US law and international law, of America's actions against Cuba, and its demands in support of these actions which had been made to Britain and other allies. Anxious to take advantage of the unpopularity of America's high-handedness in Britain, the Cuban press conducted a public opinion survey in London which showed that people from all walks of life thought the US had no right to interfere with British trade.[73]

On returning to London Douglas-Home gave a television interview during which, when questioned on his recent meeting with President Johnson and the problem of Cuba, he strongly defended Britain's position and expressed reservations about the effectiveness of the American embargo as a strategy to bring down the Castro regime.[74] But despite the Prime Minister's public rejection of the embargo, and his apparently tough stance in defending the Leyland contract in Washington, some changes were made to government policy on trade with Cuba. For example, informal warnings may have been issued to UK national shipping lines to restrict their calls at Cuban ports.[75] However, these actions were not deemed by Washington to represent 'appropriate steps' on Britain's part to cut its transportation links with Cuba, and two days after Douglas-Home's television interview Britain learned, along with a number of other offending countries, that it would no longer be a recipient of US military aid.[76] As the author of *The Times* article entitled 'Reprisal' noted, 'the termination of US military aid to Britain had been agreed in advance between the heads of state, but the timing of the announcement, only days after the Prime Minister had returned from Washington, was felt to be inopportune and designed to embarrass Britain.'

In general, the British press, including *The Times* and *The Guardian*, believed that the Prime Minister had represented Britain's interests well in Washington, and had made it clear to President Johnson that the British government would not attempt to dissuade Leyland, or any other British company, from trading with Cuba.[77] The Labour opposition, however, felt that the Prime Minister should have taken a tougher stance in defending Britain's right to trade freely with whosoever it wished, and no concessions should have been made to Washington.[78] Set against the background of a deteriorating balance of payments position, with a record one month trade deficit of £164 million in January, the opposition's claim appeared justified, and also proved to be humiliating for a government that had sought to improve its pre-election popularity by creating conditions for an increase in domestic consumption, mainly based on foreign imports.

In the months after the Prime Minister's visit to Washington further concessions were made in an attempt to mollify the US. But because of the political sensitivity of this issue, and the hostility which the British press had shown towards US efforts to curb Britain's trade with Cuba, most of these concessions were based on informal secret agreements between British government officials and US embassy staff in London. One such agreement took place in the spring of 1964 which led to restrictions being placed on any further ECGD cover for exporters to Cuba. Concerning this matter a State Department official indicated that the British government 'gave us [Washington] the signal that they might be able to do something about credits and there weren't any credits from the spring of 1964 to late-1966 from Britain'.[79] But while such issues as credit could be manipulated to satisfy Washington, the one aspect of British contact with Cuba which Whitehall appears to have been reluctant to tamper with was shipping.

The persistence of British shipowners in carrying Cuba trade overshadowed Douglas-Home's government's attempts to appease the US on other issues, and Washington continued to see Britain as the most flagrant and unrepentant transgressor of its Cuba policy. In a secret session of the NATO Council in Paris, US Under-Secretary Ball asked the members if it was their 'intention . . . that a single nation [Britain] should be able to frustrate a serious policy affecting the defense of the free world's interests in a vital area of the world'?[80] In April 1964 Ball had the opportunity to put his view directly to the British Foreign Secretary R.A. Butler, who was on an official visit to Washington at that time. However, Butler wisely avoided entering into a political debate over Cuba, either with Ball or during a later meeting with the President and Secretary Rusk, and simply emphasised the point that all of British trade was conducted on a 'purely commercial basis'.[81] Butler also indicated that Britain could not consider terminating its trade with Cuba while the British economy was experiencing balance of payments problems.[82]

Ball and other US officials spent much time during early-1964 haranguing members of the NATO council to join them in condemning British trade with Cuba, believing that once Britain was contained the rest of Western Europe and Japan would also fall into line.[83] Early in May 1964 Cuba indicated that it planned to exercise its option on its contract with Leyland and buy an additional 500 buses. This boosted Washington's case against Britain and on 7 May the NATO council voted 15 to 1 against Britain's stance on trade with Cuba and other socialist states.[84]

When questioned about the proposed new order from Cuba, Leyland officials were reticent and even claimed they knew nothing of such an order.[85] The Cuban statement, however, generated a flurry of exchanges between Washington and London. Seemingly anxious not to put too great a strain on the 'special relationship' the Douglas-Home government sent reassurances to Washington that British exports to Cuba would not be allowed to rise above certain levels.[86] Other concessions may also have been made by London as *The Times* confidently predicted on 12 May that 'Anglo-American differences over trade with Cuba are expected to be more or less resolved soon'.[87] Indeed, at this time there appears to have been a secret rapprochement between Washington and London over the issue of British trade with Cuba. For example, Secretary of State Rusk, who had earlier taken a hard line against Britain, now argued that the Anglo-American confrontation over Cuba was 'tactical and minor in character'.[88] *The New Statesman* suggested that this new understanding came about because of Rusk's willingness to 'horse-trade' more European nuclear control for curbing trade with Cuba.[89] It is also possible that the US took the pressure off the British Conservative government to ensure that the Cuba controversy did not damage its election chances. This latter explanation would seem particularly plausible in the context of the visit of Labour's spokesman on foreign affairs, Patrick Gordon Walker to Washington in February, during which, while making a number of anodyne statements concerning his party's objectives should it come to power, he made it known that he thought revolutions were inevitable and necessary in Latin America, and if Labour formed a government it would continue a policy of *détente* with Cuba.[90] Considering America's loosening political and economic grip on Latin America and the recent embarrassments over their embargo policy on Cuba one imagines that Gordon Walker's statement went down like a lead balloon in Washington.

Although Washington had made extraordinary efforts during 1964 to curb Britain's commercial links with Cuba and had achieved success in some areas such as credits, its attempts to dissuade British shipowners from calling at Cuban ports was a total failure. Soon after Washington had decided to take the heat off the British government, possibly for political reasons, a report came out which had been prepared by the US Federal Marine Administration on capitalist shipping that had traded with Cuba during the first nine months of 1964; again British vessels stood out as the worst offenders with 97 trips to Cuban ports in that period.[91] It was also noted that since the 'blacklist' had been started in January 1963 230 British vessels had visited Cuba, which was more than twice that of any other capitalist country.

Leyland and Revolutionary Cuba: A pragmatic fraternity

The Cubans were delighted with the outcome of their negotiations with Leyland; not only had they secured a supply of first-class buses to improve their ailing transport system, but they had also persuaded America's closest ally to break the US embargo.[92] Having made a firm commitment to Leyland products, and also to consolidate their snub to the US, the Cubans invited Leyland to set up a permanent office in Havana. According to Leyland personnel who were involved in the 1964 bus contract with the Cubans, this invitation was extended by the then Minister of Transport, Comandante Moira.[93] Moira was also responsible for providing Leyland with premises in central Havana from which the company could conduct its business in Cuba. Because Leyland was not only willing to break the US embargo, but also to establish an official representation in Havana, the company and the British government were held in high esteem by the Cuban media as a result.[94]

Leyland representatives who visited Cuba during the 1960s and the early-1970s claim that during the ten years in which their office in Havana was kept open, it played an important role in maintaining and developing commercial relations between Britain and Cuba. Some Leyland personnel have even suggested that in this respect it overshadowed the British embassy. Indeed, British exporters visiting Havana would often call at the Leyland office rather than the British embassy, not only because it was the only place in Havana that kept a supply of Watney's Red Barrel ale, but also to receive advice and guidance on conducting business in Cuba. One Aveling-Barford service engineer who visited Cuba in the early-1970s recalled that Leyland personnel were given a semi-diplomatic status by the Cuban authorities.[95] As well as wishing to consolidate their good relationship with Leyland, the Cubans were also anxious to impress upon the British government that they were reliable trading partners, fully deserving of the good credit terms they had been granted. To strengthen the Cuban position in this respect, Castro announced in February 1964 that his government had offered to begin discussions with the Shell oil company, with a view to paying compensation for Shell installations which had been taken over by the Cuban government in 1960. With characteristic frankness he also conceded that he had made the offer 'in the interests of strengthening Cuba's international credit position'.[96]

Having anticipated a severe US reaction to the bus deal with Cuba, Leyland did not wish to provoke Washington further by shipping the vehicles to Havana in British-registered vessels. Moreover, as noted earlier, as a concession to the Americans the British Prime-Minister had agreed to persuade Leyland to use a foreign carrier.[97] By 1964 approximately 70 per cent of Cuba's import-export trade was being conducted with the Soviet Union and its Eastern European allies, and ships from these countries were frequent callers at Cuban ports. But up to 1964 none had yet carried Western European freight to Cuba. After what appears to have been informal negotiations between a Leyland export manager, who was travelling to

Cuba on an East German ship from the DSR line, and the ship's captain, an agreement was reached with DSR to take the first batch of Leyland buses to Cuba. Subsequently DSR went on to ship the rest of the order, and a number of smaller orders for Leyland vehicles which Cuba placed during the late-1960s and early-1970s. Once it became known that an East German shipping line was to be responsible for delivering the Leyland buses to Havana, the Labour opposition began to put increasing pressure on the Prime Minister to obtain assurances from the US that British ships would not again be threatened with blacklisting and forced to surrender valuable business to foreign carriers.[98] Such assurances were neither obtained during the last few months of Douglas Home's government nor the two terms of the subsequent Labour government.

The first 15 buses to be delivered to Cuba left Dagenham Dock on the East German freighter *Heinrich Heine* on 3 July 1964.[99] They arrived in Havana 12 days later on 15 July. Leyland personnel who were in Havana at that time recalled that many Cubans came to the docks to greet the ship, and for several days after the delivery, Britain, and Leyland's role in breaking the American embargo, was praised in the press, and was the favourite topic of discussion among Cubans for some time.[100] Moreover, on 2 August when the new Leyland buses went into service, crowds in Havana lined the streets and applauded as they passed by.[101] Indeed, at this time the relationship between Cuba and Leyland could not have been better; not only had Leyland broken the embargo but had, despite US threats, also honoured their contractual obligations to the Cubans and agreed to supply a further 500 buses. This second part of the contract was signed at the Leyland plant in Lancashire on 22 June by the then Cuban Ambassador in Britain, Senor Luís Ricardo Alonso, after he and several other Cuban officials had inspected a number of buses from the earlier order that were being prepared for delivery.[102] Donald Stokes, who was present, took the opportunity to remind the press that '[Leyland] are ordinary commercial people trying to do a commercial job. We are not doing it for any political motive, but just carrying out a deal with a traditional customer'.[103] When asked if the buses could be considered as tactical weapons he replied, 'they could not be called a strategic weapon by any stretch of the imagination'.

In an interview which Donald Stokes gave to the business journal *The Director* soon after the second part of the contract with Cuba had been signed, he took the opportunity to respond to American criticisms of his company.[104] While conceding that Washington had the right to make its own business community observe the embargo, he felt it was unrealistic to expect other countries to abide by American legislation that was damaging to their business interests. He also pointed to the double standards practised by Washington concerning business with communist countries, stating as an example 'I gather they [America] are offering to send a nuclear reactor to Romania which I would have thought more controversial than sending buses to Cuba'. Concluding his comments on the American response to the Cuban sale he noted wryly that the publicity it had generated had been excellent for Leyland's business.

Between July and October 1964 several small shipments of buses, all under 30 vehicles, were sent to Cuba.[105] On the 26 October the largest batch so far delivered on the contract, consisting of 42 vehicles, was loaded onto the East German freighter *Magdeburg* at Dagenham. Soon after the *Magdeburg* left port the following morning it collided with the Japanese freighter, the *Yamashiro Maru*, and sank.[106] The *Magdeburg*'s crew of 54, and two passengers, were all saved, but most of the cargo, including the buses, was ruined, even though the ship became lodged on a sand bank and remained only partially submerged.[107]

The total value of the Leyland cargo, including spares, was £400,000, but the salvage operation realised only £27,000, leaving the insurers, who had given 110 per cent cover on the shipment, with heavy losses.[108] Leyland, on the other hand, did well out of this unfortunate incident, not only did it receive full compensation for its losses but it also had to supply an additional 42 vehicles, which were despatched to Cuba before a late delivery penalty clause came into effect.

At the time of this incident a rumour quickly spread that US secret agents had helped to bring about the collision.[109] But many Leyland staff expressed the view that poor visibility on the Thames on the morning the freighter set out, was more likely to have been the cause of the accident than the CIA. Most of the British and American press accepted this explanation, but many people remained sceptical, including a few Leyland employees, one of whom suspected that the British and American governments decided that it would be in their mutual interest to conceal the real cause of the accident.[110]

The delivery of Leyland buses to Cuba from the two orders which were signed in 1964, continued until 1967. During this period no new orders were received from the Cubans for complete buses, but the spares and service requirements which had been generated by the 1964 contract, along with the prospect of further business, ensured that Leyland maintained a close commercial relationship with Cuba.[111] The staff at the Leyland office in Havana also occasionally served as advisers to the Cuban government on the procurement of engineering goods. In this way Leyland personnel in Cuba were able to give advance warning of new business opportunities to British manufacturers, and especially their own company's new subsidiaries like the construction equipment manufacturer Aveling Barford, which was absorbed into Leyland in 1967. Aveling Barford received their first order from Cuba for dumper trucks and mining equipment, for use in the nickel mines, in late-1967. Like their new parent company, Aveling Barford went on to establish a good commercial relationship with the Cubans, and continued to receive orders for their products throughout the 1970s and the 1980s, long after Leyland's bus and truck division had pulled out of the Cuban market.

Other British companies, which were not part of Leyland Group, such as Coles Cranes, Kent Water Meters, Perkins Diesels, and the construction company Simon-Carves, were also introduced to business opportunities in Cuba by Leyland staff in Havana. In 1965, after the political quarrel between Washington and London over the bus deal had subsided, a Leyland representative at the company's headquarters in Lancashire conceded in an interview he gave to a journalist from the *Times Review of Industry and Technology* that 'we are being inundated with requests from British companies for information on business prospects and contacts in Cuba'.[112] He added that those companies which established business links with Cuba still preferred to keep quiet about their activities, for fear of American reprisals or possible unfavourable responses from their other Latin American customers.

The largest contract to be signed between Cuba and a British company in the late-1960s was the £10 million order which was received by Simon-Carves to build a fertiliser plant near Cienfuegos.[113] During the 1950s and 1960s Simon-Carves had established a good reputation with the Soviet Union and several Eastern European countries, for their construction work. This may have helped them in their negotiations with the Cubans, but the crucial factor in securing the contract was, as it had been with Leyland three years earlier, the availability of credit backed by the British government. The Americans were again incensed with the British, who had set yet another precedent in dealing with Cuba, this time by offering the largest single credit ever received by the Cubans from a capitalist nation since the Revolution.

Naturally, the Cubans were jubilant at having delivered another blow to the US, and also for having negotiated the construction of what would be one of the largest fertiliser plants in the world.[114] In a speech given by Fidel Castro at the Liberation Day ceremony held on 2 January 1967, he praised Britain for being a loyal friend of Cuba, and added that now other European countries had been given a clear lead, they might be more generous in offering credit to back up their claims that they were anxious to do big business with the Cubans.[115] Concluding his comments on Cuba's trade with Western market economies he said: 'we ask that the European countries be not misled by imperialists and monopolists [i.e. the US]. I tell Europeans that if there are revolutions in Latin America they have little to lose and much to gain from them'.[116] Privately, few European businessmen who were in a position to compare the Cuban market with the wider Latin American market at that time, would have disagreed.

Shortly after Simon-Carves began work on the fertiliser plant in Cuba in August 1967, the US convened a meeting of OAS members in Washington in an attempt to increase the pressure on Cuba and her non-communist trading partners.[117] But apart from agreeing to tighten up procedures for identifying ships that were involved in trade with Cuba, and to make further diplomatic approaches to Cuba's capitalist trading partners, little was achieved. Some OAS members, including Mexico, Ecuador and Chile also even refused to vote in favour of these token measures.

By 1969 Leyland was again negotiating large contracts with the Castro government, and in May of that year an agreement was signed in London to supply Cuba with 300 Leyland Hippo trucks for use on new agricultural projects. This order was estimated to be worth £3 million, and was again covered by a five-year British government credit guarantee. Delivery of these vehicles began in January 1970 and continued until late-1972. During 1969 a separate order was also placed with Leyland for 82 long-distance buses.

Leyland personnel who were involved in the negotiation of the truck contract recalled that they faced some stiff competition from other European bidders, and particularly the Berliet company of France which at that time was determined to improve its standing in the Cuban commercial vehicle market. Although Leyland continued to receive direct orders from Cuba in the late-1960s and early-1970s, the trend in the business of motor vehicle exporting was moving towards building assembly plants in the customer's country. Indeed, by 1969 representatives from Berliet had already discussed such a project with the Cubans, and at least one Japanese commercial vehicle manufacturer had put forward similar proposals. The Cubans, however, seemed still to favour Leyland products, and in December the Castro government invited the company to set up an assembly plant for buses and trucks near Havana. Soon after this suggestion was made a meeting was arranged between the two parties but the subsequent negotiations came to nothing. As Leyland personnel have pointed out, at that time the company was still suffering from the difficult restructuring which had taken place in 1968, which resulted in the formation of the conglomerate British Leyland. For many years after this merger financial resources as well as managerial and technical expertise from the profitable bus and truck division, were redirected into reviving ailing new acquisitions like BMC. The result of this strategy was disastrous for those sections which constituted the original Leyland Motors Ltd. At a time when a concerted effort was needed to improve the competitiveness of its commercial vehicles in export markets, the crucial resources of expertise and research and development funding were withdrawn. Largely because of these problems Leyland's bus and truck division began to lose orders and one of its first customers to switch its allegiance was Cuba.

Notes

1   For example in 1944, after four years of occupation and pillage, France's industrial output was less than a third of what it had been in 1938. During the war 900,000 dwellings, 3,125 bridges, thousands of factories, 75 per cent of locomotives, 90 per cent of road vehicles, and 65 per cent of the country's harbour installations had been destroyed. See Charles P. Kindleberger, *Economic Growth in France and Britain*, London, O.U.P., 1976, p. 33.

2   For a study of the economic recovery of Europe in the immediate postwar years see A.S. Milward, *The Reconstruction of Western Europe, 1945–1951*, London, Methuen, 1984, p. 68.

3   The following table shows Britain's declining position as an exporter of manufactures to world markets in comparison to its main competitors:

Percentage shares of world exports of manufactures of the major industrial powers

	1950	1960	1965	1970
United Kingdom	25.5	16.5	13.9	10.8
France	9.9	9.6	8.8	8.7
Germany	7.3	19.3	19.1	19.8
Japan	3.4	6.9	9.4	11.7
US	27.3	21.6	20.3	18.5

Source: F.T. Blackaby (ed.), *De-industrialisation*, London, Heinemann Educational, 1979, p. 241.

4   Information on Leyland's pre-war commercial links with Cuba was provided by Patrick Kennett who has written a series of historical studies of European commercial vehicle manufacturers, including Leyland (interview held in Cromford, Derbyshire, 21 September 1987). Patrick Kennett worked as Leyland's Sales Manager and Technical Adviser in the Caribbean in the late-1950s and early-1960s, and spent two years in Cuba from 1959–61.

5   Leyland management decided shortly after the war that the company should seek to expand its export market in the sterling area and those developing countries which had accumulated large sterling balances during the conflict, rather than attempt to increase their exports to Europe. European countries, it was believed, only offered temporary markets while their own motor vehicle industries were re-established. Latin America and the Middle East were identified as areas in which vigorous export drives should be launched. See Graham Turner, *The Leyland Papers*, London, Eyre and Spottiswoode, 1971, p. 22.

6   Pawley's business activities were not restricted to Latin America: in the 1930s and 1940s he had built, and managed, several aircraft factories and chemical plants in India and China. Indeed, Pawley was an outstanding international entrepreneur, even by American standards, and Leyland were eager to make use of his skills and influence. The relationship, however, did not develop any further after the 1950 Cuban bus contract, because Pawley was recruited by the State Department at the end of that year to work on a secret project. For a brief account of Pawley's life and achievements see *Who's Who in America*, 39th ed. 1976–1977, Chicago, Macmillan Directory Division, 1978. With hindsight if Leyland had become associated with Pawley they would almost

certainly not have been able to continue doing business with Cuba after the insurrection, because in 1958 Pawley was involved in a CIA sponsored plot to prevent Castro coming to power. Pawley was sent to Cuba three weeks before Batista fled the country in the hope that he could rally sections of the military to form a 'caretaker government', which would be anti-Batista but also anti-Castro. Having known Batista personally for almost 30 years the CIA felt that Pawley, if anyone, could persuade the dictator to step down (see '1958 Move to Bar Castro Disclosed', *New York Times*, 12 February 1961, p. 30). In 1964, at the time when Leyland was signing its first big contract with the Castro government, the Cuban daily newspaper *Revolución* published an article accusing Pawley of having been involved in corrupt business deals with the former Cuban presidents, Batista and Carlos Prío Socarrás. In particular reference was made to the alleged graft which surrounded the dismantling of the Havana tram network in 1950 and the setting up of a new bus service (see 'La guerra de los autobuses', 10 January, p. 2). Not surprisingly Pawley took a dim view of the Castro regime and became a leading figure in the Cuban Families Committee for the Liberation of Prisoners of War, which was dedicated to pressurising the Cuban government into releasing 'political prisoners' who wished to join their relations in the US.

7 Details of this contract are to be found in *The Times*, 22 June 1950, p. 6. See also Douglas Jack, *The Leyland Bus*, Glossop, Derbyshire, Transport Publishing Company, 1977, p. 204.

8 Turner, *The Leyland Papers*, p. 24.

9 The most comprehensive report on this contract is Patrick Kennett's article 'Progress in Cuba' which was published in the March 1960 issue of the *Leyland Journal*, pp. 88–93.

10 See the various articles which were published in *The Times* during September 1958 for details of this contract and especially 'Sale of Fighters to Cuba', 26 September, p. 11.

11 'Cuban Chronology, June 1958 – October 1962', Labour Party Information Paper, International Department, December, 1962, p. 2.

12 'Cuban Rebel Press Attacks Britain', *The Times*, 13 October 1958, p. 10.

13 Parliamentary Debates, *Hansard*, Vol. 597, 15 December 1958, pp. 763–6.

14 'Cuban Chronology', Labour Party Information Paper, p. 2. Once the rebels were in power the British Conservative government had to endure a number of attacks by its critics in Britain for backing the wrong side. Some argued that it had aided Batista in full cognisance of the implications of its actions, others, like the author Graham Greene, spoke of 'the extraordinary ignorance of Cuban affairs shown by the British government'. The Foreign Office meekly responded by saying its embassy in Havana had been understaffed during the crisis and it had not been fully informed of events. See 'Were the British Government Misinformed?', *The Times*, 5 January 1959, p. 8.

15 In May 1959 the British government sanctioned the delivery of the five war planes it had withheld from Batista to the new regime in Havana.

16 For a documented account of the pressures put on Selwyn Lloyd by the US see Morris H. Morley, *Imperial State and Revolution. The United States and Cuba, 1952–1956*, Cambridge, C.U.P., 1987, p. 122.

17 For details of the contract see 'Anglo-Cuban Venture – Big Shipyard Near Havana', *The Times*, 1 November 1958, p. 12. This was the first British venture into shipbuilding in Latin America.

18 According to Patrick Kennett, who was in charge of the rebuilding pro-

gramme, not only Leyland vehicles but also Leyland personnel were seen by the Cubans as valuable assets to the Revolution. Mr Kennett's own account of the two years he spent in Cuba, from 1960 to 1961, would indeed seem to verify this claim. During this period he was invited, in his capacity as Leyland's chief representative in Cuba, to provide a broad range of technical advice. This included giving a series of lectures on mechanical engineering at the University of Havana; helping to design and build a protective cladding for buses which were to be used to carry troops to the battle zone in the event of a US invasion; and a number of other services which had not been included in the initial contract. Mr Kennett also claimed that during his stay in Cuba he was asked on several occasions by Cuban government officials to remain in Cuba as their technical adviser on commercial vehicles. When Mr Kennett left Cuba in 1961 he was awarded a medal inscribed with the words 'Hero of the Revolution Class 1'. Most Leyland personnel who were in Cuba in the early 1960s also recognised the commercial opportunities which would arise from Castro's plans for economic development. For example, in his article 'Progress in Cuba' Patrick Kennett wrote: 'Present-day Cuba is making unprecedented efforts to improve the status of the nation and its people. Despite considerable adversities appreciable development is under way in the fields of industry, agriculture, commerce, social welfare and building. The progressive policy of Omnibus Metropolitanos is ensuring that public transport maintains its place abreast of national development in the story of progress that is unfolding here', p. 93.

19   For comments on Eastern European buses in Cuba see 'British Firm Sells Buses to Cuba', *The Times*, 8 January 1964, p. 10. A more comprehensive report on the unsuitability of Soviet equipment in Cuba is Anthony Sylvester's, 'Soviet Equipment Fails in Cuba', *Times Review of Industry and Technology*, December, 1965, p. 55. Some Leyland personnel who were in Cuba in the early-1960s recall travelling on Icarus buses fitted with double glazed windows and heaters that could not be switched off.

20   The value in millions of pounds sterling of British imports of Cuban sugar and its derivatives between 1957–1964 were as follows: 1957, 23.7m (total imports 25.9m); 1958, 16.4m (total 17.8m); 1959, 9.1m (total 10.2m); 1960, 6.8m (total 7.9m); 1961, 4.2m (total 5.3m); 1962, 6m (total 7.1m); 1963, 11.6m (total 13.6m); 1964, 7.9m (total 9.1m). Source, *Annual Statement of Overseas Trade of the United Kingdom*. The difference between sugar imports and total imports was made up mainly by tobacco.

21   For details of the contract see 'British Firm Sells Buses to Cuba', *The Times*, 8 January 1964, p. 10. See also 'British Sell Buses to Cuba, Defying US Trade Curb', the *New York Times*, 8 January 1964, pp. 1 and 11. The *New York Times* added that as part of the contract Leyland had agreed to invite six Cuban technicians to their factory in Britain to be trained in maintenance methods, p. 1. The signatories on the contract were A.F. Smith, Leyland's Export Contracts Manager, and Ricardo Espino the Managing Director of 'Transimport'. The signing was witnessed by Hugh Adam Watson the British Ambassador, see 'Firmó Cuba la compra de 400 ómnibus ingleses', in the Cuban Communist Party daily newspaper *Revolución*, 7 January 1964, pp. 1–2 (p. 2). He was later to join Leylands.

22   These figures were cited in the British and American press (*The Times*, 8 January 1964, p. 10 and the *New York Times*, 8 January 1964, p. 1). The Cuban press gave the slightly lower figure of $10 million for the first order

and noted that Leyland had agreed to take responsibility for the shipment of the buses, see *Revolución*, 7 January 1964, p. 1.

23 For details of this second order and for specifications of the vehicles supplied, see Douglas Jack, *The Leyland Bus*. See also 'Amplía Cuba sus compras de ómnibus ingleses', *Revolución*, 29 February 1964, pp. 1–2. This article states that the fifty long-distance buses had been specially designed by Leyland to cope with Cuban conditions. The contract was signed by A.F. Smith for Leyland and Ricardo Espino and Antonio Vinagre for 'Transimport'. John Thompson, the First Commercial Secretary at the British embassy, witnessed the signing.

24 The *New York Times*, 8 January 1964, p. 11. Keith Maddox, Leyland's sales manager for the Americas, who played a key role in securing the contract, claims that although Leyland faced competition in Cuba at that time, the company's previous contracts with the island put it in a strong negotiating position. Interview held in Oxford, 21 March 1989. There are several newspaper reports of Maddox's outstanding sale to the Cubans. See, for example, Michael Moynihan, 'Selling to Communism: Business Versus Politics', subtitled, 'The Man Who Sold Buses To Cuba', *Sunday Times*, 16 February 1964, p. 8. The Managing Director of Leyland, Donald Stokes, was also quoted in this article as saying that Leyland had been 'painstakingly building up a market in Cuba over a period of 15 years' and that with the new contract 'we have in effect cornered the bus market in Cuba'. He also pointed out, possibly as an oblique snub to the US which had put his company under so much pressure, that he had done business with Batista in the past but 'I very much prefer dealing with the present regime to the old. I find them very correct and straightforward'.

25 It is rumoured that the circumstances and events surrounding the British government's decision to instruct ECGD to grant a credit guarantee to the Leyland contract with Cuba were highly controversial, but unfortunately Leyland and ECGD personnel who were involved in the negotiations decline to give details of what happened.

26 The Cuban daily *Revolución* gave an excellent résumé of the immediate response of the international press to the Leyland contract with Cuba. See 'Repugnante el chantaje de los Estados Unidos', 10 January 1964, pp. 1, 2.

27 Morley, *Imperial State and Revolution*, p. 229. Morley cites as his source a Department of State (Assistant Secretary Ball) telegram to the London embassy dated 24 January 1964.

28 *Hispanic American Report*, Vol. XVII, No. 1, March 1964, p. 36.

29 Morley, *Imperial State and Revolution*, p. 229.

30 For a succinct account of American foreign policy in Latin America, and towards Cuba, see Walter LaFeber, 'Latin America Policy', in Robert A. Divine (ed.), *Exploring the Johnson Years*, Austin, University of Texas Press, 1981. A more extensive analysis of America's relations with revolutionary Cuba is to be found in Morley, *Imperial State and Revolution*. For a specific statement by the US government on the 'threat' imposed by Cuba see the 78-page document entitled 'Responsibility of Cuban Government for Increased International Tensions in the Hemisphere' which was issued by the US Information Service to its foreign embassies (London version dated 1 August 1960).

31 The *New York Times* on 18 January 1964, claimed that Moscow and Havana had agreed that Cuba should reduce its sugar exports to the Soviet Union, and

sell any surplus on the world market to take advantage of the prevailing high price. With the hard currency earned from these sales the Cubans would be able to buy those manufactured goods which were badly needed in Cuba, but which were also in short supply in the Soviet Union, p. 2. One must also take into account that between 1962–65, Cuba was engaged in the first co-ordinated economic plan since the revolution. At the centre of this plan was a programme for rapid industrialisation through the development of a wide range of import-substitution industries, including metallurgy, chemical products, machinery, etc. Most of the equipment for these plants was to be supplied by the Soviet Union and its Eastern European allies. But by 1963, which turned out to be the worst year for economic performance since the Revolution, with shortages of consumer goods, as well as the most basic equipment, it became clear that trading links would have to be re-established with the market economies to obtain essential manufactured goods. By this time most Cuban economists had also begun to reject the idea which had prevailed in the early years of the Revolution that industrial growth should have priority over sugar production. Now they believed that sugar production would have to be expanded first, to obtain the necessary hard currency for the importation of Western capital goods.

32   This argument was presented on numerous occasions by British politicians of all parties in their defence of the Leyland contract. The press also took up this argument, see for example the article by Clyde Farnsworth entitled 'British Defend Bus Sale as Non-political' in *The Times*, 9 January 1964, p. 6. Soon after the Leyland contract was signed with Cuba the company's managing director noted that 'we don't want to flout any embargoes or to upset Americans, but we really can't keep looking over our shoulders at the political scene every time we make a deal', see Moynihan 'Selling to Communism: Business Versus Politics', *op. cit.*, p. 6.

33.   Douglas Jack, *The Leyland Bus*, p. 38. During 1924 and 1925 Leyland dispatched 156 buses on this contract.

34   *Ibid.*, p. 157. Leyland were also one of the first British companies after the war to negotiate a barter contract with a foreign customer; this was drawn up with Poland in 1948 and involved the exchange of 200 bus chassis for several shiploads of geese.

35   'Substantial Opportunities for Trade with Eastern Europe', [British] *Board of Trade Journal*, Vol. 187, No. 3517, 14 August 1964, pp. 329–30.

36   *Ibid.*, p. 330.

37   For a detailed analysis of the problems facing British exporters during the 1960s see A.D. Morgan, 'Commercial Policy' in F.T. Blackaby (ed.), *British Economic Policy 1960–1974*, Cambridge, C.U.P., 1978, pp. 515–63.

38   It was only in 1970 that the Community overtook the Commonwealth as Britain's largest market, see A.D. Morgan, 'Commercial Policy', p. 541.

39   The British press eagerly seized on this contradiction, see for example the *Daily Mirror*, 11 January 1964, p. 3, for a cartoon and comments. The Cuban press were also anxious to bring to the attention of its readers the inconsistency in America's position on trade with communist countries, see 'Nunca ha habido boicot inglés a Cuba y no hay por qué hacerlo', *Revolución*, 8 January 1964, pp. 1–2 (p. 2).

40   'British Feel More Sadness Than Anger at Aid Cut', *Washington Post*, 20 February 1964, p. A15.

41   *The Times*, 11 February 1964, p. 11.

42 Morley, *op. cit.*, p. 229.

43 Cited in 'British Defend Bus Sale to Cuba as Non-political', *New York Times*, 9 January 1964, p. 6 – forgetting the Battle of the Marne!.

44 *Washington Star*, 20 February 1964, p. 6. Indeed many of the arguments put forward in defence of the Leyland contract with Cuba by the British government, the British press, and Leyland officials, were supported by sections of the American press. For example Arthur Krock, a *New York Times* foreign affairs correspondent frequently expressed reservations about US policy towards Cuba and sympathised with the position of Leyland and the British government. See particularly 'US Policy on Trade Is Examined in the Light of Britain's Action', *New York Times*, 12 January 1964, p. 13.

45 Although most moderate politicians in the US accepted reluctantly that buses did not constitute strategic equipment, even some of the most liberal figures in the Congress felt that the contract was a 'moral' outrage. For example Senator Stephen Young, who was known for his liberal stance on most issues, joined the Conservatives in condemning Leyland's complicity with the Castro regime, which he described as 'despicable'. Cited in Murrey Marder, 'Rusk Raps US Allies for Trade with Castro', *Washington Post*, 23 January 1974, p. A1.

46 Interview with George Maze, Leyland, 18 January 1988.

47 Information provided by Patrick Kennett. Similar claims were made in the British and American press as late as April 1964. *The Times's* Washington correspondent reported for example that a story was circulating that General Motors had concluded an agreement through its Canadian subsidiary to sell £4 million worth of parts to Cuba, 16 April 1964, p. 14.

48 'British Sell Buses to Cuba, Defying US Trade Curb', *New York Times*, 8 January 1964, pp. 1 and 13 (p. 13).

49 For example, only a month after the Leyland contract had been signed, the French motor vehicle manufacturer Berliet received an order from the Cuban government to supply 300 industrial vehicles for work on construction projects. See *The Times*, 7 February 1964, p. 10. On 24 November 1964 the *New York Times* reported that in the previous six months salesmen from the market economies had obtained between $100–120 million of orders from the Cuban government, p. 13.

50 The State Department's response to the Leyland contract was reported in *The Times*, 8 January 1964, p. 10. Referring to the Leyland contract, the US Secretary of Commerce, Luther Hodges, also reluctantly accepted the impotence of the US in the matter, stating, 'I do not like it a bit; but I do not see what we can do about it'. Cited in *Keesing's Contemporary Archives*, 22–29 February 1964, p. 19914.

51 Before the State Department had made its position clear concerning reprisals some high officials in the administration, such as Secretary of State Dean Rusk and White House aide McGeorge Bundy, had publicly expressed their support of a consumer boycott of British goods. See 'Rusk Sees Public Boycott Facing Traders with Cuba', *New York Times*, 6 February 1964, p. 3.

52 'US Restive at Cuba Trade', *The Times*, 11 February 1964, p. 9. *New York Times* had expressed a similar view on the previous day, p. 8.

53 This new legislation is mentioned in Tad Szulc, 'Spain is Cautioned by US on Rise in Cuban Trade', 21 December 1963, pp. 1 and 7 (p. 1).

54 Morley, *op. cit.*, p. 197 (footnote 88, pp. 451–2).

55 *Ibid.*, p. 197.

56   'US Fails to Curb Allies Over Cuba', *New York Times*, 16 September 1962, p. 24.

57   Flora Lewis, 'German Shippers Would Accept Western Ban on Trade to Cuba', *Washington Post*, 24 September 1962, p. A9. Although the British government officially opposed a shipping boycott on Cuba, the Transport Minister, Ernest Marples, made informal requests to 800 British shipowners through the General Council of British Shipping not to carry cargoes to Cuba which included strategic goods. See Philip Geyelin, 'US Seeks to Bolster Ban on Cuban Trade by Persuading Allies to Impose Ship Curbs', *Washington Post*, 26 September 1962, p. 3 and 'British Reluctant on Cuba Trade' p. A12.

58   Tad Szulc, 'US Ports to Bar Ships That Carry Arms Aid to Cuba', *New York Times*, 4 October 1962, pp. 1,11.

59   Walter Hamshar, 'Dock Workers Won't Handle Red Cargoes', *New York Herald Tribune*, 9 October 1962, p. 25.

60   Morley, *op. cit.*, pp. 200–1.

61   *Ibid.*, p. 200.

62   Lewis Gulick, 'Cuba Trade Perils Aid, US Warns', *Washington Post*, 12 January 1963, p. A6.

63   Max Frankel, 'US Denies Its Cargoes to Ships in Cuba Trade', *New York Times*, 7 February 1963, pp. 1,2.

64   According to a survey made by the US Department of Commerce (Maritime Administration) 385 ships from capitalist countries called at Cuban ports in 1963. Among these 133 were British, 99 Greek, 64 Lebanese, 16 Italian, 14 Norwegian, 9 Spanish, 9 Moroccan, 8 French, 1 Finnish, and 6 from other countries. See Morley, p. 374.

65   *Ibid.*, p. 230. Morley cites as his source for this information a Department of State document entitled 'Effect of Amendment of Foreign Assistance Act of 1963 on Aid to the United Kingdom and Dependent Territories', dated 11 February 1964.

66   *The Times*, 10 February 1964, p. 10.

67   Carol Kilpatrick, 'British Maintain Red Trade', *Washington Post*, 14 February 1964, pp. A1 and A8.

68   'Sir A. Home Seeking to "Keep Close to US" ', *The Times*, 13 February 1964, p. 12.

69   'Johnson and Home Conclude Parley; Hopeful on Arms', *New York Times*, 14 February 1964, pp. 1, 3 (p. 1).

70   Morley, *op. cit.*, p. 231.

71   'Johnson and Home Conclude Parley . . .', p. 3. US officials, however, were quick to point out that the $37 million in exports to Cuba in 1963 consisted almost entirely of shipments of medicines and drugs which were made in exchange for the release of prisoners taken in the 1961 Bay of Pigs invasion.

72   *Daily Express*, 8 Jan 1964, and the *Daily Mail* on the same day.

73   'Mantiene el Premier Inglés que seguira el comercio con Cuba', *Revolución*, 13 February 1964, pp. 1–2. The newspaper's correspondent in Britain also interviewed some of the workers at Leyland's Birmingham plant where the buses were being built and was told that a number of unemployed had been given work because of the new contract with Cuba.

74   Some of the most important comments made during the interview are quoted in Francis Boyd, 'Sir Alec Refuses to Rule Out March 19', *The Guardian*, 18 February 1964, p. 5.

75   If this was so then the warning cannot have been heeded because 180 British-

registered ships called at Cuban ports during 1964, which was more than for any year between 1963 and 1975. See Morley, p. 374.

76 Direct cuts of military aid were made against Britain, France and Yugoslavia, all of which were only minor beneficiaries of the aid programme. Spain and Morocco, which were both major recipients of US military and economic aid, were given a temporary reprieve in that the continuation of US support was made subject to them being able to prove that they were taking 'appropriate steps' to curb their transportation links with Cuba. Fourteen other countries which received US military aid were exempted from the action. See Tad Szulc, 'US Curtails Aid to Five Countries That Sell to Cuba', *New York Times*, 19 February 1964, pp. 1–2.

77 *The Times*, 15 February 1964, p. 9 and *The Guardian* on the same day, p. 5.

78 Parliamentary Debates, *Hansard*, Vol. 689, House of Commons, 18 February 1964, pp. 1025–1031.

79 Morley, p. 232. Morley obtained his information through a private interview with the official concerned, p. 465 (footnote, 295).

80 Morley, p. 232. Morley cites as his source Philip Geyelin, *Lyndon B. Johnson and the World*, New York, 1966, pp. 92–93.

81 Murrey Marder, 'LBJ Raps Cuba Trade in Talks with Butler', *Washington Post*, 1 May 1964, p. A14.

82 Tad Szulc, 'Rusk and Butler Look for Benefit from Red's Split', *New York Times*, 28 April 1964, pp. 1,13 (p. 13).

83 Robert H. Estabrook, 'US Bitterness at British Trade Affecting NATO', *Washington Post*, 9 May 1964, p. A6.

84 Drew Middleton, 'US – British Clash on Red Trade Due', *New York Times*, 8 May 1964, p. 5.

85 'Cuba to Buy 500 More Buses: US Displeased by British Deal', *The Times*, 8 May 1989, p. 14.

86 Flora Lewis, 'British Firm to Sell Cuba More Buses', *Washington Post*, 8 May 1964, pp. A1,A16.

87 'British Concession to US on China Trade', p. 10.

88 Cited in Sydney Gruson, 'Rusk Calls Dispute Minor', *New York Times*, 11 May 1964, p. 10.

89 'Cuban Horse-Trading', 15 May 1964, p. 1.

90 For details of the visit see 'Labourite Policy Explained in US', *New York Times*, 23 February 1964, p. 26.

91 John P. Callahan, 'British Ships Top Cuba Trade List', *New York Times*, 25 July 1964, p. 46.

92 *New York Times* was swift to acknowledge the political significance of the Leyland contract for the Cuban government. In a leading article of 14 January 1964 the author wrote, '[Castro] has managed to shoot a big hole through the US embargo with his purchase of British buses. He has had little to boast about since the Bay of Pigs, but the bus deal, which drew spirited bidding from competing firms in other Western nations, does represent a significant economic victory', p. 30.

93 Interview with George Maze.

94 An indication of Cuba's perception of Leyland and Great Britain at this time is given in an article which was written by Vicente Cubillas for *Revolución* entitled 'Hablan obreros ingleses "Muy sensata la actitud del gobierno de la Gran Bretaña en su comercio con Cuba" ', 30 April 1964. The article deals with the visit to Cuba of a number of Leyland and Metro Cammell Weighmann

workers who had been invited to Havana by the Cuban government to take part in the 1st of May celebrations, p. 4.

95   Information supplied by Bill Cowie (interview held in Grantham 10 December 1987). Mr Cowie worked in Cuba in the late-1960s and early-1970s as an engineer for the construction equipment manufacturer Aveling Barford which was taken over by Leyland in 1967.

96   *The Times*, 25 February 1964, p. 7. In the same article it was estimated that Cuba held $100 million in foreign currency reserves, and was in a position to place a number of big orders with Western companies.

97   In the frantic search for a shipping line to take the buses to Cuba, one Leyland sales manager, apparently on the suggestion of the company's managing director, Donald Stokes, approached the British Admiralty to see if they would be willing to ship the buses on one of their aircraft carriers. It transpired, however, that Donald Stokes had not been serious, and consequently he and other senior executives were amused and astonished when the sales manager reported back that his request, though eventually refused, had received a sympathetic ear. The request was in fact given consideration until an admiral decided that naval involvement in the execution of such a controversial contract might further antagonise the US. This episode was later leaked to a number of Labour politicians, including Mr Fernyhough the MP for Jarrow, who asked the Prime Minister during Commons question time if the story was true, and if so, why had the Admiralty refused to co-operate. Needless to say the Prime Minister evaded the question (see Parliamentary Debates, *Hansard*, Vol. 690, 25 February 1964, p. 621). Had the Admiralty agreed to ship the buses, and if Senator Barry Goldwater's suggestion that American warships be used to prevent the buses reaching Cuba (*The Times*, 10 February 1964, p. 10) had been heeded by the US government, one dreads to speculate what might have happened.

98   Reported in *The Times*, 19 February 1964, p. 14.

99   Reported in the *New York Times*, 16 July 1964, p. 22. A second shipment consisting of 26 buses arrived in Havana on the freighter *Dresden* on 28 July, *The Times*, 29 July 1964, p. 9.

100   The arrival of the first shipment of Leyland buses made the headlines in *Revolución* on 16 July. The article which followed praised Britain for its commitment to free trade and its 'gallant' stance against US imperialism. Also included were details of an interview given by the *Heinrich Heine*'s captain Helmut Queisser to Cuban journalists. Queisser noted that although the voyage had been trouble-free his ship was circled by a US reconnaissance plane near the Bahamas.

101   The enthusiastic response with which the buses were greeted was reported in *The Times*, 3 August 1964, p. 8. See also Evelio Telleria, 'Cuba derrota de nuevo el bloqueo con los Leylands', *Revolución*, 3 August 1964, pp. 1–2. Telleria's article described the entry into service of the Leyland buses as 'Un paso histórico, por lo que significa de derrota al bloqueo económico del imperialismo yanqui contra nuestro pueblo . . .' (p. 1). So enthusiastic were some Cubans about the Leyland buses that they even submitted poems to the press about them, see for example Bernardo Callejas, 'Homenaje a Leyland' Hoy, 12 February 1965, p. 6, which begins 'Querido autobus . . .'.

102   *The Times*, 23 June 1964, p. 6.

103   *Ibid.* Although when commenting to the press on the Leyland contracts with Cuba, Donald Stokes always emphasised the commercial and pragmatic side

of the deal and shunned politics, it was well known among his peers that personally he held strong political views and was a Labour Party supporter. See 'The Radical with a £200 million Turnover', *The Director*, August 1964, pp. 246–51. In this article Stokes claimed that in the modern world a man in his position had to be a radical, implying not that one should mix politics and business but rather that a progressive view of the world made good business sense (p. 246). In France de Gaulle was developing his foreign policy on just such a belief. By pursuing this ideal both men were able to make outstanding contributions to the export sectors of their respective countries.

104 *Ibid.*, p. 248.

105 The Cuban press eagerly reported each delivery, see, for example 'Cuba derrota de nuevo el bloqueo con los Leylands', *Revolución*, 3 August 1964, pp. 1,2, and 'Llegaron otros 30 omnibus Leyland', *Revolución*, 21 September 1964, p. 1, which included a large photograph of the East German freighter *Karl Marx* sailing into Havana harbour with rows of buses on the top deck.

106 This incident was reported in *The Times*, 28 October 1964, p. 6.

107 Reported in *The Times*, 29 October 1964, p. 17.

108 Only those buses which had been on the upper deck were still serviceable after the salvage operation and some of these were later auctioned complete. Others which were on the lower decks were more badly damaged and were sold for spares. The insurers finally abandoned the wreck and sold it to a Greek salvage firm with 14 buses still in the holds. After a difficult refloating operation the Greek salvage vessel set out to tow the wreck home but the ill-fated *Magdeburg* and its remaining cargo of buses sank again in a storm in the Bay of Biscay.

109 The controversy surrounding the incident lingered for years, see for example Jack Anderson and Les Whitten, 'CIA Accused in '64 Thames Collision', *Washington Post*, 14 February 1975, p. C31.

110 The Leyland employee who made this suggestion prefers to remain anonymous. Morley also seems convinced on the basis of investigations he has made into CIA operations against Cuba that the collision was manufactured as part of a covert operation, p. 236.

111 The spares side of Leyland's business with Cuba, according to one former employee of the company, was a substantial and lucrative trade. A reason for this was indicated by the Cuban President Osvaldo Dorticós when he reported in 1972 that Cuba had the world's highest per capita consumption of spare parts due to poor treatment of equipment. Cited by Carmelo Mesa-Lago, *Cuba in the 1970s: Pragmatism and Institutionalization*, Albuquerque, University of New Mexico Press, 1978, p. 35.

112 'Soviet Equipment Fails in Cuba', December, 1965, p. 55.

113 The Simon-Carves contract made the headlines in *The Times* on 3 January 1967. See also the article by Ian Ball in *The Daily Telegraph* on the same day, p. 6.

114 The largest fertiliser plant that Simon-Carves had constructed before the Cuban contract was one in Poland that was completed in 1965, at a cost to the customer of £2.5 million. Britain's exports to Cuba in 1966 were £7.7 million, therefore £10 million for one contract was exceptional.

115 Castro's speech was reported in full in *Revolución* on the 3 January 1967, pp. 1–3 (p. 2).

116 Author's translation.

117 Commenting on the meeting, the author of a leading article in *The Times*

wrote, 'The OAS, adopting its familiar friendly attitude to the United States, agreed to blacklist ships which no sensible industrialist would use anyway. The companies trading with Cuba use ships from, say, communist countries; trading with the free American world they use other lines. Shipping companies – most directly involved by the ban – long ago made their accommodation with American sensibilities: with scarcely a backward glance, they chose the lush American market, rather than trade with Cuba. What purpose, then, has been served by this OAS resolution? Business continues, essentially unhindered; the Cubans survive, in spite of the cordon sanitaire which is being constructed around them. But it does provide Congressmen with something to throw back at the critics who complain that they do nothing while the enemies of America gnaw at its heart', p. 21.

CHAPTER 7 | De Gaulle's France and the Cuban Revolution

George Lambie

Introduction

We have seen in chapter 6 on Anglo-Cuban relations in the 1960s that the only significant principle on which exchanges between these two countries was based, and sustained, was commercial pragmatism, and that political ideology and non-commercial ties rarely played a role in the relationship. This held true even after 1964 when a Labour government took office which was more sympathetic, at least rhetorically, to socialist Cuba than the previous Conservative administration.

With French-Cuban relations during the same period commercial pragmatism was again the main motivating force influencing exchanges between the two countries. However, there was also a political dimension in this relationship which resulted from France's wider foreign policy strategy under de Gaulle, which included a programme to form stronger economic, diplomatic, and cultural ties with selected socialist states and some Third World countries. While there is no evidence that the Castro government was targeted specifically by France for inclusion in this programme, as was the Soviet bloc, China and a number of former French colonies, the Cuban Revolution was kept under close scrutiny by de Gaulle's foreign policymakers, who hoped to use the anti-American sentiments and political divisions which it generated in Latin America to serve French initiatives in the region. Consequently, although commercial considerations remained paramount in the Franco-Cuban relationship of the 1960s, they evolved within a more political climate than that which existed between Cuba and other Western European nations at that time. In practice the non-commercial side of this relationship came to little more than a few gestures of mutual political support, a number of educational and cultural exchanges, and some minor projects for scientific and technological co-operation, but their symbolic value was important for both countries. Besides these inter-state non-commercial exchanges, one should also take into account the involvement of a number of liberal and left-wing French intellectuals with the Cuban Revolution in the 1960s. (See Chapters 1 and 2 on the role of French intellectuals in the Cuban Revolution.) Although this aspect of French involvement in Cuba cannot be associated with official Gaullist policy, and was indeed frowned upon by de Gaulle's government, such individual commitment was well received by the Cubans and further improved their view of France.

As a result of the above factors French-Cuban relations in the 1960s present a more complex picture than the relationship between Cuba and any other Western European nation during the same period, including Spain, which attempted to justify its growing commercial links with the Castro government by appealing to the numerous traditional bonds which it continued to share with its former colony.

Gaullist foreign policy in the 1960s

To understand French-Cuban relations in the 1960s one has to be aware of the ideology of Gaullist foreign policy. When de Gaulle took office as President of the Fifth Republic in January 1959 – coincidentally the same year and month as the triumph of the Cuban insurrection – France had been a great power in decline for twenty years. Because of the defeat and occupation which France had suffered in the war its international standing had been undermined, and during the period of recovery after the conflict new international alliances were formed which excluded this once great nation from a significant decision-making role in world affairs. The objective of de Gaulle's foreign policy was to restore to France its status as a leading European and world power, which would be capable of challenging the Anglo-American alliance that had emerged after the war.

In a wider context de Gaulle not only envisaged a new role for France but also for Europe and the Third World. As Cerny points out, de Gaulle developed a far-sighted vision based on a belief in 'a post Cold War world, in which the mature nations of the old world and newly-developed states of the Third World would act to counterbalance the political, economic, technological and military hegemony of the two recently emerged 'superpowers', the US and the Soviet Union'.[1]

De Gaulle's foreign policy in the 1960s was profoundly influenced by his distrust of the US. This distrust first took root during the Second World War when as leader of the 'Free French' de Gaulle experienced difficulties in convincing Roosevelt that he and his followers were the legitimate representatives of an independent France. Even towards the end of the war, when de Gaulle became head of the *Comité Français de Liberación Nacionale* (CFLN), which was widely accepted by the European allies, and the Soviet Union, as the provisional government of France, Roosevelt refused to recognise the organisation under de Gaulle's leadership until it became clear that no alternative was going to present itself.[2] Moreover, de Gaulle was furious at not being invited to the Yalta conference, during which he believed the 'big three' connived to divide up the post-war world between themselves.[3]

After the war, de Gaulle, and indeed most of the French population, felt that the US, despite its generous donations of Marshall dollars to the coalition government, treated France like a second-rate power.[4] This belief was based not only on momentous issues like Washington's willingness to share its nuclear secrets with Britain and not France, but also on more everyday matters like the bad behaviour of some American personnel who were based in France after the war.

De Gaulle was also highly suspicious of the agreements that had been reached at Bretton Woods in 1944, when the US and Britain devised a post-war fiscal strategy in which gold and the dollar were given a fixed exchange rate, thereby promoting the dollar to the status of a world currency. For de Gaulle this was simply another mechanism through which the US could pursue its imperialist objectives, and he condemned the Bretton Woods system and called for a return to the gold standard.[5]

When de Gaulle came to power in 1959 America's handling of France over the previous two decades weighed heavily on his perceptions of the superpower, which he believed was determined to bring Europe increasingly under its control. This belief was reinforced in de Gaulle's mind in 1962 when President Kennedy opportunely used his Independence Day speech to launch his 'Grand Design', which contained a 'Declaration of Interdependence' aimed at a 'concrete Atlantic partnership'.[6] Some of Kennedy's proposals, such as the lowering of tariff barriers between the Common Market and the US, and the maintenance of a US 'nuclear umbrella' over Europe, convinced de Gaulle and many of his followers that America was planning for the eventual total absorption of Europe into its sphere of influence. De Gaulle's response was to speed up the formulation of his plans to establish a truly independent Europe.

To prepare the way for this new counter orientation against US hegemony de Gaulle believed that initially France might have to act alone as an example to other nations. But he also felt that it was France's historical mission to inspire and lead Europe in what he saw was the continent's logical destiny; to create an alternative world force capable of challenging the economic and political domination of the two entrenched superpowers, the US and the Soviet Union. De Gaulle, however, did not envisage simply another bloc of superpower status, but rather an alliance of co-operative and independent nation-states which would gradually weaken and undermine the inflexible principles which were bound up in the two dominant Cold War ideologies of capitalism and communism.

The two most important initiatives of de Gaulle's foreign policy in Europe were, first, France's strategic and highly symbolic withdrawal from NATO in 1966, which was followed by the formation of an independent nuclear deterrent, the *force de frappe*. Second, France's veto of Britain's application for entry into the Common Market because of the belief that the British were still too involved with the legacy of a far flung empire to become a serious member of Europe. Moreover, de Gaulle felt that as a member of the EEC Britain's loyalties would be divided between the US and Europe, and therefore it might be open to persuasion by its superpower ally to act as a 'Trojan Horse' from which American capital could gain unrestricted access into continental Europe.[7]

De Gaulle's policy towards socialist states and the Third World, though not as grand as his European strategy, was nevertheless equally controversial. In 1966, the same year that France withdrew from NATO, de Gaulle made his first state visit to Moscow. Since the early-1960s France had been improving its relationship with the Soviet Union and its Eastern European satellites through a number of trade agreements and the strengthening of diplomatic contacts.[8] When de Gaulle met the Soviet leaders in Moscow, rapprochement between the two nations was therefore already well under way and the visit took place in an atmosphere of apparent harmony, and was regarded as a great success by both sides. Apart from a temporary cooling of the relationship in 1968 after the Soviet invasion of Czechoslovakia, the USSR and France remained on good terms throughout de Gaulle's period in office.[9]

At about the same time as the French diplomatic and commercial offensive began in the Soviet Union and Eastern Europe, de Gaulle's government was also preparing for a similar offensive in China. From 1963 to 1964 Sino-French relations underwent a complete about-face, as the two countries re-established diplomatic contact and entered into a series of negotiations to improve commercial and cultural ties. As with his policy towards the Soviet bloc, de Gaulle felt that by giving China an opportunity to open up a line of communication with the capitalist West, he was preparing for a time when the frozen ideologies of Cold War politics would begin to thaw and give way to the emergence of a more co-operative and co-ordinated world economic order. Naturally, by anticipating this process it was hoped that France would be able to gain many commercial and diplomatic advantages.[10]

A further component of de Gaulle's integrated foreign policy was his programme for improving France's relations with the Third World, and especially those nations which had recently gained their independence from a colonial power. Like his policy of rapprochement with the socialist states, this programme involved the strengthening of diplomatic ties and the negotiation of trade agreements, but also included access to French aid, both in the form of financial assistance and the provision of professional personnel such as teachers, doctors and engineers for development projects.[11]

Although retrospectively French foreign policy in the 1960s has been widely criticised, at the time de Gaulle's initiatives were being implemented, especially in the Third World and the socialist states, they were seen in France by political groups on the right, as well as the left, to represent a serious challenge to the rigid bipolar economic and political structure of the Cold War.[12] Abroad Gaullist foreign policy was largely rejected by the right, but found favour with many who were growing tired of the stagnant political environment which existed after the war.

France and pre-Revolutionary Cuba

In the years between the end of the Second World War and the triumph of the Cuban insurrection in 1959, French-Cuban relations in general had been modest and uneventful. Like other Western European nations France had accepted that Cuba was all but in name an American colony, and realised that substantial penetration of the Cuban market by another foreign power would be strongly resisted by the US government and US commercial interests on the island. French governments therefore tended to concentrate on protecting and developing trade with France's own colonies in the Caribbean, and only occasionally encouraged commercial forays into areas in the region which were in the domain of other imperialist powers. France's two most important colonies in the Caribbean were Martinique and Guadeloupe, each of which, despite their minute size, had for over 100 years consistently done more trade with France than any other island in the region, including Cuba.[13]

However, as the largest seller of raw cane sugar in the world market, Cuba had supplied France with sugar since before the war. France, like Britain which also received most of its requirements of raw cane sugar from its colonies and former colonies, bought Cuban raw sugar mainly for refining and re-export. This could be a very profitable business when refined sugar commanded a higher price than raw sugar, but if the difference in price narrowed purchases of Cuban sugar were quickly reduced.[14]

France's second main import from Cuba was tobacco, which in the 1950s averaged one tenth of the value of sugar imports. Together sugar and tobacco accounted for 95 per cent of French imports from Cuba. In return Cuba bought from France a wide range of manufactured goods of which a large proportion were luxury items such as perfumes and fashionable clothes. France's trade with Cuba since the end of the Second World War accounted on average for 5 per cent of its trade with the Americas, excluding the US and Canada. This volume of commercial exchange warranted the maintenance of full diplomatic missions by both countries in each others capitals.

Regarding cultural and political relations between France and Cuba before the 1959 Cuban insurrection information is scarce.[15] At an official level political relations between the two countries were stable, and could usually be dealt with by routine diplomacy. Regarding individual political figures there were a number of Cuban left-wing intellectuals who visited Paris during the interwar years and the 1950s, and some may have been influenced by radical French thinking.[16] Generally, since the 1920s the Latin American intelligentsia, including political theorists, writers and artists, regarded Paris as the world's most important cultural and intellectual centre, and throughout this period, except perhaps during the war years, there existed a small Cuban community in the French capital.[17]

In an interview given to French journalists in 1983, Fidel Castro made a broad historical analysis of Cuba's relations with France in which he suggested that, after Spain, France was the European country which had had the most influence on Cuban cultural and intellectual development.[18] Qualifying this statement he went on to identify a number of events and ideas in French history which had a particular resonance in Cuba; these included, firstly, the ideas of the French Revolution of 1789, and in particular the thinking of the Jacobins, which he believed influenced the liberation fighters who took part in Cuba's first war of independence which began in 1868. On a personal level he claimed that he had read the history of the French Revolution before he had read Marx, and that this was one of the most important early influences on his political formation. Secondly, Castro referred to the revolution of 1848 in France and the Paris Commune of 1871 as events that had a lasting effect on Cuban revolutionary thinking, adding that the Cuban understanding of this period of French history had been most influenced by Marx's works *The Civil War in France* and *The Eighteenth Brumaire of Louis Bonaparte*. Thirdly, he identified his own generation of Cuban revolutionaries with the members of the French Resistance who had fought against the Nazis during the Second World War.

Following this historical overview of Cuba's debt to France from a revolutionary perspective, Castro went on briefly to mention French influence on Cuban art and literature. Although it would be useful to have access to a more balanced view of French influence on Cuba, the perceptions of France as a radical and revolutionary country were to play an important role in the development of French-Cuban relations in the 1960s.

Revolutionary Cuba and de Gaulle's France: the early years

The first sign of interest in Cuban politics to be shown in France in the postwar period emerged in late-1958, a few months before Fidel Castro's guerrilla army seized power. At that time the French were occupied with their own internal political contest for a new President, but the press nevertheless still found space for regular reports on events in Cuba. With the end of the French election campaign in January 1959, and the triumph of the Cuban rebels in the same month, the Cuban insurrection became one of the most frequent foreign affairs topics to be discussed in the French media.[19] This high level of interest in developments in Cuba was, one suspects, partly because the French public were anxious to contrast events in Cuba with what was happening in their own rebel colony, Algeria. Of the four main French daily newspapers, *Le Figaro*, *l'Humanité*, *France-Soir* and *Le Monde*, it was *Le Monde* which gave the most detailed, though not most frequent, coverage of the Revolution. *Le Monde* was also the only French newspaper to send its own correspondent, Claude Julien, to report on events in Cuba. Claude Julien went on to visit Cuba on several occasions during the 1960s and became one of the best-informed French journalists on the Revolution and its developments.

Analysis of the Revolution and its leaders in the French press was, as one would expect, much affected by each publication's ideological leanings. But because of the political ambiguity of the Revolution during its early months, there were some inconsistencies. For example the right wing *France Soir* praised Castro as an individual until it became clear that he was moving the Revolution towards the left. In contrast *l'Humanité*, the French Communist Party paper, rarely mentioned Castro until they were sure that the Cuban Communist Party was going to play a significant role in the consolidation of the Revolution.[20]

From a Cuban perspective interest in France began to develop among members of the Revolutionary leadership in the early 1960s, when they realised that de Gaulle was showing signs of pursuing an independent foreign policy that would challenge the Cold War political and economic ideologies on which the Western Alliance was founded.[21] During the previously cited interview which Fidel Castro gave to French journalists in 1983, the Cuban leader conceded that his government had always sympathised with de Gaulle's 'spirit of independence'.

However, despite the growing mutual interest between France and Cuba which emerged after the Cuban insurrection, there remained a number of obstacles which precluded an immediate strengthening of relations. The most important and decisive factor which prevented increased trade between France and Cuba in the early-1960s, and indeed Cuba and the rest of the capitalist world, excluding of course the US, was the Castro government's grave shortage of hard currency. Besides, any Western market economy that attempted to expand its trade with Cuba at this time may have invited a particularly fierce reaction from the US, which was still hoping to bring about a swift demise of the Castro government by a combination of internal and external pressure. Moreover, for the first few years after the insurrection there was a shared sense of outrage among the Western capitalist powers at the Castro government's nationalisation of foreign investments without compensation. This was perhaps the only time since the insurrection when the US could claim to have enjoyed majority support from its Western allies for its policy to isolate Cuba.[22] In this respect France was no exception, and up to 1964 de Gaulle's government refused to provide credit guarantees to French exporters who wished to do business with Cuba. Government pressure was also put on French shipowners to stop carrying Cuba trade in their vessels.[23] And in March 1960 a number of French banks that formed part of a Western European banking consortium which had agreed to negotiate a $100 million loan to Cuba, decided to act in concert with their partners and accede to US demands to withdraw their offer.[24]

On a political and diplomatic level there were also a number of areas of contention between France and Cuba which precluded an early improvement in relations. Firstly, once the Castro government had made its socialist objectives clear it could not be seen to be moving closer to France while the latter was engaged in a bloody colonial war with Algeria.[25] Cuba chose Algeria's struggle against France as its Third World *cause célèbre*, and from 1960 to 1962 the state run newspaper *Revolución* carried articles almost every day on the war. During this period Cuba's support for the independence fighters of the FLN and its condemnation of France was unwavering.[26] In his meeting with French journalists in 1983, Fidel Castro indeed singled out the Algerian problem as the principle obstacle to an improvement in political relations between France and Cuba in the early-1960s.

Even after the signing of the accord of Evian in March 1962 between de Gaulle's government and the FLN, in which Algeria was granted independence and a cease-fire declared, Cuba did not moderate its attacks against France, assuming it would simply switch to a covert war against the FLN.[27] Moreover, in independence wars against colonial powers, Cuba advocated a revolutionary solution which should stop at nothing short of a total military defeat of the enemy and the seizure of all foreign assets.[28] The Evian accord, therefore, which was based on negotiations between France and its rebellious colony, was seen as a dangerous compromise for the Algerian rebels.

Secondly, as the Castro government moved closer to the Soviet Union it was obliged to register its disapproval of international decisions and actions which were detrimental to its new ally, and one of the first instances in which this kind of support was given was at the time of the Berlin crisis in 1961. During the crisis France was singled out for particular criticism by Cuba because de Gaulle, along with the West German Chancellor Adenauer, adopted an even harder line than the rest of the Western allies towards the Soviet Union.[29]

Thirdly, having begun to take note of de Gaulle's arguments in favour of the establishment of a new world order, the Cuban leadership took a dim view of France's seemingly unquestioning support of US actions during the Cuban missile crisis of October 1962.[30] For the Cubans this demonstrated clearly that while France was willing to pursue an independent foreign policy when it suited its national interests, when the capitalist system of which it was a part was threatened its only recourse was to fall in line with its natural allies. In such circumstances even neutrality was not an option.

The unfolding of de Gaulle's foreign policy: an environment for French-Cuban rapprochement

Although French-Cuban relations in the early-1960s reached a low ebb, by the end of 1963 there were developments in both countries, and internationally, which boded well for a speedy rapprochement. On the French side de Gaulle's foreign policy initiatives were beginning to strengthen France's relations with the Soviet Union, China, and a few Third World countries. For Cuba this had positive indications for an improvement of its own relations with France. The aspect of France's Third World policy which was of special interest to the Castro government was de Gaulle's treatment of Algeria after the accord of Evian. As noted earlier, initially the Cubans, like most foreign observers, had expected France to destabilise the new FLN government, but instead it acceded to almost every demand made by the Ben Bella government. De Gaulle hoped that by supporting Algeria's transition to independence France would establish valuable anti-colonial credentials which would enhance its standing in the eyes of the Third World and the socialist states. Most importantly de Gaulle's government believed that the political kudos which it gained from its support of Algerian independence would lead to economic advantages for French business in the Third World, and especially Africa where European colonial rule was coming to an end throughout the continent.[31]

The Cubans were suitably impressed by France's treatment of its former colony, and by late-1963 the Cuban state newspaper, *Revolución*, which had been the most vehement and consistent source of criticism in the Americas against French colonial policy in Algeria, began to praise de Gaulle's efforts in support of Algerian independence. In his meeting with French journalists twenty years later, Castro recalled that once the French-Algerian problem had been 'happily settled', Cuba's political and economic relations with France improved, and ever since had developed in a 'progressive manner'.

Interestingly, after the Algerians had gained their independence the new government under Ben Bella identified Cuba as its most trusted ally, and claimed that it had chosen the Cuban model for its own economic and political development.[32] Soon after this declaration was made in March 1962 the Algerians began to undertake a programme of nationalisation of foreign-owned assets. De Gaulle's government observed these developments with apparent approval, but secretly feared that communism would go too far in the former colony. However, France saw this threat coming not so much from imported Cuban ideologies, but rather from the rapidly-expanding involvement of the Soviet Union in Ben Bella's economic programme.

De Gaulle hoped that the enthusiastic establishment of official relations between the newly-independent government of Algeria and Castro's Cuba, would serve as an illustration of France's tolerance towards Third World revolutions in comparison to the chauvinism of the US. In a conversation with *Le Monde* reporter Jean Daniel in February 1964 Castro indicated that he fully accepted this view, when he argued that Algeria was fortunate to be the former colony of a capitalist power which supported its independence, adding that such a relationship between the US and one of the members of its imperial empire in Latin America was unthinkable.[33] Indeed, the French were anxious to give credibility to the idea that while the US had failed in Cuba they were succeeding in Algeria. Allowing their former colony to choose freely its allies and select its own model for development were essential elements in this strategy.[34]

As well as offering cautious support for de Gaulle's Third World policy, and especially his handling of Algeria after independence, by 1964 Cuba was also indicating its approval of de Gaulle's attempts to improve France's relations with the socialist states. For example *Revolución* registered Cuba's support for France's declaration that it would be establishing diplomatic relations with China, pointing out how de Gaulle had refused to be intimidated by US protests.[35] De Gaulle's stance against the US on various issues was, as far as the Cubans were concerned, the most commendable aspect of French foreign policy. In an article entitled 'Charles de Gaulle Attacks Politics of the Yankees', *Revolución* reported comprehensively on a press conference given by the French leader in which hé had made clear France's main objections to US foreign policy.[36] These included: America's attempts to increase its political and economic hegemony in Europe and particularly France; the desire of Washington to create an Atlantic Alliance which was subordinate to its political and military control; and US involvement in Vietnam and its belief that it was its mission to police the world against communism. On the issue of Vietnam, *Revolución* noted that de Gaulle had made it known that personally he believed that the US would never be victorious in South-East Asia, and therefore should disengage from the war as soon as possible. *Revolución* also quoted de Gaulle's assertion, which could be construed as a challenge to the US, that ' "things have changed greatly since the post-war years when the United States directed the affairs of the Western world" '. In the opinion of the Cuban daily this statement constituted 'one of the most important declarations to be made during his . . . [de Gaulle's] presidency'.

The political *rapprochement* between France and Cuba which began towards the end of 1963 was complemented by a mutual desire to improve trading relations. This was particularly noticeable from the Cuban side, as it became clear to the Castro government by this time that their plans for economic diversification would have to rely more than they had previously anticipated on the import of manufactured goods and expertise from capitalist nations. Nevertheless, there remained a number of obstacles, some of which were intrinsic to France and Cuba's economic formations, which made commercial relations between the two countries more problematic than between Cuba and some of its other capitalist trading partners.

Political rapprochement – *economic* incompatibility

Cuba's trade with the market economies plummeted in the early 1960s because of the shortage of hard currency, and the need to divert resources to improving commercial relations with the Soviet bloc and China as the US became increasingly hostile to the revolution. Trade between France and Cuba faced an additional constraint from 1960 when the EEC, of which France was a member, inaugurated a policy which encouraged self-sufficiency in sugar production within the Community. From henceforth importation of sugar was discouraged by internal subsidies to Community producers and the imposition of tariffs on sugar originating from non-EEC sources. The only exception to this policy was the dispensation given to France to continue importing sugar at pre-tariff prices from its colonies and former colonies which made up the *Communauté*. Therefore, although after 1960 France was able to maintain its sugar imports from its two *départements* in the Caribbean, Martinique and Guadeloupe, Cuban sugar was subject to a tariff and became prohibitively expensive. These tariff regulations, of course, did not apply to France's two main Western European competitors in the Cuban market, Britain and Spain, neither of whom were members of the EEC and could therefore purchase sugar from Cuba without incurring EEC tariffs. Britain, though, was obliged under the Commonwealth Sugar Agreement to give preference to Commonwealth producers, and in some years this resulted in a reduction in imports of Cuban sugar.

Concerning France's potential as a sugar importer, one should also bear in mind that in the 1960s it was Europe's largest sugar producer, and between 1960 and 1966 French sugar output was on average 32 per cent in excess of national consumption.[37] Britain, on the other hand, only produced enough sugar to supply 30 per cent of domestic demand for the same period, and West Germany could just manage to meet domestic requirements in years of good harvests.[38] In the early-1960s Spanish sugar producers were able to satisfy about 90 per cent of home demand but as the decade progressed, and living standards improved, this figure fell to 70 per cent and imports increased proportionately.[39] France's high levels of sugar production in the 1960s, along with its continuing obligation to import sugar from its colonies and former colonies, made it a poor market for Cuba and other raw sugar producers which sold on the free market, even before taking into account EEC tariff protection. Since the late-1940s France had itself been an important sugar exporter, and during the 1960s exported an equivalent of one-fifth of Cuba's total sugar exports during the decade.

As a result of EEC regulations French imports of Cuban raw sugar fell from 107,339 metric tonnes in 1960 to zero in 1961, and stayed at this level for the rest of the decade, except for 1968 when 20,637 tonnes were imported.[40] Once France could no longer offer a reliable market for Cuban sugar, Cuba lost approximately 90 per cent of its export trade to France, and was forced to reduce drastically its imports of French products in response. In 1960, total French-Cuban commercial exchanges were $23.9 million, but after the new EEC sugar tariffs came into effect trade between the two countries fell to $7.1m in 1961, $4.2m in 1962, rising to $8.5m in 1963.[41] In comparison during the same period Britain's trade with Cuba in 1960 had been $42.5m, and fell to $26.9m in 1962 which was the worst year generally for Cuban trade with market economies.[42] Even Spain, which had a poor trading record with Cuba before the 1959 insurrection, was doing more trade ($9.9m) with the Castro government than France by 1962.[43]

Given the constraints on French-Cuban trade the improvements which began after 1963 may be seen as evidence of a mutual desire to maintain a strong commercial relationship. But this relationship, despite de Gaulle's rhetorical support for Third World countries which showed an independent posture, remained an unequal one, in which Cuba obtained few concessions from France in exchange for its willingness to buy large quantities of French manufactured goods. On average, during the 1960s, Cuba had to tolerate a ratio of trade in France's favour of almost 3:1; a discrepancy which was financed by Cuba's surplus hard currency earnings from commercial exchanges with countries like Japan and Spain with which it had a positive trade balance.

From political rhetoric to commercial pragmatism: French-Cuban trade in the mid-1960s

By mid-1963 Cuba's leaders decided that the direct route towards industrialisation, which they had attempted to follow since 1959, was no longer tenable and a more protracted strategy for economic diversification would have to be adopted which included a renewed concentration on sugar production for export. This resulted in a gradual increase in sugar sales to capitalist countries, which, combined with a rise in the price of sugar, improved Cuba's hard currency earnings. French exporters, along with a number of other Western European exporters, were eager to exploit this new market in North America's traditional sphere of influence.

While there is no firm evidence that de Gaulle's foreign policy strategists had any specific plans by 1963 to include Cuba in their programme of *détente* with socialist states, some French firms, such as the commercial vehicle manufacturer Berliet of Lyon, which were already beginning to take advantage of the new markets in Africa and the East, had identified Cuba as the next logical target for their export drive.[44] Clearly, this decision was based on essentially pragmatic factors such as Cuba's improving reserves of hard currency, its ambitious programme of economic diversification, and the rare opportunity to expand French trade into a region that was previously dominated by US interests. But that some sectors of French industry should be seeking new business in Cuba at this time, gave the impression that they were acting within the spirit of France's radical foreign policy.

Berliet was the first French company to pursue new business opportunities in Cuba since Castro came to power, and in late-1963 tendered for a contract to supply the Cubans with up to 1000 buses over a number of years.[45] The contract was finally awarded to Leyland Motors of Great Britain, partly because the Cubans had already established a good business relationship with Leyland before the Revolution, and were familiar with their vehicles, but most importantly because Leyland were able to offer their customers five years credit which was backed by a British government (Export Credits Guarantee Department) guarantee to underwrite the sale in the event of a Cuban default (Chapter 6).[46] This was the first time since the US had initiated its trade embargo on Cuba in 1961, that any European government had openly offered official support to a member of its business community to enter into commercial relations with the Castro government. As indicated in Chapter 6 on Anglo-Cuban relations in the 1960s the Johnson administration was incensed by this display of blatant disregard for its policy on Cuba, and what was even worse the offence was committed by America's most trusted ally in the Western Alliance. Above all Washington feared that the British action would serve as a precedent which would be followed by the rest of their allies in the West. These fears were soon confirmed as only a few weeks after the Cuban contract with Leyland had been signed, the de Gaulle government began backing its own exporters to Cuba with credit guarantees.[47] The first French company to take advantage of this change of policy was Berliet, which signed a $7 million contract with the Cubans in February 1964, to supply 300 heavy trucks for use on agricultural projects.[48] Cuba agreed to pay 20 per cent in cash with the order and the remaining 80 per cent over three years. These were the normal repayment terms which were expected on a contract of this type which was underwritten by the French government (COFACE).

During the negotiations which took place between Berliet and the Cubans before the signing of the truck contract, the Cuban team indicated that they were also seeking to purchase a number of bulldozers.[49] Apparently they had experienced problems finding a supplier because the North American company, Caterpillar, dominated production of this type of vehicle in the capitalist West, and since the embargo came into operation in 1961 Cuba had been restricted from purchasing any equipment produced by American-owned companies or equipment which contained American parts. Representatives from Berliet suggested that the Cubans should obtain bulldozers from the Richards Continental company of Lyon, which was the only manufacturer in Europe that could build bulldozers without using any American parts. It was also brought to the attention of the Cuban team that Richards Continental's vehicles were fitted with Berliet engines, and therefore they would be compatible with the trucks they were purchasing and allow for standardisation of parts and equipment. On this advice Cuba signed a contract with Richards Continental in February 1964.[50]

De Gaulle's foreign policy towards Latin America: a role for Cuba?

What appears to have been firstly a French business-led initiative to improve Franco-Cuban commercial relations, with the submission of the Berliet tender in late-1963 for the Cuban bus contract, was soon followed by a response from the de Gaulle government. This included not only the granting of state-backed credit guarantees for exporters to Cuba, but also the beginning of wider diplomatic and political moves to improve relations between the two countries. One of the first indications that the de Gaulle government was turning its attention towards Cuba came in January 1964, when at a New Year reception in the Elysee Palace for foreign diplomats serving in France, de Gaulle took aside the Cuban Ambassador, Harold Gramatges, for a long discussion.[51] This incident was particularly noticeable because the President did not afford the same treatment to any of the other Latin American ambassadors who attended the reception. Havana radio later reported some of the details of the conversation, emphasising that de Gaulle had 'underlined his sentiments of sympathy towards Cuba' and expressed the hope that the 'traditional friendship' between the two countries would be strengthened in 1964.[52] The discussion between de Gaulle and Gramatges also made the headlines in *Revolución*, which read 'Strengthening of Friendship Between Cuba and France'.[53] The *New York Times* interpreted de Gaulle's comments as 'another example of the President's desire to demonstrate his and France's independence of United States policy'.[54]

De Gaulle's public gesture of support towards Cuba, though clearly a snub to the US, also had other implications, which can only be understood in the context of rapidly unfolding French foreign policy at that time. By the end of 1963 France had begun its *rapprochement* with the Soviet Union and Eastern Europe, it was on the point of restoring diplomatic relations with China, and was well under way with the implementation of its controversial policy in Algeria. The next phase of this integrated foreign policy strategy was to improve France's commercial, political and cultural relations with Latin America. This phase was to be initiated with a visit by the French President to Mexico in March 1964, followed by a tour of other major Latin American nations in September. Though the details and dates for these visits had not been finalised when de Gaulle attended the New Year reception for foreign diplomats in January 1964, it was widely known that they would be taking place. Therefore the special attention de Gaulle gave to the Cuban Ambassador was a clear and opportunely-timed indication that he did not accept Cuba's pariah status in the continent. Moreover, de Gaulle's action suggested that his government recognised the legitimacy of Cuba's struggle for independence and self-determination in a region dominated by the US. Indeed, given French foreign policy thinking at that time, Cuba had set an example for the rest of the region; it had reversed US imperial hegemony and was now showing a desire to strengthen its relations with Europe.

De Gaulle hoped that by presenting Europe as an alternative, and potentially more progressive, partner in the process of development than the US, it would be possible to encourage Latin American nations to seek greater political and economic independence from their superpower ally.[55] In fact the centrepiece of all Gaullist foreign policy was to lure the states of the Third World and Eastern Europe away from superpower hegemony, towards a new and less ideologically dominated relationship with a neutral Europe. Therefore before de Gaulle's visit to Mexico his information minister, Alain Peyrefitte, claimed that the trip would be the first stage in ending Latin America's 'claustrophobia', which resulted from the region's

nearly exclusive relations with the US.[56] This claim did have some substance, because before leaving for Mexico de Gaulle met with West German
leaders to establish mechanisms for the joint planning of economic aid to
Latin America.[57] Similar proposals were put to the Italians but no agreement
was signed.[58]

Immediately before leaving for Mexico de Gaulle paid his first visit
to Algeria since the country had been granted independence, and had a long
and amicable meeting with Ben Bella.[59] Although such a gesture was
diplomatically consonant with France's management of Algerian independence since the accord of Evian, it caused much controversy at home and
abroad. Sections of the right-wing French press felt that it was unwise of the
President to visit Algeria at a time when his government was planning to
strengthen relations with Latin America, because it helped to reinforce the
already growing international perception of France as a power that tolerated
and supported radical governments.[60] After Evian the new Algerian leaders
had made it clear that they intended to follow the Cuban model of development, therefore de Gaulle's meeting with Ben Bella could also be construed
as an indication of France's tacit approval of the Cuban revolution.

It appears that the Castro government wished to be identified with
France's radical proposals for Latin American development, by showing
that it had already been following some of the prescriptions that were being
put forward for the region by de Gaulle. The first indication of this was
given by Fidel Castro in an informal meeting with foreign journalists at an
Independence Day reception at the Moroccan Embassy in Havana, which
was held a few days before de Gaulle's visit to Mexico. During the meeting
Castro told his audience that the Revolution had brought stability, and Cuba
was 'now the best country to do business with in Latin America'.[61] He also
emphasised the importance of Cuba's strengthening commercial links with
Western Europe, which he suggested had created the extraordinary situation
in which socialist Cuba and the great European powers were now joined
together as allies in defence of free trade, with the US as the odd man out.
Clearly during this meeting Castro may simply have been making political
capital out of Cuba's recent successes in breaking the American blockade,
but the timing of his comments, the setting in which they were made, and
given that de Gaulle's forthcoming visit to Mexico was one of the main
topics of discussion, suggest that he was acutely aware of the French
position on Latin America. And when asked if he had invited de Gaulle to
visit Cuba later in the year, when the French leader would be making a more
extensive tour of Latin America, he said no such invitation had yet been
given but added if the President came he would be 'well received by the
Cuban people'.

De Gaulle's visit to Mexico lasted from 16–19 of March and he
returned to Paris on the 23 March after spending a day each in Guadeloupe,

French Guiana and Martinique.[62] The trip was largely uneventful but served to strengthen relation's with the Mexican president López Mateos, a key figure for France to have on its side if it was to make any headway with its new policy in Latin America. It also smoothed the way for de Gaulle's grand tour of Latin America later in the year. During the Mexico visit de Gaulle's aides were cautious when asked questions on Cuba and stressed that French policy in the region was designed to prevent more revolutions by offering a peaceful route to social and economic development.[63]

De Gaulle's visit to Mexico made headlines in the Cuban daily *Revolución* on 16 March.[64] Although it was not reported as such, one suspects that Cuba must have attached some significance to the meeting between the heads of state of two significant, friendly countries, one of which was becoming its main political ally in Western Europe and the other which was its only reliable friend in Latin America.

In the intervening period between de Gaulle's visit to Mexico and his tour of Latin America later in the year, French commercial relations with Cuba continued to improve. One of the most important and controversial contracts to be signed at this time was the Cuban order which was placed with the French engineering company Brissonneau et Lotz to supply 20 used diesel locomotives.[65] The success of this deal was again based on the availability of French government credit guarantees, with the Cubans being given three years to pay the contract price of $4 million.

Like many other areas of Cuban infrastructure which were based predominantly on American technology, the railway system was in a desperate state of disrepair by 1964 due to the unavailability of spares. At the time of the signing of the contract with Brissonneau et Lotz it was estimated that only a quarter of the locomotives which had been operating before the revolution were still functioning.[66] Among these were a few of the 15 Brissonneau locomotives which had been purchased in 1955, and for which spares had remained available after Castro had come to power. The French company were therefore in a strong position when the Cubans decided to buy more locomotives.

Although railway equipment was not regarded as strategic goods by the French or American administrations, Washington was furious with the de Gaulle government for letting the deal go ahead and for providing guaranteed credit.[67] America's forthright condemnation of this contract, which appeared excessive given its value, resulted from a belief on the part of US policymakers that the collapse of the Cuban railway system was imminent; a development which they expected would bring about a speedy demise of Castro's principal economic plans. This strategy had gained increasing importance in Washington during 1963 when the Cuban's began to put a renewed emphasis on sugar production, because the railways played a crucial role in transporting cane to the mills and sugar to the ports. The

French locomotives were to be used precisely for these operations and were therefore seen by the US government as a direct contribution to Cuba's economic survival. A few days after the contract was signed President Johnsón identified France along with Britain as the two allies which had been least co-operative in helping the US to enforce its economic boycott of Cuba.[68]

On 21 September de Gaulle left France for Venezuela, on what was the first stage on the longest and most comprehensive state tour of Latin America ever to be undertaken by a French President, lasting 26 days and including visits to ten countries.[69] De Gaulle was accompanied by his wife and his Foreign Minister Couve de Murville, as well as a party of officials and advisers. Even with hindsight it is difficult to judge if the trip was a success, though it was hailed as such by the French press at the time. In diplomatic terms it undoubtedly strengthened France's links with some Latin American countries, and this in turn led to improved commercial relations, but such developments cannot be quantified, especially considering that Latin American trade with France, and with Western Europe generally, had already been expanding for a number of years before de Gaulle's visit. As well as it being difficult to measure the success of the trip it is also not easy to identify its failures. Sections of the Western press, however, put forward the view that de Gaulle and his advisers had failed to anticipate the full extent of the affinity between some Latin American governments and the US. One particular incident which was chosen to support this claim was the speech given in Bogotá by Colombia's President, Guillermo León Valencia, at a banquet in honour of de Gaulle, in which the Colombian leader was so fulsome in his praise of the US that even American officials who were present were embarrassed.[70] Apparently the French were nonplussed by the speech and described it as 'strange'.[71] Clearly de Gaulle and his party would have been briefed before leaving France on the political alignments of the various governments they would be visiting in Latin America, but nevertheless such incidents must have been discouraging.

During the tour Latin American support for US policies in the region was also made clear when government officials in several countries indicated to de Gaulle that they disapproved of France's apparent eagerness to trade with Cuba. In Venezuela President Raúl Leoni even insisted on having a special discussion with de Gaulle on this matter.[72]

The Cubans, who supported a revolutionary solution to Latin America's problems, kept their official comments on the trip to a minimum, but their silence can be taken as a sign of tacit approval. *Revolución* published several short articles on the visit, none of which attempted to analyse de Gaulle's policy on Latin America or the significance of his personal tour of the region.[73] While the French President was in Latin America, however,

Revolución took the opportunity whenever possible to suggest that France supported Cuba's attempts to trade with Western Europe. For example, while the French party were in Colombia, whose government was particularly hostile to Cuba, *Revolución* eagerly quoted Couve de Murville, who, in defending France's trade with Cuba had stated, 'France only imposes boycotts when it is at war with a country'.[74] During de Gaulle's visit *Revolución* also published a report claiming that France was planning to expand its trade with socialist countries by offering long-term credits.[75] Finally, while de Gaulle was in Latin America a large shipment of trucks arrived in Cuba, which formed part of the order that had been placed earlier in the year with the French company Berliet. Taking advantage of the coincidental but opportune timing of this delivery from France, *Revolución* saw fit to report the event on its front page, emphasising how the ships captain had been unmoved by American planes which had flown reconnaissance missions over his vessel.[76] The article also gave information on the models of vehicles that had been sent, the quantity, and the price that the Cuban's had paid for them.[77] This was followed by a statement which was clearly directed at the US: 'The delivery of this modern machinery, whose acquisition proves yet again that Cuba is expanding its external trade in conjunction with the numerous European nations which believe in the politics of free trade, represents an important boost to the tasks of development that face our country'.

Returning to a broader view of de Gaulle's policy on Latin America it was Brazil which was perhaps intended to be the focal point of his strategy in the region. Soon after de Gaulle became President of France, a nationalist reformist government under the leadership of Jânio Quadros came to power in Brazil. Quadros in many ways became Latin America's equivalent of de Gaulle, as he took a tough line at home to protect Brazilian business against foreign capital, and pursued an independent foreign policy which included a programme of *détente* with the socialist states, including Cuba. In 1961 Quadros resigned and power passed to his vice-president João Goulart. Goulart continued to pursue most of his predecessor's policies but was a far more radical and populist leader than Quadros, and soon speeded up the pace of domestic reforms and *rapprochement* with the socialist camp. De Gaulle's foreign policymakers observed these developments with interest, paying particular attention to the growing animosity between the Goulart government and the US, which they believed would result in new business opportunities for France in Brazil. By early 1964, at the time of de Gaulle's visit to Mexico, Franco-Brazilian relations were the strongest they had been for many years, and great hopes were held out by both sides that the French President's visit to Brazil during his forthcoming tour of Latin America would lead to new commercial, political, and cultural ties between the two countries. Such plans, however, were shattered only days after de Gaulle had returned from Mexico when Goulart was deposed by a military coup, which had been partly inspired by the US.[78]

Immediately on gaining power the military dictatorship fell in line with American policy in the region by breaking diplomatic relations with Cuba and other socialist states, and dismantling the progressive reforms which had been enacted by the Goulart government. With pro-American regimes in power in most of Latin America after the fall of Goulart, de Gaulle must have felt far less sanguine about the outcome of his approaching tour of the region.

It is difficult to speculate what would have happened if Goulart had remained in office, but one possible scenario may have been that not only would Franco-Brazilian relations have become stronger but relations between Brazil and Cuba may have also made significant advances. Indeed, Goulart had made overtures to the Castro government soon after he had come to power and by 1963 these gestures were being enthusiastically reciprocated by Cuba. France may have been able to take advantage of this situation by using Brazil and Cuba as an embryonic independent Latin American alliance through which it could demonstrate the benefits to be gained from improving contact with France, and Europe, to the rest of the region. One suspects, however, that if such a plan existed it would have been managed via Brazil, rather than Brazil and Cuba, so as not to provoke unnecessary hostility to France from the US. Once Goulart had gone France could not devise an alternative strategy based on Cuba alone, precisely because any friendly approaches to the Castro government provoked a disproportionate response from Washington.

French policy on Cuba from the time of de Gaulle's tour of Latin America to the end of his period in office was therefore little different in practical terms than that of France's neighbouring European powers, apart from a possible attempt in 1968, based on a joint initiative from Cuba and France, to establish a higher level of commercial relations.

France becomes a market for Cuban nickel

As Cuban purchases of French goods began to increase in 1964 de Gaulle's government was obliged to seek ways of expanding France's imports from Cuba, especially if they wished to continue supplying the Cuban market in subsequent years when Cuba's general trading position might not be so strong. Because of Cuba's improved hard currency earnings in 1964 arising from high prices for raw sugar and a reasonably good harvest, it had been possible for the Castro government to bear a trading ratio in France's favour of 6:1 ($20.9 million : $3.4 million), but clearly this imbalance could not be sustained indefinitely. After France ceased to buy Cuban raw sugar in 1961, it had continued to import other sugar products such as honey and molasses from Cuba, but there were limits to how much this trade could be expanded. In 1963, for example, although French purchases of these products were at the highest level for many years, and accounted for 30 per cent of imports from Cuba, their total value was only $1.2 million. France's two other main imports from Cuba, tobacco and various types of preserved sea food, which averaged a value of $1.1 million and $0.67 million per annum respectively from 1959–64, were also commodities with a static market in France.[79]

By the autumn of 1964 it was becoming clear to Cuba's capitalist trading partners that the dramatic fall in raw sugar prices which had taken place over the past year – from 13 cents a pound in October 1963 to 3.6 cents in September 1964 – would soon be felt in reduced orders for their products from the Castro government. This fear was confirmed when the Cuban leadership announced on 17 September that due to reduced hard currency earnings it would be postponing some of its plans to buy machinery and consumer goods from non-communist countries.[80] For capitalist countries which were regular importers of Cuban sugar like Britain and Italy, the decline in the world price simply meant that the Cuban market for their goods might contract temporarily until prices of sugar rose again. And for Spain, which had negotiated a long-term contact with Cuba to supply sugar at fixed prices, no decline in trade was expected. France, on the other hand, because it had stopped importing raw sugar from Cuba and had not expanded its imports of any other Cuban product to compensate for the loss, was obliged to wait until the world price for sugar rose sufficiently for Cuba to earn surplus hard currency in other capitalist markets before it could expect to receive new orders.

In an attempt to overcome this constraint on French-Cuban trade, in 1965 de Gaulle's government gave authorisation to the French company 'Société le Nickel' to begin importing Cuban nickel. For the next seven years nickel became France's principal import from Cuba, and though the quantities purchased were insufficient to bring about a balance of trade between the two countries, the Cuban's were encouraged to continue purchases of French products.[81] De Gaulle's concession to Cuba, although an indication of his government's political determination to uphold Franco-Cuban trade in the face of mounting pressures from the US, was based principally on commercial pragmatism, and in exchange for France's willingness to bear the increased risk of US retaliation, the Cuban's were obliged to sell nickel to French industry at or below the world market price.

The Berliet contracts with Cuba

As France's share of the Cuban market increased from the mid-1960s its main exports consisted of commercial vehicles, railway equipment (including locomotives), industrial machinery, chemicals, fertilisers, and some foodstuffs such as maize and dried milk powder. This pattern continued throughout the second half of the 1960s and the early-1970s. Among the French companies trading with Cuba during this period it was the commercial vehicle manufacturer Berliet of Lyon which established the longest and most fruitful relationship with the Castro government. As we have seen this relationship began in 1964 with the export to Cuba of 300 trucks worth approximately $7.3 million. During the subsequent nine years Berliet conducted business with Cuba that amounted to $70 million, which was equivalent to 20 per cent of the value of all French exports to Cuba for that period. For Berliet its Cuba trade represented annually on average 4.7 per cent of the company's total business and 15.5 per cent of exports.[82]

Berliet's second big Cuban order came in 1967 when the company signed a contract to supply the Castro government with additional trucks and equipment to the value of $17 million. Again, French government credit guarantees were made available for the transaction. During these first years of contact between Berliet and the Castro government, the French company earned a good reputation with the Cubans not only for the reliability of its vehicles but also for its after-sales service and technical assistance. At that time Berliet was also gaining notoriety for its products and services in other socialist and Third World countries including China, Algeria, and some Eastern European states. In Algeria and China the company had also been invited to set up maintenance and service workshops for their vehicles, and assembly plants with facilities to produce a number of components and special equipment from local resources.

Partly because of the success of Berliet equipment in Cuba, and also perhaps due to recommendations from Cuba's socialist allies who had dealt with the company at a more advanced level, in February 1968 Castro invited Managing Director Paul Berliet to Cuba to discuss a number of projects. During the subsequent meeting between Berliet and Castro the Cuban leader indicated three main areas in which he felt the French company could offer assistance, these included: giving advice on the most suitable equipment for the construction of reservoirs and dams, help with a review of the transport requirements of the nickel industry, and finally to suggest ways to improve Cuba's capacity to service and maintain its existing public transport resources. Besides these requests Castro also asked Paul Berliet to investigate the possibility of establishing an air link between Paris and Havana, and to try to arrange a meeting between de Gaulle and the Cuban leadership.

At the time Berliet was visiting Cuba relations between the Castro government and the Soviet Union, which had been deteriorating for over a year, had reached their lowest ebb since before the Revolution. Because of these tensions a split had emerged in the Cuban Communist Party, with a small group which became known as the 'micro-faction' retaining what they claimed was a pro-Soviet position, while the main body of the Party, including key figures in the leadership like Fidel Castro and his brother Raúl, temporarily distanced themselves from some of the arguments supported by Moscow. The exposure and public denunciations of the 'micro-faction' by the Castro brothers and their followers took place during a meeting of the Central Committee of the Cuba Communist Party which was held only days before Berliet arrived in Cuba.[83] This coincidence is interesting because during the meeting documents were produced by Raúl Castro containing the accusations of Anibal Escalante, a key figure in the 'micro-faction', against the leadership. Among these was a claim that some members of the Party, who were close to the Castro brothers, were planning for Cuba to move away from the Soviet Union and strengthen its ties with France.[84]

Given that Fidel Castro had invited Paul Berliet to Cuba to discuss a number of large projects involving French technology, and that he was also seeking to arrange a regular flight between Paris and Havana, and a meeting with de Gaulle, it would appear that Escalante's claim had some foundations. Berliet was also not the only French industrialist to visit Cuba at that time. In late January Pierre Richards, the President and Director of Richards Continental also of Lyon, spent a number of days on the island during which he visited the headquarters of the Che Guevara Invasion Brigade to which his company was supplying bulldozers for clearing new land to plant rice and sugar cane.[85] Further evidence of French involvement in Cuba was also suggested by the American industrialist Cyrus S. Eaton, who visited Cuba a few months after Berliet and Richards. In a conversation he had with Fidel Castro, Eaton claimed that the Cuban leader had told him that plans were being drawn up to modernise Cuba's dairy industry with French computers. Eaton also said that he had heard that the de Gaulle government had extended a $100 million dollar credit line to Cuba so it could purchase industrial equipment from France.[86]

One can only speculate on the extent to which Castro envisaged turning towards France to counterbalance the influence of the Soviet Union. However, that France should be chosen for this role indicates that not only had French technology impressed the Cuban leadership but so also had de Gaulle's independent foreign policy. Perhaps Castro had in mind for Cuba a similar situation to the one which existed in Algeria where the Soviet Union and France vied for markets and influence, with the Algerians themselves gaining many advantages from the competition. It is also interesting to note that at the time accusations were being made against the Cuban leadership for moving towards France, Castro was also encouraging a strengthening of relations between Cuba and Romania.[87] This may have been a coincidence, but it is interesting that among France's attempts at *rapprochement* with the Soviet bloc it had had its most spectacular success with Romania. Among the Eastern European states which had fallen under Soviet control after the Second World War, Romania had the lowest levels of industrial development. Despite Romania's incorporation into CMEA this position did not improve because it was encouraged by Moscow to increase agricultural production to compensate for other states which had been allowed to give priority to industrialisation. Because of these restrictions on its development Romania had attempted to gain some independence from CMEA, and France's offer of new trading opportunities was seized upon eagerly. Moreover, in 1968 de Gaulle made an important state visit to Romania during which relations between the two countries were further strengthened.[88] Given the above developments in French-Romanian relations it could be argued that Cuba was seeking to establish a similar, and perhaps more advanced, relationship with France in which it would continue to play its role as a supplier of agricultural produce to the Soviet Union and Eastern Europe but at the same time attempt to develop its industrial sector with the co-operation of a friendly capitalist power. For both Romania and Cuba, France under de Gaulle presented a unique opportunity to pursue such an economic programme because it was felt that France's commercial pragmatism was underpinned by a deep ideological commitment to confront superpower hegemony. If these assumptions are correct then the strengthening of Cuban-Romanian relations in 1968 may have been part of a more complex strategy, possibly involving France, than was suggested in the Cuban press.

To some extent Castro's plan to bring about closer ties between Cuba and France did materialise as French exports to Cuba increased for a few years after 1968, and the Berliet company became involved in significant projects on the island. But the meeting with de Gaulle and Castro which had been requested by the latter failed to take place, and no progress was made towards the establishment of a regular air link between Paris and Havana. The reasons why French-Cuban relations did not develop further in the late-1960s may never come to light, however, such factors as the internal political problems suffered by both Castro and de Gaulle at home in 1968, the failure of France to balance its trade with Cuba, and the growing moderation of de Gaulle's foreign policy in the late-1960s, must all have played a part in preventing the establishment of a more advanced relationship between the two countries.

The involvement of the Berliet company in Cuba from 1968–71 remains, however, perhaps the most outstanding attempt, during the first 15 years of the Revolution, to integrate European technology into Cuba's plans for economic diversification. After Paul Berliet's meeting with Fidel Castro in early-1968 it was decided by both parties that plans could be drawn up immediately for the proposed project to improve Cuba's capacity to service and maintain its commercial and public transport system. By the autumn of 1968, after the arrival of 17 Berliet technicians and engineers, work was started on the first phase of the project which comprised of a training centre for mechanics and welders, and an engine rebuilding plant in Holguín. The French team worked with the Cuban organisation CESETA which provided local technicians, planners and manual labour for the building work. When the training centre was completed in mid-1969 it had places for 680 full and part-time students, and was run by 21 full-time teachers.

The engine rebuilding plant, which began operating at the end of the year, covered an area of 6,348 square metres and employed 150 workers. This plant was a specialised unit which was dedicated to the maintenance of Berliet engines. Two other similar plants were constructed the following year in Havana and Santa Clara. Between 1969 and 1971 ten smaller workshops were also built in various locations around the island to service and maintain Berliet equipment. In total these workshops employed 275 workers and had a capacity to deal with 1,000 vehicles a year.

The second and most significant phase of the project involved the construction of an industrial complex at Mariel. It was estimated at the time of signing the contract for this part of the project in December 1969 that the entire complex would take 15 years to complete. By then Berliet planned to have provided Cuba with sufficient plant and expertise to produce its own buses. Naturally these vehicles were to be based on Berliet models, but it was anticipated that after the construction of a foundry and a metal pressing plant the Cubans would be able to produce some of the main components, including the chassis and bodywork. The complex would also eventually include factories for manufacturing tyres, batteries and other components. But to ensure that buses could start being made as soon as possible, the first factory to be built was an assembly plant, which would gradually become increasingly independent as more of the complex was completed. When the assembly plant was finished in 1972, it began production at a rate of two buses a day and employed 1,100 people. By this time, however, commercial relations between France and Cuba were suffering a number of set-backs, and work on the complex began to slow down until it finally ceased in 1973.

The principal reason for the deterioration in French-Cuban commercial relations in the early-1970s, and which undermined Berliet's position in Cuba, was the French government's curtailment of imports of Cuban nickel in January 1972. Although the loss of the French market for nickel was not as serious in commercial terms to Cuba as its exclusion from France's raw sugar market a decade earlier, it created a deficit in trade with France which the Castro government found unsustainable. Moreover, when de Gaulle had first authorised nickel imports from Cuba in 1965 his action was seen as an important gesture of political defiance against the US, although in purely financial terms the Cubans were offering France nickel at a discount price. Therefore when France terminated its imports of Cuban nickel in 1972, this was seen partly as a political action, which in turn invited an appropriate response from Cuba. Unfortunately for the Berliet company, perhaps because they were representative of the most advanced stage in French-Cuban relations, it was their business which was cut to reciprocate the French action.[89]

The decision by the Pompidou government to stop imports of Cuban nickel was based on a combination of political and commercial factors. Firstly, Pompidou, who had assumed the Presidency after de Gaulle stepped down in April 1969, was not so enthusiastic as his predecessor in promoting an independent French foreign policy. This was particularly true in the case of France's relationship with the socialist states which he felt had caused too many problems with the US. Consequently, as American pressure increased on France to stop importing nickel from Cuba, a pragmatic response was favoured by the Pompidou government rather than an ideological one. Furthermore, the Société le Nickel, which was responsible for Cuban nickel imports into France, feared that by persisting in its trade with Cuba it might endanger its joint nickel-mining operations with two US multinationals in New Caledonia.[90]

It has also been suggested that Pompidou was much influenced in his decision to stop Cuban nickel imports by the Rothschilds, who had investments in nickel mines in New Caledonia, and did not wish to face competition from low-priced Cuban nickel in their own share of the French market as demand for nickel declined.[91] In fact the most important economic factor facing the Cubans and other nickel producers in the early-1970s was the world-wide slump in nickel consumption. This was caused by both a cyclical downturn in the steel industry, and the introduction of new methods of steel production which required less nickel. In 1971, for example, France imported 30,000 tonnes of nickel but by 1972 this had fallen 13,000 tonnes; a decline for which the Cuban's were forced to make a disproportionate contribution compared to France's other suppliers.

Despite the strains on French-Cuban relations which were felt in the early-1970s France began again to enjoy a good market for its products in Cuba by the middle of the decade.[92] But taking into account inflation, business was perhaps not as good as it had been in the second half of the 1960s. By the mid-1970s the form of commercial relations between the two countries had also changed drastically from the previous decade. Now French business with Cuba was no longer based on a mixture of commercial pragmatism and ideological independence, but rather on Cuba's success in negotiating international financial loans, and France's ability to capture sections of Cuba's hard currency market against stiff international competition. France was one of the first capitalist powers to offer the Castro government a substantial loan in the mid-1970s. And throughout the rest of the decade, and into the 1980s, French banks such as Crédit Lyonnais remained important sources of credit for Cuba.

France's willingness to make loans to Cuba, it may be argued, played an important role in lessening the problem of the discrepancy in trade which had existed between the two countries since the early-1960s, because in the 1970s Cuba's criteria for trading with a capitalist power was based more on the loans it was receiving from that power than on existing trading balances.

Although it is clear that France's relations with Cuba in the 1960s were, like those of other capitalist powers, based on commercial pragmatism, there are indications that France under de Gaulle could have offered Cuba a unique opportunity to partially reintegrate its economy into the capitalist West. De Gaulle's foreign policy, with its key principal of a France/Europe which charted its own course in world politics independent of the US, which in turn would allow for the formulation of a new deal for the Third World and *rapprochement* with the socialist states, was clearly a plan in which Cuba could have played a part. In retrospect it may be argued that if certain developments had not taken place such a relationship between France and Cuba could have materialised. Firstly, the severest blow to de Gaulle's Latin America strategy was the collapse of the Goulart government in Brazil, which weakened the possibility of a strengthening of French-Cuban relations. Secondly, France could not, or would not, solve the problem of its trade discrepancy with Cuba. Thirdly, as the penetration of American capital into France increased in the late-1960s the de Gaulle government felt itself under increasing pressure from Washington to restrain its relations with Cuba.

The events which took place in 1968 involving the accusations of the 'micro-faction' against the Cuban leadership for planning to strengthen Cuba's relations with France, and the subsequent signing of a number of large contracts with French industrialists, does suggest, however, that even towards the end of his term in office de Gaulle still saw the possibility of a French-Cuban commercial alliance. Had de Gaulle stayed in office into the 1970s such an alliance, whose foundations were being put in place by the Berliet company until France ceased nickel imports from Cuba, may indeed have been consolidated.

Notes

1   Philip G. Cerny, *The Politics of Grandeur: Ideological Aspects of de Gaulle's Foreign Policy*, Cambridge, C.U.P., 1980, p. 1.

2   For details of de Gaulle's relations with the US during the war see Jean-Baptiste Duroselle, *France and the United States from the beginnings to the present* (trans. D. Coleman), Chicago, University of Chicago Press, 1978, pp. 147–175.

3   See Arther Conte, *Yalta ou le partage du monde*, Paris, R. Laffont, 1964.

4   Because of fears of a possible communist takeover in France after the war the US gave the French government a high priority when handing out Marshall aid. Of $13.8 billion Marshall aid that was distributed between 1948 and 1952 France received $2.76 billion. See Duroselle, p. 181.

5   See Michael Moffitt, *The World's Money: International Banking from Bretton Woods to the Brink of Insolvency*, New York, Simon and Schuster, 1983, p. 32. Because of the status of 'global currency' which had been conferred on the dollar at Bretton Woods, de Gaulle believed that once America could no longer back up its currency with gold reserves it would simply go on issuing dollars because of its privileged status. This indeed began to happen by the 1960s because of enormous increases in US expenses abroad, particularly to finance the war in Vietnam. Once this precedent had been established it became very tempting for the US simply to issue dollars for foreign investment. As far as de Gaulle was concerned this 'extravagant privilege' resulted in a 'sort of expropriation of certain [foreign] enterprises to the benefit of American firms' (Duroselle, p. 237). De Gaulle's response to this development was to convert a large amount of France's currency into gold. This accelerated the erosion of American gold reserves and made the whole Bretton Woods system even more precarious.

6   Duroselle, p. 220.

7   The 1960s saw a massive increase in US investment overseas, and especially into Western Europe. This investment consisted mainly of US multinationals establishing subsidiaries abroad from where they could take advantage of local markets. For those with operations in EEC countries there was also the opportunity to benefit from the community's expanding share of world exports. Most European governments, including France, found this kind of investment acceptable because it created local employment and in some cases helped to boost national economic development. However, American attempts to make investments which were more highly integrated with European capital were usually not so well received. Because of the weakness of the French economy after the war it had been particularly susceptible to this latter type of investment and by the time de Gaulle took office American capital had gained significant footholds in French industry. De Gaulle hoped to control the rate of this penetration, and one of the ways of doing this he believed was to delay the entry of America's main ally in Europe, Great Britain, into the EEC. French foreign policy towards the communist states during the 1960s can also be seen partly as a response to the encroachment of American capital in France's industrial sector. By expanding market opportunities in such states it was believed that French national business interests would be able to steal a march on US-dominated businesses in France, which were still subject to ideological directives from Washington which constrained their trading activities with socialist countries. Ironically, because of economic difficulties at home, by the end of

the 1960s France became the main point of entry for American capital into Europe, and by 1975 US investors held a majority interest (20 per cent or more of shares) in major French companies accounting for 10 per cent of the country's industrial sales, see F. Roy Williams, *The French Paradox*, Hoover Press (USA), 1982, p. 26. For a detailed analysis of the complex subject of American investment in France in the 1960s see Robert B. Dickie, *Foreign Investment: France a Case Study*, New York, Oceana Publishers, 1970. Dickie has calculated that American investment in France between 1959 and 1967 rose from $640 million to $1.9 billion. But he also points out that despite this rapid increase during the 1960s total US investment in France since the war had been less than in some other European countries; most notably Germany and Britain which by 1967 had accumulated $3.5 billion and $6.1 billion of American investment respectively. For an account of the French attitude to American investment and the US generally see Jean-Jacques Servan-Schreiber, *Le Défi Américain*, Paris, Denoël, 1967. American investment in France was such a burning issue when Schreiber's book came out that it immediately became a best-seller.

8   Among the most important commercial initiatives between the Soviet bloc and France in the mid-1960s was the involvement of Renault with the Soviet Union's state run commercial vehicle sector. For example by 1966 Renault had taken over from Ford (USA) and Daimler Benz (West Germany) as the principal Western contractor for the Kama lorry factory. France also signed contracts with the Soviet Union and its Eastern European satellites to supply components and technical expertise to install the colour television system SECAM. To the chagrin of the US and West Germany this system was chosen in preference to their own PAL system which they had been promoting in the Soviet bloc for a number of years. See Cerny, *The Politics of Grandeur*, pp. 154–155.

9   De Gaulle's commercial and diplomatic initiatives in the Soviet bloc, and his willingness to act independently of the US, invited respect from Moscow for his foreign policy and even tacit support for his domestic policies. During the 1967 French legislative elections, for example, the Soviet Union made it clear that it favoured a Gaullist victory. This caused confusion among communists in France, some of whom felt obliged to temporarily desert their party to vote with their class enemies for a Gaullist candidate.

10 Despite the growing tensions in Sino-Soviet relations at the time de Gaulle was unfolding his China strategy, there are no indications that the Soviet Union objected to this further extension of French foreign policy into the socialist world.

11 France also used its influence in international forums to support the Third World. For example at the World Trade Conference in Geneva in 1964 France put forward a plan for stabilising the prices of raw materials. This was welcomed by many developing countries but was rejected by the US on the grounds that such a plan would be technically unworkable. During de Gaulle's period in office France also gave a larger proportion of its GNP in foreign aid than any other Western power.

12 A debate on Gaullism and Gaullist policies from a political perspective, which considers whether the movement was of the Right or the Left, is to be found in William Safran, *The French Polity*, London, Longman, 1979, pp. 68–74.

13 During the 1950s France's annual trade both with Martinique and Guadeloupe was on average three times more in total value than its annual trade with Cuba.

Below are the values (in millions of dollars) of French trade with the three islands in 1957, 1958 and 1959:

| | French exports | | | French imports | | |
	1957	1958	1959	1957	1958	1959
Martinique	35.8	32.5	29.1	44.7	39.4	39.8
Guadeloupe	32.3	31.1	27.9	40.9	40.1	37.3
Cuba	12.9	9.4	14.5	18.6	7.4	8.5

All foreign trade figures for France since the beginning of this century can be found in the annual trade statistics journal *Commerce de France: Tableau Général du Commerce Extérieur*, Paris. For the sake of consistency, and to facilitate the comparison of trade values between different countries, all financial sums cited in this chapter will be given in US dollars. Exchange rates are based on the information provided in the International Monetary Fund, *Annual Report on Exchange Restrictions*.

14   Below are listed the sources and values (in millions of dollars) of French imports of cane sugar for the years 1957 and 1959. The figures in parentheses indicate total sugar cane imports for the year.

	Réunion	Guadeloupe	Martinique	Cuba	Brazil
1957 ($81m)	34.7	17.9	10.0	13.9	0.3
1959 ($62m)	24.8	15.4	8.3	7.4	3.7

Throughout the 1950s a similar pattern prevailed with occasionally Cuba or Brazil replacing Martinique as France's third most important supplier. See *Tableau Général de Commerce Extérieur*.

15   Cuba was rarely mentioned in the French press and any references that were made were usually concerned with Cuba's sugar harvests, see for example the listings under Cuba in *Le Monde Index Analytique*, 1949–1958.

16   The Cuban communists Juan Marinello and Júlio Antonio Mella both visited Paris in the 1920s and Carlos Rafael Rodríguez, another communist, had a short sojourn in Paris in the 1950s, as did Nicholas Guillén in the 1930s.

17   The most distinguished Cuban writer to have lived in Paris was Alejo Carpentier. His main period of residence in France was in the 1930s, but he continued for many years after to make occasional visits to Paris. For an account of Carpentier's view of France, as represented in his journalistic writings, see Claire Cadillon-Alvárez Rios, 'Vision de la France dans l'oeuvre journalistique d'Alejo Carpentier' (1928–1939) in *Cuba et la France: Francia y Cuba*, pp. 227–238. This publication consists of a compilation of papers which were given at a conference that was organised by 'Le Centre Interuniversitaire d'Etudes Cubaines' (C.I.E.C.), which was held at the University of Bordeaux in December 1982.

18   The French journalists were headed by Foreign Minister Claude Cheysson and their meeting with Fidel Castro took place on 6 August 1983. A transcript of the discussions is include in *Granma*, 10 August 1983, p. 5.

19   For a survey of the response of the French press to the Cuban Revolution during the first three months after the rebels had seized power see Liliane

Hasson, 'La Révolution Cubaine et la Presse Francaise' in *Cuba et la France: Francia y Cuba*, pp. 435–53.

20   For an analysis of the political positions that were adopted by the French press to the Cuban Revolution and its leaders see Liliane Hasson, 'La Révolution Cubaine et la Press Francaise', pp. 437–52.

21   Interview with Sr Raúl Becerra, Director of the Department of Trade with Western Europe, MINCEX (Ministerio de Comercio Exterior), Havana, Cuba, 4 April 1988.

22   While the US could feel satisfied with the decline in trade between its Western allies and Cuba during the early-1960s, and the support of capitalist powers in general for its official policy to undermine the Castro government, they found it particularly disturbing that some allies were still engaged in supplying arms to Cuba. Belgium was the worst offender.

23   See Morris H. Morley, *Imperial State and Revolution: The United States and Cuba, 1952–1986*, Cambridge, C.U.P., 1987, p. 223. Morley cites as his source for this information a telegram from the US Department of State to the American Embassy in Paris dated 5 February 1964, p. 461 (footnotes).

24   See Morley, *Imperial State and Revolution*, p. 88.

25   For an account of French policy in Algeria during the period in which it was at war with its colony from 1954–1962 see, E.A. Kolodziej, *French International Policy under de Gaulle and Pompidou*, Ithaca, Cornell University Press, London, 1974, pp. 447–80.

26   A particularly vitriolic attack against French colonial rule in Algeria and France's conduct in the war of independence is to be found in *Revolución*, 5 March 1962, pp. 11,13.

27   An analysis of the first years of Algerian independence after the Evian accord is given by I.W. Zartman, in 'Les Relations entre la France et L'Algerie depuis les accords d'Evian', *Revue française de science politique*, XIV, December, 1964, pp. 1087–113.

28   This view was stated with reference to Algeria in *Revolución*, 5 March 1962, p. 13.

29   See *Revolución*, 18 June 1961, p. 5. Cerny suggests that the establishment of closer relations between France and West Germany was the centre-piece of de Gaulle's European strategy, and this meant offering West German leaders support at every available opportunity, even to the detriment of other elements of French foreign policy, *The Politics of Grandeur*, p. 169.

30   Although de Gaulle had made declarations of solidarity with the US during the missile crisis, he was later to complain that the US had acted unilaterally and without consultation with its Western allies, simply assuming that they would support its position in an emergency. For de Gaulle this assumption had seriously compromised European defence during the crisis and demonstrated that ultimately the US placed its own security above that of its allies. This argument was later used by de Gaulle to support the view that Europe should act independently to challenge the narrow bipolar view of the world on which superpower Cold War politics was founded, see Kolodziej, pp. 115–16. The Americans on the other hand saw the outcome of the crisis as a vindication of the existing system, p. 174.

31   Kolodziej, p. 466.

32   One of Ben Bella's first statements indicating that Algeria would follow many of the precedents of the Cuban revolution was made in March 1962. This took place a few days after the signing of the Evian Accords, during a meeting in the

Moroccan capital Rabat, with the Cuban Ambassador to Morocco E. Rodríguez Loeches and the editor of *Revolución* Carlos Franqui. In this meeting Ben Bella declared 'We live in Algeria but our hearts are in Cuba . . . this is the truth, not an empty phrase; the fundamental line which we have chosen is the same as the Cuban one and this will determine the proximity and the unity of our countries and our revolutions' (author's translation), cited in *Revolución*, 1 April 1962, p. 2. This position was reaffirmed during Ben Bella's visit to Cuba in October 1962, see *Revolución* on 16, 17 and 18 October for coverage of the visit and comments by the Algerian leader on his country's relations with Cuba. Before visiting Cuba, Ben Bella had been in the US where he had met President Kennedy. In this context Castro hailed his visit as 'an act of courage in the face of US imperialism'. Several days later the US State Department instructed the Agency for International Development to suspend all economic aid to Algeria. See Jane Franklin, *The Cuban Revolution and the United States, a chronological history*, Melbourne, Victoria, Ocean Press, 1992. In 1964 Ben Bella was still arguing that the Algerian and Cuban revolutions were inseparable, and that Algeria was much influenced by what was happening in Cuba, see for example 'Jámas dos pueblos han estado mas unidos que Cuba y Argelia' *Revolución*, 6 January 1964, p. 2. Also in 1964 an Algerian-Cuban co-operation society was opened in Algiers and during the inauguration ceremony Ben Bella proclaimed that his country's unity with Cuba 'would remain unbreakable, whatever the price', *Revolución*, 17 April 1964, p. 4.

33 See 'Le mythe Gaulliste dans le *tiers monde, Le Monde*, 5 February 1964, pp. 1–2.

34 See Kolodziej, p. 464. Despite the bitterness which remained in Algeria because of France's ruthless treatment of the rebels during the anti-colonial war, after independence the new Algerian government readily acknowledged that they now had a unique and indeed beneficial relationship with the power that once controlled and dominated their country. At the time of de Gaulle's meeting with Ben Bella in March 1964 one Algerian high official is reported to have stated '*c'est la grande chance de la France de prouver qu'il est possible de réussir avec l'Algérie ce que les Etats-Unis n'ont pas su faire a Cuba'*, *Le Monde*, 14 March 1964, p. 3. From a French perspective one might argue that de Gaulle's post Evian policy had succeeded in Algeria, not only because of the positive image of France that it gave to the Third World, but also because it protected France's markets and investments in Algeria. Most importantly French oil companies were able to retain control over their investments for some time after independence. Some might argue that these privileges had to be paid for by France in aid, loans and grants to the Algerian government, but at least de Gaulle could claim that his government had managed its crisis in Algeria better than the US had dealt with Cuba where its business community had lost all its markets and investments. Moreover, Washington had saddled itself with an expensive destabilisation strategy towards Cuba which only served to damage the image of the US in the Third World.

35 'Rechaza De Gaulle protesta yanqui', *Revolución*, 22 January 1964, p. 6.

36 'Charles de Gaulle ataca política de los Yanquis', *Revolución*, 24 July 1964, p. 3.

37 For details of French production and consumption of sugar between 1960 and 1966, see the International Sugar Council, *Sugar Year Book*, 1966, p. 78.

38 *Sugar Year Book*, 1966, p. 265 (Britain), p. 98 (West Germany).

39 *Sugar Year Book*, 1966, p. 229.

40   Below are listed Cuban raw sugar exports in metric tonnes to France, Britain and Spain in the 1960s. The figures in parentheses indicate French imports of other Cuban sugar products such as molasses and honey.

	France	Britain	Spain
1960	100,400 (43,592)	173,368	33,247
1961	107,339 (1,000)	79,382	53,208
1962	0 (21,000)	76,143	58,312
1963	0 (28,000)	173,698	102,737
1964	0 (256)	94,144	275,704
1965	0 (14,322)	113,237	173,771
1966	0 (19,740)	61,646	145,343
1967	0 (5,555)	70,290	158,581
1968	20,634 (19,770)	20,065	175,678
1969	0	42,912	181,577
1970	0	0	143,407

Source: Sugar Year Book, 1966 and 1973.

41   See Appendix 1, p. 342.
42   For Britain's trade with Cuba in the 1960s see the *Annual Statement of the Trade of the United Kingdom* for relevant years.
43   See *Estadística de Comercio Exterior de España*, 1962.
44   This was suggested by Paul Berliet, who, in the 1960s was Managing Director of his family's company Berliet of Lyon. Interview given to the author in Lyon 16 November 1987. Berliet was one of the first French companies to follow in the wake of de Gaulle's foreign policy initiatives. For example, contracts were being signed in Eastern Europe from 1962, and shortly after Sino-French diplomatic relations were re-established in January 1964, Paul Berliet visited Peking where he initiated a long and fruitful business relationship between his company and the Chinese. The best history of the Berliet company is J. Borge and N. Viasnoff, *Berliet*, Paris, 1981. Pat Kennett's book *Berliet* (number 12 in his 'World Trucks' series) also provides some useful historical information on the company.
45   Interview with Paul Berliet.
46   Morley also suggests that Leyland's strongest advantage over Berliet was their ability to offer British government-backed credit to the Cubans (p. 223), and cites as his source the (US) Economic Intelligence Unit, *Quarterly Economic Review of Cuba*, No. 45, March 1964, p. 2 (p. 461, footnotes).
47   The French were indeed to claim that their change of policy on granting credit guarantees on trade with Cuba had come about because of 'precedents established by other Western powers', see Drew Middleton, 'French Complete Cuba Truck Sale', *New York Times*, 8 February 1964, p. 2.
48   For details of the contract see *Le Monde*, 8 February 1964, p. 1.
49   Interview with Paul Berliet.
50   The signing of the contract was reported in *Le Monde*, 6 February 1964, p. 1, and the *New York Times*, 7 February, p. 10. Neither report gives the number or value of the vehicles sold.
51   'Havana Reports Gesture by Paris', *New York Times*, 4 January 1964, pp. 1 and 3.

52   *Ibid.*, p. 3.
53   'Fortalecimiento de la amistad cubano-francesa', *Revolución*, 4 January 1964, p. 1. It is notable that the above article included a complimentary photograph of de Gaulle, which shared the front page with photographs of Nikita Khrushchev and Palmiro Togliatti.
54   'French Say Cuba Exaggerates De Gaulle's Chat With Envoy', *New York Times*, 7 January 1964, p. 6.
55   Interestingly the most ardent supporter of de Gaulle's plans for the Third World, and especially Latin America, was Franco's Spain which saw itself playing a key role in any reorientation of its former colonies away from the US and towards Europe. Indeed de Gaulle's policy on Latin America and his visits to the region received more comprehensive and supportive reporting in the Spanish press than the French. See for example 'De Gaulle: Veintiseis días alrededor de Hispanoamérica' in the Spanish commercial journal *SP*, No. 244, 15 October 1964, pp. 15–19. Spain, which by this time was being put under pressure from Washington for its growing commercial relations with Cuba, was also eager to give de Gaulle its support in his challenge to US hegemony in Latin America.
56   *Le Monde*, 8 February 1964, section IV, p. 1.
57   *New York Times*, 16 February 1964, Section IV, p. 1.
58   'De Gaulle Fails to Sway Italians', *New York Times*, 22 February 1964, p. 2.
59   An account of the visit is given in *Le Monde*, 14 March 1964, p. 2.
60   See, for example, the account of the visit in *France Soir*, 14 March 1964, p. 6.
61   See Juan de Onís, 'Castro Ridicules US on Blockade', *New York Times*, 5 March 1964, p. 3.
62   For coverage of the visit see *Le Monde*, 15/16 March 1964, pp. 1–2. See also *Le Monde* on subsequent days up to 23 March.
63   See Drew Middleton, 'Aiding US, the French Say', *New York Times*, 20 March 1964, p. 3.
64   'De Gaulle en Guadelupe; va hoy a Mexico', *Revolución*, 16 March 1964, pp. 1–2.
65   Details of the contract are given in *Le Monde*, 7 May 1964, pp. 1 and 3.
66   *Ibid.*, p. 3.
67   See the *New York Times*, 5 May 1964, p. 19, and 6 May, p. 2.
68   The *New York Times*, 7 May 1964, p. 1.
69   For a full coverage of the visit see *Le Monde* from 21 September 1964 to 18 October 1964.
70   See Henry Giniger, 'Latins Receive French Leader Warmly but Indicate no Shift Away from US', *New York Times*, 28 September 1964, p. 8. Giniger, however, does acknowledge the difference between the official response of Latin American leaders to the French visit and the popular response. Of the former he states 'on an official level South Americans have made it plain that a French presence in Latin America, which President de Gaulle is trying so hard to promote during his tour, can be no alternative to the United States'. But he also points out that when the French party were travelling through the streets of Latin American capitals they were greeted with such cries as 'Viva la Francia' and 'France si, Yankee no'.
71   *Ibid.*
72   *Le Monde*, 22 September 1964, p. 2.
73   See, for example, 'Inicia de Gaulle el día 20 gira por la América', *Revolución*, 10 September 1964, p. 8.

74 *Revolución*, 25 September 1964, p. 8.
75 *Revolución*, 19 September 1964, p. 8. *Revolución* identified its source of information as the French journal *Combat*.
76 Javier Rodríguez, 'Llegó un embarque de camiones franceses de los 300 comprados', *Revolución*, 17 September 1964, pp. 1 and 2.
77 According to *Revolución* the cargo comprised of 18 heavy dumper lorries (camiones de volteo pesado), 6 mobile service stations (estaciones de servicio), 4 trailers (cuñas tractoras). This consignment of equipment was part of the 6.5 million peso contract that had been signed with Berliet earlier in the year for a total of 250 dumper lorries, 24 mobile service stations, 16 concrete mixers (concreteras-mezcladoras), 18 trailers and 18 drags (arrastres) for use with the trailers. These last items had been supplied by another company (Trailor) but were included in the contract price. The equipment was obtained through the Cuban organisation for the import of transport equipment and other vehicles, TRANSIMPORT, and was destined for use by the Instituto Nacional de Recursos Hidráulicos, Ministerio de la Construcción y Plan de Obras Viales.
78 For an account of US involvement in the overthrow of Goulart see Morley, *Imperial State and Revolution*, pp. 167–72.
79 For more detailed information on the structure and values of French imports from Cuba from 1961–64 see *Commerce Extérieur de la France* for these years. During this period sugar products (other than raw sugar), preserved fish, and tobacco, accounted for an average of 93 per cent of French imports from Cuba.
80 See Tad Szulc, 'Cuba to Reduce Buying in West', *New York Times*, 18 September 1964, pp. 1 and 4.
81 French imports of Cuba nickel were as follows for the period 1964–1973:

	Weight (tonnes)	Value (dollars)	Percentage of all imports from Cuba
1964	0	0	0
1965	6419	6,413,469	56
1966	4848	4,882,857	47
1967	9233	10,146,938	64
1968	4481	6,551,224	44
1969	(figures not available)		
1970	3330	6,448,108	41
1971	2060	3,434,296	26
1972	5	11,507	00.1
1973	0	0	0

Source: *Statistiques du Commerce Extérieur de la France*.

82 Information given in company documents supplied to the author by Paul Berliet. All subsequent information on the Berliet company's activities in Cuba is taken from these documents or from the transcript of the author's interview with Paul Berliet, unless otherwise stated.
83 Extensive reportage of the denunciation and trial of the members of the 'micro-faction' is to be found in the Cuban state daily newspaper *Granma*, starting on 28 January 1968 and on subsequent days up to and including 3 February 1968. A translation into English of most of the information given in *Granma* is

available in the Foreign Broadcast Information Service, *Daily Report: Latin America* from 30 January to 6 February.

84   Raúl Castro's denunciation of the 'micro-faction' to the Central Committee of the Cuban Communist Party is reported in *Granma*, 29 January 1968, pp. 1–3, 30 January, pp. 1–3, 31 January, pp. 2–3. Excerpts from the Escalante document which includes the statement on Franco-Cuban relations is to be found in *Granma*, 30 January, p. 2. The text is as follows: 'in view of de Gaulle's new attitude in France after his failure in Vietnam and Algeria, his repeating to the world of last century's slogan of liberty, equality, and fraternity, and his adoption of a correct position towards peaceful coexistence and free trade with all countries, including tactically speaking, opposition to Yankee imperialism (but agreeing with it strategically because of his belief in class division), a pro-French current has taken root in our country which has been further stimulated because of a loan France has given us in an attempt to draw us closer politically. Also, in view of this, a series of activities has been organised, both social and cultural – the May salon, tourist tours, and so forth – thus making it easier for groups on both sides to come closer to one another. This group [in Cuba] is directed by Llanusa, Marcelo Fernandez, Alfredo Guevara, and Carlos Franqui. Logically, this follows the policy of trying to separate us more and more from the Soviet Union. Recently, Régis Debray's book, *Revolution in the Revolution*, was added to the list of reading materials in party cells. Debray was expelled by the French Communist Youth because he was suspected of belonging to the French intelligence service. His book ignores the role of the party and the working class in the struggle for power.' This translation from Spanish is taken from *Daily Report: Latin America*, 31 January 1968 (p. 4). In further material produced by Raúl Castro which included statements by Octavio Fernández, another important figure in the 'micro-faction', more comments were revealed on the Franco-Cuban 'conspiracy'. Defending the position and arguments of the 'micro-faction' Fernández argued: 'with regard to the Soviet Union, we would draw much closer to it in all of our policy, eliminating a whole series of discrepancies which currently exist, since life would serve as the example in this case. This would occur, furthermore, because the group working to bring us closer to France would fail in its efforts despite everything, because France is a capitalist country which, in dealing with us, would not abandon its class position. Moreover, it did not have as great resources as the Soviet Union'. See *Granma*, 31 January 1968, p. 2. English version is to be found in the *Daily Report: Latin America*, 1 February, (p. 12). The above statements are consistent with a number of other accusations levelled against the main Castro group by members of the 'micro-faction', which aimed to prove that the Cuban leadership was composed of petty bourgeois elements who were abandoning the proletarian cause and intending to move the Revolution away from the Soviet Union and back towards the capitalist West.

85   Details of Richards' visit to Cuba, and quotations from a favourable commentary he gave on Cuban use and maintenance of equipment supplied by his company, were broadcast on Havana Radio on 29 January 1968. A transcript of the broadcast is included in *Daily Report: Latin America*, 31 January, (p. 1). For a description of the work being undertaken by the Che Guevara Invasion Brigade see Juan de Onís, 'Castro's Problem: Matching Promises with Cuba's Economic Performance', *New York Times*, 11 March 1968, pp. 1 and 16. In this article the author claimed that in the land clearing teams from the brigade were using Soviet tanks to knock down trees in advance of the French bulldozers

which then levelled the ground, p. 16.

86   See Gerd Wilcke, 'Eaton Hints that Cuba Seeks US Ties', *New York Times*, 2 June 1968, p. 28 (F. supplement). Eaton also noted that there were limitless opportunities for US business in Cuba, and when asked how the Castro government would find the hard currency to pay for American imports he suggested that the Cuban tourist industry should be revitalised.

87   See *Granma* from December 1967 to February 1968 for numerous articles dealing with various aspects of Cuban-Romanian relations including: agreements on technical and scientific collaboration, plans for increasing trade, statements on ideological compatibility, and coverage of visits by Romanian delegations to Cuba.

88   For details of the visit see Corneliu Manescu, 'Romania in the Concert of Nations', *International Affairs*, 45, 1, January 1969, p. 1.

89   Though French imports of Cuban nickel terminated in 1972, the decision to stop this trade was made in December 1970 when 'Société le Nickel' failed to renew its three year import agreement with Cuba. See Morley, *Imperial State and Revolution*, p. 274.

90   *Ibid.*, p. 274. Morley cites as his source an article entitled 'US Maintains Tough Strictures on Cuba Trade', which was published in *Business International*, 13 August 1971, p. 258.

91   Interview with Paul Berliet. Apparently Berliet attempted to persuade Pompidou to reverse his decision on the curtailment of Cuban nickel imports, but his efforts were countered by the Rothschilds.

92   See Appendix I, p. 342.

CHAPTER 8

Franco's Spain and the Cuban Revolution

George Lambie

Introduction

While in France the first ten years of the Cuban Revolution coincided with a controversial political and economic experiment under de Gaulle, in Spain during the same period Franco's government was engaging in an unprecedented attempt to modernise the Spanish economy. As we have seen in Chapter 7 de Gaulle's policies had significant repercussions on France's relations with Cuba, and the same is true of developments in Spain in the 1960s which also played an important part in shaping Spanish-Cuban relations. It will also be argued in this chapter that the changes which were taking place in Spain, and in Cuba, in the 1960s brought about a degree of compatibility between the two economies which was not equalled in Cuba's relations with any other Western power during the same period. This mutual attraction, however, while providing Cuba with many advantages did not prove to be entirely beneficial to Spain. On face value Spanish-Cuban trade statistics for the 1960s show what appears to be an expanding and harmonious commercial relationship, but in reality this picture belies a series of problems which put the Franco government at a trading disadvantage with what should have been its most lucrative market in Latin America.

The commercial side of Spain's relations with Cuba in the 1960s will be assessed firstly in the context of Spain's economic strategy and the concomitant changes in its trading patterns. This will be followed by an analysis of the part played by Cuban sugar exports to Spain in determining the form and composition of commercial exchanges between the two countries.

Besides examining Spanish-Cuban commerce during the 1960s, this chapter will explore the political and diplomatic ambience surrounding trade between the two countries. A study will also be made of Spain's wider foreign relations in the 1960s, which will focus mainly on the response of the US to Spain's strengthening links with Cuba.

Owing to the lack of published works on Spanish-Cuban relations

during the 1960s and the difficulty in obtaining access to Spanish government documents after 1959, the researcher has to rely to a large extent on
the press as a source of information. These constraints are further compounded because while reports on Cuba in the Spanish press were plentiful
as a result of the strong historical and cultural links between the two
countries, they were excessively shaped and controlled by the system of
censorship under the Franco government. Therefore while one can find
numerous articles in Spanish newspapers and journals dealing with such
subjects as the internal problems faced by the Castro government, the plight
of Spanish nationals in Cuba, and Cuba's commercial and political ties with
other countries, the treatment of Spain's own relationship with Cuba, especially in commercial terms, is almost non-existent. Clearly Franco wished
to play down his country's expanding commercial links with communist
Cuba, and especially at home where the legitimacy of his government had
been founded and sustained on its anti-communism. This censorship, or
perhaps more precisely, selective reporting, is frustrating for the researcher
examining Spanish-Cuban relations in the Franco period, but thankfully
such was the controversy surrounding Spain's trade with Cuba that some
foreign newspapers, and especially the American press which missed nothing concerning Castro's attempts to break the embargo, help to compensate
for omissions of the Spanish media.

While the Spanish media was reluctant to allow coverage of Spain's
links with Cuba, the state-controlled media in Cuba similarly did not wish
to emphasise Cuba's links with Spain.

The United States and the 'Spanish Economic Miracle'

As a result of Franco's collaboration with the fascist powers during the
Spanish Civil War, his gestures of goodwill towards the Axis in the Second
World War, and his proclamations in support of Spanish fascism up to the
early-1950s, his government was vilified not only by the socialist states but
also most of the world's capitalist democracies. One of the most serious
consequences of Spain's unpopularity among the international community
was its exclusion from the US backed European Recovery Programme
(Marshall Aid) after the war. This exacerbated the Franco government's
isolation from the rest of Europe.

However, as the ideological positions of the Cold War began to ossify
Franco's impeccable anti-communist credentials encouraged some capitalist nations to view his dictatorship in a more favourable light. Some
right-wing Latin American governments were first to register their acceptance of the Franco regime, but it was only its later *rapprochement* with
the US which secured Spain's eventual reprieve from pariah status

among the European democracies.[1] US approval of Franco's ideological stance towards communism in the early-1950s was complemented by a US military interest in Spain's strategic location on the southern flank of the NATO alliance.[2] In 1953 Spain and the US signed a ten year mutual defence agreement, which granted the US permission to establish military bases on Spanish soil, in exchange for substantial economic aid. Besides direct financial assistance the US also agreed to re-equip the Spanish military with American weapons. The components of the agreement, which became known collectively as the Bases Pact, gave the Franco government greater political credibility among the international community and in 1955 Spain was accepted as a member of the United Nations.[3] Spain's improved relations with the US and the main capitalist powers was also a crucial prerequisite for its economic development. US aid, which was given with a generous but guiding hand, played a key role in the country's first steps towards modernisation.

US government aid to Spain between 1953 and 1962 amounted to $1,200 million.[4] This huge injection of foreign capital persuaded Franco to gradually abandon the policy of economic autarky which had prevailed since the end of the Civil War, and embark on a programme of industrial expansion based on liberal economic principles. However, it was not until 1957, after a cabinet reshuffle, that the liberal group in the Franco administration, most of whom were members of the Catholic secular order 'Opus Dei', were strong enough to gain full control of economic planning from the diehard falangists who had steered Spain along its isolationist course for the previous two decades.[5] Among the most important changes in the cabinet reshuffle was the handing over of foreign affairs to the progressive liberal Fernando Castiella. But while the change in economic affairs met with US approval, the independent foreign policy which Castiella charted for Spain soon took a course which caused concern in Washington, as communist China, the Soviet bloc, and revolutionary Cuba were all offered the hand of friendship.

Between 1957 and 1959 plans were drawn up by Franco's new liberal economists for the transformation of the Spanish economy. In 1959 Spain submitted a memorandum for approval to the International Monetary Fund and the Organisation of European Economic Co-operation (later renamed the Organisation of Economic Co-operation and Development – OECD) which became known as the Stabilisation Plan. This Plan, though prepared by Spanish economists, may have been influenced by American officials responsible for administering the US aid programme in Spain. Since the signing of the Bases Pact in 1953 the US had encouraged the liberal elements in the Franco government and had frequently offered suggestions on how Spain's economic performance could be improved. Indeed, in retrospect American aid to Spain in the 1950s, though ostensibly part of a direct exchange for the right to build bases on Spanish soil, appears to have been intended from its inception primarily as a means to gain influence over the course of Spain's economic development.[6]

During the period of the so called 'Spanish economic miracle', which ran from 1959 to the oil price rise in 1973, Spain became the second fastest expanding capitalist economy in the world after Japan.[7] In these years Spanish imports rose thirteen-fold, exports four-fold and the value of the country's GDP more than doubled. This accelerated growth was partly based on increased labour productivity and the improving competitiveness of Spanish firms on the world market, but above all it was underpinned by the availability of new financial resources. These were provided from an expanding tourist industry, massive foreign investment which was attracted to Spain because of low wages and stringent labour controls, and the financial remittances of emigrants who had left to find work abroad.[8] Although between 1959 and 1973 the Spanish economy grew at an unprecedented rate the distribution of wealth remained very uneven. Thus while the bourgeoisie enjoyed large rises in their standard of living the majority of the working classes continued to suffer from low wages, draconian labour laws, and the uncertainties of seasonal employment.[9]

As the 'Spanish economic miracle' took off in the late-1950s and early-1960s not only did Spain's foreign trade expand but the pattern of its commercial relations also began to change. After the signing of the Bases Pact in 1953 the US became Spain's most important single trading partner, largely because of the aid package which Washington granted to the Franco government. By the time this programme of US state aid was terminated in 1962, it had been replaced by private American investment in the Spanish economy. For the rest of the decade the US remained the largest foreign investor in Spain, accounting for 40.3 per cent of total external investments.[10] Its nearest rival was Switzerland with 20.7 per cent. The expansion of Spain's trade with the US in the second half of the 1950s and the 1960s was extraordinary: in 1954 trade between the two countries had a total value of $35 million, by 1961 this had risen to $343 million, and in 1965 stood at $642 million. Throughout the above period Spanish imports from the US averaged 76 per cent of all commercial exchanges between the two countries, which left Spain with a large trading deficit. During the 1960s Spain's trade with the US accounted for 18 per cent of its total foreign trade. Spain's most important trading partners in the 1960s after the US were: West Germany, which accounted for 13 per cent of Spanish foreign commercial exchanges, France, 10.3 per cent, and Britain with 9.8 per cent.[11] In this list Cuba took twelfth position at 1.6 per cent. Although Spain's trade with all of Latin America amounted to barely 16 per cent of its total trade in the 1960s, the region was of special commercial importance because it was the only part of the world where the ratio of Spanish exports to imports was improving throughout the period.[12] Moreover, during the 1960s Latin America became Spain's most promising market for its new industrial products.

As can be seen from the above figures, in the 1960s Spain conducted a higher percentage of its external trade with the US than with any other capitalist economy. Although commercial exchanges between the two countries were lopsided, with Spanish imports accounting for over two-thirds of the total value of joint trade, Spain's economic development, especially in its early years, depended heavily on access to US products.[13] A similar imbalance was evident in the political and diplomatic relationship between the two countries, where the US also took the lead, but again Spain derived benefits from its subordinate position. Given the concord and interdependence which existed between Spain and the US, at least up to the mid-1960s, along with the Franco government's staunch anti-communism reputation, it would seem extraordinary and contradictory that during the same period Spain was also developing strong commercial and diplomatic links with Cuba; the *bête noire* of American foreign policymakers. Spain's relations with the Castro government placed a strain on Spanish – US relations, but as will be seen later the mutual dependency which was initiated with the Bases Pact put the Franco government in the unusual position, at least for a small power, of being guaranteed a minimum level of US support even if aspects of its foreign policy did not meet with Washington's approval.[14]

Franco's Spain and Castro's Cuba: political antithesis and commercial harmony

No two nations could have been further apart ideologically than Franco's Spain and Castro's Cuba. The first incident which reflected this divergence occurred in January 1960 when Castro expelled the Spanish Ambassador to Cuba for suspected collaboration with counter-revolutionaries.[15] At the same time the Cuban Ambassador to Madrid was recalled. This incident precipitated a severe deterioration in Spanish-Cuban relations at all levels, except in the sphere of commercial activities where it was business as usual. In particular the press from both countries seized on this diplomatic breakdown to vilify each others' governments and their leaders. For example on 23 January, a few days after the Spanish Ambassador had left Cuba, an article in the Havana daily *Revolución* examining US President Eisenhower's politics, concluded that his most odious crime was to have 'embraced the butcher Franco' on his recent visit to Madrid (p. 1). The Spanish press, still preoccupied with denying the embarrassing accusations which had been made against Franco's Ambassador, was not so swift off the mark as its counterparts in Cuba, but regular articles soon began to appear in such pro-government newspapers as *ABC* attacking Castro and his government.[16]

Throughout 1960 and 1961 non-commercial relations between Cuba and Spain continued to deteriorate as new political conflicts kept arising. In August 1960 the Catholic church in Cuba issued a pastoral letter criticising the Revolutionary government for strengthening its ties with Moscow and moving towards communism at home. Castro responded by accusing the church hierarchy of 'systematic provocations' against his government, adding that the US and Spain were behind this intrigue, and that Franco was playing a special role in mobilising the 'fascist priests'.[17] Soon after this incident the Cuban leadership began to pressurise the church to accept the Revolution and its objectives. Inevitably this gave many members of the clergy no choice but to leave Cuba. The first exodus, which was mainly voluntary, came in May 1961, when 140 priests, nuns, and monks, most of whom held Spanish passports, set sail for their mother country.[18] This exodus was followed in September by the official expulsion of over 100 Spanish priests, and a bishop who along with many of the priests stood accused of counter-revolutionary activities.[19] While the Spanish press had treated the June exodus with calm dismay, it responded to the September expulsion with vitriolic attacks against the Castro government reminiscent of the treatment given by Spain's right-wing newspapers to the left's abuses against the church during the Civil War.[20]

In December 1961 a potentially more serious political dispute threatened relations between Cuba and Spain, as it was rumoured in the US press that a new organisation had been formed in Cuba called the 'Spanish Army of Liberation' (CELE) whose objective was to undermine the Franco government by guerrilla tactics. Among the members of this organisation was Santiago Carrillo, the leader of the Spanish Communist Party in exile, and Alberto Bayo who had been a Republican army commander during the Civil War. It was also rumoured that a communist training camp had been set up in Havana under the command of Carlos Rafael Rodríguez (then editor of the Cuban daily newspaper *Noticias de Hoy*) to prepare cadres to carry out 'terrorist' activities in Spain.[21] For almost two years after these reports had been circulated the pro-government press in Spain continued to identify Cuba as the main haven for Spanish communists, and a breeding ground of violent plots against the Franco government. These perceptions were further reinforced when the Spanish communist Enrique Lister, who had commanded the famous Communist Fifth Regiment during the Civil War and had briefly been in charge of the International Brigades, was reported to have been appointed to a senior military post in Cuba.[22]

As a result of the divergent political philosophies held by Madrid and Havana minor crises continued to arise between the two governments for the duration of Franco's term in office, but it appears that both sides were anxious that such disagreements should not be allowed to interfere with the all important commercial side of their relationship. Consequently, while one finds that the state-controlled popular press in both Cuba and Spain continued to berate each others' governments and their leaders up until Franco's death in 1976, rarely did these ideological squabbles affect trade. In fact it was only in 1961 when political tensions were at their height that trade relations may have been damaged as a consequence. During most of that year Spain refused to import tobacco from Cuba until the Cuban government paid compensation to the Spanish owners of tobacco firms on the island which it had expropriated.[23] After negotiations a compromise was reached and Cuban exports of tobacco to Spain were resumed.

While British and French commerce with Cuba decreased dramatically during the first few traumatic years of the revolution, Spain managed to maintain relative consistency in its trade with the Castro government.[24] This was perhaps because trade between the countries was small and included many essential foodstuffs and basic products, but it also suggests that there was some correlation between the take-off of the 'Spanish economic miracle' and the Cuban revolution. During the 1950s Britain, West Germany and France had all conducted more trade with Cuba than Spain, but by 1964 Spain was Cuba's most important trading partner in Western Europe. The rate of expansion of Spanish-Cuban trade was impressive: from 1954 to 1958 the value of annual commercial exchanges between the two countries averaged $15.5 million, but in the subsequent five years the annual average for the period leapt to $34.3 million.[25] During the same two five-year periods Britain's trade with Cuba averaged $77.2 million and $38.0 million per annum respectively.[26] For the first half of the 1960s Spain's foreign trade was expanding generally, and especially with Latin America, but its increase in Cuban trade was exceptional.

When comparing the value of trade conducted by Britain, France and Spain with Cuba in the first half of the 1960s one should note that the total output of the Spanish economy was far less than that of its rivals, therefore any increases in its trade with Cuba were proportionately more significant for the economy as a whole. For example, in 1965, even after a number of years of rapid growth, Spain's GDP was still only equivalent to 22 per cent of that of France.[27] Moreover, despite the extraordinary expansion of Spain's foreign trade in the 1960s, even by the end of the decade its export-import to GDP ratio was still low in comparison to other Western European nations. Hence although the total value of trade which Britain, France and Spain conducted with Cuba during the 1960s did not vary greatly, for Spain Cuba represented an important trading partner, while for France and Britain commercial relations with Cuba formed an insignificant part of their total world trade. Taking the decade as a whole the value of Spain's trade with Cuba amounted to 1.7 per cent of its foreign trade (1.2 per cent of imports and 2.2 per cent of exports).[28] In 1966, which was Spain's best trading year with Cuba for the period, this figure stood at 2.8 per cent (1.3 per cent of imports and 6.1 per cent of exports). On the other hand for Britain its commercial exchanges with Cuba during the 1960s represented only 0.15 of 1 per cent of its foreign trade, and for France 0.16 of 1 per cent.[29]

Spain's trade with Cuba in the 1960s was particularly impressive when compared to its commercial exchanges with the rest of Latin America. For most of the decade Cuba was of equal importance for Spain as a trading partner as the economic giants of the region, Brazil, Argentina and Venezuela. And in a number of years, most notably 1964, 1965 and 1966, Cuba took a clear lead, commanding on average 24 per cent of Spain's total trade with Latin America.[30]

As the Spanish economy began to grow and diversify not only did this mean increases in the value of foreign trade but also changes in its composition. In the 1940s and most of the 1950s Spain's exports consisted mainly of traditional products from the agricultural sector such as olive oil, wine and citrus fruits. Imports were made up largely of wheat, fuel and oils, and some capital goods.[31] By the mid-1960s Spain's foreign trade had begun to reflect its transition from an agricultural to an industrial nation, as manufactured goods and chemicals took up a growing proportion of exports, while imports consisted mainly of capital equipment, semi-finished goods, and raw materials for the new industries.[32] Indeed this combination of imports, along with the capital earnings from the expanding tourist industry and foreign investments, was itself necessary to sustain Spain's economic growth.

The change in the composition of Spanish exports between the late-1950s and early-1960s, is represented particularly clearly in a comparison of Spain's commercial relations with Cuba before and after Castro came to power. Between 1955 and 1959 Spain's ten main exports to Cuba, measured in monetary value, were, olive oil, wine, brandy, confectionary, canned and other forms of preserved fish, books, hand tools, garlic, and timber for building.[33] During the period 1960–65 the value of Spanish exports to Cuba increased significantly. This increase was based predominantly on the sale of new products which were becoming available because of Spain's rapid industrialisation. Consequently in the first five years of the Revolution the most important ten imports to arrive in Havana from Spain were: commercial vehicles, electric and combustion engines, mechanical equipment, pharmaceutical products, welding equipment, olive oil, fruit and vegetables, cotton, books and stationery, and preserved fish.[34] In the 1960s Cuba was not only Spain's most rapidly growing market in Latin America, but also the best customer in the region for the new industrial products that were being manufactured by Spanish industry.

If one examines Spanish exports to Cuba in the 1960s rather than total trade between the two countries, Cuba's importance as a trading partner for the Franco government becomes even more apparent. For example, during this period Cuba was the best market for Spanish exports in Latin America, and was Spain's tenth largest customer in the world. When making these calculations it should also be remembered that during 1961 and 1962 Spanish trade with Cuba though higher than at any time in the 1950s was still small. As a final example to illustrate the importance of the Cuban market to Spanish exporters, in 1966, which was Spain's best trading year with Cuba, sales to the Castro government amounted to over half the value of Spanish exports dispatched to the US in the same year.

As the Spanish economy expanded and diversified in the 1960s the most significant problem which the Franco government faced was the imbalance on its foreign trading account. While imports of industrial products, semi-processed goods and industrial raw materials were the key resources which fuelled and sustained the 'economic miracle', this massive influx of foreign goods also created balance of payments difficulties for Spain. During the decade Spain's total merchandise imports valued $25 billion while exports totaled $11 billion; a ratio of more than 2:1 in favour of imports.[35] The severity of this discrepancy in merchandise trade was partly offset by earnings from tourism and remittances back to Spain by nationals working abroad. However, even with these substantial sources of invisible earnings the Franco government continued to run a deficit on its current account.[36] Among Spain's principal trading partners its import to export ratio was worst with Saudi Arabia, Iraq and the US. Its most favourable balances were with Cuba, Brazil and Holland.

Spain's commercial relationship with Cuba in the 1960s is particularly interesting because as both nations pursued programmes of economic diversification, although these were based on very different ideological foundations, they encountered similar structural problems in their respective economies. In particular, as the demand for imports of capital equipment and industrial raw materials increased in both countries, their export sectors were unable to generate sufficient earnings to balance their foreign accounts. For Cuba this problem was partly alleviated by the Soviet Union's willingness to grant aid and long-term loans. But this arrangement increasingly committed Cuba to Soviet technology which in many areas of the economy proved to be unsuitable. The Cubans, therefore, had to continue engaging in trade with capitalist nations, even though this meant exposing their economic plans to the vicissitudes of the world market price of their main export commodity, sugar.

Although Spain's imbalance on its foreign merchandise trade in the 1960s was lessened by various sources of invisible earnings, these were never sufficient to bring about equilibrium in the current account. Consequently, while there were significant differences between the Cuban and Spanish economies in the 1960s, for example unlike Cuba, Spain was fully integrated in the capitalist world market and had a convertible currency, shortages of foreign exchange persisted as a common problem for both countries. Based on this fact, and the compatibility of the two economies – with Cuba requiring Spain's new industrial products and Spain demanding increasing quantities of Cuban sugar as consumption at home grew – it became possible for Spain and Cuba to enter into a number of trading agreements founded on comparative advantage.

Spain and Cuba: the sugar connection

Cuba has been an important supplier of sugar to Spain since colonial times, and often for long periods Cuban exports have made up almost entirely the shortfall between Spanish sugar production and consumption. Indeed, for most of the nineteenth century Spain had relied on Cuba to provide around 50 per cent of its sugar needs. But in the 1890s the ravages of the Cuban War of Independence adversely affected supplies, and Spain began to expand its own production.[37] For the first 35 years of the twentieth century Spain became almost self-sufficient in sugar production, except for the last three years of the First World War when it turned temporarily to Latin America to supply its needs, and particularly to Cuba and Brazil.

During the Spanish Civil War, which lasted from 1936–1939, sugar production declined from around 300,000 tonnes per annum (average 1931–35) to about 150,000 tonnes, and along with the rest of Spanish agriculture only made a slow recovery after the conflict, with output averaging 163,700 tonnes per annum for the duration of the 1940s. However, consumption during this period was also low and Spanish imports of sugar remained negligible. Indeed, only in the mid-1950s did Spain begin to import significant quantities of sugar.[38] As the Spanish economy started to expand and diversify in the early-1960s, sugar consumption increased at a rate that quickly outstripped domestic output, although harvests continued to improve from year to year.[39] At this time Cuba, which was going through the first stages of revolutionary change, was identified by Spain not only as a good market for Spanish products but also as a potentially long-term supplier of sugar.

In October 1959, less than a year after Castro had seized power, Spain and Cuba signed a commercial agreement, the *Modus Vivendi Comercial y de Pagos*, which replaced an earlier trading pact which had existed since 1953. This agreement put into operation the financial and commercial mechanisms by which a system of bilateral trade based on clearing could be conducted.[40] To prevent any significant imbalances in trade between the two countries it was written into the agreement that each party would allow the other a maximum deficit of $3 million. But by the end of 1960 it became clear that this limit had been set too low when Spanish-Cuban trade surged to over $20 million, which was a 220 per cent increase on the previous year. During the negotiations which had been held in 1959 neither side had anticipated the severity of the deterioration in Cuban – US relations during 1960, and the disruptions this would cause to Cuba's external trade. After Washington cancelled Cuba's sugar quota in July 1960 and began to apply a selective embargo on US exports to the Castro government, the Cuban's were forced to expand their trade with other countries. Among the European market economies Spain was particularly well placed to respond to Cuba's needs, not only because both countries' trading requirements were compatible, but most importantly because a system of bilateral exchange was already in place which allowed for an immediate expansion of trade without undertaking the usual commitments to guarantee payment in hard currency. As noted earlier, at this time both Spain and Cuba were suffering from shortages of hard currency so conducting trade through clearing appeared to be the most appropriate response to a common problem.

In 1960 the commercial section of the Spanish embassy in Havana reported back to Madrid that the Revolution had opened up new commercial opportunities, and developments under the Castro government would guarantee a reliable market for Spanish manufactured goods well into the future.[41] However, as Cuba's demand for Spanish products increased it was not matched immediately by a similar demand in Spain for Cuban sugar, or any other Cuban export commodity. The problem for the Franco government was that while Cuba could select from a wide range of Spanish export products, it was restricted to expanding its imports from Cuba on the basis of only a few commodities. The first step that Spain took to attempt to balance its trade with Cuba was to ensure that the maximum possible quantity of its sugar imports came from this source. Therefore, while in 1958 46 per cent of Spanish sugar imports were of Cuban origin, and in 1959 only 8.5 per cent, in 1960 Cuba supplied 95.4 per cent of Spain's requirements.[42] For the remainder of the decade Cuba provided on average 79.2 per cent of Spain's sugar imports.

The Franco government further attempted to balance its trade surplus with Cuba by engaging in triangular trade through the re-exportation of Cuban sugar imports. This method of equalising trading accounts was practised in 1960 and 1961 by Spain, but Cuban disapproval prevented it from being used in subsequent years. Despite the measures taken by the Franco government to avoid a trade imbalance, Cuba still accrued a deficit in 1960 far in excess of the $3 million limit agreed in 1959. Recarte suggests that this figure was as high as $10 million (p. 164).

After 1960 Spain had to take firmer measures to reduce Cuba's deficit. This included placing restrictions on the issue of export licences to Spanish firms doing business with Cuba. The new trading restraints which were put on trade with Cuba by the Franco government in 1960 not only led to a more manageable balance of trade for Spain, but also prevented Cuba from using the system of clearing to its advantage during the Revolution's leanest years of 1961 and 1962 when hard currency reserves were dangerously low. At this time Cuba had to obtain most of its imports from socialist countries with which it had established trading relations based on various systems of barter, and other forms of bilateral exchange. Had it not been for the controls which were put on such trade by Madrid, Spain, which was the only market economy, apart from Morocco, to have a bilateral trading agreement with Cuba, could have provided a unique opportunity for the Castro government to obtain much coveted Western goods without expending any hard currency.

Because of Spain's action to curb Cuban access to Spanish goods, trade between the two countries fell from $20 million in 1960 to $13 million in 1961, and $10 million in 1962. In 1961 and 1962 Spain also ran large deficits on its trading account with Cuba in an attempt to reduce the $10 million Cuban deficit which had been created in 1960. Both by restricting exports to the Castro government and engaging in some triangular trade, at the end of 1962 Spain was able to restore the balance on its clearing account with Cuba.

Once this equilibrium had been achieved Spanish-Cuban trade began to expand and in 1963 reached $31 million. Spain, however, continued to maintain a large deficit on its trade with Cuba, with imports at $22 million while exports were only $9 million. The main reasons for this imbalance were: firstly, in 1963 Spain's sugar harvest produced below average yields and imports of sugar had to be increased to compensate for the shortfall. Secondly, the world market price for sugar soared to record heights in 1963, so Spain had to pay more for this import than in previous years.[43] Finally, as the market price for sugar rose Cuba found that it had more hard currency at its disposal than in previous years with which to buy goods from the capitalist economies. This gave the Castro government greater choice both in what it purchased and with whom it did business. In 1963 Cuba was also seeking to purchase some goods which Spain was not yet able to supply, such as earth-moving equipment. But although Spanish exports to Cuba in 1963 continued to include large quantities of traditional foodstuff commodities such as olive oil and pulses, almost half of all exports were now made up of manufactured products from the new industries. Most notably in 1963 Spain sent its first batch of Pegaso trucks to Cuba, and in the same year the Castro government entered into negotiations with Spanish shipbuilders to build a number of merchant and fishing vessels for the Cuban fleet.

By June 1963, as sugar prices began to rise and forecasts predicted another poor sugar harvest in Spain in 1964, the Franco government became anxious to ensure a guaranteed supply of sugar at a fixed price for at least two years. After protracted negotiations with the Cubans a three-year contract was signed in November in which Spain agreed to purchase Cuban sugar on a yearly basis at the following quantities and prices: 1964 – 150,000 metric tonnes at 11.42 cents a pound (imperial) to be paid in convertible currency, plus 100,000 metric tonnes at 9.83 cents a pound paid through the clearing account. 1965 and 1966 – 100,000 each year at 9.83 cents a pound paid through clearing.[44] In sharp contrast to the political acrimony which had existed in earlier years between Cuba and Spain, and which had been voiced mainly through each country's state controlled press, the Cuban daily *Noticias de Hoy*, reporting on the agreement, spoke of the 'cordiality and broad mutual comprehension' which prevailed during the negotiations.[45]

With the average raw sugar price on the open market at 13 cents a pound at the time the contract was signed, and continuing predictions of a world shortage of sugar for the following year, the Spanish negotiating team must have felt satisfied with the terms they had agreed with the Cubans. Indeed, according to Recarte instructions were given to the Spanish delegation before it left for Havana to obtain a guaranteed supply even if it meant paying over the world market price (p. 166).

Unfortunately for Spain shortly after the signing of the November agreement the sugar price on the world market began to fall. At first it fell quite slowly as it went down to 11.8 cents per pound in January 1964, but after that the decline gained pace so that by August it stood at 4.3 cents.[46] In 1965 and 1966 the price fell even further with a yearly average of 2.03 cents and 1.76 cents respectively.[47] The collapse of the sugar price during the period of the Spanish-Cuban agreement put the Franco government in a difficult position, because although it had planned to increase its exports to Cuba it did not expect to do so under such unfavourable circumstances. With sugar accounting for 85 per cent of the total value of Spain's imports from Cuba between 1964 and 1966, and being paid for at approximately two and a half times the world market price, the Franco government was in effect subsidising its exports to Cuba. During these years Cuba was receiving better terms on its trading agreement with Spain than it had with the Soviet Union, which was only paying 6.11 cents for Cuban sugar.[48] Moreover, Cuba's agreements with the Soviet Union had been negotiated purposely to its advantage, which reflected the commitment of the socialist states to the Cuban Revolution. Clearly the same objectives were not shared by Franco's policymakers when they signed a sugar agreement with Cuba but the results were similar.[49]

In late-1964, as the world sugar price slipped below three cents a pound Cuba agreed to accede to Spanish requests for a renegotiation of the 1963 contract. During the subsequent meetings which were held in Havana, Cuba insisted that if it was to agree to a lower fixed price for sugar for the remaining years of the existing agreement, then Spain would have to accept an extension of the original contract for a further three years up to 1969. This modified agreement, which was signed on 8 February 1965 after two months of negotiations, stipulated a new fixed price of 6.71 cents per pound, and that Cuba would deliver the following quantities: 1965 – 160,000 metric tonnes; 1966 – 130,000 metric tonnes; 1967 – 140,000 metric tonnes; 1968 – 150,000 metric tonnes; 1969 – 160,000 metric tonnes.[50] Payment for all deliveries would be made through the mechanism of clearing. Finally, Spain was offered the option in each year of the contract to expand its sugar imports up to 200,000 metric tonnes, with the extra quantity being paid for at the agreed fixed price.

Even with a lower fixed price for its purchases of Cuban sugar one may wonder why Spain was willing to renegotiate and extend a contract which had proved to be so disadvantageous. There are a number of possible reasons why such a choice was made: firstly, there are risks involved in buying large quantities of sugar on the open market, or on short-term contracts at prevailing market prices, because sugar prices can fluctuate wildly and accurate decisions regarding the best purchase price and quantity are impossible. Moreover, in the 1960s as Spain began to experience rapid economic growth, it became increasingly necessary to have advance knowledge of import commodity quantities and prices to undertake the more accurate budgetary calculations and forecasts which are demanded of a modern economy.[51] Indeed, for this and other reasons, almost all industrial nations have access to a dependable raw sugar supply at fixed prices. For example, in the 1960s Britain imported within the system of Colonial Preference (British Commonwealth Sugar Agreement); France from the *Communauté* (this arrangement was solely to supply part of France's requirements of cane sugar, France itself was a net exporter of sugar); the US operated a quota system with the Philippines, Hawaii and several Latin American nations; the USSR had bilateral agreements with its partners in CMEA and Cuba; and the EEC had its own internal pricing structure. All these nations paid on average over the years above the world market price for their sugar imports, but clearly regarded this as an acceptable extra cost in exchange for a reliable supply at a pre-determined price.

Secondly, by in effect taking over a portion of the former US quota, Spain was gaining access to one of the most reliable sugar supplies in the world: a privilege it could not have expected to be given before the Revolution, not only because of the enormous influence and control which the US had over Cuban sugar, but also because Spain's sugar imports were never sufficiently large for it to negotiate a priority supply from Cuba or any other large sugar producer. But as Spain became Cuba's principal market for sugar in Western Europe its negotiating position was strengthened.

Thirdly, as noted earlier, Spain became acutely aware soon after

Castro came to power that the Revolution would create new market opportunities for Spanish exporters; to secure this market, however, it was necessary to allow Cuba to balance its trade with Spain, which it could only do through the export of sugar. This obligation did not fall so heavily on some of Cuba's other capitalist trading partners because their industrial products were often more sought after by the Cubans than those which were being produced in Spain. Hence they were able to attract hard currency payments for their products without always committing themselves to reciprocal purchases of Cuban exports.

Fourthly, one must take into account a number of problems which Spain faces as a sugar producer that restrict it from increasing its output, and which consequently makes access to reliable external sources of supply all the more important. The most fundamental of these problems is that only a small proportion of Spain's land area is suitable for growing sugar.[52] In their determination to overcome the climatic and geographical constraints on sugar production, Spanish farmers have taken the unusual step of growing sugar beet in dry regions with the aid of irrigation. This has allowed the planting of this crop as far south as the provinces of Granada and Seville. Although sugar beet can be encouraged to grow on irrigated land its output per hectare is sometimes lower than in its natural environment. In fact the output per hectare of Spanish sugar beet in general compared unfavourably with the rest of Europe in the 1960s, where the average was 33 tonnes per hectare while in Spain it was below 24 tonnes.[53]

Poor output per hectare in Spanish sugar harvests up to the late-1950s was partly offset by low wage, labour-intensive farming methods, which helped to keep down the cost of production. However, in the 1960s as wages began to rise labour-intensive sugar production became a liability and forced some restructuring of the industry. This led to increased mechanisation, a decrease in small-scale sugar farming, and the expansion of larger producers who could take advantage of mechanisation and economies of scale.[54]

Despite these improvements Spanish sugar production in the 1960s remained inefficient and expensive by European standards. Moreover, cane sugar, especially from the Caribbean and Latin America, is generally cheaper to produce than beet sugar. Therefore Spain's imports of Cuban sugar, even when paid for at over twice the world market price, were still probably cheaper in the 1960s than domestically produced Spanish sugar.

Finally, although the political ideologies of Franco's Spain and Castro's Cuba were diametrically opposed, both governments could claim some legitimacy for their expanding trade, besides commercial pragmatism, by appealing to the nebulous concept of *Hispanidad*. One may argue that calling on *Hispanidad*, especially on the part of Spain, as a justification for its strengthening commercial relations with Cuba was simply a convenient obfuscation of purely material objectives. However, it must be acknowledged that Castro's ejection of the US from Cuba, and the subsequent expansion of Spanish trade with the island, held a great symbolic value for both countries, when seen in the context of Spain's humiliating defeats in 1898 at the hands of the US. As well as playing the role in Spain of justifying the expansion of its trade with Cuba, perhaps the most important function of *Hispanidad* as a concept was to act as a convenient justification for a series of disastrous sugar contracts which left Spain at a trading disadvantage.

After the re-negotiation of the Spanish-Cuban sugar agreement in February 1965 both parties believed that the sugar price, then at 2.4 cents a pound, had passed its lowest point and was on the upturn. This, however, was a miscalculation which proved expensive for Spain because prices did not begin to rise until 1969, which was the last year of the contract, and then only reached 3.2 cents a pound on average for the year.[55] Once committed to paying 6.71 cents a pound for the duration of the contract, Spain again found itself at a disadvantage in its trade with Cuba.

The only positive aspect for Spain of its sugar contract with Cuba was that the annual quantities ordered proved to coincide approximately with demand. Firstly, in 1965, as predicted, the Spanish sugar crop was poor, so having a guaranteed external supply ensured that there were no shortages.[56] In subsequent years the Spanish sugar harvest improved, but rapidly expanding domestic sugar consumption meant that high levels of imports had to be maintained.

In 1966, when it became clear that the upturn in the price of sugar was not going to take place as predicted the previous year, Spain attempted to persuade the Cubans to lower the contract price which had been agreed in 1965. To put pressure on the Cubans to accede to its demands the Franco government instructed the members of the negotiating team who were sent to Havana to bring up the issue of compensation for Spanish assets seized during the first months of the Revolution, and the question of Spanish political prisoners still held in Cuba.[57] Despite these pressures the Cubans refused to lower the price of sugar sold on contract to Spain. In fact their only concession was to release a few prisoners with Spanish nationality and allow them to return home.[58] After Spain's failure to persuade the Cubans to lower the contract sugar price in 1966 no further attempts were made to alter the agreement, which remained unchanged until its completion in 1969. In 1968, however, the Franco government notified the Cubans that after the existing sugar contract was terminated, they would not enter into any more fixed price agreements. Needless to say the Cubans took a dim view of this proposal.

By March 1970, with the 1965 contract terminated and the future of Spanish-Cuban commercial relations still undecided both sides came to the negotiating table. This resulted in Spain agreeing to purchase the following quantities of sugar: 1970 – 120,000 metric tonnes, 1971 – 70,000 metric tonnes, and 1972 – 70,000 metric tonnes.[59] A new pricing mechanism was also devised in which 70 per cent of the final price was based on a fixed rate of 5.5 cents a pound, with the other 30 per cent being determined by the annual average world market price. To obtain this concession on pricing Spain had to agree to purchase all its requirements of raw sugar which could not be satisfied by domestic production, from Cuba. Additionally, the Franco government gave Cuba credits worth $30 million and extended the deficit limit on the clearing account from $3 million to $10 million.

The above contract served Spain reasonably well for its duration, and offered favourable trading conditions which had proved so elusive in the 1960s. But by 1973, when the world sugar price began to climb sharply, Spain was forced to enter into a contract that would again prove to be disadvantageous.

An analysis of Spain's trading relations with Cuba from 1959 to the mid-1970s based on sugar contracts alone, can only conclude that during this period the Franco government failed to maximise the commercial opportunities which emerged because of the Revolution. However, it could be argued that between 1965–68 Spain was able to compensate for the high prices it was paying for Cuban sugar by charging above market prices for the ships that it manufactured and delivered during these years to the Castro government. It should also be remembered that even when Spain was trading with Cuba at a commercial disadvantage it was increasing its share of the Cuban market for Spanish products and especially manufactured goods. By the late-1970s when the system of clearing was abandoned, Cuba had incorporated so much Spanish technology into its economy that it was obliged to continue buying its requirements of Spanish products with valuable hard currency. In these terms Spanish penetration of the Cuban market, though costly, can be seen as an impressive and enduring achievement.

Spanish foreign policy in the 1960s and the US response to strengthening Spanish – Cuban relations

Among Western European nations that continued trading with Cuba after the imposition of a trade embargo on the Castro government by the US, Spain presented Washington with the most serious and embarrassing problem. Serious because in the 1960s Cuba became a more important trading partner for Spain than it did for any other Western European market economy. Moreover, of all the capitalist nations that maintained commercial relations with Cuba beyond the first few years of the Revolution, Spain was the only capitalist state along with Morocco to set up a formal trading agreement with the Cubans. This was especially distressing for the US because it meant that unlike Cuba's fair weather friends in the rest of Western Europe, Spain had to continue doing business with the Castro government even when the Revolution fell on hard times.

Spain's commercial relationship with Cuba was embarrassing for the US, firstly, because in the 1950s and early-1960s Washington had nurtured the Franco government on the path to economic modernisation and expected in return Spanish compliance with the demands of American foreign policy.[60] Secondly, US aid to Spain, and the general *rapprochement* which had taken place between the two countries since the early-1950s, had, as far as Washington was concerned, been premised on Franco's staunch anti-communist stand at home and abroad. With Britain, France, Japan and any other large and independent capitalist economy, the US had to accept some disagreement and non-compliance with aspects of its foreign policy, but such conduct was not expected from a small and partly dependent ally like Spain.

In the early-1960s the US continued to regard itself, with justification, as Spain's most important economic and political ally, but at that time the Franco government was beginning to pursue an independent foreign policy.[61] Although Franco himself was still deeply involved in all aspects of government, his Foreign Minister Fernando Castiella seems to have been the driving force behind Spain's foreign policy in the 1960s. Castiella's strategy, which included the strengthening of Spain's relations with the EEC, Latin America, the Arab states, and most of the communist world, was clearly based on the belief that Spain's association with the US was becoming too claustrophobic. Therefore Spain's improving relations with Cuba can be seen as part of a wider plan of integration with the international community, which was premised on a desire to weaken US hegemony in the peninsula. Moreover, in a period when Spain was switching its economic energies from reconstruction to export-led growth it became crucial to find new and expanding markets for its products. As noted earlier, Spain's trade with the US grew throughout the 1960s, but remained unbalanced as Spanish exports performed poorly in the US market, and as a percentage of total exchanges showed a gradual decline. For example, in 1960 Spain's exports to the US accounted for 34 per cent of all trade between the two countries but by 1969 this figure had fallen to 26 per cent. On the other hand, during the same period Spain's export to import ratio was improving in its commercial relations with Latin America, some Western European countries, and a number of socialist states.[62]

Increasing economic independence from the US through the expansion of foreign trade also led Spain to seek new political alliances. Among these the most important was France which Spanish policymakers believed could supersede the US as Spain's chief ally: a partnership in which, it was envisaged, Spain would be less compromised.[63] Franco's decision to seek improved relations with France coincided with the first stages of the implementation of de Gaulle's independent foreign policy in the communist states and the Third World. Franco was impressed by de Gaulle's foreign policy initiatives, and especially his view of the Third World and his treatment of former French colonies like Algeria. Indeed, Franco may have wished to join forces with France to implement de Gaulle's strategy in the Third World, with Spain playing a special role among the Hispanic nations.[64] If this was so it suggests that the expansion of Spanish-Cuban trade in the 1960s had a further dimension than simply commercial pragmatism.

Spain's support of French foreign policy and its attempts to bring about closer collaboration between the two countries was well received by de Gaulle's government, which reciprocated by sending a number of economic advisers and high officials to Madrid with the purpose of finding ways of improving commercial relations. De Gaulle also gave his full support to Spain in its (unsuccessful) attempts to join the EEC in the 1960s.[65]

Moreover, de Gaulle's foreign policy towards the communist states met with Franco's approval and may again have encouraged Spain to make its own cautious attempts to improve its relations with the USSR and Eastern Europe. The thaw between Spain and the European socialist states began in 1962 when Franco sent aid to the victims of an earthquake in Yugoslavia.[66] This was followed by a number of exploratory Spanish trade missions to Eastern Europe which resulted in the signing of trade agreements with Romania and East Germany in 1967. However, relations between Spain and the Soviet Union were not so easily improved because of the legacy of the Spanish Civil War, and Franco's sympathies for the Axis powers during the Second World War.[67] But despite these obstacles to an early *rapprochement*, there were potentially numerous political and economic advantages to be gained by both sides from an improvement in relations. For Spain the Soviet Union promised not only to be a good market for its exports, as indeed were the other European socialist states from 1965, but also a powerful bargaining counter against US hegemony. Moreover, Spain's lack of natural oil reserves made it strategically and economically necessary to have access to several external sources, and the Soviet Union was seen as an important contingency supplier.

Spain's geographical position between Europe and Africa, and the command which its south-west tip offers of the entrance to the Mediterranean, gave it a strategic military importance which was recognised by both superpowers. Clearly the Soviet leadership never expected Franco to allow any appreciable loosening of his commitments to the US, but perhaps hoped that by moving closer to Spain it would be better placed to encourage and influence those figures in the government like Castiella who sought to reduce American military strength in the area. As well as trying to moderate US influence on the Franco government, the Soviet leadership was also anxious to prevent Spain's entry into NATO and the EEC. While Spain remained outside of these organisations it was felt by Moscow that Spanish neutrality, its ultimate goal, remained a possibility. Finally, Moscow saw Spain as the gateway through which it would gain more political influence and commercial opportunities in the Hispanic world.

During the first half of the 1960s there were numerous low level contacts between Spain and the Soviet Union. These included: informal discussions between respective embassies in several European capitals; the encouragement by both countries of cultural exchanges; and a few tentative reciprocal trade missions.[68] Small numbers of Russian tourists also started arriving in Spain from 1965. Perhaps the most surprising development in this relationship occurred during a speech Franco gave in Bilbao in 1964 in which he praised the Soviet Union and Premier Khrushchev. This was indeed an extraordinary gesture from a leader who had built his reputation on being Europe's most vehement anti-communist. Some of Franco's opponents at home and abroad saw his statements as further justification of their belief that the *caudillo* was not an ideologue himself but simply admired strong governments and other *caudillos* – perhaps this also serves as a partial explanation of why he so readily allowed his government to establish a strong relationship with the Castro government in Cuba. Franco and Castro were also both *gallegos* and apparently the two leaders shared an empathy which transcended politics.[69] A former American diplomat in Cuba has even suggested that they maintained a private personal correspondence for a number of years.[70]

Although it is probably correct to assume that Franco admired strong leaders and this affected his response to individuals like Castro, one also finds that Falangist newspapers in the 1960s such as *Arriba* and *Pueblo* were openly advocating an improvement in relations between Spain and the socialist states, including the Soviet Union and Cuba.[71] This would suggest therefore that Franco's increasing tolerance of such governments was consistent ideologically with progressive elements in the Falange.

Reciprocal gestures of friendship between Madrid and Moscow in the mid-1960s did lead to a modest improvement in relations, but because of the profound contempt with which both countries had viewed each other since Franco came to power, there seems to have been a mutually accepted limit as to how far the relationship could develop.[72] In fact although diplomatic links were established between Spain and most of the socialist states, including East Germany (1973) and China (1973), during the later Franco years, it was not until 1977, two years after the *caudillo's* death, that

Madrid and Moscow exchanged ambassadors.

Despite the lingering acrimony which continued to exist between Madrid and Moscow during the Franco period the Soviet Union did not impede its allies from strengthening their contacts with Spain. Indeed, Moscow may have even encouraged the Castro government to expand its trade with Spain.[73] If so there were good reasons for this. Firstly, Spain was the only Western European market with which Cuba could balance its trade, thereby relieving the Soviet Union from what could have been an even weightier obligation to provide aid to prevent Cuban indebtedness to the capitalist world. Secondly, Moscow must have felt satisfaction at seeing Cuba, which was then the world's most revolutionary state, establishing favourable commercial relations with Washington's staunchest right-wing ally in Europe.

Before the re-negotiation of the Bases Pact in September 1963 the US did not challenge Spain openly on its foreign policy, and most notably made no attempt to block improving Spanish-Cuban commercial relations, although trade between the two countries grew from $9.2 million in 1959 to $31 million in 1963.[74] Even after the US had hardened its policy on Cuba with the implementation of a total trade embargo on the Havana government during early 1962, Spain was still left almost unhindered to carry on its commercial links with Cuba. This uncharacteristic caution on the part of Washington in matters concerning revolutionary Cuba, may have been adopted because its bargaining position with Spain for an extension of the Bases Pact was by no means as strong as it had been ten years earlier. In fact, as Spain's economic and foreign policy had become less dependent on the US during the early 1960s, the US had, in contrast, become more reliant on its military facilities in Spain. This was especially so from 1962 when the US naval base at Rota became a vital stopover for Polaris equipped submarines travelling between North America and the Middle East.

Because of Spain's improved leverage in the 1963 re-negotiation of the Bases Pact, it was able to persuade the US to accept several changes to the original agreement.[75] The two most important of these were: firstly, whereas previously Washington had been able to make unilateral decisions concerning the installation of new weapons systems in its Spanish bases, it now had to consult with Madrid before taking such action. Secondly, rather than only being responsible for the protection of its own military installations in Spain, the US was persuaded to enter into a mutual defence agreement in which any threat to either country from a foreign power would be treated as 'a matter of common concern', and lead to 'appropriate' joint action against the aggressor.[76] This fell short of the 'fully fledged' alliance which Franco's Ambassador in Washington, Antonio Garrigues had argued for, but nevertheless was seen in Spain as an acceptable compromise.[77] The new agreement was also signed for only five years, instead of ten, but this had been decided earlier and was not part of the 1963 negotiations. Finally, although Washington was in the process of disengaging from some of its financial commitments to Spain by the early-1960s, it sanctioned a $100 million Import-Export Bank loan as part of the agreement. Franco and his ministers were delighted with the outcome of the negotiations because they believed that they had proved to their critics at home and abroad, who felt Spain was little more than a satellite of the US, that the government could negotiate on equal terms with its superpower ally.[78] This view was not shared by some of Spain's other allies and trading partners, least of all the Cubans, who felt that Franco had simply delivered his country into American hands for another five years for the sake of a $100,000 loan.[79]

Once the US had secured an extension to the Bases Pact pressure began to be applied more vigorously on Spain to curb its relationship with Cuba. In response to Washington's disquiet Spanish officials insisted that Spain could justify its trade with Cuba on commercial and political grounds. Firstly, they claimed that because Spain was still weak as an exporter of manufactured goods it could not afford to cease trading with Cuba which was emerging as an excellent market for these products. Moreover, this trade depended on Spain maintaining substantial sugar imports from Cuba. Secondly, it was argued that Spain was obliged to support good relations with the Castro government to ensure that it could continue to defend the interests of the 40,000 Spanish citizens living in Cuba.[80]

Washington remained unmoved by Spain's attempt to justify its trade with Cuba, and their continuing concern was compounded by reports that Spanish shipbuilders were attempting to secure a large Cuban order for fishing vessels. Faced with Spain's intransigence and rumours that Britain and France were also planning to sign large contracts with the Cubans the Johnson administration decided to step up the blockade on Cuba. This was achieved through an amendment to the Foreign Assistance Act, which was made on 16 December 1963 allowing the US to halt economic and military aid to countries failing to take 'appropriate steps' to cut off their transportation links with Cuba.[81] The deadline by which offending parties had to comply with the new ruling was 14 February 1964.

For Cuba's capitalist trading partners like Britain and France this new legislation was of little economic concern because the only aid they received from the US took the form of an insignificant contribution to their military expenditure. But for Spain, with receipts of over $30 million in military aid in 1963, and expectations of an increase in 1964, it was a serious threat.[82] Furthermore, Washington quickly pointed out to the Franco government that the $100 million Import-Export Bank loan which had been granted as part of the agreement for the renewal of the Bases Pact, might also be in jeopardy if Spain failed to comply with the new ruling.[83] Spain naturally felt victimised by Washington's stance, because it stood to lose more than Cuba's other capitalist trading partners.

This feeling was compounded because Spain also had to make greater sacrifices to carry out Washington's demands. For example, since November 1962, after the Cubans had given the Spanish national airline, Iberia, permission to land its planes at Havana airport, Spain had been the only Western European nation to have a scheduled air service to Cuba.[84] This service was curtailed for most of 1963 because of various problems, but was resumed again at the end of the year.[85] Iberia's flights to Cuba were defended by the Franco government on the basis that it was essential to maintain contact with the large Spanish community on the island, and provide a link with the homeland for those who wished to return. Due to the high levels of trade which Spain conducted with Cuba it was also in Spain's commercial interest to let as much of this trade as possible be carried by national shipping companies. However, from as early as 1961, under pressure from Washington, the Franco government had reluctantly begun to reduce the number of Spanish ships involved in trade with Cuba, and by 1964 only a few Spanish registered vessels were calling at Cuban ports.[86] Although it was clear by the time of the US imposed deadline of 14 February 1964 that Spain had made efforts to stop its ships from carrying Cuban trade, five Spanish-owned vessels were still found by that date to be under charter to the Castro government.[87] But the most severe breach of the US ruling was committed by Iberia, which ignored Washington's directives and continued with its weekly scheduled flights to Havana up to and after 14 February.[88]

Soon after the deadline had passed it became clear to Washington that Cuba's European trading partners had largely disregarded the call to cease their transportation links with Cuba.[89] Consequently action was taken to cut off military aid to the offending countries.[90] In the cases of Britain, France and Yugoslavia, which were only receiving small amounts of aid, the cut was made immediately. But Spain and Morocco, which relied more heavily on US military assistance, loans and development grants, were given a second chance, being told simply that no new aid would be available until they could prove that 'appropriate steps' were being taken to comply with Washington's directives.

Despite the US administration's conciliatory attitude towards Spain, the Franco government felt humiliated to be put, as it perceived, on trial in front of the international community. A few days before the deadline of the 14 February the Spanish Ambassador to Washington, Antonio Garrigues, apparently under direct orders from Franco, visited President Johnson to present Spain's case on trade with Cuba, and to give account of the efforts which were being made to curb transport links with the Castro government.[91] Once it was clear that Garrigues mission had failed the Ambassador was recalled to Madrid, and later sent on to represent Spain in the Vatican.

This may be seen as a retaliatory action, not only because of the timing of the transfer, but also because Garrigues was well respected by the Johnson administration for the role he played in preparing the diplomatic and political conditions for the extension and modification of the Bases Pact.

Since the Johnson administration had initiated the amendment to the Foreign Assistance Act in December 1963, which required non-communist nations to curtail their transportation links with Cuba or face cuts in American aid, the Spanish press began to display an unprecedented degree of opposition to US policy towards Cuba. Given that only three months earlier the agreement for the extension of the Bases Pact had marked a high point in US-Spanish relations this change of attitude towards policies emanating from Washington appeared all the more abrupt. Interestingly, but perhaps not surprisingly, the most severe condemnation of Washington's handling of the Castro government, and its attempts to force other non-communist countries to adhere to its anti-Cuban strategies, came from the Falangist press. For example, *Arriba* claimed that because it wholeheartedly supported the view held in the non-communist West that Cuba should not be permitted to become a satellite of the Soviet Union, it could not comprehend American policy towards the Castro government, which

> . . . rather than support a return of Cuba to the fold of the Hispanic family, rather than encourage those elements within the Castro government which want a closer alliance with the West – which surely exist in Havana – consistently serves to push Cuba towards the arms of Russia. . . . Consequently it is extremely difficult to see how they [the US] expect to gain any support for such a contradictory strategy.[92]

The article goes on to suggest that Washington's incomprehensible handling of Cuba could only be explained as 'a kind of national neurosis', which stemmed in part from the humiliating defeat of US-backed forces by the Cubans at the Bay of Pigs in 1961. Fortunately, it was pointed out, 'North America's Western allies do not suffer from the same 'neurosis' and therefore are well placed to help the superpower to view the Castro government in a more rational light.' Thus, *Arriba* concluded, that instead of condemning its allies for their policies towards Cuba, Washington would do well to learn from their example, and modify its own attitude towards the Castro government.

The more restrained Madrid daily *ABC*, which despite its monarchist leanings was usually a reliable indicator of the mainstream views of the Franco government, also began to question the wisdom of US policy towards Cuba once it became clear that reprisals might be taken against Spain for its links with the Castro government. On 13 February, which was the eve of the US imposed deadline and the day Ambassador Garrigues was recalled from Washington, A*BC* noted, concerning the immanent implementation of aid cuts, that 'it would be difficult to imagine a more effective way of sowing seeds of dissension among the Western allies'.[93] The following day *ABC* indicated that 'unprecedented, urgent and profound problems' existed between Washington and Madrid.[94]

Once Washington announced its decision on 19 February not to take immediate action against Spain, but to give its ally a chance to clarify what steps it was taking to curb its transportation links with Cuba, there were some signs of relief in the Spanish press but the general mood continued to be one of dismay and indignation. *ABC*, for example, took the view that Washington's decision to put Spain on trial in this fashion was indicative of the general confusion and uncertainty which existed among US policymakers regarding the implementation of reprisals.[95] The Madrid daily also eagerly pointed out that this view was supported by sections of the US press. Furthermore, this was one of the few times during the Franco period when Fidel Castro was quoted with apparent approval by the Spanish media. In an interview the Cuban leader gave to reporters from Reuters he had insisted that the US response towards its allies for trading with Cuba was 'absurd', and that Cuba offered 'magnificent commercial opportunities' for capitalist countries.[96] Such statements met with sympathy in Spain.

At the same time that the US announced its decision to put Spain's relations with Cuba under official scrutiny, with a view to taking possible retaliatory measures against the Franco government, Washington and Madrid entered into high level diplomatic negotiations. Some indication of the stance adopted by Spain in these negotiations was given by one of the chief participants, Manuel Fraga Iribarne, Franco's Minister of Information and Tourism. In a press conference for foreign journalists given by the Minister on 21 February, he claimed that while Spain was unequivocal in its opposition to communism one had to remember that Spain's ties with Latin America, including Cuba, were complex and deeply rooted, and were composed of elements which transcended politics.[97] On a more pragmatic note Fraga also pointed out that the Castro government was an important and reliable customer for Spanish products and his country had no intention of abandoning its 'firm commitments' to Cuba. He also made it clear that if Washington decided to cut off any military aid to Spain, or rescind the recently agreed Import-Export Bank loan, then the US would be held by his government to be in breach of the contract signed the previous September between the two countries to extend the 1953 Bases Pact.[98] Such action therefore could jeopardise the future of US military facilities in Spain. Fraga indicated furthermore that the negotiations with the US were concerned not only with Spain's relations with Cuba, but also with finalising the details of an agreement with the Americans that would allow them to use their present naval facility at Rota as a base for Polaris-carrying submarines, rather than simply a stopover and refuelling point between the US and the Eastern Mediterranean.[99] The implication of this final statement was that Spain was doing some hard bargaining with Washington over the issue of Spanish relations with Cuba. All these points had been explained in more detail a few days before the Minister's press conference, in the Ministry of Information and Tourism's journal *El Español*. The question of extended US facilities at Rota had also been under discussion for some months, and had become public knowledge in December 1963 after an American naval commander at Holy Loch in Scotland had spoken to the press about the matter.

The day after Manuel Fraga's news conference there was a minor embarrassment for the Minister, when in response to his statements, and the contents of the article in *El Español*, the Spanish-born wife of a former Cuban Ambassador to Spain (who had served under Batista) circulated an open letter to the press which contained a scathing attack on the Franco government for its 'scandalous commercial partnership' with the Castro government.[100] Not surprisingly only brief, severely edited, résumés of this letter were published in the Spanish press.[101] Foreign newspapers, however, eagerly pointed out these omissions which included the claim that 'very high government quarters' in Spain had been infiltrated by communists and pro-communists.[102]

As far as Washington was concerned, among the Western European states Spain was the worst offender against its Cuba policy. Even after grave warnings had been given to the Franco government by the State Department to curb its trade and transportation links with Cuba, which included threats of retaliation, Spanish airlines had continued to run a weekly scheduled flight to Havana, and trade between Spain and the Castro government, both in imports and exports, had continued to expand faster than between any other of America's Western allies and Cuba. During 1964, in fact, Spain's trade with Cuba exceeded the Cuban trade of Britain and France combined.[103] In particular the US viewed Spain's contract to supply the Cuban's with freighters and fishing vessels, which was being negotiated at the time Washington was threatening to cut off military aid to Franco, as the most serious contravention of their Cuba policy. Not only would this contract amount to over $100 million worth of Spanish business with Cuba over the subsequent four years, but also many of the vessels supplied would be used to relieve Cuba from the maritime isolation which the US was attempting to impose.

But, despite Spain's blatant transgressions of Washington's Cuba policy there was little the US administration could do to punish the Franco government while it wished to retain and develop its military and naval bases on Spanish territory.[104] Clearly Franco never underestimated the strength of this factor and realised that no US government would ever jeopardise its access to these vital strategic facilities for the sake of gaining satisfaction on a minor area of its foreign policy; albeit in the case of Cuba one which it pursued with an unprecedented vigour. Spanish confidence that the US would not take retaliatory measures, as implied in the press and through official government statements, proved to be justified when in late February 1964 Washington indicated that it intended to exempt Spain from any previously proposed loan or military aid cuts. After this climb down the US were, however, anxious to find a 'face-saving formula', under which aid could be continued.[105]

Having won the main diplomatic argument Madrid showed some willingness to help Washington to legitimise its retreat, and in early March it announced that Iberia would be reducing its cargo service to Cuba.[106] Madrid also agreed to continue cutting back on the number of Spanish registered vessels trading with Cuba. But despite these concessions, the fact remained that the US had stopped short of implementing to the full its stated policy on Cuba against the most blatant transgressor of that policy. By failing to carry out its threats the US was in effect endorsing the continuation of Spanish trade and transportation links with the Castro government. From this moment Washington's whole argument advocating a Western embargo on Cuba lost a great deal of its 'moral' and practical credibility. Thus it became clear to Spain, and the rest of Cuba's capitalist trading partners, that America's policy on Cuba, which had gained a dramatic legitimacy during the autumn of 1962 at the time of the missile crisis, was, in the absence of a direct threat to Western security, a mere chimera which even the US itself would not defend when more important interests were at stake.

After Spain's diplomatic victory over the issue of its trading links with Cuba, American foreign policymakers were careful to avoid further embarrassments of this kind. And for the rest of the decade Spain, despite continuing to be Cuba's most important trading partner in Western Europe, was given a relatively easy time compared to Cuba's other capitalist trading partners, who faced unrelenting US diplomatic pressure to cease their commerce with the Castro government. Naturally, Spain continued to be subject, like all other market economies, to the legislation of the US embargo on Cuba such as the blacklisting of ships which engaged in Cuban trade, but by the mid-1960s most countries, including Spain, had found ways of bypassing Washington's 'cordon sanitaire'.

Further weakening of Washington's bargaining position with the Franco government

Because of Spain's defiance of Washington's Cuba policy resentment was felt in the US against the Franco government, and especially by right-wing groups and Cuban exile organisations. Most of these were content to attack Spain through the press but some hard-line anti-Castro factions, mainly among the Cuban exiles, who were already engaged in sabotage operations against Cuba and traffic carrying goods to Cuba, must have put Spain high on their 'hit list'. Among the armoury of sabotage equipment available to these terrorist factions were a number of armed motor launches, which were used sporadically to threaten or attack foreign vessels bound for Cuba. Between early 1963 and September 1964 although several such attacks took place no serious damage was caused to any Cuba traffic. By 1964 it was also widely believed that Washington had instructed the CIA – which was often the sponsor of these factions – to discourage such activities because it was feared that in the event of a vessel being sunk or immobilised with the loss of life, the repercussions could far outweigh the effect it would have on the Castro government. Washington's fears were confirmed in September 1964 when a Spanish-owned vessel the *Sierra de Aránzazu*, en route to Havana, and only a few hours sailing from its destination, was subject to a night attack by two armed launches. The incident resulted in the death of three Spanish sailors, including the captain, many injuries, and the crew of twenty having to abandon ship.[107]

The whole of Spain was incensed by the attack, and for the first time since the signing of the Bases Pact in 1953 the Spanish authorities allowed anti-American demonstrations to take place in several cities, including Madrid where a crowd of about 700 marched passed the American embassy shouting such slogans as 'Cuba sí, Yankee no!' and 'Yankee go home'.[108] The moment the news of the attack was received, Madrid's ambassador to Washington demanded an immediate audience with the Secretary of State Dean Rusk to be given an explanation of how such an incident could have happened in waters that were policed by the US navy. Rusk tried to mollify the Spaniards by insisting that the attack was a renegade action in which no official organisation in the US was involved. This did little to appease Madrid, and especially after an article appeared in the American newspaper *The Daily News* claiming the attack had been carried out by a Cuban exile group called 'Fuerza X', which had been trained, financed, and given protection, by the CIA.[109]

Washington suffered a further humiliation when the Spanish press raised the question of why a ship like the *Sierra de Aránzazu*, which was carrying products for Cuba's Christmas celebrations, should be attacked instead of British-owned oil tankers which were supplying the Castro government with a vital economic requirement. After posing this question the Madrid based commercial and foreign affairs journal *SP* made two suggestions: firstly, that the attack was political rather than strategic, and was designed to serve the purposes of the Goldwater camp in the forthcoming

American election, by providing a dramatic reminder to the American public that the allies were trading openly with Cuba under the Johnson administration. *SP*'s second suggestion was even more condemnatory as it was directed at the whole US political establishment: '. . . this act of piracy has again shown the lack of co-ordination which exists between the diverse departments of the American government. This is a grave problem for a power that has assigned to itself the role of leader of half the world's nations and could lead to tragic consequences.' (author's translation)

One of the consequences of the unfortunate *Sierra de Aránzazu* incident was to increase Spain's determination to continue its trade and transportation links with Cuba. This was made clear by *SP* which stated in conclusion to its article on the incident that 'Spain has established the right to trade with its brother country in the Caribbean and will continue to do so despite provocations' (p. 19).

Spain's bargaining position with the US was further strengthened in 1966 because of the Palomares incident, in which a Spanish-based American B52 bomber carrying a nuclear payload collided with its tanker plane while attempting to refuel in flight. Both aircraft fell to the ground near the village of Palomares on the south-east coast of Spain. Of the four atomic bombs which were being carried by the B52 three fell on land and were quickly recovered but the fourth, which fell in the sea, was only located after a massive search which attracted much media attention.[110] The incident weakened America's standing in Spain in two ways: firstly, since the Bases Pact had been initiated in 1953 one of the main concerns of Franco's negotiators was the possibility of Spain becoming a target in a nuclear war, or an American nuclear device being set off by accident. The US had constantly reassured the Franco government that both scenarios were only a remote possibility, but the Palomares incident was a warning that could not be easily dismissed. Washington had to accept that in future diplomatic bargaining between the two countries, Spain would use the risk element involved in hosting US bases to gain concessions. Secondly, since 1953 there had been some public resentment to the establishment of American bases on Spanish territory. This discontent grew during the 1960s and came to a climax with the Palomares incident, which opponents of the US bases claimed was a vindication of their arguments. Feelings ran so high that the incident led to unprecedented demonstrations against the Franco government by left-wing and liberal students. The concerns expressed by the students were also shared by a large, but less vociferous, sector of the Spanish population.[111] Again Franco was able to use this factor to strengthen his negotiating position with the Americans.

Largely because of the Palomares incident Spain was able to gain favourable terms from the Americans during the third renewal of the Bases Pact which was negotiated between 1968 and 1970. As well as loans and aid to purchase military equipment the US agreed to change some of the fundamental wording of the Pact. For example the term 'joint use bases' was changed to 'US facilities on Spanish bases'.[112] Although difficult to prove one suspects that after Palomares Washington's ability to influence Spanish-Cuban relations also further declined. An oblique indication of this was given by the then Secretary of State, Dean Rusk, who, referring to US post-Palomares relations with Spain stated: 'although we and other countries in this hemisphere were trying to bring economic pressure upon Cuba, we thought that it would be important to continue certain "windows" for Cuban contacts with the outside world . . . both Spain and Mexico would be examples of that idea'.[113] It is curious why Dean Rusk should make such a statement considering that at no time in the 1960s, or even the 1970s, did Washington give any indication that it was pursuing such a policy. Perhaps Rusk was just simply acknowledging indirectly that after Palomares the US could do little to prevent Spanish-Cuban trade.[114]

As a final point concerning the American response to Spanish-Cuban trade it should be remembered that during the 1960s the US enjoyed an extraordinarily good market for its products in Spain, and maintained a large trade surplus in its favour. If Washington had pressured Spain too hard to curb its commercial links with Cuba the Franco government could have responded with a cut back in American imports. Perhaps again, as with the bases, Washington felt that this was an aspect of American-Spanish relations that was too important to place in jeopardy in order to gain satisfaction on its Cuba policy.

Spanish industry and the Cuban market

Spain's perception of Cuba as a market for its new industrial products during the 1960s must be seen in the context of the Franco government's wider commercial objectives in Latin America at that time. With the take off of the 'Spanish economic miracle' in the late-1950s Latin America was identified as a key market for the manufactures that were being produced by the new Spanish industries. Although Spain's trade with the US and Europe far overshadowed its trade with Latin America during the 1960s, the region became an increasingly important market for Spanish products as the decade progressed. The idea of forming a common market of Hispanic nations was also one of the most popular topics of discussion among the Spanish business community. This idea was expressed particularly forcefully by the commercial and foreign affairs journal *SP* which was associated with Opus Dei. One article, written in 1963 by *SP*'s editor, Rodrigo Royo, referred to the question of the commercial unity of *Iberoamérica* as 'our favourite theme'.[115] In the same article Royo also pointed out that given current trends for population growth in the Americas, by 1983 Spanish America would have 500 million inhabitants, making the region more populous than the US. To this he added: 'if these 500 million people of which we [Spain] are a part do not unite together and begin progressing in the same direction, if we do not weigh our common interests on the same scales, if we do not co-ordinate our future together . . . then we are fools' (p. 9). Finally he suggests, possibly with Cuba in mind, to achieve the unity of *Iberoamérica* . . . 'it is essential not to let politics and ideologies interfere with such a plan' (p. 9).

Spain's hopes of playing a leading role in a Hispanic commercial union received a boost in November 1963, when during an exposition of Spanish products in Mexico City a number of leading Latin American businessmen proposed to the Secretary General of the Spanish Association of Chambers of Commerce, that Spain should become a member of Latin American Free Trade Association (ALALC). In the opinion of *SP*, which represented the views of the most progressive elements in the Spanish business community, 'the ALALC, the common market of Latin America, is of far greater importance for Spain than the European Common Market'.[116] To support its argument in favour of Spain joining the ALALC *SP* argued that this organisation offered several important opportunities for Spain. Firstly, as a member of ALALC, Spain would play a leading role whereas in any commercial agreement with the EEC or the US it would be in a subordinate position. Secondly, Spain could become Europe's economic and cultural 'bridgehead' in Latin America. Thirdly, it was felt that Spain's new industrial products were in many cases better suited to the needs of Latin America than the high technology products of the advanced industrial nations, which often could not be adapted satisfactorily to suit the conditions in developing countries.[117]

It is interesting to note that among the supporters of Spain's entry into the ALALC *SP* claimed could be included presidents López Mateos of Mexico and João Goulart of Brazil, as well as the Argentine economist Raúl Prebisch. These progressive 'paladins' of Latin American economic integration, as *SP* described them, had also been identified by de Gaulle's government as potentially key elements in its unfolding Latin American policy. It is not surprising therefore that from 1963 onwards Spain was enthusiastic about French policy towards the region. With justification Franco felt that Spain was in a unique position to lead Europe into a commercial 'reconquest' of Latin America, and to play this role it realised that, despite pursuing staunch anti-leftist policies at home, in its foreign policy it had to form allegiances with the most progressive elements in Europe and Latin America if it wished to wield any influence in the Hispanic world. In this context Spain's relationship with Cuba in the 1960s was not just an example of commercial pragmatism, but also a political strategy which gained it legitimacy among those nations and individuals in Latin America and Europe which sought to challenge US hegemony in its own back yard.

Notes

1   In December 1946 the Soviet bloc, France and Mexico had pressed the United Nations General Assembly to instruct member states to break diplomatic relations with Spain. This motion was carried but some Latin American states, comprising of Argentina – which took the lead – Paraguay, Peru, Brazil and Colombia defied the recommendation and in May 1949 these nations called for a withdrawal of the 1946 resolution. Their request was defeated but notably the US and Britain abstained from the vote. The 1946 resolution was finally revoked in October 1950 and among Latin American nations only Guatemala, Uruguay and Mexico voted in favour of its retention. Britain and the US, who again abstained from the vote, sent their ambassadors to Madrid the following March. See George Hills, *Franco the Man and his Nation*, London, Hale, 1967, pp. 407–10.

2   Although strategic and political concerns were the main reasons why the US opened official diplomatic channels with Franco's Spain, one must also acknowledge the influence of a pro-Spanish lobby which had been at work in the US since the end of the war. This pro-Franco group were well organised and employed a professional American lobbyist. The 'lobby's' first significant success was in 1951 when it played a key role in persuading the Truman administration to sanction a \$62 million Export-Import Bank loan to Spain. The activities of the 'Spanish lobby' are dealt with in Ronald F. Hadian, 'United States Foreign Policy Towards Spain: 1953–1970', unpublished Ph.D. thesis, University of California, Santa Barbara, 1976, pp. 25–9.

3   Basic details of the Bases Pact are given in Benjamin Welles, *Spain: the Gentle Anarchy*, London, Pall Mall Press, 1965, pp. 286–312. A more controversial and penetrating study, which also includes an account of the developments which preceded the negotiations as well as details of the 'Pact', is Angel Viñas, *Los pactos secretos de Franco con Estados Unidos: bases, ayuda económica, recortes de soberania*, Barcelona, Grijalbo, 1981. Bases were built at Rota (Cadíz, navy), Torrejón de Ardoz (Madrid, air force), Morón de la Frontera (Seville, air force), and Zaragoza (army). Several other centres were also established to provide services and gather intelligence.

4   A list of all US government loans to Spain between 1953 and 1957 is to be found in R.J. Harrison, *The Spanish Economy in the Twentieth Century*, London, Croom Helm, 1985, p. 133. Harrison notes that private US banks were making loans to Spain as early as January 1949, with the tacit approval of Washington, p. 126.

5   A good analysis of Spanish capitalism during the first twenty years of the Franco dictatorship is Joan Clavera *et al.*, *Capitalismo español: de la autarquía a la estabilización, 1939–1959*, Madrid, Edicusa, 1978. For a study of Spanish fascism, and the divisions within the movement, in the late-1950s and early-1960s, see Sheelagh M. Ellwood, *Spanish Fascism in the Franco Era: Falange Española de las Jons, 1936–76*, Basingstoke, Macmillan Press Ltd., 1987, pp. 118–61.

6   This view is put forward by Charles W. Anderson, in *The Political Economy of Modern Spain*, University of Wisconsin Press, 1970, p. 92.

7   For a comprehensive study of Spain's economic development during this period see Sima Lieberman, *The Contemporary Spanish Economy*, London, Allen and Unwin, 1982, Chapter IV, 'The Spanish Industrial Revolution of the 1960s', pp. 199–264.

8   Statistical data on these three sources of finance are given in R.J. Harrison, *The Spanish Economy in the Twentieth Century*, pp. 154–57.

9   These inequalities are described poignantly by Max Gallo in *Spain Under Franco: a History*, London, Allen and Unwin, 1972.

10   A table listing foreign investments in Spain during the period of the 'economic miracle' is to be found in J. Muñoz *et al.*, *La economía española*, Madrid, Edicusa, 1973, p. 361.

11   Calculations based on statistics supplied in *España: anuario de estadística*, 1961, 1964, 1967 and 1970, which give figures for three years before the date of publication and therefore together cover the 1960s. Those nations which occupied fifth to eleventh place in Spain's league of trading partners in the 1960s were, Italy (5.5%), Holland (3.4%), Saudi Arabia (2.8%), Switzerland (2.6%), Sweden (2.4%), Belgium and Luxembourg (2.2%), Argentina (2.1%).

12   See *España: anuario de estadística*, 1960–69.

13   The most comprehensive analysis of Spain's commercial relations with the US in the 1950s is to be found in Angel Viñas *et al.*, *Política comercial exterior de España (1931–1975)*, 2 vols, I (Madrid, 1979), pp. 741–849.

14   In his dissertation entitled *United States Foreign Policy Towards Spain: 1953–1970* Hadian suggests a number of reasons, besides the direct interdependence created by the Bases Pact, why Spain was often able to manipulate its superpower ally to its advantage. The two most important of these were, he argues, firstly, the 'Cold-War anti-communist syndrome' which canalised and blunted American foreign policy. Consequently some less important allies like Spain only attracted serious attention from US policymakers when they became components in a wider strategy. Allies in this position often found themselves with a free hand in much of their decision-making, and even when they played a role in a major aspect of US policy they were occasionally able to anticipate and take advantage of this process. Secondly, Spain, along with some other small powers, has utilised divisions within the American bureaucracy to achieve its objectives. Spain in particular was able to cultivate important contacts in the American military establishment, pp. 1–12. Hadian claims the 'analytical framework' on which these hypotheses are based is derived from Robert Keohane's article 'The Big Influence of Small Allies', *Foreign Policy*, Spring, 1971, pp. 161–182.

15   The circumstances in which the Spanish Ambassador, Juan Pablo de Lojendio, Marquis of Vellisca, was expelled were unusually dramatic: during a live television and radio broadcast which was being given by Castro the Cuban leader implied that the Spanish Ambassador – who was known to have falangist sympathies – was involved in counter-revolutionary activities in Cuba. Incensed by this accusation the Ambassador made his way to the television company and demanded an immediate 'right to reply', when this was refused he burst into the studio from where Castro was making the broadcast and challenged the Premier to his face while he was still on the air. During the fiasco which followed President Osvaldo Dorticós, who was also present, declared the Ambassador 'persona non grata', and gave him 24 hours

to leave the country. The most comprehensive report on the incident, and its possible implications for Spanish-Cuban relations, is to be found in the Spanish commercial and foreign affairs journal *SP* (Revista de información mundial), 25 January 1965, pp. 15–19. See also the Spanish daily *ABC*, 22 January 1960, p. 1., and R. Hart Phillips, 'Castro in Clash Ousts Spanish Aide', *New York Times*, 21 January 1960, pp. 1 and 12.

16 *ABC* has always been regarded as Spain's leading monarchist newspaper, but it rarely challenged the policies of the Franco dictatorship and indeed lent its wholehearted support to the government on most issues.

17 In the same article in which these statements were published Castro is also reported to have talked of the 'crimes and murders of Franco', *Revolución*, 11 August 1960, p. 6.

18 See Richard Eder, 'Cuba Church Group Departs for Spain', *New York Times*, 14 May 1961, p. 27.

19 See Richard Eder, 'Havana Deports 135 Priests and Accused Bishop to Spain', *New York Times*, 18 September 1961, pp. 1 and 16.

20 See 'Obispo expulsado de Cuba', *ABC*, 19 September 1961, p. 31.

21 See Benjamin Welles, 'Anti-Franco Plot is Laid to Cubans', *New York Times*, 22 January 1961, p. 28. Apparently this new organisation replaced Revolutionary Directorate for the Liberation of the Iberian Peninsula (DRIL) which had existed since the 1940s. These events were not reported in the Spanish press because of the censorship of the media under Franco, which exclude all references to any forces which might threaten the government.

22 See Tad Szulc, 'Ex-Soviet General Said to Aid Castro', *New York Times*, 6 March 1962, pp. 1 and 5. Lister was in fact not linked to any organisation in Cuba dedicated to the overthrow of Franco but had been sent by the Soviet Union to train Cuban army officers in the use of advanced Russian and Czechoslovakian military equipment and the techniques of modern warfare. This was a particularly important task because the officers who were selected for training were the most trusted revolutionaries, whose only practical military experience had been in guerrilla warfare. Though Lister was apparently not engaged in anti-Franco activities while in Cuba, Madrid felt uneasy that the Spanish Republic's most successful general during the Civil War, and subsequently the organiser of many plots against the Franco government, should be given a high military office in Cuba.

23 Alberto Recarte, *Cuba: economía y poder* (1959–1980), Alianza, Madrid, 1980, p. 164.

24 For this and all other statements in the chapter which refer to Cuba's annual trade with Spain, Britain or France, but are not supported by relevant figures see Appendix I, p. 342, which includes data for the period 1957–1975.

25 See Appendix, p. 342.

26 *Ibid.*

27 Lieberman, *The Contemporary Spanish Economy*, p. 231.

28 Calculation based on figures given in the *Estadística de comercio exterior de España*, 1960–69.

29 Calculations based on figures given in the *Annual Statement of Trade of the United Kingdom*, 1960–69, and *Statistiques du Commerce Exterieur de la France*, 1960–69.

30 *Estadística de comercio exterior de España*, 1964, 1965 and 1966. The 1966 volume includes two useful pie charts, expressed in pesetas, of Spain's trade with the rest of the world, p. XXIII.

31   Between 1954 and 1957 Spain's main imports and exports, in order of import-
     ance according to their monetary value, were as follows:

Imports	Exports
1) oil and its derivatives	1) iron ore
2) machinery	2) oranges and mandarins
3) raw cotton	3) petrol and diesel oil
4) vegetable oil	4) olive oil
5) unworked iron and steel	5) wine
6) wheat	6) olives
7) motor cars	7) preserved fruit, beans, and vegetables
8) electrical machinery	8) books

Source: *España: anuario de estadística*, 1955–58

32   For a short analysis of the composition of Spain's foreign trade in the 1960s,
     see Lieberman, *The Contemporary Spanish Economy*, pp. 227–29.

33   *Estadística de comercio exterior de España*, 1955–59.

34   *Estadística de comercio exterior de España*, 1960–64.

35   *Estadística de comercio exterior de España*, 1960–69. In comparison British
     imports in the 1960s totalled $153 billion, while exports less invisibles stood
     at $129 billion, which represented a far more balanced trading ratio than the
     one sustained by Spain during the same period. Calculation based on figures
     given in the *Annual Abstract of Statistics*, No. 106, (1969), p. 234, No. 107
     (1970), p. 242.

36   Among these two sources of finance tourism was by far the most important
     and earned for Spain in the 1960s $7.7 billion. See Harrison, *The Spanish
     Economy in the Twentieth Century*, for statistics on Spain's tourist trade in the
     1960s, p. 155. Receipts from remittances from Spaniards working abroad are
     more difficult to calculate but were probably in excess of $1.5 billion for the
     period.

37   For data on Spanish imports of Cuban sugar in the last two decades of the
     nineteenth century and the second half of the twentieth see *The World Sugar
     Economy in Figures, 1880–1959*, FAO. An annual listing of Cuban sugar
     production from 1770 to 1970 is given in Hugh Thomas, *Cuba: or The Pursuit
     of Freedom*, London, Eyre and Spottiswode, 1971, pp. 1560–64.

38   For all of the 1950s Spanish sugar imports remained below 50,000 except for
     1958 when they rose to 150,000 tonnes. In this year pre-revolutionary Cuba
     was the main supplier. Other main sources included Czechoslovakia, Poland
     and Mexico, all arch enemies of Franco but they seemed to have little com-
     punction in supplying his government with an essential commodity. See
     International Sugar Council, *Sugar Year Book*, 1960 for a breakdown of
     Spanish sugar imports by country in 1958.

39   Figures for Spanish sugar production, imports and consumption in the 1960s
     are taken from the International Sugar Council, *Sugar Year Book*, 1966 and
     1970 which together supply data to cover the decade. For a listing of such data
     and other relevant statistics on the Spanish sugar market in the 1960s see
     Appendix II, p. 344.

40   Recarte, *Cuba: economía y poder* (1950–80), pp. 162–63. The usual proce-
     dure for operating a clearing system is for each country's national bank to

open an account in the other's name. The value of all trade between the two countries is recorded by the banks, which at the end of the year draw up a balance. Whichever country is in debt can either pay the difference in hard currency or incorporate the sum owed into the next year's trading account, or a combination of the two options, depending on the nature of the bilateral agreement. To operate the financial side of this system the parties involved rarely use their own currency to make the necessary calculations, but rather a major world currency like the US dollar, (in Spain's transactions with Cuba the Canadian dollar was used) the value of which fluctuates independently of the performance of their own economies.

41 Recarte, p. 161.

42 See Appendix II, p. 344, for data on Spanish sugar imports. During the 1950s Cuba was Spain's main supplier of sugar. See *Sugar Year Book*, 1960, which gives data back to 1954.

43 In 1961 Spain imported 53,000 tonnes of sugar from Cuba at an average price per pound (imperial) of 4 US cents. In 1962 the average price paid for the year fell to 3.5 cents per pound but in 1963 Spain had to pay on average for the year over 9.0 cents per pound. Calculation based on import quantities and prices given in the *Estadística de comercio de España* for relevant years. Average world market prices for these years were: 1961 – 2.75 cents, 1962 – 2.83 cents, 1963 – 8.34 cents.

44 For details of the contract see Recarte, p. 166.

45 See 'Comprará España 100,000 toneladas anuales de azúcar durante 3 años', *Noticias de Hoy*, 17 November 1963, p. 3.

46 These prices are given in 'Cuba Reported Ordering Halt in Buying Abroad', *New York Times*, 22 August 1964, p. 10.

47 Average yearly prices for raw sugar (No. 4 World Contract f.a.s. Cuba) from 1952–66 are to be found in the International Sugar Council, *Sugar Year Book*, 1966, p. 355.

48 For details of the Soviet-Cuban sugar agreements in the 1960s see Jorge F. Perez-Lopez, 'Cuban-Soviet Sugar Trade: Price and Subsidy Issues', *Bulletin of Latin America Research*, Vol. 7, No. 1, 1988, pp. 123–47 (pp. 124–27).

49 A possible indication of Cuba's delight in 1964 at having capitalist Spain tied to a contract to pay over 9 cents a pound for sugar when the world price was slipping below 6 cents, was when in that year the Castro government decided to break its ban on the import of luxury goods and place large orders for Spanish wine and spirits. These orders were also accompanied by reassurances from Havana that Cuba would remain a reliable market for these Spanish products, see Recarte, p. 167.

50 The signing of the contract was given brief coverage in the Cuban press, see 'Renuevan acuerdo comercial por un año Cuba y España', *Noticias de Hoy*, 10 February 1965, p. 1. The report points out that the negotiations took place in Madrid, and that the Cuban delegation was headed by the Director of Commerce for Europe, Raúl Roa Kouri. The Spanish negotiating team was led by Carlos Gamir the Director of Bilateral Economic Relations. For details of the contract see Recarte, p. 168.

51 Part of this process of modernisation included the influx into Spain of several million high sugar consuming Northern European tourists every summer. This not only increased the demand for sugar generally but also, because of the importance of the tourist industry to Spain, made a reliable and stable external supply of sugar even more important.

52   For a survey of sugar production in Spain in the 1960s, see 'La dulce vida', *SP*, no. 214, 15 July 1963, pp. 41–5.

53   *Ibid.*, p. 44.

54   Besides the problem of increased labour costs small sugar farmers were also forced to sell their sugar beet to the state for a fixed price of 975 pesetas per tonne. While this price had provided an incentive to farmers to expand sugar production in 1957 when it was set, by the 1960s as costs increased it had the opposite effect, except for large producers who were able to cut costs.

55   Average annual world market sugar prices from 1965–69 (1965–67 No. 4 World Contract f.a.s. Cuba, from 1968 International Sugar Agreement price) were: 1965 – 2.03 cents per pound, 1966 – 1.76 cts.lb, 1967 – 1.93 cts.lb, 1968 – 1.90 cts.lb, 1969 – 3.2 cts.lb. *Sugar Year Book*, 1966 and 1973.

56   See Appendix II, p. 344, for quantities produced in Spanish sugar harvests in the 1960s.

57   Recarte, p. 170.

58   See, 'Cuba Frees Nine Spaniards', *New York Times*, 14 August 1966, p. 26. The remainder of the Spanish prisoners which were held on charges of political subversion (about 24 in number) had to wait until 1974 before another attempt was made to secure their release.

59   See Recarte for full details of the contract, p. 174.

60   During the 1950s Franco frequently acknowledged the important role the US was playing in Spain, and occasionally openly expressed his gratitude to Washington. For example in 1959 after the US granted a large credit to Spain and approved an Import-Export Bank loan, he sent a profuse message of thanks to Eisenhower through the Spanish Ambassador in Washington. See Max Gallo, *Spain Under Franco*, p. 266.

61   Spanish foreign policy during the 1960s is dealt with most comprehensively by Benny Pollack, *The Paradox of Spanish Foreign Policy: Spain's International Relation's from Franco to Democracy*, London, Pinter, 1987, see especially Chapters 3–5, pp. 47–128.

62   During the second half of the 1950s and the 1960s Spain's trade with the EEC and Great Britain expanded considerably. By the mid-1960s the EEC replaced the US as Spain's main export market. Between 1958–65 Spain's exports to the US fell from 24 to 17 per cent of total exports, while its exports to the EEC expanded in value from $186 million to $937 million, or from 21 to 37 per cent of all exports (Hadian, p. 53). Spain's export to import ratio with the EEC and Great Britain was, however, nearly as poor as it was with the US during this period and as Morris H. Morley (*Imperial State and Revolution: The United States and Cuba, 1952–1986*, Cambridge, C.U.P., 1987) points out, if one takes the decade of the 1960s as a whole the performance of Spanish exports as a percentage of its total trade with the region did in fact decline (p. 225). One must take into account, though, when making such calculations that if one includes Spain's invisible earnings from Europe in the form of tourism, then its trade with the region as a whole was probably in the black from the early-1960s onwards. Spain's trade with Latin America in the 1960s, though small compared to its trade with the US and Europe during the same period, was impressive if seen in terms of exports to the region which rose from 7 to 12 per cent of total Spanish exports during the decade. Calculation based on trade figures given in *Anuario de estadística*, 1961, 1966 and 1970.

63   The extent of the Franco government's interest in France during de Gaulle's period in office can perhaps best be gauged by consulting the Spanish press in

the 1960s. For example between 1961 and 1966 Spain's main newspapers (all of which supported the government despite their identification with different political groups) including the Monarchist *ABC*, the Falangist *Arriba* and *Pueblo*, and the commercial and foreign affairs journal *SP*, which reflected the views of Opus Dei, all carried information on France, and especially French foreign policy, in almost every issue. The treatment of de Gaulle's policies in all these publications was nearly always sympathetic, and occasionally laudatory. See, for example, the article 'Los dos hombres del año, de Gaulle y "El Cordobés" ' (*SP*, No. 249, 1 January 1965, pp. 15–20) in which de Gaulle and the great bullfighter "El Cordobés" are praised in equally glowing terms for their respective achievements.

64 Some support for this view can be found in the Spanish press during 1964, the year de Gaulle visited Latin America. From February when the visit was announced through to September when it took place, *ABC* reported every development and incident relating to the trip, and while de Gaulle was in Latin America the coverage was more comprehensive than in the French press. Of the many articles that were written during this period, Spain's possible future role in Latin America as part of a French-led 'new deal' for the region was often discussed. See, for example, the *ABC* editorial entitled 'Pleno acuerdo en las conversaciones entre de Gaulle y Erhard' which deals with the agreement between the West German Chancellor and de Gaulle concerning a joint aid programme for Latin America (16 February 1964, p. 71). See also the extraordinary article by Pedro Massa, 'De Gaulle se prepara a conquistar Hispanoamérica' which is more sanguine about the outcome of the visit than even the Gaullist press in France, and contains the statement 'Europa se prepara para hacer el redescubrimiento de nuestra América', *ABC*, 22 February 1964, pp. 55–6 (p. 55).

65 France also saw Spain as a potentially important supplier of natural uranium for use in its expanding nuclear power programme. With this objective in mind the French Foreign Minister Couve de Murville visited Madrid in May 1964, and after a series of negotiations a contract was signed to build a Spanish-French nuclear power station in the south of France which would use Spanish uranium. See Welles, *Spain: the Gentle Anarchy*, p. 270. The previous year France had given the first indication of its willingness to improve relations with Spain by providing export credits to the Franco government for a number of industrial projects. The most important of these was a joint Spanish-French venture to build a natural gas pipeline from Algeria to Spain. See *New York Times*, 11 November 1963, p. 11.

66 See Welles, p. 271.

67 This view is most convincingly argued by J. Lee Schneidman in J.W. Cortada (ed.), *Spain In the Twentieth Century: Essays on Spanish Diplomacy 1898–1978*, London, Aldwych, 1980, p. 155.

68 A study of the development of Spanish-Soviet relations in the 1960s and 1970s is in Pollack, *The Paradox of Spanish Foreign Policy*, pp. 63–8.

69 In 1985 Castro acknowledged Cuba's debt to Franco with the words 'Franco no se portó mal, hay que reconocerlo. Pese a las presiones que tuvo, no rompió las relaciones diplomáticas y comerciales con nosotros. No tocar a Cuba fue su frase terminante. El gallego supo habérselas. Que se portó bien, caramba', 'Declaraciones a EL PAIS de Fidel Castro', *El Pais*, 20 January 1985, (p. 4). Castro visited his father's birthplace in Galicia in 1992 and also addressed the Meeting of Latin American Heads of State in Madrid.

70   Author's correspondence with Wayne Smith.

71   See for example Guy Bueno, ' "The New York Times" defiende el supuesto propósito español de negociar con Cuba y la URSS', *Arriba*, 7 February 1964, p. 13. To ensure that none of its readers would suspect that *Arriba*, or the government, were making any concessions to either socialist state the main heading was followed immediately with the words 'These initiatives do not imply in any way a softening of the ideological opposition of General Franco against communism' (author's translation).

72   Besides ideological differences there were also important practical factors which prevented the formation of more convivial relations between Franco's Spain and the Soviet Union. Firstly, over 500 tons of Spanish gold remained in Soviet possession which had been transferred to Moscow during the Civil War when it appeared that Nationalist forces might capture Madrid. In reality Stalin had seen this transfer as a part payment for Soviet aid to the Republic; a view which was shared by his successors. Secondly, Spain's willingness to allow US Polaris equipped submarines to use its naval base at Rota was an affront to Soviet policy on denuclearisation of the Mediterranean.

73   There are also some indications that the Cuban Ambassador to Moscow played an important role in helping to improve Spanish-Soviet relations, see Pollack, *The Paradox of Spanish Foreign Policy*, p. 55. See also the *New York Times*, 6 June 1963, p. 10.

74   It should be pointed out, however, that while Spain increased its trade with Cuba with impunity in the early-1960s, it was heedful not to antagonise the US in other matters concerning Cuba. For example the Spanish cabinet gave fulsome support to the Kennedy administration during the missile crisis (See *New York Times*, 27 October 1962, p. 9). In July 1963 Spain also took the precaution of seeking the advice of the US before acting on plans to increase its shipping to Cuba (*New York Times*, 12 July 1963, p. 7). A similar consultation took place at the same time regarding plans for additional flights between Madrid and Havana (*New York Times*, 13 July 1963, p. 7). In 1962 and 1963 Spain did in fact cut back on its shipping links with Cuba partly in response to US directives (Recarte, pp. 165–6).

75   Details of the renegotiation of the Bases Pact are given in Hadian, pp. 55–8.

76   The precise wording of the most important sections of the agreement are given by Sam Pope Brewer 'Spain and US Extending Bases Pact for Five Years', *New York Times*, 27 September 1963, pp. 1–2.

77   Garrigues' statements concerning his proposed negotiating stance were published in the *New York Times*, 20 March 1963, p. 2.

78   For the Spanish response to the agreement see the editorial entitled 'Renovación del convenio defensivo Hispano-Norteamericano por cinco años', *ABC*, 27 September 1963, pp. 31–3. The tenor of the article is summed up by the statement 'we have passed on from collaboration from necessity in 1953 to cordial co-operation in 1963' (p. 31). Even the Falangist press, which had been critical in the past of US influence in Spain, hailed the agreement as a success, stating 'we march on to vast new horizons', see *Arriba*, 27 September 1963, p. 1. A good independent analysis of the implications of the agreement for both sides is Hugh Thomas, 'The Balance of Forces in Spain', *Foreign Affairs*, October, 1962, pp. 215–24.

79   See 'Nueva entrega franquista a EE.UU', *Revolución*, 27 September 1963. Interestingly Cuban scepticism was shared by sections of the US press which expressed the view that Spain had gained little from the negotiations, see for

example the *New York Times* editorial on 2 October 1963 entitled 'Keeping the Spanish Bases', p. 40. In particular it was pointed out that the new joint consultative committee, that had been established to give Spain more influence over US military decisions at the bases, had in fact been meeting informally since 1953. The editorial also argued that the Import-Export Bank loan which had been granted to Spain as part of the agreement could not be regarded as a concession because Spain was entirely credit worthy.

80   In a sympathetic editorial the *New York Times* acknowledged the importance of this aspect of Spain's relations with Cuba stating, 'So far as Cuba is concerned, the United States would do well to remember the special and powerful sentimental and racial ties between the "Mother Country" and her lost island. Cuba is culturally Spanish. There are between 40,000 and 50,000 Spanish nationals in Cuba today. Hardly a Spanish family is without relatives in Cuba and vice-versa'. See 'Spain, the USSR and Cuba', 5 February 1964, p. 34.

81   This amendment to the Foreign Assistance Act is mentioned with reference to Spain in Tad Szulc 'Spain is Cautioned by US On Rise in Cuban Trade', *New York Times* 21 December 1963, pp. 1 and 7.

82   Hadian suggests that $100 million in military aid was promised to Spain by the US as part of the contract for the renewal of the Bases Pact which was signed in 1963. This sum apparently was contingent on Spain purchasing $50 million in additional military equipment. See *United States Foreign Policy Towards Spain: 1953–1976*, p. 58.

83   See Tad Szulc 'Spain is Cautioned by US On Rise in Cuban Trade', p. 1.

84   The resumption of Spanish air links with Cuba was reported in *ABC*, 4 November 1962, p. 39.

85   Recarte, p. 165.

86   In a dispatch sent in January 1964 by the US State Department to the American Embassy in Madrid, Spain was described as 'stand[ing] out among free-world countries in that, according to present data, all indicies of economic ties with Cuba, except shipping, moved up [between 1962 and 1963]. See Morley, *Imperial State and Revolution*, p. 225.

87   Morley, p. 226. Morley cites as his source Vincent J. Burke, 'US Studies Policy on Cuban Traders', *Washington Post*, 15 February 1964, p. A13.

88   Even after the US had passed the amendment to the Foreign Assistance Act demanding that other non-communist countries cut off all transportation links with Cuba, Iberia were still putting full page advertisements in the Spanish national press for their flights to Latin America, including Cuba. See for example *ABC*, 22 December 1963, p. 34.

89   An indication of the ineffectiveness of the new US legislation can be gauged from the fact that in 1963, before the new ruling came into effect, 358 ships from non-communist countries were involved in trade with Cuba, in 1964 this number had risen to 383, see Morley p. 374. Among European countries Britain was the worst offender with respectively 133 and 188 ships calling at Cuban ports in 1963 and 1964. In comparison only 9 Spanish ships were engaged in trade with Cuba in 1963 and 17 in 1964. But after 1964 Spanish ships ceased to engage in Cuba trade and only resumed again in 1975. During the second half of the decade the number of non-communist vessels sailing to Cuba declined because of improved implementation of the US policy of blacklisting ships that called at Cuban ports. Once a ship was on the blacklist it, and all other vessels in its owner's fleet, were prohibited from carrying

American government financed cargoes.

90   See Tad Szulc, 'US Curtails Aid to Five Countries That Sell to Cuba', *New York Times*, 19 February 1964, pp. 1–2. Apparently fourteen countries were deemed by the State Department to have taken 'appropriate steps' to curb their transportation links with Cuba and were therefore exempted from the action, p. 1. Among these fourteen were the Lebanon, Greece, Italy and Norway, all of which appear in reality to have taken little heed of Washington's call and continued to send their ships to Cuba throughout 1964. Indeed, Lebanon's share of non-communist shipping trading with Cuba increased from 18 per cent in 1963 to 24 per cent in 1964.

91   See José Maria Massip, 'Mensaje del Jefe del Estado español al Presidente Johnson', *ABC*, 13 February 1964, p. 47.

92   Author's translation of a section from an article entitled, 'La actual política Norteamericana empuja a Fidel Castro hacia Moscú', *Arriba*, 22 December 1963, p. 13.

93   *ABC* editorial, 13 February 1964, p. 50.

94   See José María Massip, 'Las relaciónes entre España y los Estados Unidos son de la máxima importancia para la estabilidad occidental', *ABC*, 14 February 1964, p. 31.

95   See José María Massip, 'Confusión, incertidumbre y contradicciones en torno a la suspensión de la asistencia exterior', *ABC*, 29 February 1964, p. 31.

96   Castro's statements are included in José María Massip, 'Agudas divergencias entre Estados Unidos e Hispanoamerica sobre Cuba', *ABC*, 25 February 1964, p. 31. The Falangist newspaper *Arriba* also cited Castro's comments on the same day.

97   See 'España reitera su posición ante los Estados Unidos respecto a nuestros relaciones con Cuba', *ABC*, 22 February 1964, pp. 55–7.

98   As Hadian points out though, the Americans could equally claim that by trading with Cuba, Spain itself had violated the 'spirit' and 'intent' of the Pact of which Article IV of the original agreement stated 'Spain will co-operate with the Government of the United States in taking measures designed to control trade with nations which threaten the maintenance of world peace'. The 1963 agreement extended Article IV. See *United States Foreign Policy Towards Spain: 1953–1970*, p. 152.

99   For an analysis of the benefits which would be afforded to the US if it stationed its nuclear submarines at Rota, see Guy Bueno, 'Nuevas negociaciones Hispano-Norte-Americanas sobre la base naval de Rota', *Arriba*, 21 December 1963, p. 1. These included, it was suggested: an excellent strategic location giving access to both the South Atlantic as well as the Mediterranean; improved ability to police political instability in any of the numerous countries bordering on the Mediterranean; provide compensation for the Jupiter missiles which were being withdrawn from Italy and Turkey, and for bases which were to be vacated in Morocco.

100   The former ambassador in question was Sr. Rosendo Canto Hernández, who, after Castro came to power became editor of the journal *Acción Cubana* which was the organ of anti-Castro Cuban refugees in Spain. His wife, Sra. Juana Maria de Gregorio de Canto was a former national secretary of the Franco government's student organisation. This information was supplied to the author during a conversation with Cuban expatriates at the 'Centro Cubano de España' in Madrid in 1988.

101   This letter had been sent initially to *El Español* but the journal had only

published a few selected sentences. Dissatisfied with this response the author made the contents of the letter available to the international press.

102 See for example 'Spain is Denounced for Policy on Cuba', *New York Times*, 23 January 1964, p. 3.

103 See Appendix I, p. 342.

104 The State Department begrudgingly acknowledged that they could only exert 'limited' pressure on the Franco government to cease its trade with Cuba because of America's 'national security' interests in Spain. See Jack Raymond, 'US Acts to Avoid Halt in Aid to Spain Despite Cuba Trade', *New York Times*, 23 February 1964, pp. 1 and 8.

105 Cited by Tad Szulc, in 'Foreign Aid Curb to Exempt Spain', *New York Times*, 26 February 1964, p. 14.

106 Reported in 'Spain to Cut Back Air Cargo to Cuba', *New York Times*, 3 March 1964, p. 14.

107 For a comprehensive report on the incident see 'USA, imponente en la policía de los mares', *SP*, No. 243, 1 October 1964, pp. 15–19.

108 See 'Spanish Marchers Denounce the US', *New York Times*, 20 September 1964, p. 33.

109 See 'USA imponente en la policía de los mares', *SP*, p. 18.

110 A comprehensive account of the Palomares incident is given by Christopher Morris, *The Day They Lost the H-Bomb*, New York, Coward-McCann, 1966, see especially pp. 22–37. See also the Spanish, American and Cuban press from 18 January 1966 to April 1966 for numerous articles on the incident.

111 In 1974 a survey was conducted of the long-term effect of the Palomares incident on Spanish public opinion towards the US bases. This resulted in 48 per cent of Spaniards that were interviewed saying the bases should be removed from Spanish territory. Only 16 per cent felt they should stay, and the remaining 36 per cent gave no reply. See Hadian, pp. 88–91.

112 For details of the agreement see the *New York Times*, 7 August 1970, pp. 1 and 2.

113 See Hadian, p. 132. This statement was made in a personal letter sent by Dean Rusk to Hadian, 1 September 1976.

114 Although the Palomares incident strengthened Spain's hand in its negotiations with the US, it should be pointed out that from the mid-1960s onwards the American Air Force bases in Spain started to lose their strategic importance as America began to rely more heavily on ground and sea launched missiles as a means of delivering nuclear warheads rather than bombers. The Polaris base at Rota, however, possibly became more valuable to the US because of this changing strategy.

115 'El mercado de los 300 milliones', *SP*, No. 220, 15 October 1963, pp. 9–10 (p. 9).

116 See 'Puente entre Europa y América', No. 222, 15 November 1963, pp. 9–10 (p. 9).

117 See 'España debe ingresar en la ALALC', *SP*, No. 222, 15 November 1963, pp. 11–15.

CHAPTER 9

Western Europe and Cuba in the 1970s: The boom years

George Lambie

Introduction

Although Cuba attracted much international attention in the 1960s, concrete information on the island's relations with Western European countries is hard to find and often unreliable. Unfortunately this problem increases as one extends research on this topic into the 1970s, because once Washington's allies had established a precedent for successful breaches of the US economic blockade of Cuba in the 1960s, the continuation of such acts of defiance into the 1970s was taken for granted by the international press. Even the North American press, which had been extraordinarily sensitive to Western European-Cuban relations in the 1960s, only commented on the most controversial issues after the early-1970s. Generally during its second decade the Cuban Revolution attracted far less international attention than it had in the 1960s.

Given the above constraints on the study of Western European-Cuban commercial relations in the 1970s, this chapter will concentrate on trends in the international economy which affected Cuba's trading position with capitalist powers, and place less emphasis on the Castro government's commercial relations with individual firms and countries than in the chapters on the 1960s.

Consistent with Cuban history of the previous two hundred years, during the 1970s the market price of sugar played a crucial role in determining the island's fortunes. This chapter begins therefore with a short analysis of Cuba's sugar policy since the early years of the Revolution, and shows how by the mid-1970s the Castro government was able to take full advantage of temporarily high sugar prices to boost economic development. This will be followed by brief assessments of Cuba's trade with individual Western European countries in the 1970s.

A further trend which will be explored is the effect of changes within US capitalism in the late-1960s and 1970s on America's economic and political relations with the rest of the world, and the consequences of these developments for Cuba and Cuba's relations with Western Europe and Japan. One of the most important repercussions of the restructuring of US capitalism was its influence on the world's financial markets. In the 1970s, this restructuring, combined with the OPEC oil price rises, allowed commercial banks to channel billions of dollars in credit and loans to the Third World and the socialist countries including Cuba. This marked the beginning of a new kind of relationship between Cuba and Western Europe, which integrated the Revolution even more closely with America's capitalist competitors than had the bilateral trade deals of the 1960s.

By analysing the above trends it will be shown that Cuba's economic and political development in the 1970s was shaped not only by changes in domestic policies and the strengthening of its relations with the Soviet Union, but also by the convulsions within international capitalism during the decade.

Cuban sugar policy and the world sugar market 1959–75

When the revolutionaries of the Castro generation came to power in 1959 they took over a country whose economic and social potential had been distorted and under-utilised for four and a half centuries; first, under Spanish colonialism, and then from the beginning of the twentieth century by US imperialism. The avowed aim of these young revolutionaries was to break from this stultifying legacy by installing economic and social mechanisms which would allow Cuba to become master of its own destiny.

Against enormous odds, among which the most debilitating were: the flight of many members of the professional middle classes to the US, the lack of experience of the revolutionary leaders, the US embargo and US aggression, and the legacy of social and economic underdevelopment itself, Cuba's new leadership embarked on a series of audacious experiments which they believed would transform their country and its people.

In the sphere of economics the most important debate centred on industrialisation. Guevara and his followers argued that for centuries Cuba had been prevented from pursuing a strategy of integrated economic development, because it was of greater value to its colonial and imperialist masters as a producer of one commodity, sugar. Guevara argued that Cuba should gradually disengage from sugar production and concentrate on building an industrial base, which he believed was essential to sustain the Revolution and provide the appropriate environment for the construction of a socialist society.

By 1963 this policy became increasingly difficult to sustain because of mounting internal and external pressures.[1] Externally two factors in particular impeded Cuba's attempts to industrialise. First, because of the US embargo, Cuba lost its access to North American manufactures and technology, on which most of its economy was based. Second, the transition from North American to Soviet bloc technology was fraught with problems. Primarily Soviet equipment was of inferior quality and unsuitable in many Cuban applications.[2] This meant that if Cuba wanted to sustain a programme of industrial and infrastructural development it would need to supplement Soviet imports with purchases of appropriate equipment from capitalist suppliers. Such equipment, however, had to be bought with hard currency which Cuba could only obtain in any quantity by selling its traditional export crop, sugar, in capitalist markets. The exception being the bilateral trading agreements based on clearing which it negotiated with Spain in the 1960s and 1970s, in which sugar and other Cuban products were exchanged for Spanish industrial goods.

Consequently, as the sugar price began to rise in 1963 – partly because Cuba had re-directed most of its sugar exports from the US and the world market to the Soviet Union in the previous three years – the Cuban leadership was obliged to reconsider its strategy of direct import substitution and the running down of sugar production. Although sugar monoculture had been identified as the cause of the backwardness and distortion of the Cuban economy in the past, it was begrudgingly accepted by the Revolutionary government that the sugar industry would have to be adapted to serve the Revolution's immediate needs rather than allowed to decline. A policy to expand sugar production was initiated in 1963, and in 1964 exports were increased to capitalist markets. Because of this policy Cuba was able to improve its hard currency earnings and gain access to vital industrial goods from market economies. This, along with its stabilising commercial relations with the Soviet bloc based on the exchange of sugar for Soviet technology and assistance, encouraged the Cubans to seek to further exploit their comparative advantage as sugar producers. From 1965 Cuba became fully committed to a strategy of export-led economic growth in which the earnings from a dynamic and expanding sugar sector would finance industrialisation in other sectors of the economy, and indeed the sugar sector itself, which could only be made more efficient through increased mechanisation.

Between 1964 and 1966 one could argue that the strategies of industrialisation and expanding sugar exports ran in tandem with some success, but by 1966 when the sugar price reached its lowest ebb for over a decade Cuba was forcefully reminded of its continuing status as a Third World exporter whose fate is determined by the vagaries of the world commodity markets. Cuba's response to low market prices was to increase production not only to ensure that it continued to provide a reliable supply to its socialist and other bilateral trading partners who were paying higher than market prices, but also to use its 'comparative advantage' as a sugar producer to strengthen its position in the sugar market. In the medium term it was believed that high levels of Cuban sugar production would possibly force some marginal producers out of business which would leave Cuba with greater sway in the world sugar market in future years. The results of this strategy are difficult to assess but expanding sugar production in Brazil and the EEC must have reduced its impact.

Cuba's policy of expanding sugar production was taken to its limits in 1969–70 with the drive to produce 10 million tons in the 1970 harvest. The failure to attain this target, by a shortfall of 1.5 million tons, was not only an embarrassment for the revolutionary leadership but also highlighted all the limitations and problems of pushing the theory of comparative advantage and export-led growth to extremes.[3] Even after ten years of socialist revolution, in which many of the evils of the past had been eliminated, sugar had again succeeded in distorting the Cuban economy and Cuban society. Although this did not result in any gross injustices as it had before the Revolution it proved to be a tremendous waste of resources, and nowhere more so than in the use of labour which had been redirected from all professions into the sugar harvest.[4]

In retrospect Cuban sugar policy from 1963–70 failed to achieve the desired results of sustained economic growth and the reorientation of labour into a socialist mode of production. One important element of this failure was Cuba's inability to establish reliable commercial relations with its capitalist trading partners through sugar exports.

The economic and political problems experienced by Cuba in the 1960s, which had resulted partly from its excessive focus on the export sector, led to a shift in strategy in the 1970s. However, most of the restructuring took place internally and policy towards its external trading partners remained similar to that adopted in the second half of the 1960s, but based on more stable levels of sugar production and export.[5] The drive towards mechanisation of the sugar industry was also stepped up.

The Cuban sugar boom of the mid-1970s

More significant for Cuba's economic relations with the market economies in the 1970s than its own restructuring were such external factors as: the rise in the free market price of sugar, modifications to the US embargo, and changes in the world economy.

The rise in the world market price of sugar from 3.68 cents a pound in 1970 to an all-time high of 56.6 cents in November 1974 (average price for the year 29.66 cents) gave Cuba an extraordinary opportunity to increase its hard currency earnings and develop sectors of its economy through the import of technology and expertise from capitalist economies. After 1974 the price of sugar began to fall but even by 1977, when the world price was around 8 cents, it was still more than twice what it had been in 1970. However, inflation during the 1970s made this price only marginally better in real terms than in 1970.

While Cuba's sugar export sector performed well generally in the 1970s if one includes exports to socialist countries, it was only in the mid-1970s that it enjoyed good terms of trade based on sugar exports to capitalist countries. For most of the 1970s Cuba's sugar exports to the market economies earned between $200 to $350 million per annum, but in 1974 to 1975 earnings rose to around $800 million and $1200 million respectively.[6] In 1975 total exports to hard currency areas earned the Castro government approximately $1400 million and its total imports from the West amounted to approximately $1800 million.[7] Between 1971 and 1975 Cuba's imports from the market economies increased from 30 per cent of total imports to just over 40 per cent.[8]

Western Europe cashes in on Cuba's years of plenty

While Cuba was able to increase its imports from all of its capitalist trading partners in 1974 and 1975 because of exceptionally high sugar prices, it was the Western European economies that benefited most from Cuba's spending spree. If one excludes the years 1974 and 1975, the main Western European countries including France, West Germany, Britain and Italy (Spain is not included because of its special trading arrangements with Cuba based on clearing) had an average trading ratio with Cuba of 2.6:1 in their favour in the 1970s.[9] But in 1974 and 1975 this ratio increased to 4.7:1. The value of exports to Cuba by these four countries combined, which averaged $216 million per annum for the decade excluding 1974 and 75, rose in these two years to an average of $360 million per annum.

Clearly for Cuba to sustain such a high negative balance of trade with the major Western European economies it had to have access to sources of surplus hard currency. In the first half of the 1970s it was its trade with Japan which provided a large proportion of this surplus, which after 1973 was supplemented by loans and credits from Western banks. In the second half of the decade, as sugar prices fell and Cuba's trade with Japan declined, credits and loans became increasingly important as a means of financing Cuba's hard currency import requirements. But despite the availability of this new source of funding, and a commitment by Cuban planners to a strategy of debt-led growth, imports had to be cut back drastically after 1975. Had the Cuban government decided to sign a fixed price five-year sugar agreement with Japan in 1975 it may have been able to cushion itself against the dramatic fall in the market value of sugar after 1976. In late-1975 Japan offered to buy one million tons of Cuban sugar per annum up to 1980 at a fixed price of around 17 cents. But with the market price still over 25 cents a pound Cuba insisted that 19 cents was the lowest it could accept. Later in the year Japan signed a contract with Australia to pay 17 cents per pound until 1982. After this Japanese imports of Cuban sugar were cut to 1960s levels. As the market price fell to below 8 cents in 1977 Cuba realised the extent of its mistake.

From 1970 onwards Japan became Cuba's largest capitalist trading partner and its best hard currency market for sugar. Up to 1975 the trading ratio between Japan and Cuba stood at 1:1.5 in Cuba's favour. This discrepancy appears small when compared to the ratios given for Cuba's trade with Western Europe but one has to remember that in the first half of the decade Cuba's trade with Japan was greater than its total trade with the four major European economies cited above. Between 1970–75 Cuba earned a surplus of approximately $450 million in its merchandise trade with Japan. Some of this must have gone into paying for its deficit of around $960 with the main European economies which was accumulated in the same period. Part of the surplus Cuba earned on its merchandise trade with Spain during the first half of the 1970s, which amounted to approximately $290 million, may also have helped to offset its negative trading balances with other market economies, but an estimate is difficult to calculate because most trade between the two countries was conducted through clearing and involved few direct hard currency transactions.

In the crucial years of 1974 and 1975 when Cuba almost trebled its hard currency imports over previous years it was able to revitalise many sectors of its economy. As in the 1960s it was the transport sector which received the greatest amount of inputs. Huge imports of lorries, tractors, bulldozers, railway engines, boats, and all kinds of associated equipment, lubricants and spares were made from capitalist countries.[10] Imports were also increased of such products as office equipment, fertilisers, pesticides, chemicals, milk products, ships and electrical equipment. Often complete industrial plants were ordered so that products such as chemicals and fertilisers could be manufactured domestically.

From 1974 to 1976 Cuba imported an astonishing 18,561 trucks at a total value of 159 million pesos ($193m).[11] The two main suppliers to Cuba among the capitalist nations were Spain and Japan which dispatched 5,730 and 3,910 vehicles respectively.[12] Most of the remaining vehicles were supplied by the Soviet Union. During the same period Cuba imported 5,664 buses at a total value of 350 million pesos ($426m). Again Japan and Spain were the main suppliers among the market economies sending 562 and 586 vehicles respectively.

As Cuba's biggest and most reliable hard currency markets for sugar, Spain and Japan enjoyed a privileged position as suppliers to the Cuban transport sector. In the 1960s when the US embargo was more rigid, and Cuba's sugar markets among the capitalist economies were smaller and less reliable, the Castro government had to obtain its hard currency imports from almost any available source. But by the 1970s, having found two dependable capitalist markets for sugar, Cuba could build up long-term trading relationships in which its main export could be exchanged for its main import requirement, transport equipment. Although this arrangement was logical and necessary in commercial terms it meant that the Cuban's had to cope with the introduction of yet more ranges of transport technology, some of which was incompatible with existing equipment. Having made a shift from American technology to Russian, British and French technology in the 1960s, in the 1970s it was Russian, Spanish and Japanese equipment that dominated the transport sector. However, of the vehicles that were imported from Spain most were supplied by the Pegaso company which used some Leyland designs.[13] The Pegaso buses in particular which were supplied to Cuba in the 1970s were essentially updated models of the Leyland buses which had been sold to Cuba in the 1960s. Moreover, most of the trucks and engines supplied by Spain's second biggest motor vehicle exporter to Cuba, Barreiros, were based on designs used by the Berliet company in France in the 1960s, which had also been a significant supplier of vehicles to Cuba in previous years. Japanese motor vehicle technology (mainly Hino) on the other hand was not compatible with existing equipment in Cuba, but having such a substantial market for sugar in Japan the Castro government could afford to import enough vehicles to warrant the setting up a separate servicing and maintenance network.

With imports other than vehicles for the transport sector Cuba appears to have maintained a flexible purchasing policy in hard currency areas during the 1970s, as it had during the 1960s. And with surplus hard currency earnings from its trade with Japan and Spain for much of the decade its business was eagerly sought by other capitalist countries, and especially the main economies in Europe.

Cuba's trade with individual Western European countries in the 1970s

France

During the 1970s France obtained a number of orders to build complete plants in Cuba. A contract was signed in 1974 with the engineering firm Speichim to build six yeast processing units.[14] The following year another engineering company KEBS won a contract to construct a chlorine producing plant. Between 1974 and 1977 these contracts were worth 50–60 million pesos ($62–74m). Richards Continental, the manufacturer of heavy earthmoving equipment which had done business with Cuba in the 1960s, received orders in 1970 and 1971 for a total of 612 bulldozers worth 16 million pesos ($16m).

Perhaps the most important potentially long-term new business France received from Cuba in the 1970s was the orders for data processing and computing equipment that were placed in 1975 with the firm CII Honeywell Bull. Since the early-1970s Cuba had attached great importance to the use of computers for simplifying and co-ordinating centrally-planned economic strategies, and to enter the Cuban computer market in the mid-1970s when such plans were being put into motion was a unique opportunity for a computing company,[15] especially given that almost all the earlier equipment had come from the Soviet bloc.

In 1978 a large contract was signed with the engineering firm Creusot-Loire to build a factory to produce paper out of sugar cane waste (*bagasse*). Interestingly France's most consistent export to Cuba in the 1970s was dairy foods and especially dried milk. During the decade Cuba imported over $60 million in value of these products from France. The average annual value of French exports to Cuba in the 1970s was $57 million. Imports averaged $21 million. 1975 was France's best year of trade with Cuba with exports of $105 million and imports of $24 million.

In early 1975 Cuba's deputy Prime Minister, Carlos Rafael Rodríguez, made an important visit to France principally to sign a trade and economic co-operation agreement between the two governments.[16] In an interview given to *Le Monde* correspondent Alain-Marie Carron, Rodríguez spoke of Cuba's 'great hopes' of especially fruitful relations with France in the subsequent five years. He estimated that during this period Cuba would make investments in the region of 12–15 billion dollars and it was intended to spend a large proportion of this on foreign imports. Rodríguez indicated that because France was already an important supplier to Cuba there were good grounds for an expansion in trade over the coming years. Among the companies he named that were already doing business with Cuba were those mentioned earlier up to 1975 and also the engineering firm Sofresi. He further indicated that several other companies including Renault, Berliet, Sifar and Sofralta were negotiating with Cuba for new business, and Creusot-Loire was advising on the possibilities of constructing a plant to convert *bagasse* into paper. Apparently French companies had also shown an interest in other Cuban projects; one to build two plants to produce ammonia fertiliser; another to build a tyre factory (for which Britain was also tendering) and finally a joint venture in the field of petrochemicals.

Having outlined the opportunities for French business in Cuba

Rodríguez stressed that if France wanted to take full advantage of these opportunities it would have to be more forthcoming with long-term credits. He also pointed out that if Cuba was capable of proving itself to be a good credit risk when the price of sugar was 6 cents a pound, then there was no excuse for failing to give full credit backing to trade with the island when sugar was at its current 40 cents. The second obstacle to the expansion of French exports to Cuba, Rodríguez suggested, was France's failure to increase its import of Cuban products. In particular he noted that the reduction in nickel imports was a serious problem. He also indicated that high French tariffs on Cuban rum made it impossible to compete with Guadeloupe and Martinique which did not face any levies on their rum exports to France.

In a subsequent article by Alain-Marie Carron summing up the main issues to arise out of the Cuban deputy Prime Minister's visit, the author pointed out that a further obstacle to the improvement in Franco-Cuban relations was the lack of an airline connection between the two countries.[17]

Italy

In the late-1960s Italy began to export large quantities of fertilisers to Cuba which came to a total value of 27 million pesos ($32m) between 1970 and 1975. Chemical exports during the same period exceeded 10 million pesos ($12m). In the first five years of the decade Italy also exported agricultural equipment to Cuba to the value of 40 million pesos ($48m) which included over 2500 tractors. In 1971 and 1972, 1007 lorries, 523 buses and 1073 motor cars were sold to Cuba at a total value of 22 million pesos ($22m). Italy's annual exports to Cuba in the 1970s averaged $58 million. Imports averaged $22 million.

West Germany

During the 1970s West Germany's main exports to Cuba were fertilisers, animal feed, herbicides and pesticides and steel tubing. For the period the value of herbicide and pesticide exports alone amounted to 84 million pesos ($105m). West Germany's annual exports to Cuba averaged $69 million and imports from Cuba averaged $13 million.

Britain

Britain's principal exports to Cuba in the 1970s were fertilisers, pesticides and herbicides, chemicals, milk products, motor vehicle tyres and spare parts. In the early-1970s Britain was still exporting buses and trucks to Cuba and between 1970 and 1973, 217 buses and 644 trucks were despatched to Havana. But after 1973 this business, which was mainly with British Leyland, ceased. Aveling Barford, a subsidiary of Leyland, continued however to supply dumper trucks and transport equipment for the nickel mining industry into the 1980s. Britain's annual exports to Cuba in the 1970s averaged $60 million and imports averaged $24 million at this time.

After the successful Leyland contracts with the Castro government in the 1960s British business and the British government took a positive view of Cuba as a trading partner in the 1970s. In 1975 the then First Commercial Secretary at the British embassy in Havana, Michael Marshall, wrote an enthusiastic article outlining the opportunities for British business in Cuba.[18] He began by pointing out that in the 1970s Cuba had become the seventh most important market for British goods in Latin America and the Caribbean. It was further noted that according to the Cuban's their new five-year plan would require £2000 to £2500 million of investments of which 60 per cent would be spent on imported goods, a good proportion of which would be obtained from capitalist countries, especially while sugar prices were high. In particular Marshall felt that the Cubans would seek 'complete plant and specialised equipment' from the market economies, adding that British manufacturers were well placed to supply these needs.[19] Among the problems and restrictions that were listed which a British company doing business with Cuba could face, the US embargo was not included.

Flourishing commercial relations between Britain and Cuba were further consolidated when the Cuban deputy Prime Minister, Carlos Rafael Rodríguez, was invited to Britain to sign an Anglo-Cuban Economic and Industrial Co-operation Agreement in London in 1975. This agreement provided for the establishment of a Joint Commission to meet annually to review the prospects for economic co-operation.[20] During his visit Rodríguez also met a group of British businessmen from a wide range of industries who were interested in the Cuban market.

A few months after the Cuban deputy Prime Minister's visit to London, Peter Shore the British Secretary of State for Trade accepted an invitation to go to Havana to discuss Anglo-Cuban co-operation and trade, becoming the first member of a British cabinet to visit the island since 1959.[21] On returning from Cuba the minister gave an enthusiastic speech to the London Chamber of Commerce and Industry emphasising the opportunities for British business in Cuba.[22]

One of the most fascinating aspects of Britain's commercial relations with Cuba in the 1970s was the set of contracts which were obtained by the Seadrec company of Paisley in Scotland to supply a number of harbour dredgers to the Castro government.[23] By the early-1970s Cuba's dredging equipment, like most other American technology which had survived from the 1950s, was becoming old and unreliable. Demands on harbour facilities had also begun to grow during the 1960s as Cuba was forced to diversify its trading relations because of the US embargo. In particular, the replacement of North America by the distant Soviet Union as Cuba's main trading partner meant that the size of ships entering Cuban ports increased substantially.

Seadrec's first contract with the Cubans (Empresa Navegacion Mambisa de Havana) was signed in 1969 and had a value of £3 million. During the following two years Seadrec supplied Cuba with a cutter suction dredger, two tug boats, spare parts, and some workshop equipment. The company was also asked as part of the contract to re-equip one of the old American dredgers that were still in use. Apparently one of the main problems the Cuban's faced with heavy motorised American equipment like dredgers was that they were usually powered by Caterpillar engines for which it was impossible to obtain spare parts because of the embargo. To overcome this problem Seadrec used British engines both in its new equipment and in any refits it undertook. These were supplied by the Mirrlees Blackton company in Stockport. During the contract several Cuban's were invited to Seadrec's works at Paisley for in-house training. As with all other big Cuban orders placed with British companies in the 1960s and 1970s the Seadrec contract received ECGD backing.[24]

During the two years from 1969 to 1971 in which Seadrec was carrying out its contract with the Cubans a good rapport was developed between the two parties, and in contrast to the unfortunate Simon Carves contract, which possibly served to deter Cuba from seeking new business with British companies, Seadrec completed its contract on time and to the full satisfaction of its customers. Seadrec's initial success led to the signing of a further contract with Empresa Navegacion Mambisa de Havana in 1974 which was valued at £7.5 million. This time the Paisley company supplied the Cubans with a total of 27 dredgers, barges, boats and tugs, as well as ancillary equipment and spare parts. Again ECGD support was forthcoming. In 1981 the Cubans placed a third order with Seadrec worth £20 million.

What is of interest concerning the Seadrec contracts with Cuba is not so much their value but rather their importance for both parties. For the Cubans the equipment they obtained not only proved to be effective and reliable but they also found in Seadrec a medium-sized company which greatly valued their business and was willing to respond to Cuba's needs. Seadrec on the other hand, once established in Cuba after the first contract, was almost assured subsequent orders because of the expertise it had gained in a specialist section of the Cuban market. A representative of Seadrec stated that since 1969 'Cuba has been the company's most important customer taking about one-third of total business'. He also indicated that Cuban orders probably saved the company in the mid-1970s when it was experiencing difficult times.

Unlike many large Western European companies which have tended to make forays into the Cuban market when conditions were in their favour, small to medium-sized companies, and especially those like Seadrec with specialist expertise, have often established more lasting relations with Cuba. There are several possible reasons for this. First, the Cubans tend – perhaps more than many other Third World countries which are less stable – to prefer doing long-term business with satisfactory suppliers. Second, the Cubans have a reputation for being prompt and reliable payers, there is also very little, if any, corruption to contend with, these factors can be particularly important to a small company with limited resources. Third, small companies doing business with Cuba perhaps do not face the same political pressures from the US as do large ones. Paradoxically, however, it may be that it is the small Western European companies that have established the most enduring commercial relations with Cuba and will be the most difficult for American business to dislodge from the island if there is a *rapprochement* between Washington and Havana in the future.

Spain

During the 1970s Spain remained Cuba's most important and reliable trading partner in Western Europe and the high levels of trade which had been established between the two countries in the 1960s was further expanded. In the chapter on Spanish-Cuban relations in the 1960s it was suggested that because of Spain's commitment to a number of highly-priced medium-term sugar contracts, Cuba benefited most from the relationship. This was also true for most of the 1970s when again widely fluctuating and unpredictable sugar prices left Spain at a trading disadvantage.

After the termination of Spain's 1965 sugar agreement with Cuba in 1969 the two parties arranged a series of meetings to establish a new agreement. In March an accord was signed in which Cuba would supply Spain with 120,000 metric tons of sugar in 1970, 70,000 in 1971 and 70,000 in 1972. The basic price per pound was set at 5.5 cents which was subject to a formula in which 30 per cent of the final price paid was responsive to market prices.[25] Spain also granted Cuba $30 million in credits. Almost all transactions between the two countries at this time were still based on 'clearing', as they had been in the 1960s, with allowances for an annual discrepancy in merchandise trade of $3 million. The 1970 agreement, however, gave Cuba a special dispensation to surpass this limit by $7 million in 1970 and $14 million in 1971. But by the end of 1970, partly because of a fall in Cuban exports to Spain other than sugar, such as tobacco, coffee and shellfish, the island's deficit stood at $21 million. On its invisible account with Spain, Cuba also had a deficit of $12.7 million.[26] Because of these problems, and a number of other factors, including the Castro government's strong links with members of the Spanish Communist Party both in Spain and Cuba, relations began to deteriorate between the two countries. The discord reached its nadir in August 1971 when Cuba closed its embassy in Madrid and recalled the entire staff back to Havana after negotiations between a visiting Cuban delegation and the Franco government broke down.[27] Negotiations were resumed in Havana at the end of the year and resulted in an extension of the 1970 agreement for an additional two years up to 1974.[28] Cuba had to make some concessions during these negotiations to reduce the deficit which it had accumulated, including an undertaking to pay part of its debt in hard currency.[29]

Up to 1974 Spain maintained favourable trading terms with Cuba, having negotiated a series of partially fixed prices for Cuban sugar which remained below the rapidly escalating world price. In late-1974 when the sugar price was at its height Spain began negotiations with Cuba to establish a new commercial agreement. Because Spanish domestic sugar production had fallen well below national consumption in 1974 it was decided to increase imports from Cuba to 220,000 metric tons each year up to 1977. Minimum prices were fixed at 30 cents a pound for 1975 and 23 cents for 1976 and 1977. Because of the extraordinarily high sugar prices which prevailed in the market Spain also granted Cuba a credit of $300 million and agreed to pay some of its sugar account in convertible currency. Despite a number of modifications to the agreement between 1974 and 1977 as the price of sugar fell on the world market the Castro government enjoyed an unprecedented trading advantage with Spain in these years. In fact Cuba continued to benefit from favourable trading relations with Spain until the end of the decade when the system of clearing, which had existed since 1959, was replaced by a total liberalisation of trade between the two countries. By this time Spain was also reliably self-sufficient in sugar production and purchases from Cuba ceased.

The history of Spanish-Cuban relations in the 1970s was based, as it had been in the 1960s, on commercial compatibility and a continuation of strong cultural ties despite enormous political differences. Even after the death of Franco in 1975 and a return to democracy in Spain very few changes took place in relations between the two countries until the end of the decade. The Cubans, in fact, did not respond noticeably to the end of the Franco period, and in 1978 when Adolfo Suárez became the first Spanish premier to visit Cuba the crowds that met him at the airport did not greet him as a symbol of the end of dictatorship in Spain but rather as a representative of continuing Spanish-Cuban 'friendship'.[30]

Cuba's relations with the Soviet Union in the 1970s

Naturally a vital component of Cuba's external relations in the 1970s continued to be its links with the Soviet Union, which remained throughout the decade by far the island's most important trading partner. By the early-1970s, although American equipment still played an important role in the Cuban economy, Soviet and Eastern European technology had reached a commanding level in the most crucial sectors. In 1972 the Castro government requested to join the CMEA and was accepted. This formalisation of links between Cuba and the Soviet bloc resulted in a greater co-ordination in an already flourishing relationship. In return for Soviet promises of increases in technical assistance, credits, and the price paid for Cuban sugar, Cuba agreed to stabilise its sugar exports to the communist bloc.[31] At the time of the signing of the 1972 agreement the Soviet Union was paying the equivalent of 6.11 cents per pound for Cuban sugar while the market price for the year averaged 7.27 cents. The following year when the market price began to rise, averaging for the year 9.45 cents, the Soviet Union paid 12.2 cents. Although responsive to world commodity prices the CMEA attempted to apply pricing strategies among its members which would smooth out the erratic fluctuations experienced in capitalist markets. Therefore, while the Soviet Union paid lower than the market price for sugar in 1974, from 1975 to the end of the decade it was paying well above the market price. This was fortunate for Cuba because after the sugar boom of the mid-1970s was over and its levels of hard currency earnings fell, it continued to enjoy excellent terms of trade with the Soviet Union.

Soviet oil sales to CMEA members were also subject to a progressive pricing structure which meant that Cuba was paying far less for its oil imports after 1973 than any other sugar exporter not in the CMEA.[32] In the years 1973–75 when the sugar price and oil prices were both high in the market, Cuba experienced an exceptional trading advantage over other Third World countries. Beginning in the late-1970s the Soviet Union also allowed Cuba to sell its surplus oil on the market, which further enhanced the island's capacity to earn hard currency. All these advantages which Cuba enjoyed in the 1970s allowed it to reap the maximum benefit from its trading relations with the capitalist economies. A relationship which Moscow undoubtedly encouraged.

The 1970s: a new phase of American imperialism

During the first decade of the Cuban Revolution US economic and political power was at its height, but by the late-1960s the seemingly inexorable rise of American hegemony in the world began to slow.[33] After the great boost which was given to the US economy by the Second World War, and its aftermath during which most of America's pre-war capitalist competitors remained severely weakened for several years, US capitalism became the motor of the world economy. This supremacy was embodied in the 1944 Bretton Woods agreement in which the Allied powers conceded that a post-war world recovery could only be achieved by liberating the US dollar to become a world currency, and by tying the fortunes of international capitalism to the performance of the American economy. The US enjoyed disproportionate advantages from the Bretton Woods arrangements but its success, as predicted (especially by John Maynard Keynes), led to the regeneration of other capitalist powers and particularly those which had experienced extensive war damage like Germany and Japan, and to a lesser extent France and Italy. By the early-1950s, as a result mainly of Marshall Aid, the recovery in these countries was well advanced, but for a further decade they could not effectively challenge the US in world markets because of the supremacy it had established in previous years when competition was weak.

However, in the second half of the 1960s, the productivity levels and the rate of profit of US companies began to fall in comparison to its competitors. These problems were caused by several factors including: higher than average rises in the cost of US labour; an over-valued dollar; a dramatic decline in investment in research and development after the mid-1960s; an older and less efficient industrial base than its Western European and Japanese competitors. These insidious factors, along with the escalating cost of the Vietnam war, began to constrain the US economy, and resulted in the loss of foreign markets, increased import penetration, a shrinking share of world investments, rising inflation and an alarming growth in balance of payments deficits.[34] The US government responded by printing more dollars to pay for its internal and external deficits, causing the disparity between its gold stocks and dollars in circulation to increase to dangerous levels. All this put unbearable pressures on the Bretton Woods system.

During the late-1960s the US balance of payments continued to deteriorate, and the amount of dollars held in foreign hands grew to unmanageable levels. Finally, in 1971, the year when for the first time since the beginning of the century the US trade balance went into the red, the Nixon administration took the momentous but essential measures of devaluing the dollar, renouncing the gold parity pledge, and placing a 10 per cent surcharge on imports, thereby putting an end to the Bretton Woods system. The result of these measures was to give the US a temporary trading advantage over its competitors but the problems of American capitalism, declining productivity and a shrinking rate of profit, remained.

In the 1960s the expansion in Western European trade with Cuba, although in part opportunist, was also indicative of the growing strength and confidence of America's competitors. Cuba was an American market par excellence in the 1950s, and with the curtailment of trading relations between the two countries in the early-1960s an unprecedented opportunity was created for America's competitors. Never before had such a highly-integrated and lucrative US market simply been abandoned and thrown open for new business.

Naturally, such factors as the US embargo, Cuba's shortages of hard currency, the strengthening of relations between Cuba and the Soviet Union, all restricted the trading opportunities that were open to America's competitors, but nevertheless it gave them an important material and psychological foothold in Latin America. Indeed, when companies found that they could break the American embargo almost with impunity it strengthened their resolve to go out and challenge US business in other parts of Latin America. Some firms which secured contracts with Cuba in the 1960s even went so far as to use Havana as a base from which their sales executives could make forays in search of new business into the rest of the continent.

In the 1970s America's competitors, and especially the main Western Europe powers and Japan, began to significantly expand their commercial interests in Latin America. This not only reflected the improving competitiveness of Western European and Japanese industry, but also the inability of the US to sustain the economic supremacy it had enjoyed in the region in past decades.[35] The war in Vietnam, the falling productivity of US industry, and the economic restructuring which took place after the 1971 devaluation of the dollar all contributed to the contraction of US commercial power in the world. This decline in America's strength was reflected in US-Cuban relations in the 1970s.

The US and Cuba in the 1970s

When Nixon became President of the United States in 1969 his initial response to Cuba, which was encouraged by his National Security Council adviser Henry Kissinger, was to continue to work towards the isolation of the Castro government and increase destabilisation tactics.[36] During the 1960s Washington's policy of preventing Cuba from enjoying the benefits of commercial relations with market economies through the imposition of an embargo was a failure, because its main industrial competitors chose to put commercial pragmatism before inter-capitalist political solidarity. Washington enjoyed some success, however, in isolating Cuba from the rest of Latin America. In economic terms this was a negligible victory because of the limited potential for significant trade between Cuba and the rest of the region. However, as a means of quarantining Cuba to prevent it spreading its revolutionary ideology, Washington could claim to have achieved its objectives, especially after the death of Guevara in Bolivia in 1968.

When Nixon vowed to maintain Cuba's isolation into the 1970s he must have realised that there was no hope of curbing Western European and Japanese trade with Cuba; that was a lost cause. But he probably believed that he could continue to isolate Cuba within the Americas. If so this was a miscalculation. The failure of the Alliance for Progress to satisfy popular expectations, combined with America's loosening commercial hold on Latin America, helped to bring to power a number of nationalist democratic governments in the region which sought greater economic independence from the US, and improved economic relations with Western Europe and Japan.[37] These strivings for economic independence also gave rise to a demand for greater political liberty. In this new environment Cuba was able to emerge from its pariah status in the region and establish diplomatic and commercial relations with nationalist Latin American governments.

However, this process was not only a response to external conditions, but also the result of Cuba's willingness (partly because of pressure from Moscow) to soften its hard line of the 1960s and accept that progress towards socialism could be achieved without revolution. The governments of Velasco in Peru, Allende in Chile, Perón in Argentina, Torres in Bolivia, Rodríguez in Ecuador and others, strengthened their ties with Cuba at various times between 1969 and 1974. Peru was particularly vociferous in the OAS in support of putting an end to sanctions against Cuba, but all such proposals were countered by the US and its allies who continued to insist that Cuba was a destabilising force in the region.

Argentina's relations with Cuba created particular problems because Washington favoured cautious and even supportive treatment of the Perón government which came to power in 1973, in the belief that the only alternative lay to the left.[38] Anxious to take advantage of its privileged position, and also assert its independence from the US, one of the first actions of the Perón government on assuming office in May was to re-establish diplomatic relations with Havana. This was followed in August by the extension of a $200 million credit to Cuba to purchase Argentine agricultural machinery.[39] Four months later, in December, Argentina offered the Castro government a second credit of $1.2 billion for the purchase of Argentine products.[40] During the negotiating stage of this credit the Cubans expressed a particular interest in purchasing motor vehicles that were manufactured by the subsidiaries of Ford, General Motors and Chrysler based in Argentina. The Perón government welcomed this request and responded to subsequent US protests by threatening to nationalise the subsidiaries if Washington attempted to obstruct the sale.[41] On the horns of a dilemma of its own creation the US decided to issue the firms concerned with licenses to export to Cuba. Although insisting that this was a special case Washington had in fact set a dangerous precedent within its embargo policy.

Clearly one of Washington's main reasons for granting this concession was to prevent any damage to its delicate relations with the Perón government. However, one also suspects that given the declining markets for American manufactures in Latin America, US business could not afford to lose such a big contract. Indeed, at that time Brazil's Volkswagen subsidiaries were rapidly expanding their share of the Latin American motor vehicle market mainly at the expense of US motor vehicle manufacturers based in Argentina, and this could have been a crucial factor influencing Washington's decision. Washington's refusal in 1975 to repeat the concession it had granted to subsidiaries of US companies in Argentina, prompted the Association of American Chambers of Commerce in Latin America to argue that the continuing restrictions on trade with Cuba, which still affected US business abroad, could jeopardise America's corporate stake in the region.[42]

In the first half of the 1970s the US found it could do little to check the trend towards *rapprochement* between Cuba and the rest of Latin America, and even after it had manufactured the replacement of most independent nationalist governments in the region with dictatorships it still could not revive the anti-Cuban attitude which had prevailed in the continent during the 1960s.[43]

Changes in US policy towards Cuba in the 1970s and its effects on Cuba's trade with Western Europe

Throughout the 1970s, despite a few minor gestures of goodwill which were extended to Cuba during the Carter administration, the US refused to soften its economic and political hostility towards the Castro government which had existed since the early-1960s. But while maintaining its own puritanical stance against Cuba, its ability to police Cuba's relations with the international community, though already limited from 1964, weakened even further in the 1970s. The most flagrant breaches of the US embargo on Cuba in the 1960s were made mainly by America's competitors in Western Europe, and also towards the end of the decade by Japan and Canada. During the 1970s these same countries continued to flout the embargo, but with three important differences in comparison to the previous decade. First, the levels of trade they conducted with Cuba were higher; second, they extended financial loans to Cuba; third, whereas previously they at least paid lip-service to US preoccupations about the Castro government, in the 1970s they dispensed with such courtesies and treated the embargo almost as if it did not exist.

An initial gesture to indicate a strengthening of relations between Cuba and America's competitors in the 1970s was taken by Britain, which in late-1971 sent its first trade mission to Cuba since 1959.[44] This was soon followed by trade missions from other market economies including France, West Germany and Japan. Another boost to Cuba's relations with Western Europe was given in 1972 when EEC foreign ministers agreed to extend trade preferences to a selection of Third World countries, including Cuba.[45] The Castro government's already fruitful relations with Spain were also further improved in 1971 when a contract was signed between the two countries, which resulted in reciprocal trade to the value of $890 million dollars over the subsequent four years.[46]

Despite the almost total freedom with which most of America's competitors were able to trade their own manufactures with Cuba, the US did have the small satisfaction of being able to assert effective pressure on foreign countries which attempted to re-export American-made goods to Cuba. The special section which was attached to the US Department of Commerce to police these activities was kept busy in the 1970s with numerous complaints, often registered by US manufacturers, against Western European, Canadian and Mexican companies that were involved in this re-export 'racket'. French companies were the most persistent offenders and frequently incurred penalties. France had also caused irritation in Washington during the second half of the 1960s because of its large purchases of Cuban nickel (about one-third of the island's production), and in this period all French products that contained nickel were barred from entry into the US. In 1970 the Nixon administration agreed to accept such products if France could guarantee they contained no Cuban nickel. The French company Le Nickel, possibly on the advice of the Pompidou government, which may have been required to make additional concessions to Washington for its permission to renew the export of previously banned products, decided in December 1970 to cease its purchases of nickel from Cuba. This was a damaging blow to an important source of hard currency earnings for Cuba, and was consequently deemed as a successful enforcement of the embargo by Washington.

Apart from the minor irritations that were caused to some Western European and Canadian companies by Washington's policy of preventing the re-export of American-made goods to Cuba, and the favourable outcome of the disagreement with France over Cuban nickel, the US found it could do little to prevent Western Europe from developing its relations with the Castro government. Even high US officials conceded that the embargo failed to achieve the desired 'political objectives' but supported its retention because of its 'symbolic value'.[47] In 1975 the US Commerce Department carried out a survey of the embargo to assess its effectiveness 13 years after its implementation.[48] The two main conclusions which the survey reached were: first, while sugar prices were high and Cuba had plenty of hard currency to spend the embargo had little effect on the island. Second, it was estimated that with each additional year it was in operation the embargo became more expensive to administer and also resulted in ever increasing lost opportunities for American business. Despite such reports Washington believed that America's own adherence to the embargo was essential, because over time it had restricted the rate at which the Castro government could progress along the road towards economic diversification.[49]

When Ford replaced Nixon as President in August 1974 the US adopted a slightly more accommodating line towards Cuba. A year after Ford entered the White House one significant and three minor modifications were made to the embargo.[50] The most important of these was a withdrawal of the ban on the subsidiaries of American companies abroad exporting to Cuba (after this facility had been granted as a special concession to US business in Argentina, there was a clamour from other American manufacturers, with subsidiaries around the world, to be given the same privilege). The minor modifications comprised of: lifting of the restrictions on third-country ships carrying Cuban trade from using docking facilities in US ports; an end to the prohibition on aid to nations that permitted their ships or aircraft to carry goods to and from Cuba; and a request to Congress to repeal legislation that prohibited credit food sales to nations trading with Cuba. Commenting on the new changes to the embargo the *New York Times* noted that State Department officials were hoping that by allowing subsidiaries of US multinationals abroad to trade with Cuba it would 'improve the climate' for their operations in Latin America where they were increasingly becoming seen as 'agents of US foreign policy'.[51] It was also pointed out by the newspaper that the most significant benefit to be derived from allowing foreign subsidiaries of US companies to trade with Cuba was that it would help curb the free run of the island which America's competitors had had since the early 1960s.

In the first year of the Carter administration, from January 1977 to January 1978, the embargo policy on Cuba was pursued with less vigour than at any time since it was initiated, but significant changes were not made to its basic structure. Indeed, from 1978 Washington began to increase pressure on Cuba again, ostensibly because of the Castro government's growing involvement in Africa.[52]

During the 1970s there were many pressures from within the United States to re-open commercial links with Cuba. Some of the strongest of these came from the business community which was aggrieved to see their Western European and Japanese competitors picking up valuable contracts with the Castro government.[53] In general, by the 1970s, US business had begun to express concern about the rate at which their competitors abroad, and especially in Japan and West Germany, were expanding their export markets at America's expense.[54] After the oil price rise of 1973 it had been hoped by the US business community that America's greater self-sufficiency in oil would give it an advantage over its competitors which would be faced by increased import bills. However, a concerted export drive by Western Europe and Japan, combined with the tendency of Third World and socialist countries to spend their petro-currency loans on non-American technology dashed this hope.[55] In the first half of the 1970s the value of US exports increased at a rate of about 10 per cent per year which was roughly equivalent to the export performance of its competitors, but one should remember that America is a major exporter of raw materials (especially foodstuffs), and these commanded a high price for most of this period. On the other hand countries like West Germany and Japan export few raw materials and their increase in exports was based almost entirely on manufactured goods. In 1974 the value of West German exports exceeded that of US exports for the first time this century, an achievement based mainly on the superior performance of German manufacturing industry.

After America devalued the dollar in 1971 and abandoned the gold parity pledge the relationship between currencies became more unstable.[56] This resulted in increased inter-capitalist rivalry and fiercer competition in international markets as each country adopted the philosophy of every man for himself.[57] In such an environment it was hopeless for the US to try to persuade its competitors to observe the embargo on Cuba, especially when most believed anyway that Washington's Cuba policy was simply a contrived ideological position for domestic propaganda purposes. Indeed, some members of the American business community began to feel by the 1970s that their government's ideological opposition to Cuba took far too little account of prevailing economic realities.

Particular distress was felt by American exporters when foreign companies entered into contracts with Cuba to supply products in which American industry had a technological lead, as when the French firm Honeywell Bull secured an order for computing equipment from the Cuban government in 1975 while it was widely accepted that IBM was the clear leader in the market. Those sections of the US business community that could have benefited from a lifting of the embargo on Cuba could not understand why the Castro government was excluded from the policy of *détente* which prevailed for most of the decade. This argument was expressed most forcefully by the American industrialist Cyrus Eaton who had been visiting Cuba and advocating an end to the embargo since the mid-1960s. Eaton was also fond of expressing the view that Washington's ban on trade with Cuba was nonsense in economic terms and was simply aimed at pacifying domestic opponents to Castro's communist government.[58] Some US politicians also offered open support to a lifting of the embargo on Cuba. The leading figure among these was Senator Edward Kennedy who, echoing Eaton, stated that 'US policy toward Cuba . . . should be based on US interests rather than on residual antagonisms'.[59] However, despite complaints against the embargo from sections of the US business community, and some liberal politicians, they never joined together to lobby Washington to reconsider its policy. US multinationals in particular did not wish to be seen pressing for the lifting of trading restrictions with Cuba when they were working in conjunction with US governments to roll back 'communism' in other parts of the world. Multinationals had also lost the most property during the Cuban nationalisations of the early-1960s and some actively opposed any relaxation on the embargo until they had received compensation. Supporters of this stance also argued that to renew trading relations with Cuba before the issue of compensation had been settled would set a dangerous precedent which could endanger American investments in other countries.[60] Ultimately, after years of anti-Cuban propaganda and even longer of Cold War rhetoric no US businessman or politician could risk being seen as a champion of improved relations with Cuba. Indeed, in the spring of 1976 President Ford's advisers who were preparing for the primaries against Ronald Reagan became worried that any gestures of friendship towards Cuba at that time could jeopardise their candidate's position.[61]

Cuba and the international money markets in the 1970s

From the mid-1970s Cuba began substantially to increase the number and value of financial loans and credits which it contracted with international banks. This development in Cuban economic policy can be seen both as part of a trend among Third World and socialist countries, which in the 1970s were given unprecedented access to loans from Western banks, and also to supplement its hard currency earnings when the price of sugar began to fall after 1974. Washington found Cuba's entry into the financial markets particularly galling because it gave the Castro government a higher level of international legitimacy and increased its integration into the capitalist economic structure.

From Bretton Woods up to the late-1960s most international banking, including loans, credits, and other financial transactions was conducted by national banks and organisations such as the World Bank. During the 1950s and the first half of the 1960s a few privately-owned banks entered the international banking business. These newcomers formed an elite club which was dominated by a handful of big American banks whose main function was to service the needs of multinationals, and their attitude towards granting loans to foreigners, and especially the Third World, was staid and cautious. The first important stimulus to private international banking came with the US government's decision to restrict the flow of capital out of the country in the mid-1960s, in an attempt to alleviate balance of payments problems and encourage more investment in flagging American industry. This was a severe blow to home-based American banks involved in international finance, and they responded by increasing the number of branches they had abroad, because these were exempt from the new legislation and could trade freely in dollars. Washington's attempts to stem dollar flows out of the national economy also gave a boost to the Eurodollar market, which soon began to attract large numbers of new investors and borrowers who wished to avoid US restrictions.[62]

The greatest expansion of American banking abroad came in 1968 after the Johnson administration made mandatory the Voluntary Foreign Credit Restraint Program which had been initiated in 1965. Henceforth US banks were compelled to put ceilings on their foreign loans. In 1968 26 US banks had 375 foreign branches with $23 billion in assets but two years later, 79 banks had 536 branches abroad with over $52 billion of assets.[63] Because of its status as the second most important financial centre after New York, London became the favourite base for American banks abroad. London was also the capital of the Eurocurrency market which was the key financial environment for raising funds and finding new customers. By the mid-1970s America's principal banks were reaping more profits from their foreign business than from domestic transactions. The influence of the US economy and the central role of the dollar in global finance initially gave American banks a competitive advantage over their European and Japanese counterparts, but this did not last for long.

The boom in global banking which had begun in the late-1960s was augmented by the OPEC oil price rise of 1973. Although American banks received huge deposits of 'petro dollars', British, Swiss, German and Japanese banks were favoured by OPEC investors because they feared that the US government might retaliate against the price rise by freezing or confiscating their dollars. Most of these deposits entered the Euromarket, which became the framework for recycling dollars from the oil producers to the oil consumers. The US treasury has calculated that between 1974 and 1980 the OPEC countries placed $117 billion into the Euromarket.[64] This was more than the total worth of the market in 1971. Faced with a seemingly interminable flood of dollars the private Euro banks embarked on a vast orgy of lending.

Guided only by the chaotic and irrational laws of financial markets, it was hoped that mass lending to the Third World for profits would prevent a world recession by creating increased demand for Western industrial products. Among Third World countries the Latin American dictatorships were regarded as the best credit risks, and were often given blank cheques to fill out at their convenience.[65] The Soviet bloc countries were also given preferential borrower status because they offered stability and their economies were based on vast undercapitalised industrial and natural resources.[66] More important still, most member countries of the Soviet trading system, the CMEA, had a good credit record with commercial banks, and it was widely believed by Western governments and private banks that the USSR would step in if any member ran into repayment problems. Many socialist countries in the 1970s were also undertaking large industrial development schemes and upgrading their technology inputs which provided good business for the West. Some socialist countries, including Cuba, were regarded by the Euro bankers as model borrowers who could play a key long-term role in the revival world capitalism.

By 1973 even US bankers were falling over themselves to lend to the Soviet bloc and in May of that year Chase Manhattan became the first American bank with a branch office in Moscow. As the world recession deepened in 1974–75 and many Third World borrowers began to experience problems with repayments, CMEA countries, which were less affected in the short term by the fluctuations in capitalist markets, became prime targets for Western creditors. For instance in 1975 bankers and finance ministers from the four major European powers, West Germany, France, Britain and Italy met to arrange credit lines to the Soviet Union of $8.7 billion in advance of its new Five Year Plan.[67]

Washington's credit policy towards the CMEA countries differed little from its European competitors, except for Cuba which remained firmly out of bounds for American bankers. Western European, Canadian and Japanese bankers, though, were eager for Cuban business by 1973. The Caribbean island was, in fact, even when compared to socialist states in the Soviet bloc, a particularly good credit risk. The government was secure and popular with its people; most of the economy was still operating with Western technology and despite substantial contacts with the Soviet Union, Cuba conducted a higher percentage of its total foreign trade with market economies than any other socialist state; a co-ordinated programme for economic development was in place and the growth rate of the economy was one of the best in Latin America; Cuba also had an impeccable repayment record with its creditors. Moreover, it was assumed by Western financiers that given the commitment of the Soviet Union to the Cuban Revolution it would never allow the Castro government to default on its loans.[68] One imagines that American bankers were even more distressed than American industrialists by their government's legislation which prevented them doing business with Cuba.

Although trade credits had been available to the Castro government from capitalist countries since the 1960s these were significantly expanded in the 1970s. From the mid-1970s, and especially after the sugar price began to fall, Cuba also began for the first time to seek untied loans from private commercial banks as a means of maintaining access to vital hard currency imports and paying off existing debts.[69] The first untied loan Cuba contracted with the private banking sector was in 1973 when it raised $30 million on the Eurocurrency market.[70] This was followed in December 1974 by a $408 million loan from the British National Westminster Bank. In 1974 a further $119 million was raised on the Euromarket, followed by $234 million in 1975, $134m in 1976 and another $100m plus between 1977 and 1978. Morgan Grenfell organised a syndicated loan of 150 million Deutsche marks ($63.4 million) in December 1976. In February 1978 a consortium of 24 Japanese banks led by the Bank of Tokyo lent Cuba 10 billion yen ($41.7 million). This was followed in 1979 by a sindicated loan co-ordinated by the Sumitomo Trust and Banking Co. for 12.5 million yen ($62.5 million).[71]

Besides untied loans Cuba also received numerous commercial credits from capitalist countries in the 1970s. The largest, as noted earlier, came from the Perón government which gave Cuba credits of $1200 million in December 1973 to cover purchases of industrial and transportation equipment, much of which was to be supplied by the subsidiaries of US companies like Ford and Chrysler which were based in Argentina.

British private banks provided a number of tied loans and trade credits to Cuba in the 1970s. One of the earliest was a syndicated loan of £2 million organised by N.M. Rothschild and Sons Ltd., to finance the first Seadrec contract with Cuba.[72] The National Westminster Bank extended a £3 million line of credit to the Banco Nacional de Cuba in early-1972 to place orders in the UK for miscellaneous capital equipment.[73] A second line of credit to Cuba, this time for £7 million, was organised by the National Westminster Bank in 1974.[74] In 1975 Williams and Glyn's Bank made available a loan of £7.7 million to Empresa de Navegación Mambisa for the purchase of four SD14 cargo vessels from the British manufacturer Austin and Pickersgill.[75] In the same year the National Westminster gave a £6 million loan to Banco National de Cuba to finance the main part of the order for harbour vessels and equipment which had been placed with Seadrec.[76] The largest credit to be extended to Cuba by British banks was also agreed in 1975 at a value of £250 million.[77] This was announced after the signing of the Anglo-Cuban co-operation agreement in May. It was anticipated that the credit, much of which was already tied to specific contracts, would be used over two years, but under the agreement further credits would be made available to the Cubans.[78] All loans and credits from British banks listed above were guaranteed by the ECGD which gave full support to trade with Cuba in the 1970s.

During the 1970s Spain gave numerous credits to Cuba, the largest having a value of $900 million which was made available to the Cuban National Bank in December 1974. French banks were also active in providing financial support to Cuba and especially Crédit Lyonnais which organised several important lines of credit in the 1970s. These included a credit of $348 million in February 1975, and a syndicated credit of 220 million Deutsche marks ($114 million) in 1979. Besides the foregoing Cuba obtained numerous other loans and credits from banks in Western Europe, Japan, Canada and other capitalist countries around the world in the 1970s.

Cuba's involvement with the Western banks in the 1970s is particularly interesting because although the island produces very little oil it was able, as a result of cheap oil imports from the Soviet Union, to adopt a similar borrowing strategy to the oil producer countries in the region. Those Third World countries which fared worst after the OPEC oil price rises were the ones which did not have their own oil reserves, and whose main export commodity was not performing well in the market. Others which were also not oil producers but whose exports were in demand simply used any surplus hard currency they earned to cover the increase in the price of oil imports. The countries which fared best were the oil producers and exporters, and especially those which also produced other commodities which commanded high prices in the market. Depending on which of the above categories a country found itself in dramatically affected its borrowing requirements in the mid-1970s. At one end of the spectrum countries borrowed just to pay for increases in the price of oil imports with little hope of channelling these funds into development. At the other end borrowing could be used almost entirely to accelerate economic development. From 1973 to 1975 Cuba was able to adopt this latter strategy of 'debt-led growth', by borrowing on the strength of its position as the world's largest sugar exporter in a period of unusually high sugar prices.

For Third World countries that produced their own oil – or like Cuba had access to cheap oil imports – and were also significant exporters of some other commodity, the period from 1973–75 was exceptional because it was the first time since the Korean war boom that the prices of many primary products rose more rapidly than the price of industrial goods. Between 1955 and 1972 the terms of trade for primary products fell from an index of 126 to 84 but in 1973 this trend was dramatically reversed as the price of some commodities such as oil, sugar and copper soared.[79] Cuba was anxious to take advantage of this window of opportunity, which was further enhanced by access to easy credit, to accelerate economic development and especially its import substitution industries. Capital goods and complete factories were therefore the most sought after imports from market economies.[80] Chemical fertiliser and food processing plants were in greatest demand because the cost of fertilisers and food products escalated in price in the early-1970s. Indeed, for some non-oil producing countries the increase in the price of these products was more damaging financially and economically than the rise in the price of oil.

Countries like Cuba which were enjoying a new prosperity based on the export of some other commodity than oil felt a special urgency to expand and improve their import substitution industries, because the high price being paid for their products was less likely to last, especially during a world recession, which had prevailed since 1972.[81] Indeed, the market price of sugar, non-ferrous metals, rubber and many other commodities began to fall by December 1974 and in 1975 many suffered a severe deterioration in their value.

For industrialised capitalist countries which were desperately seeking new markets to avert an intensification of the recession this surge of new business from some Third World and socialist countries in the mid-1970s (for many OPEC members the boom lasted from 1973 to the end of the decade), was greatly welcomed, even though the main objective of their customers was to develop to reduce their import bills in the future.

Like many other governments in the Third World and Soviet bloc, the Cuban leadership believed that by sustaining a programme of 'debt-led growth' in the short term it would be able to establish the foundations for a more self-sufficient and competitive economy.[82] Moreover, because of socialist Cuba's commitment to growth with equity, and the popularity of its government, it was in a stronger position than any other Latin American country to use the funds it borrowed from Western banks to serve national objectives. So whereas in the rest of Latin America and the Caribbean foreign loans found their way into non-productive areas such as increases in consumer goods imports for local bourgeoisies, imports of military equipment for the repression of domestic populations, prestige projects unsuited to national needs, and above all capital flight abroad, Cuba faced none of these problems.[83]

Cuba hoped to combine the two advantages of high sugar prices, and hence a high credit rating, to maximise inputs into its economy. Consequently, in 1975 and 1976 when the sugar price was high Cuba ran huge deficits in excess of $500 million on its current account with capitalist countries.[84] But by 1977 it became clear the debt burden had to be reduced as sugar prices slumped and the amount of money owed to Western banks reached dangerous levels. In late-1977 drastic measures began to be taken to reduce the country's indebtedness such as the postponement of the delivery of $100 million dollars of Japanese exports which were on the dock side ready for shipping to Havana.[85] After the unprecedented increase in the price of sugar in the mid-1970s Cuban economic planners may have become too sanguine about sugar's future earning capacity and set their import projections too high. Some evidence of this can be found in the series of requests for postponement of deliveries and renegotiation of delivery schedules which occurred after 1975, and the increase in Cuba's external borrowing requirements between 1977 and the end of the decade.[86] It has been suggested that when Cuban planners devised the first Five-Year Plan (1976–80), they prepared three variants to allow for changes in the price of sugar.[87] However, one suspects that in the late-1970s sugar prices fell lower than envisaged even in the most pessimistic of these contingency plans.

By 1980 Cuba was able, because of cuts in imports, combined with a renewed rise in sugar prices, to bring its trade balance back into the black and slightly reduce its debt to the Western banks. During this period, however, the National Bank of Cuba continued to take up new loans and credits although at reduced values to previous years.

In the early-1980s Cuba, along with many other Third World countries, began to become overburdened by its financial commitments to Western banks. Falling prices for sugar (after 1980), increases in the price of imported manufactured goods from capitalist countries, commitments to liberation struggles abroad, and escalating interest rates, all served to push Cuba onto the treadmill of rescheduling, roll overs and constant indebtedness which faced the Third World in the 1980s.[88] In 1974 Cuba's debt to the market economies stood at $660 million which at existing market prices for sugar was equivalent to about six months of exports.[89] By 1982 the debt to Western creditors had risen to $3 billion and the Cuban National Bank was forced to request a rescheduling on its principal payments which were due to mature between 1982 and 1985.[90] At prevailing market prices for sugar Cuba's 1982 debt was equal in value to six years of sugar exports to market economies.

Despite these problems Cuba performed better in the management of its debt to Western commercial banks in the 1980s than almost any other Latin American country.[91] Moreover, this was achieved without cuts in social welfare spending, which was possible mainly because of Cuba's continuing advantageous terms of trade with the Soviet Union into the 1980s.

Conclusion

The second decade of the Revolution, the 1970s, is held by some Cuban scholars, in contrast to the heady independent years of the 1960s, as a decade of compromise during which the Castro government fell more closely in line with the Soviet Union. To support this 'Sovietisation of Cuba' thesis its advocates point to Cuba's entry into the CMEA trading system in 1972, Castro's public pronouncements in support of Soviet foreign policy, the adoption of Soviet economic models and management systems, and Cuban military support for the Soviet intervention in Ethiopia.[92] While one cannot deny that Cuba moved closer to the Soviet Union in the 1970s its foreign trade policy continued to exercise a high level of independence. Indeed, Cuba stands out, even in a decade when Moscow was giving its allies greater freedom to deal with capitalist countries, as the most audacious CMEA member country in its relations with the West. It could also be argued that Cuba exhibited the greatest skill among its fellow socialist states in its dealings with the West and reaped the most lasting rewards. In the 1970s, as in the 1960s, Western European countries played a crucial role in Cuba's development strategy.

Notes

1   For a study of internal economic problems in Cuba in the 1960s and the debates which they generated see Claes Brundenius, *Revolutionary Cuba: the Challenge of Economic Growth with Equity*, Boulder, Colorado, Westview, 1984, pp. 41–56.

2   One of the most serious examples of the failure of Soviet bloc technology to meet Cuban needs in the 1960s were the 1000 Russian-made KCT-1 sugar harvesters which were sent to Cuba between 1963–65. In operation this harvester was a disaster and even Fidel Castro described it as the 'great destroyer'. Subsequent attempts to produce a sugar harvester in the 1970s using Soviet and Cuban expertise were, however, much more successful.

3   For a contemporary assessment of Cuba's 1970 sugar harvest see Richard Gott, 'Castro's Crop of Trouble', *The Guardian*, 16 October 1970, p. 4. See also Herbert Marchant [British Ambassador to Cuba, 1961–63], 'Castro's Bitter Harvest', *New Society*, 8 October 1970, pp. 627–9.

4   In 1970 more than one-third of the labour force worked in part-time agriculture. See Andrew Zimbalist and Susan Eckstein, 'Patterns of Cuban Development: The First Twenty-Five Years', in Andrew Zimbalist (ed.), *Cuba's Socialist Economy Toward the 1990s*, London, Lynne Rienner, 1987, p. 10.

5   An excellent short survey of the restructuring of Cuba's domestic political economy in the 1970s and into the 1980s is to be found in Zimbalist and Eckstein, 'Patterns of Cuban Development', pp. 12–17. See Appendix II, p. 344 for details of Cuban sugar production and exports.

6   These figures are very approximate because of the complex pricing mechanisms of the sugar market, and inadequate information on the breakdown of sugar imports of individual countries (i.e. raw sugar, refined sugar, honey, molasses and sugar derivatives). See Appendix I, p. 342 for the list of information from which these figures have been extrapolated.

7   Calculations based on figures given in *Statistics of Foreign Trade*, OECD, 1975. George Volsky, writing for the *New York Times* estimated in January 1975 that if sugar prices remained at around 50 cents per pound Cuba could earn $4 billion dollars in hard currency in that year. Included in this figure are earnings for other Cuban exports, such as tobacco, citrus fruits and nickel, all of which were commanding higher prices than in previous years, see 'High

Sugar Prices Benefiting Cuba', 26 January 1975,' p. 69.

8   Morley, p. 267.

9   All ratios, percentages and other calculations relating to the merchandise trade of capitalist economies with Cuba in the 1970s is based on trade figures given in Appendix I, p. 342.

10   A breakdown of Cuban trade in the 1970s by countries and by merchandise categories is to be found in the 'Anuario Estadístico de Cuba' for relevant years. All subsequent trade statistics are taken from this source unless otherwise stated.

11   The dollar equivalents in parentheses of sums cited in pesos are approximate because the peso is not a convertible currency, and its dollar exchange rate is set by the Cuban National Bank and does not necessarily reflect true market values. Up to 1971 the peso was given parity with the dollar. Since then the following exchange rates have been suggested by Cuba: 1972 – $1.09, 1973 – $1.19, 1974 – $1.21, 1975 – $1.21, 1976 – $1.22, 1977 – $1.26, 1978 – $1.33, 1979 – $1.38, 1980 – $1.41, 1981 – $1.28, 1982 – $1.20. Source Banco Nacional de Cuba Informe Económico, Havana, 1982, p. 61.

12   'Anuario Estadístico de Cuba', Havana, 1979, pp. 190–205. Between 1973 and 1979 the Spanish company Pegaso supplied the following numbers of vehicles (mainly buses and trucks) to Cuba:

1973	–	435	1974	–	206	1975	–	1095
1976	–	189	1977	–	22	1978	–	412
1979	–	1027						

Information supplied by Manuel Lage Marco, Product Planning Manager, Pegaso, Madrid. Interview held 13 December 1988.

13   Interview with Manuel Lage Marco, Product Planning Manager, Pegaso (Madrid), 13 December 1988.

14   This and all subsequent information provided on contracts signed by French companies in Cuba in the 1970s, unless otherwise stated, was provided by André Stell the First Commercial Secretary at the French Embassy in Havana. Interview held 22 April 1988.

15   A study of the use of computers in Cuba in the first half of the 1970s has been made by Ramon C. Barquín in, 'Cuba: The Cybernetic Era', *Cuban Studies*, 5, 1975, pp. 1–33. The CII Honeywell Bull contract with Cuba is mentioned briefly in Alain-Marie Carron 'La Visite en France de M. Carlos Rafael Rodríguez', *Le Monde*, 17 January 1975, p. 36.

16   See Alain-Marie Carron, 'La Visite à Paris de M. Carlos Rafael Rodríguez', *Le Monde*, 16 January 1975, p. 1.

17   'La Visite en France de M. Carlos Rafael Rodríguez', *Le Monde*, 17 January 1975, p. 36.

18   See 'Cuba – growing prospects for British exports', *Trade and Industry*, 11 April 1975, pp. 71–3.

19   The most substantial plant construction contract for which British firms tendered in the 1970s was the building of a tyre factory near Havana. Apparently, negotiations reached an advanced level but the bid eventually fell through. See 'Tyre Factory in Cuba', *Trade and Industry*, 6 February 1976, p. 386.

20   See 'UK-Cuban co-operation agreement signed', *Trade and Industry*, 23 May 1975, p. 469. A list of areas where there were possibilities for economic and industrial co-operation was also included in the report.

21   See 'Peter Shore to visit Mexico and Cuba', *Trade and Industry*, 7 November 1975, p. 356.

22   See 'Peter Shore expectś exports to Cuba to exceed £40m', *Trade and Industry*, 5 December 1975, p. 645.

23   All information on the Seadrec contracts with Cuba was provided, unless otherwise stated, by Mr Ivan Robertson, a sales executive with Seadrec. Interview held in Paisley on 10 February 1989.

24   Details of ECGD support for the contract is given in *Trade and Industry*, 16 December 1970, p. 1021.

25   Full details of the agreement are given in Alberto Recarte, *Cuba: economía y poder*, 1959–80, Madrid, Alianza, 1980, p. 174.

26   According to Recarte, Cuba's deficit on its invisibles account with Spain was a result of extra costs incurred by the Cuban fishing fleet which was based in the Canary islands, p. 176.

27   See 'Cuba Closes Embassy in Spain; Trade Talks Reported Broken', *New York Times*, 4 August 1971, p. 2.

28   Details of the agreement are given in 'Firman Cuba y España convenio comercial', *Granma*, 20 December 1971, p. 8.

29   See Recarte, p. 176.

30   See *New York Times*, 10 September 1978 (supplementary material), p. 111.

31   For details of the agreement see *New York Times*, 4 January 1973, p. 10.

32   In a speech given to the National Assembly in December 1977 Fidel Castro acknowledged the importance of low-priced Soviet oil to Cuban economic development in the 1970s, stating: 'In 1976 our growth rate was 3.8 per cent and in 1977 just over 4 per cent not including the trade sector. In 1978 it will be 7.8 per cent in spite of the serious international situation . . . Suffice it to say that we are using nearly nine million tons of oil . . . and by 1978 we will consume 9.5 million tons. At present world prices the bill for this would come to 800 or 900 million dollars. By exporting sugar to the capitalist world at present prices, based on a market for Cuba in the capitalist world – of course this market does not and will not exist – at present prices, five million tons would bring us just over 800 million dollars [Cuba exported 2.050 million tons of sugar to the market economies in 1978 from which it earned about $350 million]. It would hardly be enough to pay for the oil, let alone all the food, raw materials, equipment and other products the country must import [from market economies].' A transcript of the speech can be found in *Granma Weekly Review*, 5 January 1978, pp. 1–3 (p. 2).

33   In 1967 the French economist Jean-Jacques Servan-Schreiber published his work *Le Défi Américain* in which he argued that US business was poised to sweep away its weaker European competitors in world markets. Ten years later a report produced by the Harvard Business School claimed that US expansion into foreign markets peaked in 1968 and from that time European and Japanese companies began to set the pace. See 'The Continental Challenge', *Economist*, 4 February 1978, pp. 78–9.

34   In the first half of the 1960s US balance of payments deficits averaged $742 million per year. But from 1965 they rose to an average of $3 billion per year. See Michael Moffitt, *The World's Money: International Banking from Bretton Woods to the Brink of Insolvency*, New York, Simon and Schuster, 1983, p. 30.

35   During the 1960s US exports to Latin America averaged 40 per cent of the region's total imports but by 1975 this figure had fallen dramatically to 30 per cent. See Morley, *Imperial State and Revolution*, p. 245.

36   Morley, pp. 247–8.

37   In 1973, for example, Western Europe absorbed about 30 per cent of Latin

America's exports and provided about 30 per cent of its imports. This was roughly equivalent to total US trade with the region at that time. See Lawrence B. Krause, 'Latin American Economic Relations with Western Europe', in Fontaine and Therberge, (eds) *Latin America's New Internationalism: the end of hemisphere isolation*, London, Praeger, 1976, pp. 150–1.

38   See David Binder 'US, in Shift, Views Perón As Argentina's Best Hope', *New York Times*, 29 July 1973, pp. 1–2.

39   See Johnathan Kandell, 'Argentina Offers a Credit to Cuba', *New York Times*, 7 August 1973, p. 7.

40   See Lewis H. Duiguid, 'US Boycott of Cuba Tested', *Washington Post*, 13 January 1974, p. A29.

41   See David Binder, *New York Times*, 'Latin Officials and Kissinger Open Talks', 18 April 1974, p. 5. During the controversy over the Argentine credit to Cuba, the Cuban daily *Granma* published frequent articles condemning the embargo and eagerly quoted Perón's comments on the same subject. See, for example, 'Crítica Perón el bloqueo de Estados Unidos contra Cuba' in which the Argentine president is reputed to have said that the blockade was 'a tragic error in US political strategy', 7 February 1974, p. 5.

42   Theodore H. Moran, 'The International Political Economy of Cuban Nickel Development', *Cuban Studies*, Vol.7, No.2, July 1977, p. 149.

43   The replacement of independent nationalist governments in Latin America by military dictatorships in the 1970s was an attempt by the US to reassert its hegemony in the region, and also part of a more complex process associated with the restructuring of America capitalism. The declining competitiveness of American industry and a falling rate of profit, coupled with the onset of a world recession from 1973, resulted in a need to reap more profits from the Third World. Repressive regimes were therefore needed to provide a suitable environment in which to achieve this objective. An element of this restructuring process was the movement of US capital out of extractive and agro-industries into labour-intensive manufacturing and service industries – the preferred areas of investment being the newly-industrialised countries of South-East Asia and Latin America. However, investments also flowed into very underdeveloped countries if they had governments that were totally subservient to Washington, like Haiti. The cheap labour resources of the Third World not only led to high profit ratios but also replaced high cost labour in the US by simply exporting jobs. The essential vehicle for these developments was the multinational corporation. A further indication of changes within American capitalism was the enormous increase in the number of US banks operating abroad. Much of their business was based on servicing the needs of US multinationals as they scoured the world for cheap labour, advantageous trading conditions and new markets. These developments did improve the competitiveness and profitability of American business, at least in its international operations. They also prepared an environment for coping with declining markets for US manufactures in the increasingly indebted and impoverished Third World, and a reorientation towards the markets of first world countries based on cheaper prices, the rapid transference of technological innovations to mass production, and above all, easy credit.

44   Morley, p. 267. Morley does not reveal his source for this information and the author can find no reference to this mission in either the *British Board of Trade Journal* or *The Times*. No report of such a mission was recorded in the Cuban press either.

45   *Ibid.*, p. 267.
46   See 'Spain and Cuba, Expensive Friends', *Economist*, 4 December 1971, p. 102.
47   See Morley, p. 277.
48   For details of the survey see 'US Says Cuba Ban is Less Effective', *New York Times*, 19 October 1975, p. 16.
49   The Cuban National Bank estimated in 1982 that between 1959 and 1981 the embargo cost Cuba over $9 billion. See Banco Nacional de Cuba, *Informe Económico*, Havana, 1982, p. 12.
50   Details of these modifications are given in Leslie H. Gelb, 'US Relaxes Ban Against Trading With the Cubans', *New York Times*, 22 August 1975, pp. 1, 8.
51   *Ibid.*, p. 1.
52   Between January and April Cuba dispatched 17,000 combat troops to Ethiopia to give support to the Mengistu government which faced a Somali-backed invasion of the disputed Ogadan province.
53   Morley provides an excellent survey of the efforts of sectors of the American business community to open up trade with Cuba in the 1970s, pp. 287–97.
54   The following table shows the decline in America's share of world exports of manufactured products from the mid-1960s to the mid-1970s.

Percentage share of world exports of manufactured goods of the major industrial powers

	United States	West Germany	Japan	France	Italy	Britain
1964	21.5	19.3	8.1	8.7	6.3	14.4
1970	18.5	19.8	11.7	8.7	7.2	10.8
1974	17.2	21.7	14.5	9.3	6.7	8.8
1975	17.7	20.3	13.6	10.2	7.5	9.3
1976	17.4	20.7	14.6	9.6	7.0	8.8

Source: OECD statistics 1964–76

55   One reason why many countries showed a preference for European and Japanese manufactured goods in the 1970s may have been because these products were often more efficient and energy saving than their American equivalents. This became a crucial factor after the 1973 oil price rise. With its vast natural resources and low population density the US gave little attention to saving energy before 1973, whereas its competitors with far fewer natural resources and denser populations had been designing their products for efficiency for decades.
56   As the value of the dollar fell compared to other currencies after 1971 US exports became cheaper and hence more competitive. However, as a corollary the US became increasingly attractive to European and Japanese investment. Indeed, not only companies based in the US but also companies around the world operating and valued in dollars became good bargains for holders of yen, deutschmarks and other hard currencies which were stronger than the dollar. Partly because of this the 1970s saw an unprecedented expansion of European and Japanese investment abroad.
57   Despite the intensification of competition between capitalist powers for export

markets in the 1970s there continued to exist an informal agreement between OECD governments to maintain the terms of suppliers' credits (credits extended to exporters in the country's own currency) within internationally recognised parameters. Any significant deviation from this standard would invite dumping allegations from rivals.

58　See H.J. Maidenberg, 'US Move on Trade With Cuba Acknowledges Present Practice', *New York Times*, 22 August 1975, p. 8.

59　Cited by Morley, p. 280.

60　The Cubans countered claims for compensation by asserting that they were entitled to substantial reparations from the US for losses they had incurred as a result of the global economic blockade, the Bay of Pigs invasion, and CIA sponsored sabotage operations carried out during the 1960s and early-1970s. See John Goshko, 'Cuba's Money Claims Exceed Those of US Trade, Minister Says', *Washington Post*, 4 October 1977, p. A18.

61　*New York Times*, 25 April 1976, IV, p. 3. Apparently Ford's advisers had been observing the negative response of the Canadian public to Prime Minister Pierre Trudeau's visit to Cuba the previous January.

62　For history of the Eurodollar market see M.S. Mendelsohn, *Money on the Move: the Modern International Capital Market*, London, McGraw-Hill, 1980. Mendelsohn points out in his study that the origin of the modern Eurocurrencies market goes back to the late-1940s and early-1950s, when the Soviet Union and China were obliged to place their dollar earnings in Western European banks rather than New York where they risked being confiscated, p. 36.

63　Moffitt, p. 48.

64　*Ibid.*, p. 60.

65　In 1973 the Third World owed private banks about $30 billion. By 1983 this figure had increased ten-fold to £300 billion.

66　During the 1970s the Soviet Union was also in an exceptionally strong trading position with the capitalist nations, because its two main hard currency exports oil and gold increased in value 20-fold and 14-fold respectively during the decade. It has been calculated that in the 1970s the terms of trade between the USSR and the world market improved for the former by 77 per cent. See Jan Vanous, 'East European Economic Slowdown', *Problems of Communism*, July–August 1982, pp. 1–19 (p. 9).

67　See Susumu Awanohara, 'Export Drive for Japan's Plant Sales', *Far Eastern Economic Review*, 16 May 1975, p. 51.

68　Despite these auspicious conditions for creditors the Eurobanks set Cuban interest payments at 1.75 per cent above Libor, which although the average rate for loans to most of Latin America was the highest allocated to CMEA members.

69　It has been suggested that the untied loans Cuba contracted in the second half of the 1970s also helped to finance the Castro government's overseas military operations in support of liberation movements. See Ernesto F. Betancourt and Wilson P. Dizard III, 'Fidel Castro and the Bankers: The Mortgaging of a Revolution', in *Cuban Communism*, edited by Irving Louis Horowitz, New Brunswick, Transaction, 1984, pp. 191–209 (pp. 191–2).

70　Morley, p. 271. All further information on loans and credits to Cuba in the 1970s comes from the same source unless otherwise stated.

71　Betancourt and Dizard III, 'Fidel Castro and the Bankers', p. 194.

72　Details of the loan are given in *Trade and Industry*, 16 December 1970, p. 234. The syndicate of banks comprised of Bank of Scotland, Royal Bank of Scotland, Barclay's, Lloyds, the Midland and National Westminster. The loan was to be paid over five years from the scheduled date of delivery of the order.

73   See 'British £3 million credit for Cuba', *Trade and Industry*, 24 February 1972, p. 335. The credit was offered to the Cubans at a fixed rate of interest of 6.5 per cent and was to be repaid over two to five years.

74   For details see 'Second line of credit for Cuba', *Trade and Industry*, 26 September 1974, p. 645. Commenting on the previous credit it was noted that this had been extended to £5 million. Cuban purchases with this credit included orders for telephone equipment, dumper trucks, irrigation equipment, pumps, turbines and diesel alternator sets.

75   See 'Four SD14 cargo vessels for Cuba', *Trade and Industry*, 23 May 1975, p. 469.

76   For details of the loan see 'Cuba: £7.6m contract for tugs and dredgers', *Trade and Industry*, 6 June 1975, p. 579.

77   See Malcolm Rutherford, 'UK to give Cuba £250m. credit', *Financial Times*, 21 May 1975, p. 1.

78   *Ibid.* The Cuban signatory of the agreement, Vice-President Rodríguez, indicated that if negotiations with British companies to build three fertiliser plants in Cuba were successful this would absorb about £85 million of the credit. A British government spokesman also said that British Leyland had submitted a tender to build a truck and bus assembly plant on the island. When questioned on this Dr Rodríguez warned that the Spaniards would also be strong contenders for the contract.

79   For an analysis of trends in terms of trade for primary products since the Second World War see Frédéric F. Clairmonte, 'Détérioration des termes d'échange et "désaccumulation" du capital', *Le Monde Diplomatique*, September 1975, pp. 14–18.

80   In the first half of the 1970s, and especially after the oil price rise in 1973, the number of Third World orders placed with the industrialised countries for complete plant increased dramatically. For example, the value of Japan's export of plant and complete factories to the Third World and socialist countries rose from $1.5 billion dollars in 1972 to $3 billion in 1974. See Awanohara, 'Export Drive for Japan's Plant Sales', p. 51.

81   One of the reasons why the prices of some raw materials increased so substantially between 1973 and 1975 was because of speculative buying. To protect themselves against currency fluctuations, and especially the declining value of the dollar, many speculators moved their capital into raw materials which it was widely believed would be in short supply for a number of years. Escalating prices also induced many companies to begin stockpiling raw materials. Speculation and stockpiling kept prices rising until the recession began to deepen, and the laws of supply and demand came into operation again. Under these circumstances the market price of a commodity could collapse overnight.

82   In retrospect Cuba was a far better credit risk in the mid- to late-1970s than other CMEA members which followed a similar economic strategy based on extensive borrowing from Western banks. Poland is a case in point. By the late-1970s the Polish economy had already begun to lose direction, but undaunted by economic realities and extracting huge amounts of surplus value out of Polish workers via the back door of high interest rates, the bankers kept on pumping money into the crumbling Gierek regime.

83   An extreme instance of capital flight was the outflows of capital from Venezuela between 1979 and 1982 which totalled 137 per cent of capital inflows.

The average rate of capital flight from the mid-1970s to the early-1980s among Latin American nations was probably between 40–50 per cent of inflows. See Jackie Roddick, *The Dance of the Millions: Latin America and the Debt Crisis*, London, Latin America Bureau, 1988, p. 65.

84 For a record of Cuba's balance of trade with capitalist and socialist economies from 1960 to 1984 see Richard Turits, 'Trade, Debt, and the Cuban Economy', in *Cuba's Socialist Economy Towards the 1990s*, edited by Andrew Zimbalist, Boulder, Colorado, Lynne Rienner, 1987, pp. 165–82 (p. 168).

85 Eckstein, 'Capitalist constraints on Cuban socialist development', p. 267.

86 See Morris H. Morley, *Imperial State and Revolution*, p. 269. According to Carmelo Mesa-Lago, 22 major investment projects, mainly financed by Western banks, had to be cancelled in the late-1970s because of shortages of hard currency, see *The Economy of Socialist Cuba*, Albuquerque, 1981, p. 99.

87 Brundenius, *Revolutionary Cuba*, p. 58.

88 One of the most lucid studies of the Third World debt is by the outstanding Cuban economist Raúl León Torras who represented his country in the Paris Club of Western creditor governments from 1982, the year Cuba first renegotiated its debt to Western banks, until his death in 1987. See Raúl León Torras, *Antología*, Havana, 1988.

89 Figure given in Banco Nacional de Cuba, *Informe económico*, p. 18. Cited by Zimbalist and Eckstein, p. 17.

90 See Turits, *Trade, Debt, and the Cuban Economy*, p. 172.

91 For an analysis of Cuba's debt management in the 1980s see Turits, *Trade, Debt, and the Cuban Economy*.

92 See, for example, Carmelo Mesa-Lago, *Cuba in the 1970s: Pragmatism and Institutionalisation*, Albuquerque, University of New Mexico Press, 1978.

CHAPTER 10

Western Europe and Cuba's development in the 1980s and 1990s

Gareth Jenkins

Cuba's economic fortunes at the end of the 1980s stood in stark contrast to the apparent economic dynamism with which it entered the decade. Although economic malaise was an important factor in the mass emigration to the US of 125,000 Cubans from the port of Mariel in 1980, the first half of the decade witnessed consistent double digit growth rates. These were spurred by strategic investments in the previous decade, made possible by a combination of stable trading relations with the Soviet Union and Eastern Europe and high world sugar prices.

By the mid-1980s, however, Cuba was in recession, and had contracted a Latin American-style debt problem, with the West as well as with the Soviet Union. Its hard currency debt per capita amounted to some $600 by the end of 1988, which should be multiplied several times for a true comparison with other Latin American countries, since Cuba's hard currency trade was at the time only 10–20 per cent of its total trade.

The decade ended with the collapse of the East European regimes, in alliance with which Cuba had built its economy over the previous 30 years. There were soon predictions throughout the US and European press that without Soviet largesse the Cuban regime would be the next domino to fall, fuelled by reports of exiles in Miami preparing to return in triumph to the island.

As these words are written, two and a half years later, the Castro regime remains in place, with apparently only minimal coherent opposition from inside the country. Most of the dissidents call for dialogue with rather than a direct challenge to the government, claim to support its socialist aspirations, and to demand from the US an end to the economic embargo. Certainly, the scale of political repression of oppositionists has increased quite sharply, but it is remarkable that the government should appear to be still so firmly in control after the economy has been slashed almost in half in just two years.

It is now as clear to Cuban officials as it is to foreign analysts that, whatever the long-term promise of tourism and export sectors such as nickel, oil and biotechnology, substantial economic improvement will be dependent on the integration of the economy into Western markets, and specifically on the re-establishment of normal relations with the US. Yet after two years in which reports of the Cuban regime's demise have been greatly exaggerated, some unlikely observers are beginning to conclude that the Cuban regime could continue to bump along the bottom for some time to come. This, for example, was the conclusion of a Roundtable held at the US Army War College in January 1992.[1]

An issue of domestic policy in the US

The collapse of its CMEA partners has thrown into sharper relief the role Cuba plays as an essentially domestic policy issue in the US. Prompted by the thought that with one last heave the Castro regime would collapse, the right wing Cuban American National Foundation encouraged a series of legislative attempts to tighten the economic embargo. In 1991 an Amendment sponsored by Florida Republican Senator Connie Mack, which would have outlawed trade with Cuba by third country subsidiaries of US corporations, cleared both houses of Congress as part of the Export Administration Act. The Bush administration, however, chose to throw it out, presumably concerned about the extra-territorial legal implications.

The main provisions of the Mack Amendment were carried forward in a new and more far-reaching bill introduced by Republican Robert Torricelli (D-NJ) in the autumn of 1991, known as the Cuba Democracy Act. At first political observers assumed that this would go the same way as the Mack Amendment, but as a result of astute lobbying the Foundation succeeded in making it an issue in the presidential election campaign. Bill Clinton was encouraged to voice his support for Torricelli at a Miami rally in April 1992, and it was not long before George Bush also came out in support.

However, the longer the Castro regime survives, and the more non-US firms sign high profile investment deals in Cuba, the greater the momentum for a change of US policy. A conference organised by the London financial magazine *Euromoney* on investment opportunities in Cuba, held in Cancun and Havana in June 1992 and aimed specifically at US business, exemplifies the pressures which are building to allow Americans to resume business with Cuba. Ironically, the Torricelli Bill appears to have accentuated this trend, with the *Miami Herald* opposing it and coming under fierce attack from the Foundation as a 'tool of the Castro regime' – a charge which requires a lively imagination to sustain.

Increased role of Western Europe and Canada

During the 1980s the US embargo continued to hinder Cuba's development, but more through restricting access to trade and investment relations with the US directly than through hampering its trade with other Western countries. The main exception was the success of the Reagan administration in bullying West European, Japanese and Canadian steelmakers into excluding Cuban nickel from their exports to the US.

On the other hand, in the middle of the decade the embargo began to break down spectacularly as Cuba re-established relations with most of Latin America, thus ending more than 20 years of regional isolation during which only Mexico and Canada had refused to accord it diplomatic recognition. The signing in 1991 by the Canadian nickel refiner Sherritt Gordon of a $1.2 billion investment deal with Cubaniquel, despite rumoured pressure from the US, was a further indication of the limitations of American influence over other countries' trade policies towards Cuba.

European business took advantage of the strong performance of the Cuban economy in the early-1980s to increase trade, at a time when the rest of Latin America was in deep recession. Cuba in its turn suffered the vicissitudes of the international financial and commodity markets, particularly the dramatic increase in interest rates in the early Reagan years. Nevertheless, Cuba remained an essentially marginal market, with total hard currency imports of around $1 billion a year.

While Cuba has not experienced the dynamic economic growth of the South-East Asian NICs (Newly Industrialised Countries), based on intense exploitation of the workforce and ready access to advanced US and Japanese technology and markets, it has nevertheless pursued a moderately successful import substitution programme. It has developed a range of hard currency export products which include primary products such as citrus, coffee, seafoods, marble and metals, and also industrial products such as cement, iron and steel products, clothing, medicines and non-electrical machinery. Within the last few years Cuba has also begun to produce sophisticated products such as video recorders, colour televisions, software applications and, most impressively, biotech products.

High-risk biotechnology strategy

The success of the biotechnology programme, which only began in 1981, throws into relief both the strengths and the weaknesses of Cuba's industrialisation programme. In that year a nationwide programme was launched to promote biological research – the 'Frente Biológico' – and a group of leading researchers from various centres began work on producing human leukocyte alpha interferon. They received initial training in Helsinki on production techniques, and Cuban interferon was ready for use in the treatment of dengue fever in June 1981. The following year the Centro de Investigaciones Biológicas (CIB) was established. Construction of a much larger research centre, the Centro de Ingenería Genética y Biotechnológia (CIGB), was completed in the summer of 1986. Visiting two years later US Senate Foreign Relations Committee Chair Claiborne Pell remarked that he 'was struck by the fact that the medical research equipment used in the impressive high-technology Institute of Genetic Engineering, where significant cancer research is being undertaken and genetic materials are being developed, was of Japanese, Swedish and German manufacture. Better quality and less expensive equipment, especially in terms of shipping costs, is available in the United States'.[2]

The biotechnology programme received early scientific backing from Soviet institutes, such as the Mechnikov Institute for Vaccines and Sera in Moscow. Early scientific help also came from Sweden, Italy, Spain and Denmark.

Western companies began to get involved with the setting up of the CIB. The Swedish company Pharmacia LKB, which first began selling pharmaceuticals to Cuba in 1980, soon realised there was potential for the biotech sector to develop – though they candidly admit they did not foresee the scale it has now reached. Another company which has been strongly involved since the mid-1980s is the British company Amersham International which – together with Pharmacia LKB, Boehringer Mannheim of Germany, Sakura of Japan and Exportandes of Colombia – sponsored Cuba's third triennial seminar on interferon and second on biotechnology in April 1989.

This seminar marked the coming of age of Cuban biotech. It was attended by 1700 delegates from some 50 countries, including ten Nobel prize winners, and was the biggest conference to date on biotechnology in Latin America. Roughly 40 per cent of the delegates were from Latin America and another 40 per cent from Eastern Europe.

Cuban biotech products have been successfully tested in a number of foreign countries. For instance, the CIGB's AIDS diagnostic kit has been tested in Havana and Stockholm on two panels of HIV carriers, and on AIDS patients at different stages of illness. The automated immunoassay system, SUMA, which analyzes blood, sera or tissue samples using computerised techniques, has been presented at international fairs in Leipzig, Brno and Plovdiv, as well as in Brazil, Spain and Sweden. SUMA was developed by the specialist Immunoassay Centre, which was opened in 1987.

Another important achievement of the Immunoassay Centre is the development of the world's first vaccine against meningococcal meningitis type B, originally discovered by the National Centre for Biological Preparations. The results were first presented at a conference in Amsterdam in September 1986, and the results of field trials at a conference in Atlanta, USA in November 1988. The vaccine has been tested in Spain, Finland, Denmark and Brazil. Success in combating the virus in Brazil led first to exports of Cuban-produced vaccines, and subsequently, in 1991, to a Cuban-Brazilian venture to produce the vaccines in Brazil and market them jointly. The vaccines are reported to be yielding revenues of $100–200 million a year.

The United Nations Industrial Development Organisation (UNIDO), in conjunction with the International Centre for Genetic Engineering and Biotechnology (ICGEB), based in New Delhi and Trieste, sponsored a workshop in Cuba on biotechnology in Latin America and the Caribbean in February 1988. The Cuban CIGB has been accepted as an affiliated centre to the ICGEB, one of only four in Latin America.

The biotech programme receives support from the United Nations Development Programme (UNDP). UNDP funded projects for the period 1986–90 in the field of biotechnology included: the installation of a pilot fermentation plant ($1 million); training of researchers ($800,000); and development of technology for clinical reagents ($400,000).

Non-medical biotechnological research is also being carried out in Cuba. The main areas are: research into methods for diagnosing diseases in livestock and crops; plant biology research, including in-vitro tissue culture in sugar cane; research into sugar cane by-products using yeast culture and other biotechnology techniques; and the production of nitrogen fixation bacteria for use in plant cultivation.

Consistent support by a stable national state has made this programme possible where many other developing countries have failed. However, Cuba has had to begin from scratch in developing the marketing networks and promotional skills to take advantage of its research capability. Its weakness in these areas can take very simple, but devastating forms. For instance, a number of Cuba's biotech products have tested well in Brazil, Sweden and other countries, but Cuba has failed to take the most basic steps to publicise the results, without which foreign experts will not take them seriously.

Heber Biotec S.A. has been set up as an independent marketing company for Cuba's 160 or so biotech products in recognition of these problems. It has been concentrating on organising registration and clinical trials in potential markets, and has patented some products in Venezuela, Colombia, Brazil and Argentina. Its general manager, Dr Carlos Mella, has said that he hopes to have some products accepted in the European market by the mid-1990s.[3]

Cuba has adopted a niche marketing approach to its biotech exports, concentrating on Latin America (primarily Brazil) and the former CMEA countries. Plans for 1991 included biotech and medical exports to the Soviet Union of some $700 million, with another $100 million to Latin America. In the previous year, however, these Cuban products failed to show up at all in the Soviet foreign trade statistics – despite earlier Cuban projections of exports of $250–300 million.

Now Cuba must develop new niches in the former Soviet republics and elsewhere in the Third World. New deals have been signed with former Soviet republics, Mexico, China and India. In the case of one or two products – such as streptokinase, which can limit damage from a heart attack, monoclonal antibodies, various reagents and an epidermal growth factor for patients with burns – Cuba could perhaps penetrate the world market with the assistance of a foreign partner.

Developmental contradiction

A *Financial Times* survey highlighted the tension between Cuba's achievements and aspirations and the shortages and inefficiencies which hold it back from realising its potential: 'It is one thing to produce interferons, it is another to sell them to the rest of the world. Can Cuba supply its customers reliably when the workers that produce these quality products have to spend much of their time waiting for a bus, or standing in a queue for tomatoes?'[4]

This, at its sharpest, is the fundamental contradiction of Cuba's economic development. It is as though many of the mechanisms are in place for the functioning of a modern economy, but certain crucial cogs and lubricants have been forgotten. Problems arise in one sector, resources are allocated to resolve them, but only for them to reappear somewhere else.

Before the breakdown of central planning which has accompanied the crisis of the early-1990s, the reasons seemed to lie firstly in inflexibilities and lack of adequate signals to permit the efficient continuous allocation of labour, and secondly in the country's inadequate integration into the world division of labour. These are problems Cuba shares with many other developing countries, though in Cuba's case they took a specific form as a result of its adoption of CMEA style planning mechanisms. For instance, the attempt to control millions of individual prices through a central bureaucracy becomes increasingly hard as industrialisation advances. As a result labour, equipment and materials were often allocated inefficiently.

Cuba also faces other external constraints which exacerbate its internal problems of economic organisation. Although it benefited greatly from privileged access to CMEA markets for its products, it has received little comparable preference in its relations with Western economies. The one exception was Spain which throughout the period has negotiated state level bilateral trade agreements for all products except nickel. Even this special relationship, however, is now coming to an end as Spain becomes fully integrated into the EC.

Effects of the US embargo

After the partial thaw of the Carter years the US embargo continued to constrain Cuba's development in the 1980s, mainly through restricting access to US product and financial markets. A May 1981 US Commerce Department study triumphantly concluded that:

> . . . the continued denial of Cuban access to US trade and financial markets has effectively restricted the potential for trade and invest-ment by other Western countries and narrowly circumscribed Ha-vana's options for economic development, forcing increased dependence on CMEA. Thus, the US embargo has been and continues to be not only a major, but a crucial impediment to Cuba's efforts at diversifying and expanding its hard currency trade, the key to im-proved economic growth and living standards.[5]

During the last year of the Carter administration US policy towards Cuba became tougher. In late-1979 the US successfully blocked Cuba's election to the UN Security Council. The following November the US government invoked legislation dating from 1963 to ban the import of special steels from the French company Creusot-Loire which contained Cuban nickel.

The new Reagan administration tried to tighten the embargo still further. During 1981 and the first half of 1982 it exposed more than 40 companies which it claimed were 'pass throughs', set up specifically to enable Cuba to trade with US companies through third countries. The Treasury Department labelled them 'designated Cuban nationals' and with-drew licences to trade with Cuba. Morris Morley suggests that this largely explains the decline in Cuban purchases from US third country subsidiaries in 1981. These had increased from $89.4 million in 1979 to $303.2 million in 1980, but dropped back to $73.8 million in 1981.[6] However, it would seem that Cuba quickly found ways to restore this trade as it increased to $253 million in 1982, and averaged $259 million over the six years 1982–87.[7]

The US also took action against several non-US Western companies. In February 1982 all US export privileges were temporarily withdrawn from the Spanish-based company Piher Semiconductors for allegedly ex-porting to Cuba products containing US components banned under Cocom, the Nato body for the control of exports of high technology products from the West to the socialist countries. In December 1983 similar measures were taken against Toshiba Ampex of Japan for exporting US television components to Cuba, and in June 1984 against Saburo Soejima and Hiroshi Minabe for re-exporting US video recorders.[8]

The British electronics firm Plessey also became caught up in the US anti-Cuban policy, though in this case when the US invaded Grenada in October 1983. Plessey was working on the airport being built to enable Grenada to develop international tourism, on which the Cuban construction enterprise Uneca was also contracted to work.[9] One of the main reasons given by the US for the invasion was that Cuba was building a military airport. Plessey subsequently issued a statement which identified 11 facilities which any military airbase would require, and certifying that none of them were in evidence at the Grenada airport.[10]

The National Security Council extended the policy developed under Carter of tightening restrictions on the permitted Cuban content of US imports, particularly targeting sugar and nickel. It eventually dropped its attempt to enforce the ban on sugar as this would have complicated its trade with Canada too much. However, Cuba claimed that US pressure on Canada was responsible for the termination of discussions with Petrocanada for offshore oil exploration, with Canadawide for the construction of a citrus plant and with another Canadian firm bidding for a power station contract.[11]

US action to reduce Cuban nickel exports was more successful. The Cuban National Bank claimed in 1982 that at least six Western companies had suspended discussions to invest in the nickel industry and some had even cancelled signed contracts as a result of US pressure. The following year more European companies reneged on investment contracts. In 1982 and 1983 the Treasury Department obtained agreements from the governments of Italy, Japan, the Netherlands, West Germany and even the Soviet Union that steel exports to the USA would not contain Cuban nickel. These measures taken together not only slowed down the development of the Cuban nickel industry but also substantially reduced the hard currency Cuba was able to earn from its exports, forcing it to sell larger quantities to the Soviet Union.

In September 1991 the Cuban government supplied a list to the United Nations General Assembly of recent trade operations for the purchase of spare parts, medical and laboratory equipment for which the US Treasury Department refused export licences to companies from third countries which trade with Cuba. In each case the equipment contained components manufactured by US companies. The third country companies listed were Siemens (Germany), LKB Pharmacia (Sweden), Toshiba (Japan), Nihon Kohden (Japan), CGR (France) and Medix (Argentina). The Cuban UN document (A/46/193/Add. 7, 13 September 1991) went on to list 11 ways in which it was claimed that US laws infringe the sovereignty of other states.[12]

There remain many unexplained interventions of the US authorities. One of the strangest involved Cuba's Commercial Attaché at its London embassy in a shooting on a busy London street one afternoon in September 1988. What appears to have happened is that a group of five people – the Cuban defector Florentino Azpillaga and a woman friend, and three members of the CIA and the British MI5 – surprised the attaché Carlos Medina Pérez outside his apartment in a kidnap attempt. However, Carlos Medina drew a gun and shot Azpillaga in the stomach, possibly fatally. Azpillaga's minders bundled him and his friend into a car and drove off. The British authorities drew a veil of silence over the event and Azpillaga has not been heard of since.

This shooting could simply be the outcome of an abortive attempt to encourage Carlos Medina to defect, in which the US and British security services were outwitted. But some observers have suggested that the timing and location of the attempt may not have been coincidental. For several months the British shipbuilding subsidiary NESL (North East Shipbuilders) of Sunderland had been bidding for a £100 million order from the Cuban shipping enterprise Mambisa.

If it had won the contract this would not only have been the biggest single deal ever between Britain and Cuba, but it would also have saved NESL from closure. There had even been serious discussions about a consortium including Mambisa wishing to bid for private ownership of the state-owned yard should the contract be awarded to NESL. The potential bid had been the subject of a debate in the British Parliament on 21 July. Industry Minister Kenneth Clarke stated that his department would not be prepared to sanction a subsidy from its shipbuilding intervention fund to enable NESL to bid for the Cuban order so long as the company remained in the public sector. It is possible that the apparent attempt to kidnap Carlos Medina was intended to help turn political opinion further against support for Mambisa's interest in NESL.[13]

Trade with the West

Cuba's nineteenth century hero, José Martí, once defined his aspirations to national sovereignty in terms of the right 'to trade with the whole world and not with just a part of it'. Che Guevara provided an up-dated version of Martí's ideal in an article he wrote in 1964 which was published, rather surprisingly, in *International Affairs*, the journal of the Royal Institute of International Affairs in London. In his article he explained to his capitalist readers that while the days of the economic system which supported them were numbered, they could nevertheless profit from trade with Cuba as a result of the self-exclusion of their imperialist American rival from the market.[14]

Many West European firms have indeed taken advantage of the vacuum left by the Cuban expulsion of US capital, as shown in previous chapters. Their trade with Cuba expanded rapidly from the mid-1970s up to 1981, since when it has fluctuated in line with hard currency availability from exports and access to Western credits.

In 1980 and 1981 Cuba's imports from Western Europe amounted to 13.2 per cent and 13.4 per cent of its total imports, reaching 686.6 million pesos in 1981. If Canada and Japan are included, Western countries accounted for 19.5 per cent and 18.1 per cent of total imports in those two years, with the East European countries accounting for 75.5 per cent and 77.3 per cent. This performance was close to what Cuban foreign trade officials considered optimal at the time.

The share of Western Europe in total imports between 1982–7 dropped to 6–8 per cent. Large imports from Japan between 1984–6 kept the total Western share above 11 per cent, but the rescheduling impasse since then caused it to fall to 8.2 per cent in 1987 and around 7.6 per cent in 1988.

To some extent this decline was compensated for by increased hard currency imports from other Latin American countries, particularly Argentina and Mexico. These amounted to 293.7 million pesos in 1987 – 46.9 per cent of the value of Western imports – compared with 63.5 million pesos in 1982, when they were only 11.4 per cent of the value of Western imports. As relations have improved, particularly since 1986, Latin America has come to offer an alternative source of some Western industrial goods such as Volkswagen and Nissan cars for the tourist sector. They also include substantial quantities of products supplied by US third country subsidiaries.

During the 1980s the largest single component of imports from the West was complete industrial plants. In 1987 83.8 million pesos out of a total of 720.1 million pesos spent on plant imports went to Western companies. By far and away the largest supplier was Spain (54.3 million pesos), followed by France, Italy and Japan.

Despite growing import substitution, Cuba's demand for medicines and pharmaceuticals continued to grow rapidly, with the result that imports of medicines increased from 13.3 million pesos in 1980 to 40.8 million pesos in 1987. According to the published statistics, only about 15 per cent of the latter were from Western Europe. However, the big Western pharmaceutical companies are able to supply from other countries in the region – for instance, Glaxo from Panama and Hoffmann-La Roche from Costa Rica. Cuba's hard currency spending on all health care related products including hospital and laboratory equipment at the end of the decade was close to $150 million a year.

Agrochemicals are another important hard currency import. Western countries accounted for 45.1 million pesos out of total imports of 76.9 million pesos in 1987. The main suppliers in recent years have been Switzerland, West Germany and the United Kingdom.

The other main categories of hard currency imports are agrochemicals, machinery, construction equipment and transport equipment. However, Cuba's success in developing an agricultural machinery industry, especially cane cutting machines, is evident from the low level of imports in this sector – around 15–20 million pesos a year during the decade.

The main factors governing Cuba's ability to import hard currency products from the West have been the level of its sugar and nickel exports to non-CMEA markets; its re-exports of Soviet petroleum not required for domestic consumption; exports of citrus fruits and juices, seafoods and tobacco products; tourism revenues; and Western official and commercial bank credits, which dried up in the second half of the 1980s. Although before the collapse of the CMEA exports of sugar and its derivatives accounted for around 75 per cent of all exports on a peso basis, they typically generated only around $300 million a year in hard currency as most was committed to the USSR.

The most important West European importers of Cuban products over the years 1980–88 were Spain, with total imports of 713 million pesos, France (446 million pesos), Switzerland (410 million pesos), West Germany (286 million pesos), Italy (263 million pesos) and the UK (201 million pesos). Of the other Western countries, Cuban exports to Canada fell from an average of 117 million pesos a year in 1980–81 to an average of 39 million pesos a year from 1982–88, largely as a result of US pressure on Canada to reduce imports of Cuban nickel. Japan, on the other hand, maintained high levels of imports from Cuba throughout most of the period, totalling 799 million pesos between 1980–88.

Hidden in the official trade statistics are quite substantial trade transactions with the US. Under the embargo legislation US corporations have, since 1975, been able to apply to the Office of Foreign Assets Control of the Treasury Department for a licence to trade with Cuba through third country subsidiaries. A study by the Johns Hopkins University shows that between 1982–87 1279 applications were approved, an average of 183 per year.[15] This figure jumped to 321 in 1990.[16]

Between 1982-87 these licences resulted in $693 million of exports to Cuba – consisting of $406 million of grain, wheat and other consumables and $287 million of industrial and other non-consumables – and $869 million of imports from Cuba. The main imports were sugar (60.1 per cent) and naphtha (34.7 per cent). Over the five years 1982–86 the most important third country involved in this trade was the UK, which accounted for $480 million out of total two way trade of $1307 million. The most important other countries were Switzerland ($239 million), Canada ($211 million), Bermuda ($165 million), Argentina ($103 million), Panama ($27 million), France ($25 million) and Spain ($23 million).[17]

To this authorised third country trade must be added an unknown amount of trade which US corporations engaged in through companies not registered as subsidiaries, in particular companies registered in Panama. This trade has been a more or less open secret for years. One of the revelations which emerged as a result of the drug trafficking scandal which hit Cuba in June 1989 was the existence of the secret department MC within the Ministry of the Interior authorised by the government to break the US embargo, particularly for electronics and health care products. It was this department which the La Guardia brothers used as a cover for their dealings with the Medellín drugs cartel, transhipping cocaine to Florida in IBM computer boxes via the Varadero military airport.

By the middle of the 1980s Cuba's imports from market economy countries were running at around $1.2 billion a year, still some way below the $1.5 billion which Cuban economists estimated as necessary for industry to operate efficiently. After the onset of the economic crisis in 1986 these hard currency imports dropped to an average of $936 million in 1987–88, leaving industry limping for lack of materials, equipment and spare parts. Although Cuba has stopped publishing trade and many other economic statistics, the situation has since dramatically declined still further.

Return of tourism

In order to break out of dependency on sugar Cuba needs to generate substantially greater export revenues to enable it to participate more fully in the international industrial division of labour. This is why, after two decades of spurning tourism as a source of foreign exchange, the government eventually took the decision to open up the country to Western tourism. The National Institute of Tourism (Intur), set up in 1959 to rescue the industry, was dusted off and set to renovating hotels, developing infrastructure and attracting a new generation of tourists.

The number of hard currency tourists visiting Cuba rose from 78,000 in 1980 – of which 22,000 were from Canada and 35,000 from the US – to 149,000 by 1986, despite the loss of the US market when Reagan tightened travel restrictions. The main markets it succeeded in developing during this period were West Germany (23,000 in 1986), Spain (20,000), Mexico (13,000), Italy (11,000) and Argentina (7000).

The government passed its first joint venture law (Decree No. 50) in 1982 specifically with an eye on attracting foreign investment in hotel construction and other tourist facilities, but substantial investments were slow to materialise. The only major interest in negotiating a joint venture was from the French hotel chain Novotel which was interested in contracting to manage four hotels, including the Habana Libre, the former Hilton. But talks broke down in 1986 when Novotel discovered that the staff to room ratio at the Habana Libre was 2.2, compared with 0.3 in their French hotels.

This experience pushed the government to set up a new rival enterprise to Intur in 1987 which would operate outside the existing structure for foreign trade enterprises – Cubanacán S.A. There was already a precedent for this type of corporation in Cuba. In 1977 the Panamanian-registered corporation Cimex S.A. was established to take advantage of the visits of Cuban émigrés returning to Cuba from the USA to visit relatives as a result of a relaxation of restrictions under President Carter.

Cubanacán was set up with a specific brief to attract foreign investment in joint ventures. 1442 tourist rooms, mostly in hotels in Havana and Varadero, were transferred to Cubanacán from Intur, and in addition it was given responsibility for developing the eastern half of the island for tourism – Santiago, Granma, Baracoa, Holguín, Santa Lucia, Trinidad and the Isle of Youth.

The tourism of the 1950s was narrowly based on Havana and the casinos. Cuba now has the opportunity to develop tourist centres throughout the island, and on the 1600 keys and small islands which surround its coast. In terms of geography, natural attractions, historical heritage and the splendour of Havana – now being restored with assistance from UNESCO – Cuba could easily eclipse the rest of the Caribbean in the world tourist market.

However, the modern tourism industry is intensely competitive and dominated by a handful of giant tour operators. In order to advance from its current position of attracting some 600,000 tourists a year to the one million or even two million mark which is put forward as a target for the second half of the 1990s, Cuba will have to create the infrastructure, provide the international and domestic transportation and develop the level of personal service demanded by these tour operators.

More attention is being paid to staff training at all levels – including language training – smart new hotels are going up, airports are being revamped, new coaches and cars are being purchased and recreation facilities developed. So far the hotels are full and earnings per tourist are increasing steadily. Service has improved remarkably, stimulated by the return of personal tipping.

Most of the hotel construction deals have so far been with Spanish firms. For instance, in early 1989 a joint venture, Hoteles de Cuba, was set up with the Spanish firm Ibercusa. It is building two hotels with a total of 900 rooms in Havana, including the 21-storey Cohiba next to the Riviera hotel, and is participating in the 1000 room Guardalavaca Beach hotel programme in the east of the island. Another Spanish company, Cadena de Hoteles Unidas, overhauled the management of the Marina Hemingway complex in Havana in 1988 and a hotel school was opened under its guidance.

The first joint venture hotel – the Sol Palmeras in Varadero resort, with the Spanish partner Sol Melia – opened in the summer of 1990, and the Spanish management was given the right to hire and fire staff. Occupancy rates are reported as averaging over 80 per cent, and both partners expect to recover their total investment in just 2.7 years – leaving 22 years of a 25 year contract to make a clear profit after running costs.

By the end of 1991 Varadero resort had 5450 hotel and villa rooms, and another 2500 were to be added by the end of 1992. Sol Palmeras was building two more hotels in Varadero – the 490 room Melia Varadero and the 250 room Melia Las Américas.

Non-Spanish investors have followed, such as the Jamaican Superclubs hotel chain which has taken over one Varadero hotel and will build another. This Jamaican interest is in clear recognition that Cuba is emerging as a serious challenge to the regional tourism industry.

The upswing in foreign investment activity has helped to boost the number of tourists visiting Cuba, which rose from 243,000 in 1985 to 340,000 in 1990. Despite the Gulf War, which hit Caribbean tourism in general very hard, the number of tourists visiting Cuba in 1991 jumped by 24.4 per cent to 423,000. Canada, West Germany, Mexico and Spain are currently the leading markets for Cuban tourism.

Intur president Rafael Sed Pérez, speaking at a press conference before the 1991 Tourism Convention (4–7 June), said that Cuba's hard currency earnings from tourism had increased from $75 million in 1984 to $250 million in 1990. He also said that every 38 cents invested produced a return of one dollar. However, his figure of $250 million is gross, and it is likely that net foreign exchange earned did not exceed $80–90 million when allowance is made for purchased foreign inputs and the sharing of profits with foreign partners. Even if Cuba's most optimistic predictions are real-ised, net tourist income is unlikely to exceed $130 million in 1991 and $200 million in 1992 – only a fraction of the approximately $4 billion of imports from the former CMEA countries which Cuba lost between 1989–91.

In 1990 3000 new rooms were added to the tourism industry stock, and another 5000 are scheduled for completion this year. More than 20,000 construction workers are engaged in this work. The target for 1995 is 50,000 rooms, generating gross revenue of $700–800 million – probably around $250 million net a year from one million tourists.

Cuba's least-known tourism organisation, Gaviota S.A., began work in 1988. It has 850 rooms throughout the island, and has plans to build 4175 more. These include a new hotel in the Cabaña fortress next to the Moro

castle above Havana harbour. Gaviota is widely said to be a joint venture
with the Cuban army.

Interviewed in July 1991 about his experience in managing the joint
venture Tuxpan hotel in Varadero, Eamonn Donnelly replied that: 'We
have had exactly the same problems as in any other part of the world. I've
worked for six years in the Canary Islands and four years in Brazil – ten
years experience managing in Latin countries – and I don't see any difference here.'[18]

The east of the island now has 1400 hotel rooms, 1211 of them in the
province of Santiago. A major development is planned with foreign participation at Quiebra Seca, to the east of Santiago. Negotiations are also under
way with foreign partners for the construction of 3250 hotel rooms on the
Isle of Youth and another 1200 on Cayo Sabinal, off Camagüey province.

Two of the offshore Cuban keys are currently being developed for
tourism. Cayo Largo has been operating as a resort for the last decade and
was the first of a number of Cuban offshore keys to be developed for
international tourism. A short flight from Havana, it is being promoted as
the ultimate holiday hideaway. Its potential was spotted more than three
decades ago, however. A relative of President Fulgencio Batista began to
build a hotel there as the third point of his pleasure triangle, the other two
being the Isle of Pines and the Bay of Pigs. But the hotel lay unfinished until
the 1980s when Intur took over the key. In December 1990 Cayo Largo's by
then smoothly running facilities changed hands again, when a management
contract was signed with the Spanish company Oasis. The company also
has 12 hotels in Varadero.

Despite so far failing to attract foreign investors, Cuba's tourism and
construction enterprises are also pressing ahead with the development of
Cayo Coco, potentially the country's biggest resort after Varadero. Cayo
Coco lies to the north of Ciego de Avila in Camagüey province. The
construction enterprise Uneca S.A. began preparatory work here in 1988.
Cayo Coco is planned as a free port, with facilities for yachts and cruise
ships, a string of hotels and restaurants, a yachting marina, a golf course and
other recreational facilities. The Spanish tobacco monopoly Tabacalera
came close to concluding a joint venture to develop Cayo Coco, but negotiations collapsed – reportedly as a result of US pressure.

The hunt for foreign investors

Although in the early-1980s it was the desire to develop tourism which
prompted Cuba to legislate to permit foreign investment, by the end of the
decade recession and a sizeable hard currency debt was prompting a more
active search for foreign partners outside the tourist sector, particularly in

industrial activities hobbled by lack of materials, finance, equipment and parts. The collapse of Cuba's CMEA partners gave this search far greater impetus, extending it to the previously taboo area of mineral development. The Foreign Trade Ministry launched a campaign in 1988 to attract joint ventures in industrial production, aimed principally at West Germany and Japan. A West German business delegation led by honorary president of the FRG's Association of Chambers of Commerce and Industry (DIHT) Otto Wolff von Amerongen visited Cuba in October 1988 to discuss trade between the two countries and possible investments in Cuba. This was heralded by Cuba's national newspaper *Granma* as the highest ranking delegation from the FRG ever to visit Cuba. It reported Mr Wolff as saying that West German business was interested not only in joint investments in production, but also in the joint marketing of products.

However, the optimism of the Cuban press proved unjustified. The delegation's discussions highlighted the problem of identifying new products offering realistic short-term prospects for FRG/Cuba co-operation. The meetings were unable to come up with concrete joint venture proposals, despite Cuba's interest in promoting such ventures, and despite Herr Wolff's long personal experience of joint ventures as an early pioneer of West German trade with the Soviet Union and China in the 1950s. The conditions offered by Cuba for joint venture operations were seen as quite reasonable by FRG businessmen, but Cuba did not at that time offer any special attractions to them.

Cuba's foreign debt problem has led to a loss of credibility in the eyes of West German companies, many of which have had to wait two to three years for payments. Several major West German firms active in the Cuban market have stopped dealing with Cuba except for cash, leading to withdrawal from the market by such giants as BASF.

Cuba continued its joint venture diplomacy with West Germany when Chamber of Commerce President Julio García Oliveras visited the FRG in June 1989 as a guest of the DIHT. He presented a list of twelve existing factories prepared by the Foreign Trade Ministry as part of an exercise to analyse ways foreign capital could help Cuban industry. These are all plants contracted from Western Europe and Japan between the mid-1970s and the early-1980s which are working well below capacity as a result of shortages of equipment and parts, poor management or lack of access to export markets.

The list provided an important snapshot of the industrial development problems Cuba faced at the end of the 1980s and its need for greater integration into world markets. It included a stainless steel parts plant, an automotive battery plant and a textile mill – all from Japan – a semiconductor plant (Spain), a candy factory, a flat textiles plant and a bagasse board plant (all from West Germany), a paper plant (France), a medical equipment plant, an electrical apparatus plant, a dyes and paints plant and a fats and grease plant.

Cuba's attempts in the late-1980s to woo Japanese investment also fell well short of expectations. The prospects for Japanese involvement in joint ventures in Cuba were discussed when the Japan-Cuba Economic Commission met in Havana in March 1989. Few specific details emerged, but it seems that Cuban officials particularly tried to interest the Japanese in the tourism sector.

One Japanese businessman resident in Havana, Mr Yutaka Kobayashi of Mutsumi Trading, said in an interview that he was sceptical about the prospects for joint ventures.[19] He said that one of the main problems was that Cuba was not prepared to allow foreign ownership of land. Without the direct stake which land ownership would provide Japanese companies would remain wary.

Joint venture law

The Cuban government's joint venture law of 1982 (Decree No. 50) remains in force. Already quite permissive in its scope, it has been applied with ever more flexibility. In exceptional cases, and with the express authorisation of the government, the foreign partner is allowed to own 50 per cent or more of the share capital, consisting of financial and/or other assets.

According to a brief published by the Cuban Chamber of Commerce, 'the enterprise will have absolute freedom in appointing its board of directors and managerial personnel, defining the production plan, setting prices and drawing up sales plans, exporting and importing directly, deciding how many people will be hired and selecting them, signing contracts with national and foreign entities, choosing the accounting system which it considers best and determining its financial policy'. Under the law, the joint ventures carry out all their operations in freely convertible currency. The foreign partners may remit abroad their share of profits and/or of the liquidation of the association, and foreign specialists and executives may remit two-thirds of their salaries. No taxes are payable on gross income, shareholders' dividends or executives' personal income. The net profits tax of 30 per cent and customs duties may be temporarily waived by the State Committee for Finances. There is a payroll tax of 25 per cent on Cuban employees.

In its brief, the Chamber of Commerce draws attention to 'Cuba's recognised social stability and its very extensive system of education'. As a result of state social provisions wage rates 'are usually lower than those in other countries'. Nevertheless, up until 1988 only ten or so joint ventures had been established. Three were with Dutch partners, set up to market tobacco leaf and cigarettes, metals and nickel. Three others were with Spanish partners.

In 1989 Cubatabaco renegotiated its foreign distribution arrangements, taking control of long-established importers such as Knight Brothers of London (active in the Havana cigar trade since the 1860s) by turning them into joint ventures. In these cases, however, the initiative has come from Cuba which has had the negotiating advantage of the monopoly ownership of prestigious brands.

The reason more joint ventures were not established in the early-1980s was largely because the political will did not fully exist in Cuba at the time. There were certainly many foreign proposals put forward, though given the difficulty of agreeing on their likely profitability they were mostly in the form of sub-contracting arrangements. It is clear that many of the joint venture contracts being negotiated by the early 1990s were based on a flexible interpretation of Decree No. 50, particularly in regard to the 50:50 participation of the Cuban and foreign partners. The Chamber of Commerce and the State Committee for Economic Cooperation (CECE) have been actively seeking out foreign investment, and there are reports that more than a hundred agreements have been concluded, with another hundred or so in the pipeline. These range from full production and hotel construction joint ventures to joint production and/or marketing agreements in which the foreign partner supplies missing inputs, including management expertise. The details of most agreements, however, are kept quiet for fear of attracting unwanted attention from the US.

Most recently Cuba has been attracting investment in the minerals sector and the sugar industry – sectors which would only recently have been out of bounds to Western capital. The French state oil company Total began prospecting for oil in Cuban waters in December 1990, and by the spring of 1992 had found some reserves, though possibly of a low grade. British Petroleum, however, backed off from signing an exploration agreement, reportedly as a result of US pressure. Taurus from Sweden, Canada North West Energy and Petrobras from Brazil have all signed exploration contracts.

In the summer of 1991 news leaked of an investment of $1.2 billion by the Canadian refiner Sherritt Gordon in the Cuban nickel industry, which has the potential to become the number one world producer by the end of the decade. Earlier that year Sherritt Gordon had begun purchasing Cuban nickel sulphides.

A Canadian sugar company was reported in 1991 to be planning a $50–60 million investment in the Cuban industry. Discussions were also under way with both Italian and British companies on investments in the growing, processing, transportation and marketing of citrus and other fresh fruits and vegetables, and a Chilean company is involved in developing new

markets for Cuban citrus. The Italian company Fiat is reported to be investing in the manufacture of machinery and agricultural equipment.

Although it will take time for foreign investment to make a significant
impact, it seems that Cubans are beginning to rediscover the entrepreneurial
drive for which they were famous before the Revolution. Fidel Castro
recently made his own support for these trends very public when he personally opened the annual Havana International Trade Fair in November 1991
– the first time he has done so – with a speech exhorting his countrymen to
go out and sell.

Relations with the European Community

Cuba, while still a member of the CMEA, established formal diplomatic
relations with the European Community for the first time in September
1988, and ambassadors had been exchanged between Brussels and Havana
by May 1989. Officials in Havana have expressed optimism that this will
open the way for important discussions with the EC on trade and finance.

Cuba has received EC assistance in the past, but the amounts have
been small. Between 1979–85 it received only $13.2 million out of total EC
official development assistance to Latin America of $678.3 million. Net
receipts from individual EC member countries has also been slight, amounting to $163.2 million between 1980–85 compared to $28,941 million for
Latin America as a whole. Nearly all of this came from France and Italy;
flows from Belgium, Denmark and the UK were in fact negative over this
period.[20]

However, Cuba's utilisation of EC tariff concessions available under
the Generalised System of Preferences has increased. The proportion of
Cuba's dutiable exports to the EC for which it receives GSP concessions
increased from 31 per cent in 1976 to 64 per cent in 1985. In the latter year
24 per cent of all Cuba's hard currency exports were under the GSP.

Luigi Boselli, the EC's ambassador to Latin America, told *Granma* at
the time relations were established that the moves towards greater Latin
American integration, the efforts of Latin American foreign ministers to
have Cuba re-admitted to the Organisation of American States and the entry
of Spain and Portugal into the EC all contributed to opening new avenues
for co-operation between the EC and Cuba.[21]

The main outstanding trade issue between Cuba and the EC is the
impact of the EC's Common Agricultural Policy on the world sugar market.
The massive growth in productivity and output in European agriculture as
a result of EC subsidies since the early-1970s led first to a displacement of
imports and then to the EC becoming a major sugar exporter. This has not

only displaced traditional suppliers but has also led to dramatic price falls and greatly increased price instability.

Western finance

As long as the Cuban economy was expanding in the first half of the 1980s the National Bank was able to negotiate new loans from Western Europe and Japan, even though pressure from the Carter and Reagan administrations seems to have frightened off some lenders. Crédit Lyonnais organised a large Deutschmark syndicated loan in 1979 despite opposition from Washington, although the cancellation of a $30 million Swiss franc loan by Singer and Friedlander in November 1979 may have been the result of White House pressure.[22] State Department pressure is also widely credited with the cancellation in March 1981 of a DM 150 million syndicated medium-term Eurocredit loan which was being organised by Crédit Lyonnais for a group of Arab banks.

In late-1981 Cuba secured a 57.5 million francs medium-term syndicated loan managed by Société Générale for the purchase of transport equipment. More credits followed, enabling French exports to Cuba to rank second only to Spain among West European countries for the three years 1983–85. In early-1983 the French government provided credits for purchases of food and machinery worth $27 million, and in October it provided further credits worth £12 million. Soon after, Renault won a contract worth £8 million to supply heavy trucks to Cuba.[23]

Despite the advent of the Thatcher government in 1979, British government and business have for the most part not allowed ideology to stand in the way of trade with Cuba. In 1981 the ECGD underwrote a £5 million loan to Cuba by the Midland Bank to allow British exporters to receive cash payments for capital goods. The following May Morgan Grenfell headed a consortium which put together a £19 million loan to Cuba. Midland Bank established a £30 million credit line for British exports to Cuba in July 1985, and in January 1986 backed a five year agreement between Goodwood (a private sector trading company set up for the purpose) and Cuba, with the aim of increasing bilateral trade by £350 million.

Like many other developing countries Cuba was hit by soaring interest rates during 1980–82, which added over half a billion dollars to the country's hard currency debt. Even so total debt fell from 3.2 billion pesos at the end of 1980 to 2.7 billion pesos at the end of 1982, staying below 3 billion pesos up to the end of 1984. However, the slowdown of growth in 1985 created serious repayment problems for the first time, causing the debt to rise to 3.6 billion pesos at the end of the year and soar over the next three years to reach 6.5 billion pesos at the end of 1988. The increase in the debt during that year alone was more than three times the forecast hard currency earning potential anticipated from the country's main tourist resort, Varadero, when it is fully developed in the mid-1990s.

Cuba first sought to renegotiate its debt in March 1982 and immediately found that US officials were working behind the scenes to undermine its efforts.[24] Nevertheless, an agreement was reached in March 1983 with Japan and ten European governments to reschedule 95 per cent of $413 million due between September 1982 and December 1983 for repayment over eight and a half years with a three year grace period.

Commercial bank creditors agreed to reschedule $468 million on similar terms the following month. Subsequent US efforts to sabotage a further private rescheduling in December 1983 also failed and Cuba was able successfully to reschedule a further $254 million in short-term loans to Western governments at a Paris Club meeting in July 1984 and $100 million with commercial banks in December 1984. In each case Cuba received somewhat less favourable repayment terms than countries such as Mexico and Argentina received in these years, but it would be difficult to link this with US pressure.[25]

Matters came to a head in May 1986 when Cuba suspended debt service payments on all its hard currency debt except for short-term trade related payments. In July the Paris Club agreed to reschedule 95 per cent of the $116 million of principal falling due in 1986 and to consider 1987 maturities at a later date. Later that month Cuba began to fall behind on payments on its short-term commercial debt as well. The banks responded with an offer to lend an additional $85 million, extend for another year $600 million in trade credits and reschedule $75 million falling due in 1986 over ten years with six years' grace. Since July 1986 there has been no further movement in negotiations with either the Paris Club or the commercial banks, which generally follow its lead.

Return to the Americas

At the time of writing, Cuba is engaged in a dramatic restructuring of its foreign economic and political relations in an attempt to maintain internal stability. At the same time, the baby boom generation of the 1960s has grown up and is pressing for the modernisation of the economy and the consumer benefits they expect to bring.

The most striking changes in Cuba's foreign relations in the 1980s were the great increase in commitment to the war in Angola, and the rapid improvement in relations with the rest of Latin America and, to a lesser extent, the Caribbean. At its peak Cuba had 50,000 troops in Angola and played a vital part in forcing South Africa and the US to the negotiating table.

Cuba's re-establishment of relations with Latin America is of more long-term significance and represents its homecoming after years of regional isolation. It has diplomatic relations with Mexico, Nicaragua, Panama, Trinidad-Tobago, the Bahamas, St Lucia, Guyana, Venezuela, Ecuador, Peru, Bolivia, Brazil, Argentina and Uruguay, and trade relations with many more. In the 12 months following the resumption of relations with Brazil in June 1986 the leaders of Argentina, Bolivia, Uruguay and Brazil, and the prime minister of Peru, visited Cuba.

Fidel Castro has also paid a number of visits to Latin American countries, after an absence of 15 years following his visit to Chile in 1973. In the autumn of 1988 and spring of 1989 he attended presidential inaugurations in Ecuador, Mexico and Venezuela. In Caracas he met the leaders of Colombia and the Dominican Republic, with which Cuba still has no diplomatic relations. He also spent more than three hours with Jimmy Carter, the former US President.

Argentina and Mexico are the main trading partners so far, but Cuba is also fast expanding commercial ties with Venezuela, Peru, Ecuador and Brazil. Brazil in particular, with its large domestic market, is seen as an important outlet for trade and for co-operation in areas such as electronics, biotechnology, health care and agriculture, all areas where Cuba has placed a lot of emphasis on developing technology.

Cuba's economic relations with the CIS (Commonwealth of Independent States) and Eastern Europe have officially been put on a hard currency basis. The subsidy on trade in sugar with the CIS has all but disappeared, and Cuban sugar exports to the CIS have been substantially reduced. Nevertheless, there remains a solid basis for Cuba and the CIS to continue exchanging sugar for oil, as neither can quickly find substitute trade partners for these commodities.

Strains in Cuba's relations with the countries of Eastern Europe surfaced in the middle of 1989. Fidel Castro spent a large part of his annual 26 July speech attacking the pro-capitalist direction of Poland and Hungary and warning that Cuba could become even more isolated in the world. He even suggested that the reforms in the Soviet Union could lead to its disintegration and decline into civil war.

The US administration for its part has refused to give any ground to Cuba in its time of greatest crisis. The logic of US regional interests and *détente* with the Soviet Union might have been expected to point towards a more pragmatic approach towards Cuba. Now that Cuba has been accepted back into the Latin American fold, re-establishing relations with Cuba could help the US in crisis management in the region. Cuba's support for the peace process in Central America, and its renewed offers to co-operate in policing drug trafficking in the Caribbean following its own drugs scandal, suggest that it is interested in serious negotiations with the US.

However, the Bush administration has on several occasions announced that there would be no change in US policy towards Cuba until there were major changes in Cuba's political system. Bush maintained support for TV Martí which broadcasts US programmes into Cuba, and finally was even corralled into supporting the Torricelli legislation to close the loophole allowing US corporations to trade with Cuba through third country subsidiaries.

If Bush was pursuing a considered, rather than simply opportunistic, policy towards Cuba, and intended to squeeze it as hard as possible, this must have meant that his advisers anticipated a major political and economic crisis in Cuba. The former head of the Cuban Interests Section in Washington, Ramón Sánchez Parodi, said in a discussion at the Centro de Investigaciones de la Economía Mundial in Havana on 5 January 1989 that the dominant US position seemed to have shifted from trying to promote a 'national liberation war' in Cuba to a policy of trying to establish points of contact with Cuba so as to be in a position to exert influence should a crisis develop.[26]

Cuba's distancing from the CIS and its reorientation towards Western markets thus coincides with its endgame with the US. One way or another, it is highly unlikely that the US embargo will remain for much longer. What will this mean for West European business relations, which have made such an important contribution to the stability of the Cuban regime over thirty years? It seems inevitable that, while some of the stronger internationally-based companies will maintain their business with Cuba, the smaller ones are likely to find themselves squeezed out of the market by US companies within a year or two.

One study suggested that US business would capture 50 per cent of the Cuban market within two years.[27] This, however, assumes that the volume of Cuba's trade with the West remains more or less the same. In fact it is likely both that the proportion of trade with the West will increase and that the resumption of relations with the US will give the economy a substantial boost as the costs associated with foreign trade (transportation, communications, credit, insurance, etc.) are cut and new investment flows in. European business is likely, therefore, to end up with a smaller slice of a larger cake, and so on balance may even benefit commercially.

Notes

1   Donald E. Schulz, Special Report on the Roundtable 'Cuba and the Future', 16 January 1992, Strategic Studies Institute, US Army War College, Carlisle Barracks, Pennsylvania. The main conclusions of the participants were: i) 'Castro will probably survive in the short run (1992–93) and quite possibly for many years to come'; ii) 'If a serious threat to the regime should emerge, the resulting conflict could well lead to a bloody civil war'; iii) 'US policy is

counterproductive and is one of the factors enabling Castro to remain in power'.

2 A Report to the US Senate, 'The United States and Cuba: Time for a new Beginning', November 1988.
3 *Cuba Business*, Vol. 6, No. 1, February 1992, p. 5.
4 *Financial Times*, 13 February 1989, p. 37.
5 Quoted in Morris Morley, *Imperial State and Revolution*, Cambridge University Press, 1987, p. 371.
6 *Ibid.*, p. 339.
7 Kirby Jones and Donna Rich, 'Opportunities for US-Cuban Trade', *Cuban Studies Program*, Johns Hopkins School of Advanced International Studies, Washington DC, June 1988, Appendix B.
8 Morley, *op. cit.*, p. 339.
9 *Cuba Business*, Vol. 3, No. 4, August 1989.
10 Morley, *op. cit.*, p. 329.
11 *Ibid.*, p. 346.
12 *Cuba Business*, Vol. 5, No. 5, October 1991, pp. 8–9.
13 *Cuba Business*, Vol. 2, Nos. 3–5, June–October 1988.
14. Che Guevara, 'The Cuban Economy: Its Past and Present Importance, *International Affairs*, 1964.
15 *Op. cit.*
16 Donna Rich Kaplowitz and Michael Kaplowitz, 'New Opportunities for US-Cuban Trade', *Cuban Studies Program*, The Johns Hopkins University School of Advanced International Studies, Washington DC, April 1992.
17 Opportunities for US-Cuba Trade, *op. cit.*
18 *Cuba Business*, Vol. 5, No. 5, October 1991, p. 11.
19 *Cuba Business*, Vol. 3, No. 2, April 1989.
20 Instituto de Relaciones Europeo-Latinoamericanas (IRELA), 'Economic Relations between the European Community and Latin America: a statistical profile', Working Paper No. 10, IRELA, Madrid, 1987.
21 *Cuba Business*, Vol. 2, No. 5, December 1988.
22 Morley, *op. cit.*, p. 278.
23 *Ibid.*, p. 351.
24 *Ibid.*, p. 340.
25 *Ibid.*, p. 342.
26 Centro de Investigaciones de la Economia Mundial, 'Estudios sobre Estados Unidos', second semester 1988, and *Cuba Business*, Vol. 3, No. 3, June 1989.
27 Kirby Jones and Donna Rich, 'Opportunities for US-Cuban Trade', *Cuban Studies Program*, Johns Hopkins School of Advanced International Studies, Washington DC, June 1988.

EPILOGUE | Future scenarios

Alistair Hennessy and
George Lambie

As the Cuban Revolution faces the most serious crisis in its history its detractors flex their muscles for what they consider the inevitable collapse of an economically and ideologically bankrupt regime. However, in spite of the island's isolation, its racial, class, bureaucratic and military infrastructure is not likely to permit a swift demise of the Revolution.

As a result of its precarious position Cuba, after decades of neglect by the international press, now attracts reporters in droves, who, based on observations made in the foyers of Havana hotels, or in views of the city from taxi windows, prophesy the end of socialism in Cuba. Such snapshots of Cuba, underscored by assumptions about the inevitability of neo-liberalism and the 'end of history', are inadequate to judge the present crisis. Moreover generalisations should not be made on the evidence of Havana alone.

Economic survival depends on being able to market sugar and to find alternative sources of energy and also on an effective diversification of the economy by developing markets in the West which until now have been barely skimmed. However, there are serious risks involved in these new strategies. Biotechnology, for instance, has been a remarkable development and a vindication of Cuba's educational reforms and investment policy, as well as of the belief that any revolution which cannot develop its own scientific subculture will remain stillborn, nevertheless it is fraught with difficulties. Marketing new drugs requires a long lead time. The risks of even a small failure can have a disastrous knock-on effect by discrediting validation techniques, and in order to break into new markets the competition from international pharmaceutical companies will be intense as they can employ delaying tactics related to patent legislation.

In the case of tourism Cuba clearly has advantages which will make it a challenging competitor to smaller Caribbean islands; safety, unspoilt beaches, fascinating social and economic experiments, a well-preserved historical heritage, and impressive standards of environmental protection. It may also be possible to develop isolated enclave tourist centres and so avoid the experience which reduced Havana to becoming the red-light district of the Caribbean before the Revolution. The spectre of the major cities of the former Communist bloc becoming centres for vice and prostitution as they attract Western tourism and adopt capitalist values is a salutary warning for

Cuba's tourism planners. Cuban joint venture strategy implies importing Western standards and ideas which may well threaten socialist principles. Demonstration effects from Western lifestyles and habits are unpredictable. The traditional export crop of sugar poses particularly acute problems. The European market is highly protected and Europe has now become a sugar exporter. With health faddism and sugar substitutes such as corn syrup the possibilities of an expanding market are diminishing except in the Third World. The Cubans have shown considerable ingenuity in developing sugar by-products and this may offer further opportunities for diversification. Sources of energy pose acute problems and it is difficult to envisage any substitute for oil. Ethanol based on sugar is an expensive technology and the Brazilians have found that to make its production viable requires an economy of scale and high world oil prices. If exploitable off-shore oil resources are discovered in sufficient quantity to meet needs, this would clearly be a solution but the prospects for this are unclear.

Cuba has a favourable environment to grow tropical citrus products which could be marketed in Europe but this is a highly competitive field where quality control is crucial and without the latest techniques of management, marketing skills, packaging, labelling, efficient transportation and prompt delivery and visual appeal, the chances of breaking into a market which is tightly controlled by the supermarket chains are slight. The Cubans are aware of this problem as their joint venture with the Chileans, perhaps the most efficient agricultural exporters in Latin America, has shown. However, citrus juice exports, as in the case of their trade with the old CMEA, would avoid the problem of visual imperfections. Fishing is another possible export which could be expanded, although it would be difficult to match the economies of scale of the Japanese or Taiwanese.

Even the most sympathetic observers have criticised the leadership for its lack of democratic accountability common to other communist regimes. However Cuban local government is not simply an administrative function of the centre as in the former Soviet bloc. Cuba's 'popular power' exhibits a high level of participatory democracy, and if freed of elements of centralised party and bureaucratic control, could become an effective mechanism for structural reform and economic decentralisation.

A significant potential source of opposition would seem to be the younger generation. The importance which generational factors have played in previous Cuban history would suggest that this is a danger area, especially from those young highly trained technocrats impatient with inefficient bureaucracy. Communist parties, like trade unions, are structured in age hierarchies. How can the loyalty be gained of Cuban youth which has not gone through an active revolutionary experience and which has come to take for granted the social services, educational facilities, medical health and the other achievements of the regime? The past inability, or unwillingness, of the Cuban press to engage in relevant debate has accentuated the discontent among the young, and serves to make them more receptive to counter-revolutionary propaganda. Cuba presents the paradox of the most highly-educated Third World country where many young people are unable to achieve their full potential, especially in the context of domestic economic problems and the decline of Cuba's international role. Whatever thoughts may be entertained about the concept of a 'socially unattached' intelligentsia being *'fuera del juego'*, Cuba cannot afford the haemorrhage of its intellectual talent (even free ranging literary spirits) on a scale that bears comparison with the German and Spanish diasporas of the 1930s.

There is also perhaps a need for Cuba to be more responsive to allegations by the Revolution's detractors of human rights abuses although it justly feels it is being unfairly singled out for criticism especially in a continent where the grossest violations of human liberty in other countries (with 'acceptable' politics) often go unchallenged by the same detractors.

A major factor in Cuba's survival will be the attitude of the rest of Latin America. Since the Cubans have turned aside from the guerrilla activity of the 1960s, commercial and cultural links have been established and strengthened throughout the continent, and even though US-Latin American relations might seem to have improved, any false step on the part of the US towards Cuba might well once again arouse anti-American sentiment although Clinton's attitude is still unclear (mid 1993).

Key actors in the past have been the Cuban exiles in the US. They are now becoming increasingly vocal, showing themselves to be effective lobbyists in Congress as the support mustered for the Torricelli bill has shown. They have assumed that the regime has survived through the inefficacy of the blockade. So, far from believing that the solution is to accept reality and to bring it to an end, some are arguing in strident terms, that it should be tightened. Such an argument might be justified were there to be a security threat as in the past. It is difficult to see how this could now be accepted by the wider international community. There have been no comparable examples of such an unrelenting blockade carried out against another power in peace time and today more than ever it runs against the tide of business pragmatism.

The Cuban exiles are divided and the *'dialogueros'*, in favour of dialogue, are now criticising the hardliners. In any case the exiles are not the only people with an interest in Cuban affairs, although naturally their views are the most fervently expressed. There is, for example, the Mafia, so active before the revolutionary period, who presumably would like a share of the pickings. Besides these there are those non-Cuban American interests, multinationals who would wish to re-establish their position in any post-Castro regime.

There is overall the looming figure of Fidel Castro. It would be unwise for foreigners to underestimate his drawing power with the Cuban people, and the extent to which the achievements of the Revolution are identified with his leadership. Parallels should not be drawn with the grey leaders of the former Soviet bloc. Notwithstanding institutional (and now generational changes) which have occurred, Fidel, the '*Comandante en Jefe*' remains the ultimate source of power and decision-making, and has not lost the pungency of his analyses, as was shown in his speech at the Rio Summit. There is no one in Cuba who could command the same respect and affection that he enjoys, however vocal in their criticism disillusioned critics and exiles may be. The regime is unlikely to collapse because of any massive withdrawal of popular support from the '*Comandante*'. What is unclear is whether loyalties would be transferred to another leader in the unlikely event of his retirement, should he become ill, or do the seemingly impossible and die.

What position does Cuba occupy in the 'new international order'? How will it be affected by GATT, NAFTA and the EC? And what would be the attitude of the United Nations, should there be a succession crisis resulting in internal conflict when the island could become a centre of instability and disaffection throughout the region, which is going through one of the most serious crises in its history? In any event, Britain, France, the Netherlands and Spain, as powers involved in the Caribbean, could be drawn in and hence they have an interest in preserving stability and in exercising a restraining influence on outside interested parties, quite apart from the pragmatic considerations of preserving their foothold in the Cuban market.

Whatever happens in Cuba its impact on the rest of the Caribbean is likely to be greater than at any time since 1959. For decades Cuba's foreign policy objectives were fixed on the wider horizons of Latin America or Africa – partly because any forward policy in the Caribbean itself would have alienated Western Europe and so destroyed that lifeline. Should the regime collapse and there be a disputed succession or internal conflict the island could become a destabilising element in the region. If the regime were to be replaced by a free market economy, and if the collapsed Eastern bloc is a reliable guide, the island could become a haunt for freebooters, drug merchants and speculators, inaugurating a new cycle of piracy in a region already prone to nefarious activities. On the other hand, economic freedom could release the entrepreneurial talents for which Cubans in the diaspora have become renowned. In this case, the rest of the Caribbean will have to face the cold wind of the new commercial assertiveness. Similarly, if the regime survives and the current economic strategies are successful, then the smaller states of the region, especially in the Eastern Caribbean, will equally suffer from Cuban competition, particularly in the tourist industry.

While a question mark hangs over the future of Cuba it should also be remembered that the fate of the post-communist regimes of the former Soviet bloc is also uncertain. After the euphoria of escaping from grey Stalinist bureaucracies, the new democracies are beginning to realise that neo-liberalism is not just an economic mechanism but also an ideology, whose visionaries are as rigid in their faith as those whom they have replaced. Neo-liberalism is also sweeping through the Third World and especially Latin America where the promises of its ideologues need to be treated with scepticism.

Cuba has no choice; it must change. Cuban socialism, partly based on a system which has degenerated and collapsed, has to respond to rapidly changing international circumstances. How it will do so poses acute problems of choice, but whatever the shortcomings of the Revolution, attempts are being made to reform its socialist model by drawing sustenance from nationalist traditions rather than by capitulating to the ideologues of the free market. If there were a new international formula for development which combined economic growth with social justice, Cuba would be foolish not to renounce its past and subscribe to the new order. However, faced with escalating problems and the threat posed to the social gains of the Revolution, it is right to be suspicious of what is being offered as an alternative, especially when it is recalled how First World protectionism exemplified in the tortuous GATT negotiations, as well as a 30-year economic blockade, contravenes every principle of free-market economics. In Cuban eyes, neo-liberal ideology, adhered to by some of its proponents as rigidly as the Communist dogma it challenges, does not offer a way out of the impasse. Now finally, and predictably, neo-liberalism is collapsing at its core as the US, British and European economies slide into profound and seemingly incurable recession.

Perhaps ideologies should be left on one side when considering Cuba's future and an examination made of the realities of economic development. Clearly, especially in the prevailing environment, elements of the market mechanism and capitalist mode of production are essential to economic performance, but it is noticeable that the most successful economies in the first and developing world have retained significant levels of state control and state intervention: an attempted synthesis of market and state rather than a contrived conflict between them.

Once the extremes of rhetoric and ideology are stripped away there would seem to be an economic and political space in which Cuba can manoeuvre. The real challenge which faces Cuba therefore is not how to make a transition from socialist austerity to capitalist plenty – the majority of Cubans are still better off than most other Latin Americans – but to address the practicalities of re-orienting its trade and improving internal efficiency, both of which will require new skills, more effective democracy and some decentralisation of decision-making in which West European examples and support could prove instructive and helpful. This is especially relevant given the US past and present obsessional attitudes towards Cuba which continue to impair its ability to exercise any constructive influence on the Cuban issue.

It may be that if Cuba can hold out against mounting pressures by combining its specialised skills in high technology with the need to develop a 'potato economy' to serve basic needs, along with practical solutions to internal shortages such as utilising the bicycle, then its time may come. Whatever else the Rio summit of 1992 on the environment has done it has served to deflect attention more and more away from the East-West conflict to the North-South divide. Cuba's salvation could well lie in absorbing and applying new prescriptions based on alternative technology and sustainable development which have an obvious relevance for Third World countries.

The uniqueness of the Cubans' situation has risen from their geographical position which made them the fulcrum of East-West and North-South tensions. The contradictions of Cuban foreign policy have stemmed from assuming that their passionate advocacy of Third World liberation was shared by the former USSR at any more than a superficial level. Now that East-West conflict is no longer a reality, at least in the particular form it has assumed since 1917, Cuba is free to return to its self-chosen role as advocate for the nations of the Third World. To fulfil this role effectively a small power in the past has had to have a patron and it has been Cuba's fate to have been dependent on a Great Power with little imaginative understanding of Third World problems except in ideological terms. Now it will have to seek its own way and by its example attract new friends.

Ultimately, the Cuban Revolution's saving grace has been Fidel Castro's willingness (at times) to change course pragmatically in the face of the failure of ideologically driven policies. Pragmatic considerations rather than the lust for ideological purity, and the recognition that the harsh realities of the contemporary world require dialogue, moderation, and recognition that economic progress and social justice are inseparable, could provide a basis for a continuation of that relationship between Western Europe and Cuba which has been such a marked feature of the Revolution's history.

Appendices

Appendix I: The trade of major capitalist powers with Cuba 1957–1979 ($ Million)*

	GB 1		France 2		Spain 3		West Germany 4		Italy 5		Japan 6		Canada 7		USA 8	
	Imp	Ex	Imp	Ex	Imp	Ex	Imp	Ex	Imp	Ex	Imp	Ex	Imp	Ex	Imp	Ex
1957	72.2	22.7	18.6	12.8	1.1	0.9	51.0	30.5	4.0	7.0				17.2	481.9	621.6
1958	49.8	26.0	7.4	9.4	1.3	0.9	7.1	31.3	2.4	11.0				18.3	524.0	543.5
1959	28.3	43.1	8.5	14.5	0.5	0.5	12.0	29.6	1.2	8.4			12.6	16.1	474.7	438.6
1960	21.8	20.7	13.1	10.8	10.3	9.9	9.4	14.5	0.5	5.3			7.3	13.0	375.2	222.7
1961	14.6	12.9	1.2	5.9	9.2	4.4	2.0	11.8	0.3	4.1	24.3	11.8	5.1	31.1	73.3	13.7
1962	19.6	7.3	2.3	1.9	8.5	1.4	5.8	5.7	0.2	1.5	35.8	10.6	2.5	9.9	6.8	13.4
1963	34.7	6.2	4.1	4.4	21.7	9.2	1.9	6.4	1.1	0.9	22.9	2.8	11.8	14.9	—	36.4
1964	25.5	26.9	3.4	21.0	65.6	31.4			18.6	7.2	53.5	34.4	3.2	55.4		
1965	14.6	42.0	11.5	13.5	31.1	38.2	0.8	3.5	6.7	4.1	28.8	3.6	4.8	47.8		
1966	12.9	22.7	10.3	14.7	38.2	78.6	0.9	6.0	9.0	9.8	22.8	6.0	5.1	55.8		
1967	12.9	24.1	15.8	55.0	37.8	27.8	1.6	10.5	5.1	21.2	26.4	7.2	5.7	38.5		
1968	16.3	29.8	14.8	56.0	40.5	18.5	2.4	11.9	7.3	31.0	33.6	2.4	4.6	40.8		
1969	12.9	31.7	14.9	47.3	25.5	29.4	2.7	23.5	8.3	45.4	68.0	9.8	7.2	37.9		
1970	13.4	48.0	15.9	58.3	35.0	36.6	3.6	26.7	12.0	59.0	110.6	39.2	9.1	56.6		
1971	13.2	63.1	13.4	41.0	36.0	33.0	5.0	16.6	11.3	45.0	127.9	53.5	10.2	56.0		
1972	12.5	41.8	11.7	26.5	50.0	18.8	4.3	19.8	14.4	15.6	145.3	50.7	11.2	58.3		
1973	32.3	42.9	12.0	28.2	55.9	39.1	3.6	37.7	19.8	21.8	182.7	107.8	16.6	81.8		
1974	45.5	55.0	11.3	81.6	170.8	61.9	6.4	114.0	26.6	62.3	443.3	202.7	78.0	146.8		

							Imports c.i.f. / Exports f.o.b.							
1975	14.1	83.6	24.3	105.2	315.6	178.3	8.6	127.6	19.6	92.6	343.2	439.4	79.9	217.3
1976	44.0	80.0	28.8	87.7	90.5	208.0	18.4	91.3	25.2	65.0	50.0	199.0	61.0	263.0
1977	17.0	48.0	32.6	57.7	156.8	152.0	15.8	74.9	19.2	34.0	64.0	361.0	43.0	174.0
1978	15.0	53.0	29.3	43.7	105.2	99.4	37.7	72.9	30.0	39.0	106.0	212.0	53.0	192.0
1979	29.0	85.0	40.1	44.9	94.0	219.0	30.0	104.4	45.6	154.0	112.0	154.0	90.0	134.0

* Dollar value calculated from exchange rates for respective currencies given in *International Financial Statistics*, Bureau of Statistics of the International Monetary Fund (Year Book), 1957–1980

Main sources:

1 *Annual Statement of Overseas Trade of the United Kingdom*, British Board of Trade (London), 1957–79.
2 *Commerce de France: Tableau Général du Commerce Extérieur* (Paris), 1957–79.
3 *España: anuario de estadística* (Madrid), 1957–79 and *Estadística de comercio exterior de España* (Madrid), *passim*, 1957–79.
4 *Der Aussenhandel der Bundesrepublik Deutschland* (Stuttgart), 1957–79.
5 *Statistica annuale del commercio con l'estero* (Rome), 1957–79.
6 *Foreign Trade of Japan*, compiled by the Ministry of International Trade and Industry, Japan External Trade Organisation – JETRO (Tokyo), 1965–79.
7 *Trade of Canada: Exports by Countries and Imports by Countries*, Dominion Bureau of Statistics, External Trade Division (Ottawa), 1957–79.
8 *Statistical Abstract of the United States*, US Department of Commerce (Washington).

Other sources:

1 *Anuario Estadístico de Cuba* (Havana), 1965–79.
2 *West Indies and Caribbean Year Book* (London), 1965–69.
3 *Statistiques rétrospectives du commerce extérieur, 1965–80*, OCDE (Paris, 1982).
4 Table 1, Trade of selected non-communist countries with Cuba, 1961–1975 in Morris H. Morley, *Imperial State and Revolution: the United States and Cuba, 1952–1986* (Cambridge, 1987), p.373.

Appendix II: *The Spanish Sugar Market 1956–1972* [a]

Year	Imports from Cuba	Total imports	Domestic production[b]	Domestic consumption	Per capita consumption
1956	21,305	22,368	413,534	437,904	14.7
1957	23,523	39,334	397,392	460,152	15.3
1958	70,733	150,101	386,778	504,230	16.7
1959	3,585	42,175	500,724	509,704	16.7
1960	33,645	35,268	528,020	530,087	17.1
1961	50,106	51,474	526,605	573,152	18.3
1962	47,790	48,290	555,237	619,033	19.6
1963	88,080	259,424	412,870	666,742	20.4
1964	265,598	291,833	584,404	694,620	21.1
1965	120,806	142,258	506,098	726,163	21.8
1966	196,397	194,919	591,211	767,912	22.9
1967	161,717				
1968	173,117	235,730	716,118	877,750	26.0
1969	183,904	185,420	823,273	921,800	26.9
1970	124,252	126,446	887,432	978,800	28.3
1971	48,275	50,565	983,787	1,008,255	28.8
1972	109,183				

(a) i) Includes Spanish Peninsula, Balearic Islands, Canary Islands and Spanish Possessions in North Africa; ii) all figures given below are in metric tons (raw value) except for per capita annual sugar consumption which is in kilogrammes; iii) source of information International Sugar Council, *Sugar Year Book*, 1960, 1966, 1973.

(b) Spanish domestic production of sugar during the above period was composed of 7.5 per cent cane sugar and 92.5 per cent beet sugar.

Selected bibliography

The main Cuban sources are the files of *Cuban Studies* (*Estudios Cubanos*), Pittsburgh, Pittsburgh University Press, which updates publications. The files of *Cuba Business* (London) monthly are invaluable for commerce. The best European press coverage is in *Le Monde* (Paris) and the various professional Latinamericanist journals, *Latinamerican Research Review, Journal of Latin American Studies, Hispanic American Historical Review, Bulletin of Latin American Research, Caravelle*.

Any selection from the vast bibliography on the Revolution must be arbitrary. Readers are referred to R. Chilcote and S. Lutjens, *Cuba: a Bibliographical Guide to the Literature*, New York, Kraus, 1986 and Luis Pérez, *Cuba: an Annotated Bibliography*, New York, Greenwood Press, 1988. The most useful guides are the runs of *La Revolución* and its successor *Granma* and those of various reviews, *Bohemia, Casa de las Americas, Anales del Caribe, Cuba Socialista, Pensamiento Crítico, Areito. Revista de Estudios Europeos*, is the journal of the Centro de Estudios Europeos in Havana.

Readers are referred to further bibliographical references in the notes at the end of each chapter.

Abel, C. and Torrents, N. (eds) (1984) *Spain: Conditional Democracy*, London, Croom Helm.
—— (1986) *José Martí, Revolutionary Democrat*, London, The Athlone Press.
Abreu, B. *et al.* (1988) *Guerra y Nación*, Havana, Editorial de Ciencias Sociales.
Aguilar, L.E. (1972) *Cuba 1933: Prologue to Revolution*, Ithaca, Cornell University Press.
Alleg, H. (1963) *Victorieuse Cuba*, Paris, Ed. de Minuit.
Anderson, C.W. (1970) *The Political Economy of Modern Spain*, Madison, University of Wisconsin Press.
Arnault, J. (1962) *Cuba et le Marxisme*, Paris, Ed. Sociales.
Aron, R. (1957) *The Opium of the Intellectuals*, London, Secker and Warburg.
Balfour, S. (1990) *Castro*, London, Longmans.
Baliño, C. (1976) *Documentos y Articulos*, Havana, Instituto de Historia.
Banco Nacional de Cuba (1982) (August), *Economic Report*, Havana.
—— (1990a) (June), *Información estadística seleccionada de Cuba de la economía cubana*, Havana.
—— (1990b) (June), *Economic Report*, Havana.
Betto, F. (1985) *Fidel y la Religión*, Havana, Oficina de Publicaciones del Consejo de Estado.

Blackaby, F. (ed.) (1978) British Economic Policy 1960–1974, Cambridge, C.U.P.
—— (1979) De-industrialisation, Cambridge, C.U.P.
Blasier, C. and Mesa-Lago, C. (eds) (1979) Cuba in the World, Pittsburgh, University of Pittsburgh Press.
Blume, H. (1985) Geography of Sugar Cane, Berlin, Verlag Dr Albert Bartens.
Borge, J. and Viassnoff, N. (1981) Berliet, Paris.
Bourne, P. (1986) Castro: a biography of Fidel Castro, London, Macmillan Press Ltd.
Brundenius, C. (1984) Revolutionary Cuba: the Challenge to Economic Growth with Equity, Boulder, Colorado, Westview Press.
C. Czarnikow Ltd. (1961–1971) Sugar Review, London, various issues.
Cabrera, O. (1985) Alfonso López, Maestro del Proletariado Cubano, Havana, Editorial de Ciencias Sociales.
—— (1977) Guiteras, El Programa de la Jóven Cuba, Havana, Editorial de Ciencias Sociales.
Calvert, P. (1988) The Central American Security System: North-South or East-West?, Cambridge, C.U.P.
Cardoso, E. and Helwege, A. (1992) Cuba after Communism, Cambridge, Mass., M.I.T. Press.
Carr, J. (1978) Une passion pour Che Guevara, Paris, Julliard.
Carr, R. (1988) Spain, 2nd. ed., Oxford, O.U.P.
Carr, R. and Fusi, J.P. (1979) Spain: Dictatorship to Democracy, London, Allen and Unwin.
Casaus, V. (ed.) (1981) Cartas Cruzadas, Pablo de la Torriente Brau, Havana, Editorial de Letras Cubanas.
Castro, Fidel (1967) History will absolve me, London, Jonathan Cape.
Caute, D. (1974) Cuba Yes?, London, Secker and Warburg.
—— (1988) The Year of the Barricades 1968, London, Paladin.
—— (1988) The Fellow Travellers: Intellectual Friends of Communism, (revised ed.), New Haven, Yale University Press.
Cepero Bonilla, R. (1958) Política Azucarera (1952–1958), Mexico, Editorial Futuro S.A.
—— (1959) The Cuban Revolution and the Sugar Markets, Address to the Lions Club of Havana, Havana, Editorial Echevarria.
—— (1960) The Cuban-Soviet Agreement, Havana, Editorial Echevarría.
—— (1962) 'La Conferencia Azucarera de Ginebra', Cuba Socialista, 7 March, pp. 47–62.
Cerny, P. (1980) The Politics of Grandeur: Ideological Aspects of de Gaulle's Foreign Policy, Cambridge, C.U.P.
Clavera, J. et al. (1978) Capitalismo español: de la autarquía a la estabilización, 1939–1959, Madrid.
Conte, A. (1964) Yalta ou le partage du monde, Paris.
Cortada, J.W. (ed.) (1980) Spain In the Twentieth Century: Essays on Spanish Diplomacy 1898–1978, London.
Cuba Socialista (1964) Texto del convenio a largo plazo sobre suministros de azúcar a la URSS por parte de la República de Cuba, 30 February, pp. 165–6.
Debray, R. (1967) Revolution in the Revolution? Harmondsworth, Penguin Books.
—— (1981) Teachers, Writers, Celebrities, (Introduction, F. Mulhern) London, Verso Books.
Delmas, C. (1983) Crises à Cuba, Bruxelles, Editions Complexo.
Demagny, R. (1962) Cuba l'exile et la ferveur, Paris, Buchet/Chastel.

Desnoes, E. (1967) *Punto de Vista*, Instituto del Libro, Havana.

Dickie, R.B. (1970) *Foreign Investment: France a Case Study*, New York.

Divine, R.A. (ed.) (1981) *Exploring the Johnson Years*, Austin, Univ. of Texas Press.

Dóminguez, J. (1978) *Cuba: Order and Revolution*, Cambridge, Mass., Harvard University Press.

—— (1989) *To make a World Safe for Revolution: Cuba's foreign policy*, Cambridge, Mass., Harvard University Press.

Draper, T. (1965) *Castroism: Theory and Practice*, New York, Praeger.

du Genestoux, P. (1989) 'Cuba and the Soviet Union', Paper presented at the Landell Mills Commodities Studies Sugar Conference 'The Sugar Market into the 1990s', London, 24–25 October.

Dumont, R. (1962) *La Réforme Agraire a Cuba*, Paris, Editions du Tiers Monde.

—— (1964) *Cuba, Socialisme et développement*, Paris, Le Seuil.

—— (1970) *Cuba est il socialiste?*, Paris, Le Seuil.

Duroselle, J.B. (1976) *France and the United States*, Chicago.

Edwards, J. (1982) *Persona non grata* (versión completa), Barcelona.

Erisman, H.M. and Kirk, J.M. (eds) (1991) *Cuban Foreign Policy confronts a new International Order*, Boulder, Lynne Reinner.

Fagen, R.R. (1968) *Cubans in Exile*, Stanford, Stanford University Press.

—— (1969) *The Transformation of Political Culture in Cuba*, Stanford, Stanford University Press.

Fauriol, G. and Loser, E. (1990) *Cuba: the International Dimension*, New Brunswick, Transaction Publishers.

Food & Agriculture Organisation (1990) *Production Yearbook*, Rome, FAO.

Franklin, J. (1984) *Cuban Foreign Relations: A Chronology 1959–1982*, New York.

Franqui, C. (1980) *Family Portrait with Fidel*, London, Jonathan Cape.

—— (1988) *Vida, aventuras y desastres de un hombre llamado Castro*, Barcelona, Planeta.

Frayde, M. (1970) *Ecoute Fidel*, Paris, Denoël.

Gallo, M. (1972) *Spain Under Franco: a History*, London.

Geldof, L. (1991) *Cubans*, London, Bloomsbury.

Gerassi, J. (ed.) (1968) *Venceremos. The Speeches and Writings of Ernesto Che Guevara*, London, Weidenfeld and Nicholson.

Gillespie, R. (ed.) (1990) *Cuba after Thirty Years: Rectification and the Revolution*, London, Cass.

Goldenberg, B. and Esser, K. (1969) *Zehn Jahre Kubanische Revolution*, Hannover, Verlag fur Literatur und Zeitgeschehen.

González, E. (1974) *El Ala Izquierda y su Epoca*, Havana, Editorial de Ciencias Sociales.

—— (1977) *Mella y el Movimiento Estudiantil*, Havana, Editorial de Ciencias Sociales.

González, E. and Ronfeldt, D. (1986) *Castro, Cuba and the World*, Santa Monica, Rand Corporation.

Goytisolo, J. (1963) *Pueblo en Marcha*, Paris, Librería Española.

Griffiths, J. and P. (1979) *Cuba: the second decade*, London, Writers and Readers Publishing Co-operative.

Guadarrama, P. (1987) *Edel: El Pensamiento Filosófico de Enrique José Varona & Tussel Oropeza*, Havana, Editorial de Ciencias Sociales.

Guevara, E. (1987) *Che Guevara and the Cuban Revolution*, Writings and Speeches of Ernesto Che Guevara, Pathfinder Press.

Habel, J. (1964) 'Le procès de Marcos Rodríguez et les problèmes de l'unité du

mouvement révolutionnaire a Cuba', *Les Temps Modernes*, Aug–Sept, 1964.
—— (1991) *Cuba: the Revolution in Peril*, London, Verso.
Hadian, R.F. (1976) 'United States Foreign Policy Towards Spain: 1953–1970', unpublished Ph.D thesis, University of California, Santa Barbara.
Hagelberg, G.B. (1974) *The Caribbean Sugar Industries: Constraints and Opportunities*, New Haven, Conn., Yale University, Antilles Research Program.
Halperin, M. (1972) *The Rise and Fall of Fidel Castro*, Berkeley, University of California Press.
—— (1981) *The Taming of Fidel Castro*, Berkeley, University of California Press.
Harrison, J. (1985) *The Spanish Economy in the Twentieth Century*, Beckenham.
Hennessy, A. (1992) *Intellectuals in the Twentieth Century Caribbean: Unity in Variety The Hispanic and Francophone Tradition*, Vol. II, Basingstoke, Macmillan, Warwick University Caribbean Studies.
Hills, G. (1967) *Franco the Man and his Nation*, London.
Horowitz, L. (1985) *Cuban Communism*, 5th ed., New Brunswick, Transaction Books.
Huberman, L. and Sweezy, P. (1968) *Régis Debray and the Latin American Revolution*, New York Monthly Review.
Ibarra, J. (1979) *Approximaciones a Clio*, Havana, Editorial de Ciencias Sociales.
Index on Censorship (1972) 'Cuba: Revolution and the Intellectual: The Strange Case of Heberto Padilla', 1972:2, London.
International Sugar Council (1963) *The World Sugar Economy: Structure and Policies*, Vol. II, 'The World Picture', London, ISC.
Jack, D. (1977) *The Leyland Bus*, Glossop, Derbyshire.
Julien, C. (1961) *La Révolution cubaine*, Paris, Julliard.
Karol, K.S. (1970) *Guerrillas in Power: The Course of the Cuban Revolution*, New York, Hill and Wang.
Kindelberger, C. (1976) *Economic Growth in France and Britain*, London.
Kirk, M. (1983) *José Martí. Mentor of the Cuban Nation*, Tampa, University of South Florida Press.
—— (1989) *Between God and the Party: Religion and Politics in Revolutionary Cuba*, Tampa, University of South Florida Press.
Kolodziej, E.A. (1974) *French International Policy under de Gaulle and Pompidou*, Ithaca, Cornell University Press.
Lamore, J. (1982) *Cuba et la France*, Bordeaux, Presses Universitaires de Bordeaux.
Leante, C. (1990) *Fidel Castro: el fin de un mito*, Madrid, Editorial Pliegos.
Le Riverend, J. (1971) *La República*, Havana, Editorial de Ciencias Sociales.
León, R. (1963) 'El reciente acuerdo comercial cubano-uruguayo', *Cuba Socialista*, 25 (September), pp. 48–54.
Levesque, J. (1976) *L'URSS et la Révolution Cubaine*, Montréal, Presse de l'Université de Montréal.
Levine, B. (1983) *The New Cuban Presence in the Caribbean*, Boulder, Westview Press.
Lieberman, S. (1982) *The Contemporary Spanish Economy*, London.
Liss, S.B. (1987) *Roots of Revolution: Radical Thought in Cuba*, Lincoln and London, University of Nebraska Press.
Llerena, M. (1978) *The Unsuspected Revolution: The Birth and Rise of Castroism*, Ithaca, Cornell University Press.
Lockwood, L. (1969) *Castro's Cuba, Cuba's Fidel*, New York, Random House.
Maravall, J.M. (1978) *Dictatorship and Political Dissent: Workers and Students in*

Franco Spain, London, Tavistock.

Marshall, P. (1987) *Cuba Libre: Breaking the Chains?*, London, Unwin.

Martínez, F. (1989) *El Che y el Socialismo*, Havana, Editorial Nuestro Tiempo.

Meeks, B. (1993) *Caribbean Revolutions and Revolutionary Theory: Cuba, Nicaragua, Grenada*, Warwick University Caribbean Studies, Basingstoke, Macmillan Press Ltd.

Mendelsohn, M.S. (1980) *Money on the Move: the Modern International Capital Market*, London.

Menéndez Cruz, A. (1961) 'Balance de la zafra de 1961: Primera Zafra del Pueblo', *Cuba Socialista*, 1 (September), pp. 34–46.

Menton, S. (1975) *Prose Fiction of the Cuban Revolution*, Austin, University of Texas Press.

Mesa-Lago, C. (1971) *The economy of Socialist Cuba: a Two-Decade Appraisal*, Albuquerque, University of New Mexico Press.

—— (1978) *Cuba in the 1970s: Pragmatism and Institutionalization*, Albuquerque, University of New Mexico Press.

—— (ed.) (1971) *Revolutionary Change in Cuba*, Pittsburgh, Pittsburgh University Press.

Mills, C.W. (1961) *Listen Yankee*, New York, Ballantine Books.

Milward, A.S. (1984) *The Reconstruction of Western Europe, 1945–1951*, London.

Moffitt, M. (1983) *The World's Money: International Banking from Bretton Woods to the Brink of Insolvency*, New York.

Montaner, C.A. (1981) *Secret Report on the Cuban Revolution*, New Brunswick, Transaction Books.

—— (1985) *Cuba, Castro and the Caribbean: the Cuban Revolution and the crisis in the Western Conscience*, New Brunswick, Transaction Books.

Moore, C. (1987) *Castro, the Blacks and Africa*, Los Angeles, University of California Press.

Morley, M. (1987) *Imperial State and Revolution: The United States and Cuba, 1952–86*, Cambridge, C.U.P.

Muñoz, J., *et al.* (1973) *La economía española*, Madrid.

National Bank of Cuba (1975) *Development and Prospects of the Cuban Economy*.

Padilla, H. (1991) *Self portrait of the Other*, London, Faber and Faber.

Palazuelos, E. (1986) *La economía de Cuba: las Relaciones económicas entre Cuba y España*, Madrid, Fundación Banco Exterior.

Pérez, L. Jr. (1988) *Cuba: Between Reform and Revolution*, New York, O.U.P.

Pérez, (1975) *El Movimiento Estudiantil Universitario de 1934 a 1940*, Havana, Editorial de Ciencias Sociales.

Phillipe, G. (1970) *Che Guevara*, Paris, Eds. Universitaires.

Pollack, B. (1987) *The Paradox of Spanish Foreign Policy: Spain's International Relations from Franco to Democracy*, London, Pinter.

Preston, P. (1986) *The Triumph of Democracy in Spain*, London, Methuen.

Raby, D.L. (1975) *The Cuban pre-Revolution of 1933: An Analysis*, Institute of Latin American Studies, University of Glasgow, Occasional Papers, No. 18.

Radosh, R. (ed.) (1976) *The New Cuba: Paradoxes and Potentials*, New York, William Morrow.

Ratliff, W. *et al.* (1986) *The selling of Fidel Castro: The Media and the Cuban Revolution*, New Brunswick, Transaction Books.

Recarte, A. (1980) *Cuba: economía y poder, 1959–80*, Madrid, Alianza Editorial.

Ripoll, C. (1968) *La Generación del 23 en Cuba*, New York.

Roa, R. (1964) *Retorno a la Alborada*, 2 vols, Havana, Universidad Central, Las

Villas.

Roca, S. (1988) *Socialist Cuba: past interpretations and future challenges*, Boulder, Westview Press.

Roddick, J. (1988) *The Dance of the Millions: Latin America and the Debt Crisis*, London.

Rodríguez, J.L. (1990) *Estrategía del Desarrollo económico en Cuba*, La Habana, Editorial de Ciencias Sociales.

—— (1988) *Crítica a nuestros Críticos*, La Habana, Editorial de Ciencias Sociales.

Romano, V. (1989) *Cuba en el corazón: Testimonios de un desarraigo*, Barcelona, Anthropos.

Ruíz, R.E. (1970) *Cuba: The Making of a Revolution*, New York, Random House.

Safran, W. (1985) *The French Polity*, London.

Sanches-Eppler, B. (1986) *Habits of Poetry, Habits of Resurrection*, London, Tamesis Books.

Sarabia, H. (1983) *Voisin, viajero de la ciencia*, La Habana, Editorial Cientifico-Tecnica.

Sartre, J.P. (1961) *Sartre on Cuba*, New York, Ballantine Books.

Scheer, R. and Zeitlin, M. (1964) *Cuba: an American tragedy*, Harmondsworth, Penguin Books.

Schoulz, L. (1981) *Human Rights and United States Policy Toward Latin America*, Princeton, Princeton University Press.

—— (1987) *National Security and United States Policy towards Latin America*, Princeton, Princeton University Press.

Seers, D. *et. al.* (1964) *Cuba, the Economic and Social Revolution*, Chapel Hill, University of North Carolina.

Servan-Schreiber, J.J. (1967) *Le Défi Américain*, Paris.

Sinclair, A. (1969) *Che Guevara*, London, Fontana.

Smith, W. (1987) *The Closest of Enemies: a Personal and Diplomatic account of U.S.-Cuban Relations since 1957*, New York, Norton.

Soto de, L. (1985) *La Revolución del 33*, 3 Vols, Havana, Editorial Pueblo y Revolución.

Stubbs, J. (1989) *Cuba: the Test of Time*, London, Latin America Bureau.

Sutherland, E. (1969) *The Youngest Revolution: a Personal Report on Cuba*, New York, Dial Press.

Sutton, P. (ed.) (1991) *Europe and the Caribbean*, Warwick University Caribbean Studies, Basingstoke, Macmillan Press Ltd.

Szulc, T. (1987) *Fidel: a Critical Portrait*, London, Hutchinson.

Tablada, C. (1987) *Che Guevara. Economics and Politics in the Transition to Socialism*, Sydney, Pathfinder Press.

Tellería, C. (1984) *Los Congresos Obreros en Cuba*, Havana, Editorial de Ciencias Sociales.

Thomas, H. (1971) *Cuba or the Pursuit of Freedom*, London, Eyre and Spottiswoode.

Toro del, C. (1969) *El Movimiento Obrero Cubano en 1914*, Havana, Instituto del Libro.

Torras León, R. (1988) *Antología*, Havana.

US Department of Agriculture (1975) Sugar Statistics and Related Data Compiled in the Administration of the US Sugar Acts, Vol. 1 (Revised), Washington, DC, USDA, Agricultural Stabilization and Conservation Service, Statistical Bulletin No. 293.

Valdés, N. (1975) *The Ideological Roots of the Cuban Revolutionary Movement*, Glasgow, Institute of Latin American Studies, Occasional Paper 15.

Valladares, A. (1986) *Beyond all Hope: the Prison Memoirs of Armando Valladares*, London, Hamish Hamilton.

Valls, J. (1989) *Mon ennemi, mon frère*, Paris, L'Arpenteur-Gallimard.

Verdès-Leroux, J. (1989) *La Lune et le Caudillo: la rêve des intellectuals et le régime cubain (1959–71)*, Paris, L'Arpenteur-Gallimard.

Viñas, A. (1981) *Los pactos secretos de Franco con Estados Unidos: bases, ayuda económica, recortes de soberanía*, Barcelona.

—— *et al.* (1979) *Política comercial exterior de España (1931–1975)*, 2 Vols, I, Madrid.

Vitier, C. (1975) *Ese Sol del Mundo Moral*, Mexico, Siglo XXI.

Vitier, M. (1979) *Las Ideas y la Filosofía en Cuba*, Havana, Editorial de Ciencias Sociales.

Welch, R.E. (1985) *Response to Revolution: the United States and the Cuban Revolution 1959–61*, Chapel Hill, University of North Carolina.

Welles, B. (1965) *Spain: the Gentle Anarchy*, New York, Praeger.

Williams, F.R. (1982) *The French Paradox*, Stamford, Hoover Press.

Yglesias, J. (1968) *In the Fist of the Revolution*, London, Allen Lane.

Zimbalist, A. (1987) *Cuba's Socialist Economy Towards the 1990s*, Boulder, Colorado, Lynne Reinner.

—— (1989) *The Cuban Economy*, Baltimore, The Johns Hopkins University Press.

The authors of the following references in Chapter 5 are unknown:

Anon. (1963a) 'En el décimo aniversario del 26 de Julio', *Cuba Socialista*, 23 (July), pp. 1–10.

—— (1963b) 'Relación de tratados, acuerdos y convenios comerciales', *Comercio Exterior*, 1, 2 (May), pp. 55–9.

—— (1964) 'La experiencia de Cuba en comercio exterior', *Comercio Exterior*, 2, 2 (April–June), pp. 50–118.

Index